2019 EDITION

UF CASES of INTEREST

2018's best reports from the Field Investigators of the Mutual UFO Network

Roger Marsh, Editor

CASE OVERVIEWS, REPORT STATISTICS, RESEARCH INDEX

MUFON

est. 1969

Special thanks to the Field Investigators, State and National Directors, and support staff of the Mutual UFO Network (MUFON): **Jan C. Harzan**, Executive Director • **Ken St. John**, Chief Operating Officer • **Doug Wilson**, MUFON Chief Investigator • **David MacDonald**, International Business Development • **Steve Hudgeons**, International Director of Investigations • **Ruben Jose Uriarte**, Deputy Director of International Investigations • **Kathleen Marden**, Director Experiencer Research Team (ERT) • **George Medich**, Assistant Director Experiencer Research Team (ERT) • **Roger Marsh**, Director of Communications • **Robert Spearing**, Special Assignment Team (SAT) Director • **Fred Saluga**, Cryptid Coordinator • **Chuck Zukowski**, Animal Mutilation Coordinator • **Debbie Ziegelmeyer**, Underwater Research and Recovery Coordinator • Case Assistance Group (CAG) • CMS Administrators and **Marketa Klimova**, Office Manager

ISBN-978-1079373943

Roger Marsh, editor and producer

Rob Swiatek, associate editor

Calvin Owens, Mary Owens, case research specialists

Book design by Lisa Wright/Redbird Visual Communications

Front cover image by MSCornelius, michelescornelius.com

Printed and bound in the United States of America
First printing July 2019

UFO Cases of Interest is a Perfection Restoration, LLC property produced under license and in cooperation with the Mutual UFO Network (MUFON). UFO case assets are the sole property of MUFON.

© Perfection Restoration, LLC, 2019

Feedback, Roger Marsh, editor@mufon.com

Visit MUFON.com

CONTENTS

PREFACE

Finding patterns in the UFO data

It's exciting to offer the public and sci-entific community our second annual edition of MUFON Cases of Interest (COI) book. This for the year 2018. MUFON operates in 43 countries and all 50 states and receives between 6 to 8,000 cases a year or said another way 500 to 1,000 cases a month. These are investigated by trained and certified MUFON Field Investigators to ensure the witnesses are real and are not fabricating their story. Of course, there is much more that goes into a UFO investigation, but these are two import-ant first steps.

This is one thing that sets MUFON apart from other UFO reporting web-sites. MUFON has time tested process-es and procedures for investigating UFO sightings as well as trained field investigators to follow-up on each case received from the public. This informa-tion is then shared globally in real-time on our website MUFON.com. And later, after investigation, in the UFO News section on our website, our monthly MUFON Journal for members, as well as in this annual publication of the best UFO cases MUFON has received.

It has been my personal goal since accepting the position of Executive Director to make UFO information available to the public in as many forms as possible to let the world know that UFOs Are REAL and that they repre-sent advanced technology not from this Earth. Which begs the question, then where are they from? But that's a whole other discussion and one we as an organization will be spending more time on and sharing the information we have with the public as we move for-ward. The move to make UFO informa-tion available to the public started more than 20 years ago with internal dis-cussions within MUFON on what was needed to do serious UFO research.

Those discussions led to the develop-ment of the MUFON Case Management System also known as CMS. In short, ONE central database to store all the world's UFO cases and make them easily retrievable by anyone. CMS gave the public a place to report their UFO sightings through our "Report a UFO" link on MUFON.com and our field investigators a place to document their investigations for each sighting. The second part of the plan was giving the green light to our communications department to publicize cases as they were reported to us by the public. Last year the decision was made to let our field investigators do their work first and then publicize our very best cases. These became known as Cases of Interest, or COI. This 2nd edition publication and our 1st edition is the culmination of that 20-year vision.

As I've already mentioned we receive 500 to 1,000 UFO cases a month, or 6 to 8,000 cases a year. To winnow this down to the best 2-300 cases requires a dedicated team of people who pour over UFO sightings coming into CMS tagging them as "Cases of Interest." These are then followed through the investigative process and only after a thorough investigation by one of our FIs and meeting the strictest of criteria end up on the COI list. I'd like to thank Roger Marsh, our Director of Communications, and his entire team for leading this effort and making this publication
a reality.

Publishing the cases is only part of the quest. The other part is putting together an index to allow the UFO researcher, to turn this data into information. This is done by indexing the cases and calling

out the commonalities in each of them. By doing so it is hoped we will be able to find patterns in the data, and places where a great Ahaa can be heard. At a minimum one will be able to marvel at the similarity of cases reported from all over the world. Through the patterns that emerge it is hoped that answers will spring forth and a new understanding of the UFO Phenomenon and our place in the universe will occur. You have taken the first step on this journey by purchasing this landmark publication. Thank you and may we solve the UFO mystery together.

JAN C. HARZAN graduated from the UCLA School of Engineering before spending 37 years with IBM in sales and marketing. He was appointed MUFON Executive Director August 1, 2013. His interest in UFOs began with a close encounter he had with his brother at the age of 10. He has served as a Field Investigator, State Section Director, and Assistant State Director before becoming a member of the MUFON Business Board where he helped create the current mission statement and goals, as well as develop the Case Management System (CMS) for UFO reporting, tracking, and investigative follow-up. Jan currently resides in Newport Beach, California, with his wife, Annette.

INTRODUCTION

Another year of data: Learning about UFOs

The Mutual UFO Network (MUFON) had 7,665 case reports in 2018. That's more than 600 reports a month. And 5,160 were in the United States.

The Cases of Interest Team waited the 90 days allowed per case investigation and reviewed only closed cases with one of three designations: Unknown Aerial Object, Unknown-Other, or Information Only. The first two classifications are the best reports—but we added Information Only cases because many of these include important information for further study.

Only cases that occurred in 2018 were reviewed. We had a long list of criteria for choosing cases. Especially liked cases under 100 feet away; or under 500 feet, where the witness got a good look at the object. We liked two or more witnesses. We liked object details and a witness's background.

The team weeded through 1,895 cases and chose 297 for 2018. The resulting data collected supports many long-known UFO trends. The object remains mostly silent, moves through space, air and water without resistance, can hover in place, stop on a dime, travel great distances in a short time, and can be a wide range of shapes and sizes. They tend to move about in groups of two or more. Few location patterns are known as sightings seem to occur at random, lasting two to three minutes. Exit patterns continue to vary from slowly moving away until the witness's view is obscured, to the object zooming away and disappearing into space in a matter of seconds.

Calvin Owens and Mary Owens served as our Case Research Specialists this year—painstakingly moving through the larger database of cases in the first weeding-out pattern to recommend the best cases for further study. Many thanks for their endless hours of work, project dedication and timeliness.

Rob Swiatek served again as our Associate Editor, providing second edits on all manuscript, and his wonderful guidance and help on indexing and project management.

Lisa Wright returned for the second edition as our book designer from Redbird Visual Communications, Chicago, seamlessly moving manuscript, images and data from the computer screen to print format in flawless style and fashion.

Serving as editor this second year, one

feels submersed in data as each individual case is checked and re-checked and formatted and indexed. There is a wild realization in those grueling, late-night computer sessions when you stop and look around. The simple understanding that UFOs are real hits you. Only the names and locations are tweaked from year to year, from case to case.

Witness testimony continues in the same order. They will tell you exactly what they were doing at the time leading up to the sighting. Then—bam – the object suddenly appears, and they have an encounter. Most reveal inner thoughts along the lines of, well, at first, I thought I was looking at a plane about to crash, or I thought it was this or that. Then they do a second take and realize that what they are looking at is none of the above. They can't make the object and its actions fit into their known paradigm. From this point they watch with great interest and excitement. Many attempt getting a second or third witness. Some awkwardly try to record the event.

UFO encounters are generally not very long—most play out over several minutes. Watch for cases sprinkled here and there where the object lingered, where multiple objects were in view, and those instances where people began to feel ill effects. Some revealed they had somehow connected with the intelligence behind the object and communicated with it.

How close did our witnesses get to the object? The group revealed 63 cases occurred under 100 feet away; 87 cases under 500 feet; and 53 cases under 1,000 feet. Our witnesses were watching the objects at or under 1,000 feet in 67 percent of the cases.

Some of the statistics are big numbers. Our witnesses told us the object hovered in 85 cases or 28.6 percent of the time. A very common thread. In 84 cases, the witness described seeing a triangle shape—the largest shape

selection this year.

Were witnesses bothered by the experience? Simply by being close to a UFO or watching one at a distance? When we asked about physical effects, our witnesses made 24 observations from 14 different cases—just less than 5 percent of the cases—describing a wide range of odd feelings including disorientation, nausea, and panic.

Seven reports include mention of electronics affected at the ground level. While directly feeling ill effects from a UFO would be quite frightening, some witnesses were out-right afraid during their encounters. Twelve witnesses reported being at some level of fright during the episode.

The case overviews can be simply read in order from January to December. Or you can thumb through the four indexes and look for lists of cases that interest you.

ROGER MARSH is a UFO writer and media content developer. He is Director of Communications for the Mutual UFO Network (MUFON) and serves as editor of the monthly international MUFON Journal. He is a MUFON webmaster, and project producer for: Cases of Interest and the MUFON UFO Index. His UFO news reports appear at mufon.com as the daily "UFO Traffic Report." He is author of Sacred Dialogue, editor of Silent Invasion, co-editor of Ron Paul Speaks, and co-editor of Mutual UFO Network (MUFON): 50 Years, 1969-2019. Roger was a case researcher for History channel's Hangar 1: The UFO Files. He manages  case and media permissions and licensing for MUFON. Roger and his wife, Joyce, live in Scottdale, PA, restoring a 1910 Pennsylvania foursquare.

UFO
CASES OF
INTEREST

JANUARY 2018

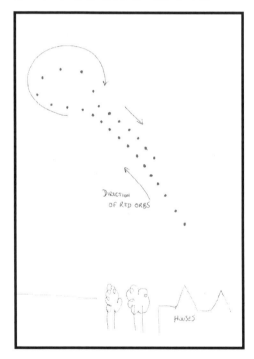

Case 91153 witness illustration.
January 26, 2018.

JANUARY 1

Three fast-moving objects reported over Las Vegas strip

A Nevada witness at Las Vegas reported watching three apparently metallic objects moving at high speed above a fireworks display, according to testimony in Case 89317.

The incident occurred just "five minutes" after midnight on January 1, 2018, along the Las Vegas strip.

"I was enjoying watching the fireworks show for New Year's," the witness stated. "I saw three objects, metal-looking type, no lights, flying very fast and noticeable in the direction I was looking."

The witness shot video and took still photos from an iPhone.

"The objects were traveling south at supersonic speed. Total time lapse of video was five seconds. Objects had no lights and were none of the following: helicopter, plane, aircraft military. Objects were just looking oval-shaped and changing directions as they were moving and defying the laws of physics and gravity."

The witness provided several photographs and has video for the investigator, too.

Nevada MUFON State Director Sue Countiss closed this case as an Unknown Aerial Vehicle.

"He said it looked 'weird' as he was filming the fireworks from the New Year's celebration on Las Vegas Boulevard," Countiss stated in her report. "He saw things that were a dull gray that moved very quickly in the sky behind the fireworks. They seemed to be within 1,000 feet and were not planes or helicopters. He took the pictures he sent in from the video, but they were not clearly defined. They seemed to be oval and changed to disc-shaped through tilting. They moved very fast, from point-to-point in a blink of an eye. The video caught the path, and they then blended into the night sky.... Moving like they were under some control from west to southwest.

"These pictures show some kind of triangular object accompanied by an undefined-shaped object in the sky over the fireworks of New Year's Eve. I do not know what these are and have decided they are not clouds from the fireworks. They keep the same shape during all the photos. Clouds would have been shifting and changing, especially at 'supersonic' speeds."

Las Vegas is the county seat of Clark County, population 648,224

Witness reports UFOs forming semi-circle

A Massachusetts witness at Lowell reported watching multiple hovering lights that formed a semi-circle, according to testimony in Case 89276.

The reporting witness stated that her husband went outside onto a deck to use a barbecue grill at 5:30 p.m. on January 1, 2018.

"He pointed out a bright light, which appeared to be hovering in the distance, on the left side of our property," the witness stated. "He then pointed to the opposite side of our property

and there were between five to seven very bright lights, which also appeared to hover."

The witness said that when looking from the right side of their home to the left, the objects were clearly forming a semi-circle.

"Since there were some trees obstructing our view outside, we ran inside to a large window in the dining room on the side of the house. From there, we were able to get a very clear view of the lights to the right of our house. None were moving. All appeared to be hovering. We questioned if they were perhaps planes, but again, they were not moving and there were no additional lights on them. Also, I'm sure planes would not even be allowed that close in proximity to each other. I assume being that close they would be considered in each other's air space."

The two sat watching for about 20 minutes and then the objects abruptly disappeared.

"They did not fly away or dim. They literally just disappeared. My husband took video from inside the house, which did not come out good, likely due to the window glare. Shortly after they disappeared (about 10 minutes), another appeared by itself. I took video of this one from our deck. It is not good quality. You can only tell that it is a bright light, but you can plainly see that it is not moving, just hovering. We're not totally sure what we saw, but these were definitely not planes. Very curious to know if anyone else in the area saw this as well. We live in Lowell, MA. The Concord River is directly to the left of our house."

Massachusetts MUFON State Director Eric Hartwig closed this case as an Unknown Aerial Vehicle.

"The witnesses (husband and wife) saw strange lights from their house, which prompted them to file a report," Hartwig wrote in his report. "The most likely earthly explanation would be that these were a series of jets in a jet path headed in the witnesses' direction with their headlights on. The reporting witness was well spoken, and I have no doubt saw something mysterious."

Lowell is a city in Middlesex County, Massachusetts, population 109,945.

JANUARY 2

'Black wing' UFO reported hovering along major highway

A Massachusetts witness at Northampton reported watching a "black wing" about 50 to 100 feet across hovering silently alongside a major highway, according to testimony in Case 89280.

The incident occurred at 5:20 p.m. on January 2, 2018, as the witness was driving home from work heading south on I-91.

"At first, I thought a new construction crane had been set up to the side of the highway because of two bright, stationary lights over top of the trees," the witness stated. "As I got closer to the object, I realized it was a flat craft just hovering in the dark sky. It was darker than the sky, so I could see its outline."

The witness described the object.

"It was a black wing maybe 50 to 100 feet across. It had two bright lights possibly on the underside and had lights along the front edge of each wing, maybe five on each side. They looked like windows. I could kind of make out an interior space. It wasn't until I drove under it that I clearly saw the wing shape. I tried to slow down as much as possible. It was rush hour and a lot of traffic, but I then realized this was something I've never seen before and it was just floating, silently."

The object was hovering at or under 500 feet and appeared to be 101 to 500 feet away.

Massachusetts State Director Eric Hartwig

closed this case as an Unknown Aerial Vehicle.

Northampton is the county seat of Hampshire County, Massachusetts, population 28,549.

JANUARY 3

UFO cluster reported low over California

A California witness at Marina reported glowing triangles they watched disappear followed by "a string of gray orbs" about 100 feet overhead and the size of yoga balls (i.e., each from 17–30 inches in diameter), according to testimony in Case 89327.

The witness and her sister were driving home from Monterey along Highway 1 near Marina at 6:40 p.m. on January 3, 2018.

"A red and blue flashing light appeared high up in the sky, moving toward a small glowing patch of yellow sky," the witness reported. "It was around 6:40 p.m., and the rest of the sky was dark. The light flashed red and blue, moving steadily toward the glowing triangle, and once they met, the flashing light disappeared. Shortly thereafter, another flashing light appeared from around 30 degrees from the horizon, moved in the same way, and disappeared after a few seconds. The same thing happened again. A few minutes later, my sister and I were both startled by a steady lead-colored orb that appeared to be the size of a basketball hovering near us, perhaps around the height of a telephone pole. When we moved our gaze slightly to the left, we saw another one, and realized that we could see about seven lead-colored orbs seemingly strung together getting farther off into the distance. We lost sight of these as we continued driving, constructing our perception that they were stationary."

California MUFON Field Investigator Jerry Gerow closed this case as an Unknown-Other.

"I checked with the local newspaper and police departments and found nothing unusual," Gerow stated in his report. "Stellarium showed the star Altair just above the horizon to the west and the moon was not up yet. MUFON showed nothing and NUFORC [National UFO Reporting Center] showed two cases at different times. I believe the sighting of two objects with blinking red and blue/green lights disappearing into a glowing opening to be possibly normal aircraft traffic flying on a cloudy day. What I cannot explain is the dark gray string of orbs 20–30 feet from their car trailing off into the distance. Both witnesses I spoke to seemed sincere and articulate."

Marina is a city in Monterey County, California, population 20,370.

Cigar-shaped UFO spotted over Illinois town

An Illinois witness at St. Charles reported watching a cigar-shaped object moving overhead with lights at both ends, according to testimony in Case 89610.

The witness and her husband were looking out a front kitchen window about 9:30 p.m. on January 3, 2018, when the incident began.

"Our window overlooks the covered deck, but we like to watch the planes coming and going into and out of the airports in Chicago," the witness stated. "From the side of the window that I was standing by, I noticed a bright light and saw a cigar-shaped object with bright lights on the front and back of the object."

The witness then alerted her husband.

"It moved so fast that by the time I told my husband to move over to my side and look up it had moved out of sight. It appeared to come from the northwest and headed southeast out of sight. It made no sound and was a dark metal color with no light between the front and back lights."

Illinois MUFON State Section Director James Wolford closed this case as an Unknown Aerial Vehicle.

"When the object was first noticed it was west-northwest of the witness and close to the zenith (almost directly overhead—80° to 90°)," Wolford wrote in his report. "It disappeared in the south-southeast while about 20° above the horizon. The object at closest approach (overhead) was about the angular size of a basketball held at arm's length or arc tan $[9.55/24.0] = 21.7°$. The witness had difficulty doing the same estimate using the 0.5° width of the full moon even though it was above the horizon at the time. Suffice it to say, the object appeared quite large.

"In the interview, the witness made it very clear that she and her husband watch airplane traffic in the St. Charles area and are familiar with the routes and patterns. The object they sighted was on an unfamiliar path that the other planes typically did not use. It would not have been taking off from or landing at any of the Chicagoland airports. She also confirmed that the front and back lights were attached to the dark gray cylindrical or cigar-shaped body. Station keeping was perfect. The object was silent and moved very fast compared to the commercial aircraft seen nearby. Distance and size could not be measured in any absolute way, but the witness's impression was that the object was about the length of a football field. This would make it 100 yards = 300 feet long. Peculiar was the fact that although the object had bright lights at front and rear, the light did not seem to reach the ground and illuminate it. The entire sighting lasted less than two minutes, perhaps as little as 30 seconds.

"I made a call to the DuPage Airport just in case this could have been a blimp. I eventually asked someone at the control tower about this and they indicated that blimp landings and takeoffs occur only in the summer. Other aircraft do have white lights in the back and front but are not a good match to the object sighted by the witness. Although the speed and general appearance of the sighted object do not match a meteor very well, I did check it. So far, the American Meteor Society does not list a fireball report for in or near St. Charles, IL, on the evening of January 3, 2018.

"My tentative disposition for this case is Unknown UAV. After a month or two the sighting data, including correlations and meteor reports, should be rechecked just to make sure that the initial opinion is correct since some of the data is not in yet at this time."

St. Charles is a city in DuPage and Kane Counties, Illinois, population 32,714.

JANUARY 4

Florida witness says low-flying object was silent

A Florida witness at Casselberry reported hovering flashing red and white lights, according to testimony in Case 89344.

The witness was checking the morning weather through a door window at 6:25 a.m. on January 4, 2018.

"First observed incredibly bright (I estimated they were LED-type lights) red and white flashing lights to the south/southwest," the witness stated. "I went outside to observe. The lights moved west/east slightly, hovering just above treetop level."

The witness could hear no sound associated with the object.

"My initial inclination was that the object was a drone because it was hovering so steadily; however, when the lights moved to a position behind a distant palm tree, I discounted that it was a drone because, if it was a drone, the size would have to be incredibly large. I also discounted that it was a blimp as there was no discernible outline of an object - I was simply

seeing lights. I also discounted that it was an aircraft (on approach or otherwise) because the lights were far too bright for any aircraft that I had ever seen (I am a former air traffic controller and flight navigator) and the object did not appear to be approaching/closing in my direction. Moreover, the lights, in the configuration I was witnessing, didn't fit any that I'd seen in my 12-year aviation career. At some point, the lights began a direct movement toward the east/southeast, remaining just above treetop level all the while. Interestingly, the light configuration and pace of flashing did not change when departing in that direction. It was then, just after departing, that I heard what seemed to be a pulsating sound, very low in intensity and at a pace of about two pulses per second. The object continued east/southeast and remained just above treetop level until it disappeared at the horizon."

Florida MUFON Field Investigator Leonard Cohen closed this case as an Unknown-Other.

"The witness is highly credible due to education and experience," Cohen wrote in his report. "Witness correctly rules out a blimp, drone, or man-made aircraft. The movement of the object rules out any natural phenomenon, like a planet or meteor. Witness has included a drawing of the lights and some of its movements. I called the Casselberry Police for confirmation, but they did not return my call. Despite the lack of any corroborating information or witnesses, my disposition is that the lights are an Unknown-Other."

Casselberry is a city in Seminole County, Florida, population 26,241.

JANUARY 6

British witness describes two different UFOs

A British witness at Darlington reported watching both a triangle-shaped and a donut-shaped object crossing the sky, according to testimony in Case 89370.

The witness was watching television at 1:50 p.m. on January 6, 2018.

"I noticed a black object in the sky flying left to right out my window," the witness stated. "I watched it and it suddenly became clear it was a triangle. I grabbed my phone to start recording and noticed a highly unusual fluorescent green at one of the edges pulsing randomly. I managed to press record on my phone."

As the witness was recording the first object, which was flying out of view, he was "absolutely shocked" to notice a second object lower in the sky flying behind it.

"The second object was a doughnut shape. It wobbled as it flew. Both objects were black. The second object was much clearer, and I could see as it wobbled that there was a hole in the middle. It was shaped exactly like a doughnut. It too had green fluorescent pulses. The second object should have been extremely clear on my camera, but when I have watched the footage back, neither object can be seen; however, I noticed on the camera footage that there are two other objects moving in the opposite direction at the same height of the first object. These two move extremely quickly and are parallel to each other. I did not see these when I was filming. I have sent the footage to a friend who is good with imaging to see if he can pull the objects from the footage. I do not know why they are not apparent in my footage. I have never witnessed anything as incredible as this in my 40 years. This was no standard craft. This was nothing like I believe the military has or anyone else."

United Kingdom MUFON Field Investigator Kevin Gorringe closed this case as Info Only.

Darlington is a large market town in County Durham, in North East England, population 105,564.

Diamond-shaped light reported over Utah

A Utah witness at Logan reported watching a red-orange light traveling northwest that stopped and hovered and then shot straight up and disappeared, according to testimony in Case 89385.

The witness and her husband were walking outside their apartment to do laundry at 10 p.m. on January 6, 2018.

"I saw a bright, fiery light coming towards us in the night sky," the witness stated. It was overcast and this was the only light in the sky. It almost looks like a helicopter that was on fire and was flying really low. It got brighter as it came closer. My husband thought that it was a meteor, but it was moving too slow. It quickly changed direction and started going northeast. Then it suddenly stopped and hovered in the same spot for about 35 or 45 seconds. Then it went straight up and disappeared. It didn't make any noise or sound at all."

Utah MUFON Field Investigator Stephen Walker closed this case as an Unknown-Other.

"The witness's information was expanded by the interview process," Walker stated in his report. "What started out as a low and slow-moving light and quite possibly a UAV became something quite different. The witness recalled that when they first noticed the light that it began to move toward them. The light passed over the Logan Utah Temple, where it was illuminated by the temple light and the witness could plainly see that it was not part of some machine. The light suddenly tumbled down in front of temple and stopped before striking the ground. It floated in front of the temple and again was illuminated by the temple lights and again no mechanical devices or structure were observed. The light was about 500 feet from the witness and was the size of a penny held at arm's length. The witness and her husband questioned what they were seeing when the light suddenly shot into the air and dissolved into the cloud deck.

"It is my opinion that the witness did observe an event that was very close in nature. The light did appear to be reactive to the witnesses. I found them to be excited and curious about the event, which eliminates the chances of guile on their part."

Logan is a city in Cache County, Utah, population 48,174.

JANUARY 8

Witness says choppers followed triangular UFO

A Wisconsin witness at Orfordville reported watching a local helicopter apparently following a low-flying object four times its size, according to testimony in Case 89435.

The witness was westbound along Highway 11 heading toward Brodhead at 5:20 p.m. on January 8, 2018.

"I saw the Green County helicopter hovering over Brodhead," the witness stated. "Pretty normal. They always come around. Then to my left I saw another chopper heading south going directly over me. Wanting to get a better look, I turned to look for the helicopter and the tree line ends at this point. When I saw 'it,' I didn't know what this was, but it was at least four times the size of the chopper and had two extremely bright, white-blue (like daylight bulb) lights coming from the rear that flashed every second or so."

The witness pointed out he grew up around an airport.

"There were no green and red lights, and it was way too big and moving way too slow to be a plane. Plus, the size of the lights would have been the entire wing of a passenger jet. I have no idea what I saw but two choppers were watching too. The one followed it all the

way to the Illinois border. I guess because the chopper flew south and stopped for a minute, then turned around and headed back. Everyone can give me garbage for not having my phone, but I was just going to grab some food quick and this is not a joke."

Wisconsin MUFON State Director Sue Brittnen closed this case as an Unknown Aerial Vehicle.

"The witness spent a lot of time with his grandfather who was a pilot," Brittnen stated in her report. "They would hang out at the airport, so he learned a lot about airplanes. He is acquainted with the local airport in Brodhead, which is approximately one mile away from his home. He thought it was strange that when he saw the object, he pulled over to the side of the road, but no one else stopped. The cars kept passing him and did not appear to see the object. He thought there was a strange quality to the object's lights. They seemed to be like LED lights and that the object might have been man-made. However, his main feelings were that the object was amazing. He has provided a computer-drawn image of the craft."

Orfordville is a village in Rock County, Wisconsin, population 1,442.

JANUARY 9

Four triangular objects spotted low over rural Pennsylvania

A Pennsylvania witness at Wrightsville reported watching four black, triangle-shaped objects moving overhead under 500 feet, according to testimony in Case 89450.

The event occurred as the witness arrived home along the Susquehanna River in York County just after 7 p.m. on January 9, 2018.

"We heard and witnessed a helicopter with a searchlight, hovering over and scanning the countryside and water," the witness stated. "As we watched it, we became aware of four other aircraft flying at a higher altitude than the helicopter."

The chopper continued moving away heading north.

"The craft flew in a pattern directly over our home. They were triangular in shape. Possessed pulsating lights. Their surfaces were black, but reflective. They flew northwest. Entire encounter took four minutes."

Pennsylvania MUFON State Section Director John Weaver closed this case as an Unknown Aerial Vehicle.

"Helicopter presence is not uncommon (checking for river ice buildup) in this area (confirmed by others who live nearby—a river rescue station is also close to this popular boating area known as 'Long Level') and evidently had no association with the four unidentified craft," Weaver stated in his report. "Helicopter continued north following Susquehanna River.

"Further description of four triangular craft: Dark surfaces, but reflective. Pulsating red/white lights noted at corners of the triangles—these lights reflected on bottom of craft. Originally observed in east, craft tracked northwest directly overhead of witness's home, passing over wooded hill above and toward town of Hellam. Craft were arranged in a 'diamond' formation throughout the event. Apparent speed was slow but steady; no sound was made by the craft; no audible reactions (barking) heard from dogs in the neighborhood.

"Witness and girlfriend had just returned from dinner and she also saw the craft from the driveway. Considered filming it with phone but could not get it to focus properly. Witness is familiar with local sky, (fairly dark here) as he and his son often look at stars, etc. on clear nights and while admits an interest in UFOs has never previously seen anything like this. (He is familiar with aircraft lights, ISS, satellites and natural celestial objects.) Personally, I am very familiar with the location of the event;

broadest part of the Susquehanna River, with a couple of large marinas—very popular in summer. Many homes—both permanent and vacation—along the river here. Opposite bank (east) of the river, directly across from witness's home are three large wind turbines, which display typical red warning lights.

"No correlating reports noted in CMS or NUFORC; additionally, I spoke to a respected colleague in the paranormal/UFO field who lives on the east side of the river here (Columbia). He made some enquiries and found no one else who had seen the objects. Other than additional details, witness's description of events mirrored his written report. Witness is a sincere, intelligent and well-grounded person; combined with his familiarity of the night sky, a most credible observer."

Wrightsville is a borough in York County, Pennsylvania, population 2,320.

Pilot: 'aircraft carrier-sized' object under 1,000 feet

A Washington witness at Ellensburg reported watching an object the size of an aircraft carrier under 1,000 feet with an estimated length of 1,000 to 2,000 feet, according to testimony in Case 89498.

The incident began at 8:45 p.m. on January 9, 2018, when the reporting witness's German Shepherd began barking insistently outside his northeast bedroom window.

"My wife and I both heard a deep, low, muffled, pulsing sound that grew louder within several seconds," the witness stated. "My wife went out the northeast bedroom door and I went out the south door. The sound we then heard was very loud and sounded like an electric turbine, similar to a hydroelectric turbine, but pulsating."

The witness looked directly up and saw a very large object moving slowly from the northeast corner of the house moving towards the southwest.

"The object appeared to be about 500 to 1,000 foot above the ground and there were two lights and one pulsating red light on both the fore and aft ends of the object. The weather that night was a bit overcast but with some stars visible, except between the two sets of lights where the object blocked out any view of the stars—or light reflected back off the low cloud ceiling."

The witness said the outline of the object was vague and hard to discern but you could clearly see a physical object extending between the sets of lights.

"I first thought that it was two aircraft moving in perfect tandem; however, the rear set of lights was directly behind the first and moving in perfect harmony at a slow but steady speed and much too slow for the objects to be aircraft, and I could clearly see some physical object between the two."

The witness's wife joined him and they both observed the object moving slowly towards the southwest.

"The pulsating sound was very loud and muffled but we could almost feel the energy as it receded as the object moved over the hills to the southwest about two miles away. Our elevation is 1,300 feet and the nearby hills are at 1,800 feet and I got the sense that the object was only 500 to 1,000 feet above us. I held both hands out pointed at the front and back and my arms were at a 90-degree angle which gave me a sense of the size. There is a major highway climbing the grade and we are able to see the lights of vehicles as they ascend and descend the grade; however, no lights were visible as the object passed over the highway."

It took about one minute for the object to reach the hills to the southwest and they viewed it the entire time.

"My wife had grabbed her cellphone and attempted to video the object; however, was only able to get some still photographs, which do show distinct light patterns and vaguely show the shape and size of the object, which I estimated to be about the size of an aircraft carrier, 1,000 feet long. As the object reached the hills, it appeared to hover for about 45 seconds to a minute and then slowly disappeared out of sight. We were amazed and a bit in shock, but were absolutely sure of what we saw and heard. As we recalled what we had seen we noted that the cloud cover had lifted slightly, and stars were very visible, which reinforced for us that it was a physical object that blocked our view of the stars above."

As the two were recapping the event, they both heard a very high-pitched wailing, screaming sound that they had never heard before.

"We do live in the country and there are coyotes, flocks of geese and other animals, but this was unlike any sound we had ever heard. The sound seemed very unnatural and I described it to my wife as similar to the sound heard in the movie "Ghost," where the bad spirits come to collect the ghost of the men who had killed the lead. Very strange and unsettling, especially as we had just witnessed something we had never seen before."

Washington MUFON Chief Investigator Daniel Nims closed this case as an Unknown Aerial Vehicle.

"The witnesses seemed to be credible and gave a very coherent description of the event," Nims wrote in his report. "They were in their bedroom in the southeast corner of the house watching TV when they heard a loud noise moving overhead. The wife went out the north exterior exit of the room to the patio, the husband went out the south exit into the hot tub patio. The wife just saw the back end of the object sticking out northeast of the roof, moving southwest. The husband saw the front of the object overhead moving southwest. He called his wife, who came to the south patio. They watched, and the craft moved toward the southwest and the aft end of the object came into view over the roof.

"The object had three lights at the front and back, a red pulsing light in the center and a white steady light on either side of it. They were not exactly in a row, with the center red light closer to the front for the front lights, and closer to the back for the back lights. Though the part of the object between the front and rear lights was not lighted, the star field and scattered clouds were obscured by the middle of the object. As it was dark, and the perimeter of the object was not clearly visible they couldn't be certain about the overall shape of the object, but they seemed to think it was oval in shape.

"The witness held his arms out in the direction of the front and back of the object and there was about a 90-degree arc between them. The witness is a private pilot and familiar with the low, scattered cloud layer common in the valley. Based on that, he estimates the object was approximately 500–1,000 feet AGL. Based on the angle between the front and back of the object and the estimated height, the object would be quite large—1,000-2,000 feet long. They watched for two to three minutes as the object moved off to the southwest and out of sight over the nearby ridge.

"The sound it made was quite loud, loud enough to be heard indoors. They said it had a slow, pulsing rhythm, not steady. The witness was aware of the Yakima Training Range, 10 miles southeast of them. They said they had occasionally seen and were familiar with helicopter traffic operating on the range. They said the sound did not sound like helicopter engines. The wife was able to get several pictures with her cell phone, an LG K8. The pictures show the lights, but they are streaks due her unsteady pointing of the camera. After the object passed, and they were discussing what they had seen, they heard a very high-pitched, wailing, screaming sound. They said it was not like a coyote or any other animal with which they were familiar.

"A possible option other than an Unknown would be a formation of aircraft (i.e., helicopters). The witnesses said they had never observed night helicopter operations in the area. The lighting pattern does not conform with known helicopter lighting configurations (green right side, red left side, white tail, with an anti-collision beacon. The path of the object was toward the southwest, not southeast toward the range area. The area between the two light groups obscured the stars and cloud sky background. These facts do not support the formation of aircraft option. The loud pulsing noise associated with the passing of the object might support the helicopter thesis, but the witness said it did not sound like a helicopter. It sounded more like an electrical turbine. No natural cause would fit the description of the object. It is concluded that this sighting is an Unknown.

"Amended, February 9, 2018: The vice-commander of the Yakima Training Range called and confirmed that there was no training scheduled the whole week of January 9, 2018. That seems to preclude range helicopter traffic as being the object sighted."

Ellensburg is a city in and county seat of Kittitas County, Washington, population 20,326.

JANUARY 13

Indiana witness describes chevron-shaped object

An Indiana witness at Indianapolis reported a low and slow-flying, chevron-shaped object moving silently overhead, according to testimony in Case 89544.

The witness was westbound along 82nd Street at 9:05 p.m. on January 13, 2018.

"Saw V-shaped aircraft flying at very low altitude and at a low speed heading southwest," the witness stated. "Viewed object for approximately six to eight seconds. No blinking or colored lights. No trail. No sound. No altitude change. Speed mimicked that of a B-2 flyover at the IMS on race day. Completely stunned me. Out of place and very large compared to typical aircraft. As I followed it and lost sight of it, I saw the blinking colored lights of other aircraft in the distance. They didn't compare at all to the object I saw. Very curious what it was. Saw nothing related on any newsfeeds."

Indiana MUFON Field Investigator Philip Leech Jr. closed this case as Info Only.

"Witness observed a V-shaped aircraft flying at very low altitude and at a low speed heading southwest," Leech wrote in his report. "Viewed object for approximately six to eight seconds."

Indianapolis is the state capital and most populous city of Indiana, population 872,680.

JANUARY 17

British 'aircraft enthusiast' describes triangular UFO

A British witness at Hemel Hempstead reported watching a triangular-shaped object under 500 feet with an inverted, lit-up dome, according to testimony in Case 89653.

The event occurred beginning at 3:35 a.m. on January 17, 2018.

"A bright light came through bedroom curtain," the witness stated. "A triangular vehicle was spotted gliding in a straight line. Underneath the vehicle was an inverted, lit dome virtually touching the three sides. The inverted dome had arched ribs from bottom to top with a center pillar projecting a bright light."

The witness said he had a perfect view of the object until it disappeared over nearby buildings.

"My first reaction was it was a strange plane out of Luton Airport, then immediately realized it was not a normal aircraft."

United Kingdom Assistant National Director Michael Price closed this case as an Unknown Aerial Vehicle.

"Having reviewed the information, this case provides me with a somewhat difficult assessment to make," Price wrote in his report. "The witness is an aircraft enthusiast, and being one myself I know how accurately we can identify known aircraft both civilian and military with a lot of accuracy even in the dark. This for me rules out mis-identification of a known aircraft and type.

"The second interesting point to note is the description of the central light, not only in its shape and luminosity, but also the fact that it was clear enough for the witness to notice that it almost touched the three sides of the triangle. The arched ribs description is very interesting with a central pillar of light. I have heard this described before by whistleblowers out of AREA 51 and Lockheed that state that bright light given off is plasma charging through the anti-gravity drive, which could have a wave expulsion pattern similar to a black hole forcing out light from the top and bottom of the center. This could explain the pillar of light observed with the arched ribs providing the skeleton for the plasma charge containment.

"Without any additional evidence or secondary observed sighting, it is difficult to investigate further, but I think based on the short description what was viewed was either a known AV (TR3B or Aurora project) or an Unknown Aerial Vehicle of ETV classification. I have classified the case as UAV in the absence of any reliable identification of TR3B or Aurora military craft."

Hemel Hempstead is a town in Hertfordshire, England, located 24 miles northwest of London, population 94,932.

JANUARY 24

British witness felt seen by UFO 'pilot'

A Scottish witness at Glasgow reported watching a fast-moving object emitting three lights that formed into a single beam, according to testimony in Case 89841.

The witness was inside playing Xbox at 8:04 p.m. on January 24, 2018, when an extremely bright light that flashed from the UFO caught his attention.

"I thought the object was a military aircraft or a normal jet," the witness stated. "The object was small, looked weird and had a blue-grayish tint to it. It had three beams going across it to the front, which was circular. Its lights then twisted, turned and got brighter as if to focus on something. It then created a thick, white light as the three lights merged at the front. It started to move northeast before abruptly changing direction and strangely seemed like it was going in one direction before cutting away in another direction, then back to northeast."

The witness said that he "felt confused" at first as to what was going on.

"When I saw the UFO move, I felt threatened; however, I also had another strange feeling. I felt that whatever was in the craft had seen me, or something else and was also scared, trying to make a swift escape. This could explain the various quick movements it was seen making. After seeing the craft, I felt weird, like it hadn't really happened. I also felt a connection with the craft and felt like it was not evil. I lost visual contact when it managed to do five or six quick movements, seemingly defying what direction it had intended to go in, before hovering and vanishing."

United Kingdom MUFON Field Investigator Robert Young closed this case as an Unknown-Other.

"Quite an interesting report," Young wrote

in his report. "Doesn't seem to behave like a normal aircraft and the witness seems to feel a strange atmosphere from the sighting; whether it was a real affect or just was feeling unnerved because of the unknown is unclear. He also states that there was static from physical items. Possible genuine anomaly."

Glasgow is the most populous city in Scotland, population 621,020.

British witness describes low-flying triangle

A British witness at Droitwich Spa reported watching a black, triangle-shaped object under 100 feet, according to testimony in Case 89780.

The witness was driving at 10:30 p.m. on January 24, 2018.

"I was travelling from the Swan Pub at the top of the lane," the witness stated. "As I started down the lane towards the Copcut Pub, I noticed a white, static light come over the tree tops, and over the top of my car; thinking it was a shooting star, I looked up to see a triangle, jet-black craft going overhead. A light was at each corner. Its length was that of a large plane. I thought it was one. So I wound the window down to hear no engine noises. As it passed quietly overhead, I slowed to watch it move at speed about 100 feet up...in a straight line, heading away towards Redditch...only seeing the rear corner light as it went...the others were not visible. I clearly saw the shape and its body was dense black...to blend in with the darkness...but the city lights showed its shape as it kept away from our town... travelling across country in the dark.

United Kingdom MUFON Field Investigator John Noyce closed this case as an Unknown-Other.

"Stellarium showed a full moon to the southwest, 40 percent elevation, although with the cloud cover it's possible the witness might not have seen this," Noyce wrote in his report.

"Although there is a large airport (Birmingham) 26 miles southwest, if aircraft were to fly over the witness position, they would be higher than the sighting. And there are no takeoff and landing flight paths in that direction. There are no military bases of interest in the area. The witness did mention there were high power electric cables that seem to run in the direction of the sighting, and upon checking with Google Earth I found this correct."

Droitwich Spa is a town in northern Worcestershire, England, on the River Salwarpe.

Montana Air Base loses power as UFO hovers overhead

A Montana witness near Great Falls reported that a contact on the Malmstrom Air Force Base described a 10-minute power outage after a circular-shaped object "over a half-acre in size" hovered over the base, according to testimony in Case 89785.

The event occurred on January 24, 2018.

"My base contact described the object only as black," the reporting witness stated. "If contacted, Malmstrom AFB will confirm the power outage but nothing more. Investigators are on their way. Last sighting was in May 2017. This source is reliable and confirmed as am I."

The witness describes himself as a retired police detective "not given to exaggerations."

The filed report indicates the object was black in color with no structural features. The object size was larger than 300 feet. No exterior lights. No emissions. The object was hovering at less than 500 feet in altitude. The object was over one mile away from the witness. No landing was observed.

MUFON CAG Investigator Marie Cisneros and Montana State Director John Gagnon closed this case as Info Only.

Investigators contacted the media relations department at Malmstrom and did not receive a reply.

"Ruled out for astronomical or weather anomalies," Cisneros and Gagnon stated in their report. "Ruled out for bolides or fireball activity. Ruled out for obvious hoax.

"Our conclusion: Unidentified object. Size, shape, flight pattern and path do not fit with known conventional aircraft. Because this was reported by someone other than the witness, this case has to be filed as an Info Only unless further information is forthcoming by the witness."

Malmstrom Air Force Base is in Cascade County, Montana, adjacent to Great Falls. It is the home of the 341st Missile Wing (341 MW) of the Air Force Global Strike Command (AFGSC). As a census-designated place, it has a population of 3,472.

JANUARY 26

'String of red orbs' reported over UK

A British witness reported watching a "string of spherical red orbs" rising into the sky, according to testimony in Case 91153.

The witness was walking home at about 8:15 p.m. on January 26, 2018.

"I live in a small town about 25 miles east of London," the witness stated. "As I walked along the pavement, something in the night sky caught my eye. I stopped, turned to the west and looked into the sky. I saw a string of small, bright red orbs rising up into the sky at an angle (not vertically). They were as many as 20 small red orbs, all the same size, all constantly moving at the same speed, close together, moving as if attached to a cord (like a string of red Christmas tree lights). The orbs were a constant bright red, constant spherical shape, and constant speed. They were quite some distance away, maybe 10 miles away, so it is difficult to estimate the speed, but these objects were covering quite a distance in the sky, so I judged them to be moving fast, at a steep angle and much faster than planes, and very nimbly."

The witness described their movement.

"As I watched, they rose up from 30 degrees, following each other up into the sky to about 60 degrees up, then moved in a circular motion at the same speed, swirling around within a large cloud that was in the sky, some traveled back down again. The red orbs were some miles away, which would put them above East London area. The red orbs were much bigger than aeroplane lights that I'm well used to seeing in the night sky above my hometown. I live directly under a busy flight corridor, so I am used to looking at planes gliding overhead (east-west), flying to several major airports in the London area. These red orbs moved fast, and swirling around in a tight turning radius, nothing like how a plane would move, and there were so many of them packed together, up to 20 all following each other. I got my phone out of my pocket and checked the time. I stood, rooted to the spot, watching these red orbs fly around the sky for several minutes. I was surprised by what I was seeing in the sky, it caught me by surprise. I did not stop to think that this might be worth taking a picture or video of. I wanted to get home, so I continued walking back home, leaving the red orbs still moving around the sky."

British MUFON Field Investigator James Dallas closed this case as an Unknown Aerial Vehicle.

"Although there was a warning to pilots that someone was shining a searchlight, I believe this is not what our witness saw," Dallas wrote in his report. "I believe he saw an object, one of which made him contact us wanting to know answers."

No town name was given for this report.

JANUARY 28

Fasting moving triangle reported over Pennsylvania

A Pennsylvania witness at Buffalo Mills reported watching a "double, triangle-shaped" object silently moving south to east, according to testimony in Case 89867.

The witness was outside in front of his home, overseeing his dogs at 7:30 p.m. on January 28, 2018.

"Waiting for them to finish, looked straight in front of me saw big, red-white lights randomly pulsating in double triangle pattern," the witness stated. "Could not see actual surface of craft. It moved at a very fast pace from south to east. The sky was cloudy, seemed like low cloud cover. Could see the glow of the moon to the northeast but couldn't actually see it."

The object was moving toward the mountain to the southeast, so the witness yelled out for his wife to come look.

"We both saw it moving before it went behind the mountain. The mountain is part of State Game Lands Number 48, which comprises slightly over 11,000 acres. It made one more appearance between mountain tops and disappeared again. At first, I thought it was the Space Station but knew the cloud cover would prohibit that. I knew that based on cloud cover, apparent size, and speed, no noise, it was a UFO. I would guess the size to be as big as our house or more, which is 40 x 60 feet. Four minutes later I saw two white lights, like LEDs, move just north of our house from east to west. Once it passed and I could see the tail, there was one blinking white light. I thought maybe it was a plane, but it was silent and had two front white lights not one light. I made this report right away so I could remember it as accurately as possible."

Pennsylvania MUFON Field Investigator Jason Geis closed this case as an Unknown-Other.

"First, I contacted the Johnstown Airport via email to ask about any maneuvers that may have been occurring in the area that evening," Geis stated in his report. "I did not receive an answer or response. I also did some research on various planes that might have had these kinds of lights or actions. And I could not find anything that would easily explain what the witness reported seeing.

"I then looked for similar type UFOs reported. There have been many triangle-shaped UFOs reported in just this year on the CMS. Just to cite a few (Case #s 90959; 90901; 90583). These were similar in size and color. I also researched triangular UFOs from 2018 and found an interesting video of another case from England.

"The object and actions of the object described by the witness do not adhere to known objects or known astronomical phenomena."

Buffalo Mills is an unincorporated community in Bedford County, Pennsylvania.

FEBRUARY 2018

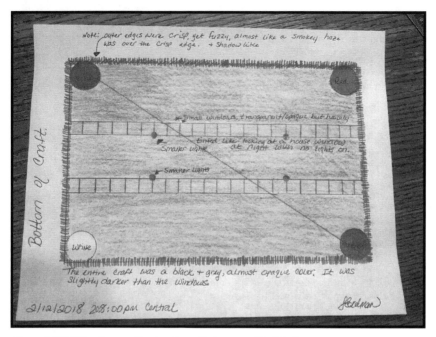

Case 90205 witness illustration. February 12, 2018.

FEBRUARY 4

PA witness says bright orbs moved in unison

A Pennsylvania witness at Mt. Pleasant reported watching a series of orbs in an alignment that seemed to move as a single unit, according to testimony in Case 90057.

The witness woke up at 1:38 a.m. on February 4, 2018, to take his dog outside.

"I always look outside at the bird feeder to check for deer," the witness stated. "This extremely bright orb appeared. I thought it was a Life Flight helicopter. It didn't move. Then two other orbs appeared, and they were in a perfect alignment with each other (straight up and down). They started to move as if they were attached to each other. Then another identical line of orbs, three in each line, a total of four lines evenly spaced."

The witness then ran out his back door calling for his wife.

"She joined me outside. I pointed at the formation. We stood there and watched this formation travel from the southeast towards a northern track. It was like they were all connected. The spacing between each orb and each line was evenly spaced. The middle orb would just disappear, then in a blink of an eye they would be there."

The group of orbs then suddenly turned to the northeast as a single unit.

"They traveled towards Kecksburg, Pennsylvania, then in a single movement, each line suddenly disappeared as fast as they appeared. It was like watching Star Trek. My wife turned to me and said these words: 'I thought Ancient Aliens and Hangar One are farces. We are not alone. They are real.' We were barefooted and in our pajamas standing on ice and we didn't realize this. She stated there is a reason people don't get these events on film. You don't think of it. You just stand there in amazement of it all. She doesn't want to talk about it nor wants anybody to know about it."

Pennsylvania MUFON Field Investigator Jason Geis closed this case as an Other.

"While outside with his dog, the witness witnessed anomalous orbs moving in formation for approximately eight minutes. He was looking out of the kitchen window when odd and extremely bright orbs appeared hovering. They were in a perfect alignment. While watching them others appeared.

"During the interview I was struck by the witness's knowledge of airplanes both civilian and military. Witness came across as very credible and explained what he saw and that he knows he witnessed something odd and not normal. Witness explained locale in detail (on Chestnut Ridge, near highway 982). Explained that the airport tower light was off to the right of what he witnessed. Object did not blink but did seem to grow bigger and bigger. Object was moving south-southeast and then it stopped. Then he saw three more orbs all the same color (reddish orange). They lined up one on top of the other. Objects were evenly spaced, moving slowly (almost like one object). They were spread out to cover at least three-quarters of a mile. Reported there was no sound. Objects then did an angular turn and lined up vertically. Then changed to horizontal and then 'warped out of there' and disappeared almost instantly.

"I began by looking into military bases and airports within the area. I found over 15 airports within 100 miles of the sighting. I also looked into possible planes that would have these kind of light formations and could find nothing that looked like this. I also looked into drones and drone lighting. Although theoretically the witness could have seen a number of drones flying in formation, I dismissed this due to the time of the sighting and the desolate area of the sighting. I also dismissed the usual culprit for orangish-red orbs, the Chinese lantern, due to the time of the sighting. Also, lanterns do not change formation instantly.

"After looking at the probable causes, and none of them being able to explain the things seen by the witness, I concluded that the objects he saw were unknown in origin."

Mt. Pleasant is a borough in Westmoreland County, Pennsylvania, population 4,454.

Florida rectangular UFO disappears behind tree line

A Florida witness at Port St. Lucie reported watching "a black, hollowed-out, rectangular object" moving against the wind and that quickly disappeared behind a tree line, according to testimony in Case 90015.

The witness was in his backyard having coffee on the patio when a "floating object" was first observed at 7:40 a.m. on February 4, 2018.

"It flew in a straight path for about 10 minutes and suddenly disappeared after passing a tree line in my view," the witness stated.

Florida MUFON Field Investigator Marc D. Barbieri closed this case as an Other.

"The size described as approximately four to six feet, rectangular, dark in color, leaving no visible signs of propulsion," Barbieri wrote in his report. "Object was observed at a distance of less than 500 feet at an elevation of 45 degrees moving in a south to southwest direction, speed less than 25 mph. No sound could be heard from the object. Object was observed for approximately 10 minutes traveling in a straight-line path.

"While the witness appears credible, there is just not enough collaborating evidence to make a determination at the time of this writing. Some additional information taken from the phone interview led to some observations concerning the object witnessed. The object was stated to be 'floating slightly faster than a balloon.' I took this to mean wind speed, which was confirmed via the phone interview. The object appeared to be maintaining a constant speed of approximately 15 to 20 mph in a south to southwest heading, according to the witness. Weather records for the area show prevailing winds of 12 to 17 mph with gusts as high as 25 mph coming from south-southeast. This would put the object traveling almost directly against the wind."

Port St. Lucie is a city in St. Lucie County, Florida, population 164,603.

British witness describes shapeshifting UFO

A British witness at Windsor reported watching and photographing multiple triangle-shaped craft with external lighting, according to testimony in Case 90097.

The witness was a passenger in a car at 6:30 a.m. on February 4, 2018, driving from Windsor toward Maidenhead.

"I saw aircraft lights on my left, which were descending at around 1,500 feet, landing west-east at Heathrow," the witness stated. "I looked again and saw what I thought was another plane with flashing lights; however, this craft was closer to me, much lower and travelling east-west. I observed the craft, which flew across the fields in my direction and then banked left to fly parallel with the road I was travelling along, directly left of me. The car was travelling at around 50 mph and was moving alongside the craft for quite some time."

The witness got a good look at the object.

"At one point the craft was so close I could see its shape was triangular, with bright, white lights at each point. I could see that the craft seemed to have a dome underneath its center. I noticed what looked like gold-colored foil around a domed part underneath that glowed slightly. I also recall that the craft seemed not to be flying flat but leaning slightly to the left for some time. I couldn't make out much at the top of the craft. I remember that there were red and blue flashing lights around the base of the circular center exactly like the strobing lights on an airplane. I recall there seemed to be more blue lighting more than red. "

The witness thought that the object appeared solid and slightly reflected the glow from road lights below.

"It seemed to be a matte gray. I tried to take some pictures through the side window with my mobile phone, but my view at this point was partially obscured by trees and bushes and reflections on the glass, although you can see a gray triangle with a white corner in all the blurriness. The craft continued in the same general direction, but farther from the road, where I struggled to keep my eyes on its movement due to the houses that lined this stretch of the road. The craft was flying low on the other side of the houses. When I could see the craft, it was moving between the houses."

The witness then lost sight of the craft and continued home, which was only a minute away.

"I exited the car and scanned the sky to see if I could see it again. It was then I saw it, this time travelling back towards Windsor. It was crossing in front of me, very close and very low. I was standing in the center of my car park, and it was directly in front of me at around 80 degrees from the horizon. As I went to take photos, the craft turned into an orb of light; the orb seemed to be smaller than when it was in its triangle state. One photo shows the craft in this orb state. My phone didn't seem to want to work very well, and it seemed frozen when trying to take the shots. When I next looked up, the craft had changed back to the triangle shape. It took a long time to actually get the shots; the ones that I did get were very shaky, apart from one showing the orb. The craft was silent and very dark this time. Although I could see the blue and red flashing lights, there was no sign of the glow underneath as I had seen earlier. I could still make out the triangular shape of the craft. It moved onwards very slowly and continued flat and straight into the distance until I lost sight of it. As it moved away, I could see two white lights at the rear, as shown on the photos submitted. I thought I saw it a minute or two later in the distance, but it could have been an airliner.

United Kingdom MUFON Field Investigator Kevin Gorringe closed this case as Info Only.

Windsor is a historic market town and unparished area in the Royal Borough of Windsor and Maidenhead in Berkshire, England.

FEBRUARY 7

Idaho witness videotapes large hovering object

An Idaho witness at Shoup reported watching a hovering, teardrop-shaped object that quickly moved away, according to testimony in Case 90127.

The witness and an assistant were parked near the intersection of Colson Creek Road and Salmon River Road at 8 a.m. on February 7, 2018.

"This location is extremely rural but has several cabins located along the river to the south of our location," the witness stated. "As we exited the vehicle my assistant pointed to an object in the air. I immediately looked up and observed this object approximately 500-feet AGL to the northeast of our location. At first it appeared to be small in size, but I soon realized it was larger than appeared as compared to trees and brush at a similar distance. I first believed it to

be a balloon, but thought otherwise after realizing the size and the actions of the object."

The witness began to film the object with a cell phone while the object hovered for several minutes.

"I felt slightly overwhelmed and found it difficult to operate my phone. Not normal as I use my phone daily. I dropped the phone, and the object ascended until it disappeared. Nothing further to report, video attached."

Idaho MUFON State Director James Millard closed this case as an Unknown Aerial Vehicle.

"Witness observed a teardrop-shaped object," Millard stated in his report. "It hovered and ascended. It appeared to be larger than a basketball. There were no lights, nor did it make any sound. This appears to be an unknown-UFO."

Shoup is an unincorporated community in Lemhi County, Idaho.

FEBRUARY 8

WA witness says disc-shaped UFO cloaked as a cloud

A Washington witness at Valley reported watching a disc-shaped object inside a cloud; moreover, the object appeared to be having trouble with a cloaking device, according to testimony in Case 94350.

The witness was sitting outside on a warm, sunny day at 1:07 p.m. on February 8, 2018.

"I was looking across the lake I live on towards the southwest sky and watching the clouds and was sort of gauging the wind, which was hardly any, maybe 4–5 miles an hour," the witness stated. "The clouds that day were various sizes but all oval."

As the witness watched, the biggest cloud started to blink.

"One second it was a giant, disc-shaped craft, then it was a cloud. I kept looking away at other clouds then looked back at this phenomenon, because I was questioning what I was seeing. It looked to me as though its cloaking was not working properly. This was enormous. I could see at least four stories of windows that were along the edge of the craft. The color was a metallic silver/chrome. After about 5-8 minutes it stopped blinking and looked like a cloud again."

Washington MUFON Chief Investigator Daniel Nims closed this case as an Unknown Aerial Vehicle.

"MUFON reports no similar large vehicle sightings in this vicinity," Sims wrote in his report. "A NUFORC case on January 22, 2018, at 3:30 a.m. reported a similar, large object that seemed to be able to generate a 'cloud' camouflage.

"The witness reports she stepped out to her west porch to have a cigarette and enjoy a pleasant early spring [sic] afternoon. She saw several strange oval-shaped clouds several miles away to the southwest high in the sky (about 45-degrees elevation). One of the clouds then changed from its cloud look and took on the appearance of a large disk-shaped object, which appeared oval looking at it from the side. The craft had a metallic surface. It also had what looked like four rows of rectangular-shaped windows that went around the craft. (See drawing.) The object was large, with an approximate width of seven inches and height of two inches at arms-length, or 14 degrees wide by 4 degrees tall. The object flickered back and forth from the cloud appearance to the disk-shaped object several times over a period of several (five to eight) minutes. She says it was like it had a 'cloaking' device that was malfunctioning. It finally assumed the cloud appearance. The object stayed fixed relative to the other clouds as they drifted off to the southeast in a mild breeze of a few miles per hour.

"No lights were noted. No sound was associated with the object, although it was quite a distance away.

"An object this large is too big to be an aircraft. An Internet search was run to see if any airship (blimp) operations were occurring in the northwest. The Internet gave no evidence of that. FlightRadar24 showed no aircraft in the vicinity of Valley for that time period.

"The unique characteristic of switching from cloud appearance to craft appearance would not be from any normal aircraft. The disposition of this case is: Unknown – UAV."

Valley is a census-designated place and unincorporated community in Stevens County, Washington, population 146.

Multiple witnesses report triangular UFO over Arkansas

Arkansas witnesses in two cases near Mena reported watching low-flying, triangle-shaped objects, according to testimony in Cases 90133 and 90181.

In Case 90133, the witness was driving on Polk Road 74 near Mena at the Ouachita River Bridge about 8:30 p.m. on February 8, 2018.

"I sighted a large triangular object in the sky at about 1,000 feet with three yellow lights at each point, about 100 feet wide and 150 feet long. I just noticed a bright yellow-colored light that I had never seen before in the sky. I thought the object was a large triangular aircraft, or maybe three planes flying in formation, but then I noticed that all three lights stayed together when the object moved, and that's when I started to think it was a UFO. All I could see was three yellow, bright lights formed as the points of a triangle. I did not see a craft, but it was the three lights that appeared to be on the points of a black object. The object moved extremely fast. Best way to describe it is when you're following an airplane, and it disappears behind a cloud, you expect to see the airplane again at an expected location when it reappears from behind a cloud, but this object did not act that way. The object seemed to move more side-to-side instead of a straight line."

The witness saw the object appear three times.

"It appeared, then disappeared, and, unlike the airplane, it reappeared where I did not expect to see it. It was like it was moving in two directions at once. It was flying more of a southwesterly direction from my location. I felt a state of awe. I was driving and tried to follow it. The object seemed to be heading in a southerly direction toward a small community called Board Camp or Nunley, where there have been other recent sightings. I called a friend who lives there to see if he could see the object. He told me later that he did and would report it. The object just disappeared while I was trying to keep up with it during driving. I drove five to seven miles trying to follow it before I lost sight of it."

The witness in Case 90181 was with a group of three other people outdoors on the grounds of the Board Camp Crystal Mine in the community of Board Camp, near Mena, Arkansas at 8:30 p.m.

"The group and I were investigating anomalies that have been occurring regularly at the site for nearly one year," the witness stated. "This is the same site investigated by MUFON nearly one year ago and featured in the October 2017 issue of the MUFON Journal. One person in the group was training us on how to use specialty equipment in our investigation, such as a night vision scope and radiation detection device. At approximately 8:30 pm, I received a cell phone call from a friend who said, 'Quick, run outside. We are following a triangular ship from Ink and it's heading your way.' The community of Ink is located north of where I was located in the community of Board Camp, so we expected

to see the object coming toward us from the north. Although I could not see the actual object itself, I could see the effect of the object as it approached and flew over. The night sky was clear and full of stars, so I could see that a portion of the sky and stars was blacked out as it flew over. It did not fly directly over my head but was more east of me. I did not see any lights on the object, only the black out and reappearance of the stars as it flew over.

"From the first time I began seeing the stars black out and reappear, the flyover lasted approximately 4–6 seconds and the object was approximately 1,000 feet in elevation. The group I was with had heard dogs and coyotes barking earlier, but all sound stopped during the flyover. It was very quiet. I saw it pass over and the estimated size was probably 150-200 feet long. I was facing east and it was moving south.

"After it passed over, I caught the quick glimpse of stars blinking out and coming back to my right, which led me to believe the anomaly changed course from south to a southwest direction. After I received the phone call from my friend who first saw the anomaly in Ink, the people in my group and I were excited and immediately started scanning the skies.

"I also quickly texted another friend of mine who lives between Ink and Board Camp and told him to go outside to watch. Before the flyover, I had a radiation detection device in my pocket. It was set to the highest setting and was picking up normal background radiation, indicated by an occasional beep sound emitted from the device. I noticed the flyover approximately five minutes after my friend called to notify me to look for it. During the flyover, the radiation detector in my pocket went off making a constant beeping noise, and the other three people in my group heard it, and were amazed and said, 'It must be right overhead!'

"After about six seconds, the detector went back to normal. After the object flew over, it disappeared past the horizon. Immediately after the flyover at approximately 8:40 p.m., I called my wife, who was inside the house on the same property, and told her to call a friend of ours who lives southwest of us around the Cove and Hatfield communities located south of the city of Mena to see if she could see it, after we determined it was possibly heading in her direction.

"Later, when my wife and I talked to our two friends whom we had notified to watch, both confirmed they saw something in the night sky, either the blacking out and reappearing of stars, or they saw three yellow lights. My background is—I am a US Army veteran, formerly worked as an investigator for the Department of Homeland Security, am a volunteer trained firefighter and certified instructor for Dept. of Labor.

Arkansas MUFON State Investigator William Brown and State Director Norm Walker closed these cases as Unknown Aerial Vehicles.

"I conclude that, without any other material evidence, this witness believes he observed a silent, triangle-shaped object with multiple lights and no obvious means of propulsion, as described in his report, moving slowly to the southwest near Mena, AR," Brown and Walker stated in their report.

Mena is a city in Polk County, Arkansas, population 5,737.

FEBRUARY 9

Rural Pennsylvania witness videotapes diamond-like UFO

A Pennsylvania witness at Derry reported watching and videotaping a "semi diamond-shaped object with what looked like an enormous spotlight in the sky," according to testimony in Case 90175.

The event occurred beginning at 11:18 p.m.

on February 9, 2018.

"I saw a very bright light in the sky, at first I truly thought it was a plane," the witness stated. "As the object got closer the lights and object became brighter and larger in size. It looked like an enormous spotlight in the sky heading towards us. It moved fast until it came close to us, and it moved almost in slow motion until I stopped in the middle of the road, just staring at it."

The witness pulled into a gas station and told her husband to grab her phone and record.

"Repeatedly asking him, 'what is that? What is that??' I could see the entire bottom of it. It was a semi diamond-shaped object. I say 'semi' because it wasn't exactly a diamond shape. Under the object there were dozens of fluorescent lights, ranging in color, blue, green, red, and orange. Underneath there was a semicircle of lights, blue and red. Around the semicircle was a shape of a diamond or square, depending on the viewpoint. The lights outlining the square/diamond shape underneath were green and orange in color. I am a person of sound mind, but this had me completely shaken. I was screaming at my husband, and honestly thought I was going insane. Never in my life have I seen anything like this. Ever. There's not a soul in this world that can tell me, nor convince me, that this was a plane. It appeared to be eight times bigger than any plane I've ever seen in my life. I am still very confused and shaken over this. I will never in my life forget this experience. For it has made me really think, over and over... what did I see in the sky that night?"

Pennsylvania MUFON James Krug and John J. Doucette III closed this case as an Unknown-Other.

"Witness and her husband spotted a brightly-lit, unidentified object to the north of the road on which they were traveling," Krug and Doucette stated in their report. "The object then passed over the road and interfered with the radio in their car. The witness and her husband may have become disoriented, and then arrived at her mother's house far later than they were expecting.

"Witness described a 100 to 300-foot-wide object that was less than 500 feet high, potentially as low as treetop level. When she had turned the radio the whole way down, but then all of a sudden it got really loud when the object was above them."

Derry is a borough in Westmoreland County, Pennsylvania, 45 miles east of Pittsburgh, population 2,688.

FEBRUARY 10

Former military pilot describes Texas UFO activity

A Texas witness at Granbury reported watching "a narrow, delta-shaped" object followed by four "fuzzy" orbs, according to testimony in Case 90355.

The witness was outside walking two puppies at 11:15 a.m. on February 10, 2018.

"In a restaurant district, 400 hundred yards from residence, just happened to look up," the witness stated. "Did not compare it to anything. It was that different. The lead object, very narrow delta shape. Did not see cockpit. One side gold and other black. Four round, disc shapes that were a gray color with a fuzzy look and edges not distinct. These four shapes were following behind main craft. The surface areas of discs and triangle appeared to be approximately the same.

The triangular craft was long, about 1.75 percent longer than the diameter of the orbs."

The witness said that all objects were traveling at the same rate and holding relative positions.

"Looking at the four orbs, I thought of positions on a clock face. From top right, first was at

about a 2:00 o'clock position, the next, lower orb was at about a 4:30 position but closer to the center, the third was at about a 7:30 position and the last at about 10:30. I did not think of a rectangular formation, but the circle I earlier stated."

Then something very unusual happened.

"The orb at about the 4:30 position suddenly, without the appearance of turning, rose vertically. I am a very avid believer of UFOs and the movement of the orbs reminded me of multiple orbs I have seen on film where orbs seem to be playing and moving around. All craft then went in front of the sun. I had to leave. Wish I had waited for them to go past the sun. There were no signs of propulsion, as they moved steadily. They were moving too slowly to be very low and keep flying. But they were too close to be moving at a high rate of speed. I would estimate the altitude to be 5,000 feet. I am a past military pilot. These were not conventional aircraft like anything I have seen before. Greatest eyewitness event I ever saw. Again, in my opinion, they were not conventional."

Texas MUFON State Director Gary A. Neitzel closed this case as an Unknown Aerial Vehicle.

"When talking to the witness over the telephone, the witness seemed to be very credible," Neitzel wrote in his report. "He talked a little about flying helicopters during the Vietnam War. The witness was very familiar with aircraft and he could not figure out what this aircraft was. The most unusual thing was that it was followed by fuzzy orbs. The delta-shaped object was flying so slow the witness could not figure out how it stayed in the air, especially since the sides were so long and narrow. The case is closed as an Unknown – UAV. During the telephone interview the witness was asked to send a drawing or a sketch."

Granbury is a city and the county seat of Hood County, Texas, population 7,978.

FEBRUARY 12

Missouri witness describes craft hovering at tree line

Missouri witnesses at St. Peters reported watching multiple, square-shaped low-flying objects, according to testimony in Cases 90205 and 90206.

The Case 90205 witness was driving along Sutters Mill Road towards Jungermann at 8:05 p.m. on February 12, 2018.

"Myself and my passenger observed hovering crafts with lights in the distance," the witness stated. "The crafts were about 200 yards apart and were rotating. We continued to drive until we reached Jungermann Road, where we pulled into a Walmart parking lot. We observed the crafts flying and hovering above."

The witness got out of his car to take a photograph.

"When I walked behind my car, a craft slowly approached from the south side of the lot and lowered quietly down to approximately 200 feet above me. The blinking lights on the craft turned off and the craft went 'dark.' At first, I was thinking it was a drone, but when it got closer it was too large and quiet to be a drone, but too small and quiet to be a plane. The appearance was square/rectangular and dark gray/black in color. It was about the size of a small car and was almost opaque, like looking at dark tinted windows hovering in the sky above me. I looked back at the passenger door of my car and then looked back up, the lights turned back on, the craft started to rotate and then 'glided' across the sky ascending about 200 feet up and to the north. About the time it was close to 200 yards away, the next craft was coming close."

After a few minutes all of the craft disappeared.

"We drove back down Sutters Mill towards Mexico Road. About 15 minutes later, I looked outside and saw the same lights/crafts. I called my daughter out and then my husband. We all observed three crafts moving in the same manner above the houses in the neighborhood. This continued for about 5–10 minutes and then they disappeared again."

Missouri MUFON State Section Director Dana Simpson West closed this case as an Unknown Aerial Vehicle.

"On the witness's report, the witness indicated seeing three to five objects that changed direction, hovered, descended, ascended, spun, blinked and appeared solid," West wrote in her report. "She indicated a dark patterned surface, with a size larger than a basketball and an actual size of 4–10 feet. She indicated a gray/black surface and white, gold, and green lights that brightened and flashed sequentially. She indicated a beam, but no sound at various elevations. There were other aircraft in the area, and the unknown objects flew in a circular path, with each one rotating or spinning clockwise, then counterclockwise. The crafts were spotted in the north and as far as 501 feet to one mile away, to 101-500 feet away with the lowest altitude at treetop level or 200 feet above the witness at a 90-degree angle. During the interview she indicated that the craft was the size of her SUV without the engine. She indicated it ascended, descended, and was itself rotating as it was moving in a circular pattern with the other craft. They were first spotted in the north but as they rotated and moved in a circular pattern were at various directions.

"Her daughter's report on this case (Case #90206) indicated 3 to 5 objects that changed direction, hovered, descended, ascended, spun, blinked, and appeared solid. She indicated a dark surface, larger than a basketball with an actual size of 4-10 feet. She marked a gray/black surface and exterior lights of red, red-orange, green, green-white, blue-green, blue, and blue-white (due to the spinning). The lights brightened, flashed sequentially, and flashed randomly with no emission or sound. She indicated it being at 90 degrees at an altitude of treetop level and 500 feet or less, with the distance from the witness being 101–500 ft. She indicated a path with directional change and then hovering in a north direction. She submitted her own sketch with her report (Case #90206).

The witness (of Case #90205) submitted a 58-second video (uploaded to File 2) that tracks at least three of the craft. This video was submitted to Joe Palermo for analysis. The witness submitted two sketches. One sketch delineates the rotation and flight path of the craft (uploaded to File 4), another sketch indicates what the bottom of the craft looked like when it was directly overhead, about 200 feet in the air (uploaded to File 3). Her daughter also did a sketch which she attached to her report Case #90206.

"The witness was very detailed in her description of what she saw, had video, and made sketches. Her daughter's and husband's descriptions of what they saw supported her report. I found her to be extremely credible, particularly with her background in aerospace and her husband's engineering background. It was so unusual to both of these individuals who have considerable expertise. The movement of the craft, their ability to rotate in both directions, and change rotational directions, their ability to maintain a flight pattern with other craft, and the close distance of the encounter all lead me to classify the sighting as Unknown UAV."

St. Peters is a city in St. Charles County, Missouri, population 52,575.

FEBRUARY 13

Pennsylvania witness describes 'four brilliant white lights'

A Pennsylvania witness at Grantville report-

ed watching "four brilliant white lights" that appeared to be cigar-shaped, according to testimony in Case 90221.

The witness was traveling eastbound along Early Mills Road at 6:40 p.m. on February 13, 2018.

"It had four brilliant white lights, no pulse, blinking or color change," the witness stated. "They were equally spaced apart. At arm's length, they appeared about the size of a shirt button. The lights illuminated an upper and lower edge above the lights. Above that edge, it appeared to curve into a cigar shape. The lights didn't illuminate far enough to tell. It moved very slowly and smoothly in a constant direction, east. I heard no sound."

The witness then drove along Pheasant Road as fast as possible to show the object to his wife, but once home, the object was no longer visible.

Pennsylvania MUFON Field Investigator Julia Weiss closed this case as an Unknown Aerial Vehicle.

"It was not a copter because it did not hover or bounce up and down," Weiss wrote in her report. "It was moving slowly and unwavering. It did not have red or green blinking lights. It did not look like a copter or plane. It could have been a blimp of some kind. However, blimps do have blinking lights. The white lights would have been blinking. That night the wind was going southeast at 10 miles an hour. The craft was moving in the direction of the wind and slow. So, I thought it could be some kind of long balloon or zeppelin. But again, we have the blinking lights. There has been a lot of triangle sightings and other craft like this seen in the area over recent years. It could be a new craft from Fort Indiantown Gap. As of now, I don't see it being a Black Manta. It was going too slow."

Grantville is an unincorporated community in East Hanover Township, Dauphin

County, Pennsylvania.

British witness describes slow-moving triangle

A British witness at Newbury reported watching a silent, black triangle slowly moving overhead, according to testimony in Case 90452.

The witness was outside at 9:35 p.m. on February 13, 2018.

"Black triangle over Boxford, West Berkshire (UK), travelling west to east approximately 30-40 mph, parallel to M4," the witness stated. "Weather cold (3 degrees C), with clear skies, constellations clearly visible, moon just a tiny sliver, maybe 8 percent lit, very dark night. Altitude: Approximately 2-3000 ft (1km). Silent. Size: approximately 35–50 meters tip to tail (medium-sized airliner length.) The two leading edges looked longer than the rear edge (60-40 percent.) The rear edge appeared to be a light strip looking a bit like a classic sci-fi light drive. A bit like football stadium lights but not as bright, a yellow/white color. Flashing red and white lights at the tips. (White may have been constant, red was flashing.) No lights underneath. Body appeared to be satin/matte black. Observed from approximately 30-degree angle at distance of approximately one mile, south of my position. (Triangle flying approximately two miles south of M4.) Observed for approximately three minutes before being obscured by houses and trees. Dog was disturbed and jumped around three or four times and made a squeaky disturbed dog noise. She's never done this before when I've taken her out."

United Kingdom Field Investigator Karl Webb closed this case as an Unknown Aerial Vehicle.

"Quite an accurate description of the triangular-shaped UFO close to the M4 in Berkshire," Webb wrote in his report. "Having checked for other sightings possibly of the same object on that date, I have unfortunately found nothing in terms of corroboration. The description given is similar to the descriptions of a possible terrestrial vehicle, which goes by the name of the TR-3B, inasmuch as the propulsion and light array on the rear edge of the triangle fits some descriptions. Other elements that would not lend themselves to the TR3B are the lights, described as one flashing and the other not, these being on the tips of the triangle but not underneath. In my experience, the more curious and more likely non-terrestrial triangles tend to be equal in their side lengths with the three bright circular masses towards the tips of the triangle underneath and a center red mass. Either way we are still at a loss as to whether this is terrestrial or not, despite much hypothesizing. In this instance I would be confident that the witness was sure as to what he saw, given his profession and interest."

Boxford, West Berkshire, is a village and civil parish in the unitary authority of West Berkshire, part of Berkshire in England.

FEBRUARY 15

Rectangular UFO reported low over Georgia

A Georgia witness at Woodstock reported watching a large, cylinder-shaped object moving at low altitude, according to testimony in Case 91313.

The witness was driving east along Eagle Drive just past Bells Ferry Road at 9:30 p.m. on February 15, 2018.

"Large, long rectangle-shaped object, glowing with various shades of bright orange through surface covered in octagon-shaped windows/exterior shell," the witness stated. "Appeared far ahead on horizon, flying low and north, having just come from the ridge of Putnam Ford Drive. At about Eagle Drive, it takes a wide turn to the west, taking it over the Etowah HS and Booth MS complex and football stadium, then flies due west, slightly north and parallel to Eagle Drive. I'm still driving east on Eagle Drive, and it passes to my left just before I reach Rose Creek Drive. I look up to my left and I can see it through the tree tops as it passes. It was so big and orange that I couldn't process in the moment what I was seeing. It seemed whimsical, or psychedelic, like out of a carnival, as it glided by. My first thought was that maybe it was a huge long balloon with orange burners inside, but soon realized that it was too massive and moved too quickly to be a balloon. Its path would've taken it over Bells Ferry Road, over Jersey's and Walmart. Many others had to see it."

Georgia MUFON Chief Investigator Jerry Carlson closed this case as an Unknown Aerial Vehicle.

"It is clear the witness believes he saw something," Carlson wrote in his report. "His initial CMS report was very detailed. For such a significant sighting in the middle of a heavily populated urban area, at an early evening time, one would expect numerous witnesses to come forward. However, no other reports were filed.

"It is clear that no currently known military or civil aircraft exhibit the properties reported by the witness. Additionally, no other research has identified any natural or manmade objects that could be confused for the object seen by the witness. While there was a report of an orange-colored drone spotted in the area of Hartsfield International Airport the next evening, this only opens the possibility that an orange-colored object in the Atlanta area does in fact exist; however, there is no evidence that ties this aircraft to this particular sighting.

"Therefore, in absence of any evidence to the contrary, the object has been classified as an Unknown UAV."

Woodstock is a city in Cherokee County, Georgia, population 23,896.

FEBRUARY 21

Witness says UFO 'appeared out of thin air'

A California witness at Sacramento reported watching a rectangle-shaped object hovering over nearby buildings, according to testimony in Case 90347.

The witness was driving to get food at 12:30 a.m. on February 21, 2018.

"I was driving down the road when out of no-where I see this big craft appear out of my top left field of view," the witness stated. "I didn't have time to think. I was almost dumbfounded at what I was looking at. The craft appeared from out of thin air and hovered at this spot above the buildings about 300 feet away or so."

The witness described the object.

"It had two blue lights that were parallel to each other. The blue lights followed from the front of the craft to the back and were on the sides of it. They were very bright, and I saw this craft the second it appeared. I could make out some sharp features of the craft, but it was like it had some form to it, and at the same time was almost transparent. Then before I could process what had happened, it shot off in a straight line and immediately disappeared as it set into motion. I still can't believe what I just saw. I had to Google 'report a UFO' and sure enough I found this place. I'm really struggling to make sense of this. I hope you guys can use this information and maybe provide me with some information of your own if you have some. I'll try and draw a sketch later."

California MUFON Field Investigator Valerie Benko closed this case as an Unknown Aerial Vehicle.

"The witness discussed the general area where he saw the craft and explained he was headed to Jack in the Box for food," Benko stated in her report. "The witness did state if he had not noticed the blue lights on the side of the craft, he probably would not even have noticed it. The witness was very shaken up over this experience. He explained they teach you in school this stuff is not real. If you talk about UFOs people will label you as crazy."

Sacramento is the capital city of California and the seat of Sacramento County, population 501,334.

New York witness says UFO 'just disappeared'

A New York witness at Rochester reported watching a triangle-shaped object with white lights at each tip that suddenly disappeared, according to testimony in Case 90647.

The witness and friends were walking across their college campus to get food at 8:30 p.m. on February 21, 2018.

"My one friend pointed to it in the sky and got our attention," the witness stated. "At first, we thought it was a drone but the more we thought about it after the fact, we realized it maybe was something else. The object was a triangle. It had a white light on each of the ends. I also noticed some gray lines on the triangle. The object was moving fast, and then all of a sudden it disappeared.

The witness stated that the group was "mesmerized" watching it.

"I was trying to get a good look at it. I was about to take out my phone, but then it disappeared. The object disappeared out of thin air. We were watching it and then it just disappeared."

New York MUFON Field Investigator Mary Fancher closed this case as an Unknown Aerial Vehicle.

"It seems clear the witness saw something highly unusual in the sky," Fancher wrote in

her report. "As per one of his replies to my questions, he is fairly familiar with planes and drones since his father was in the navy. It hardly seems likely that this was a military plane flying so low over a large city, although the possibility of the object being a drone is not completely out of the question. The fact of its sudden disappearance is also interesting. I would have to classify this as an unknown."

Rochester is a city on the southern shore of Lake Ontario in western New York and is the seat of Monroe County, population 208,046.

FEBRUARY 23

Nevada UFO described as 'several football fields' long

A Nevada witness at Summerlin reported watching a large, slow-moving craft the size of "several football fields," according to testimony in Case 90404.

The witness left home at 7:15 p.m. on February 23, 2018, and began driving west up the hill on Del Webb Drive to the Summit Clubhouse for an event.

"I immediately noticed the large craft in front of my car above the houses in front of me because it was flying too low and I thought it was going to crash into the neighborhood," the witness stated. "I was going 30-35 miles per hour and the craft stayed the same distance from me, so it was also going very slow. I thought when it didn't crash into any homes that it was perhaps in trouble trying to land at the Las Vegas airport. However, it continued to move at the same speed but just a tad higher, all the way to the top of the hill where I was going. When I pulled into the parking lot, I saw that the craft turned a little more to the north since it had been traveling west all the way up the hill. The craft had three red lights—one on the left side, one on the right side and one in the middle. This is why I originally thought it might be a large military aircraft, but it was flying too low and there was not a sound coming from the craft. Then as I attempted to make out the shape, it reminded me of the very large V-shaped object I had seen when the craft was over Phoenix, Arizona. The entire sighting took about 12 minutes and the night was very clear."

Nevada MUFON State Director Sandra Countiss closed this case as an Unknown Aerial Vehicle.

"I called the witness and she was happy to talk about the experience," Countiss stated in her report. "She was going to dinner at Summit Club in Summerlin along Dale Webb Boulevard when she saw a large, two-to-three blocks wide black plane above her, looking like it would crash into the neighborhood. It made no sound, had no emissions, and had only three red lights on the sides and at the apex of it. It was triangular-shaped, not a chevron, and huge. The red lights were on each side, no wings, and it was going about 35 miles-per-hour, as she was. It did not get ahead of her with speed, just travelled along at the same speed as she did. It was under 500 feet high, close to the ground and just over the roof tops, going from west to northwest. She kept expecting it to crash since she didn't hear any engine noise and thought it must be going down, but it didn't. Reminded her of the Phoenix lights, after she thought about it for a while. It went over the summit, changing direction slightly to the northwest, and then was gone. She heard no noise and no emissions were seen. She said she kept trying to make it fit into an airplane or drone mold, but it didn't, and it was gone when she realized it might not be one of 'ours' at all. She followed it for about 10-12 minutes until she got to the club and stood in the parking lot, watching it go over the summit and disappear. Very interesting and good description by witness.

"Witness was very descriptive and did not exaggerate at all. Very interesting craft and the third one seen of this nature in the past eight months in this area. We are seeing many chevron-shaped objects."

Summerlin is an affluent master-planned community in the Las Vegas Valley of Southern Nevada, population 100,000.

New Las Vegas witness: UFO was 'massive'

A Nevada witness at Las Vegas reported watching and videotaping a "long, flat craft" with three lights, which was hovering and making no sound, according to testimony in Case 90398. The report appears to have followed Case 90404 by several minutes.

The witness and a fiancée were driving home after picking up food at 7:17 p.m. on February 23, 2018.

"We noticed three lights in the sky, which from a distance, at first glance, appeared to be three planes flying in unison," the witness stated. "Once the craft came closer and as we got a better view, we saw it was one massive craft. I took my phone out and tried to video it. We were moving, so it was difficult to capture. The craft made no noise, and its lowest altitude appeared to be around 1,000 feet. It stopped and hovered abruptly and then continued on its path west towards Red Rock."

Nevada MUFON State Director Sandra Countiss closed this case as an Unknown Aerial Vehicle.

"Triangle, hovered over building, turned abruptly and changed direction," Countiss wrote in her report. "Appeared solid, surface was dark, no other structural features, basketball-sized, blue-green exterior lights and red exterior lights. No emissions or sounds. Possibly a military craft or airplane being tested at Nellis, 15 degrees above the horizon, would flash sequentially, 500 feet at lowest, southwest to west pathway. Background: Mountains."

Las Vegas is the county seat of Clark County,

Nevada, population 648,224.

FEBRUARY 26

Glowing disc-shaped UFO low over California

A California witness at Wilmington reported watching and videotaping a disc-shaped object with green and white lights, according to testimony in Case 90708.

A family member filed a report for two others who were driving at 3:47 p.m. on February 26, 2018.

"My sister-in-law and my daughter were driving down on C Street in Wilmington, CA, at 15:45pm, when they observed a flying object heading north on C Street parallel to Harry Bridges Boulevard. The object appeared disc-shaped and emitted green lights/white lights (think a glowing white, greenish saucer) and hovered horizontally across Harry Bridges northbound. My daughter, who couldn't get the phone video to start, took two snapshots of the flying object (on the left in the photos, not the right, that is a lamp under a tree). Then she proceeded to record the object as soon she was able to get the camera to work. The footage is only a few seconds, but details its movements. The object disappeared behind a lumber building. My family members were shocked and startled. They phoned me immediately and sent me the video shortly thereafter."

Southern California MUFON State Director Jeff Krause closed this case as an Unknown Aerial Vehicle.

"The two witnesses were driving in a car when they spotted an unusual, glowing, disc-shaped object," Krause stated in his report. "The witnesses stopped and took photos and a short video of the object.

"The witnesses described the object as being the size of a golf ball held at arm's length and estimated that it was a little over 500 feet from them when first spotted. The witnesses were unable to determine the altitude of the object, but described it as moving in a northwest direction. The witnesses were unable to determine its angular size.

"I evaluated the photographs and video myself, and all had the EXIF data intact, and were not edited in any way.

"After evaluation of the photos and video submitted, and interviewing the witnesses twice, I find their testimony to be 100 percent credible. My investigation showed that there were no blimps or other types of airships in the area on that particular night that could be mistaken for a disc. I am closing this case out as Unknown – UAV."

Wilmington is a neighborhood in the Los Angeles Harbor Region area of Los Angeles, California. The above witness testimony was edited for clarity.

MARCH 2018

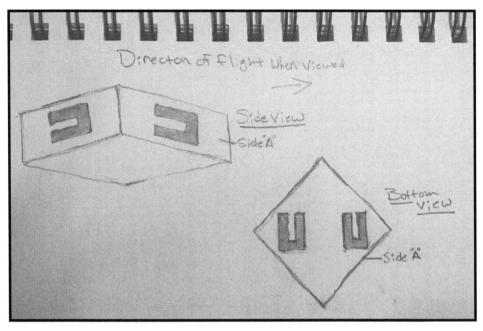

Case 94597 witness illustration. March 2, 2018.

MARCH 2

Low-flying triangle reported over Philippines

A Philippines witness at Dasmariñas reported watching a low-flying, triangle-shaped object, according to testimony in Case 90499.

The witness was walking along a highway at 5:25 a.m. on March 2, 2018.

"I noticed something in the sky," the witness stated. "There were a couple of dim lights on that flying thing in a V-shape. At first, I thought it was just an airplane, but airplanes do not have that kind of shape. I also thought it was just birds in formation, but it was still too dark for birds to fly. It flew right above me. It was so huge, so it seemed like it was flying low. It moved quietly with no sound at all. And when it went past the trees, it was gone. I was out of words. I jogged so I could check the sky, but it wasn't there anymore. I was really in shock

and I felt weird. I told my boyfriend about it."

CAG International and MUFON Field Investigator Eric Smith closed this case as an Unknown Aerial Vehicle.

"I could find no corroborating reports of a sighting near the reported time or location," Smith stated in his report. "I could find no evidence of it being attributable to a weather phenomenon. Calls and emails to local police, military and airports were unreturned."

Dasmarinas is a city in the province of Cavite, Philippines, population 659,019.

Square-shaped UFO reported over Michigan

A Michigan witness at Muskegon reported watching a low-flying, square-shaped object with U-shaped lights, according to testimony in Case 94597.

The witness stepped outside his garage's side door at 8:30 a.m. on March 2, 2018, and immediately noticed the object.

"Only because a small aircraft was crossing it in the sky at the same time," the witness stated. "Which is why I noticed it. Then I noticed the object. It was square or cube-shaped but flying point first. It had four U-shaped lights, but they were turned at a 90-degree angle. Open end facing left of me, and to the west. It came from the west and went east. It moved slow, like watching a satellite move across the sky. When it finally went beyond the trees and out of sight, I turned around for less than 30 seconds. When I looked back, it was overhead again. And then went to the southeast."

Michigan MUFON CAG Field Investigator Sue Gerberding closed this case as an Unknown Aerial Vehicle.

"The witness stated the strange object he saw was crossing the sky from west to east, and the small plane was passing behind it from the south-southwest. The object had 'strange' lights and a very black surface; so black that the witness could see the outline of the object against the night sky, lit only by a less than quarter-moon on a clear night. The witness said he has never seen anything like it; he is familiar with the small planes from the local airport, the medivac planes/choppers in the area, and he is a former Army Apache helicopter flight-ops technician (served in the Army from April 2005 – December 2006). The object also had four dark-red lights, in an elongated backwards 'C' shape; it had a square, flat bottom and was moving point first; the front and back red lights alternated in slow flashing, rhythmic, but not like those on aircraft. The object did not seem to be that 'tall,' and moved slowly across the sky, much like a satellite, but it was only at about 1,000 feet or so. It appeared to be the same size as the small plane in the sky (Cessna), though they were at different altitudes; he estimated actual size at between 31–300 feet—it was difficult to

judge. It took the object about 10 minutes to cross the sky, before it went over the trees and out of the witness's field of view. The witness turned and went back into the garage for just a second, and when he turned around and came out again, the object was again in his sky following the same path, but a little farther north this time, not directly overhead. Then the object departed from its path and left, moving to the east/southeast. The object had made no sound. The witness did not report this for months, because he had never seen anything like this and was a little hesitant about reporting such.

"In this case there was no obvious explanation. The visual characteristics and travel speed of the object in this case are somewhat unique. Until further evidence is discovered, this object cannot be identified, and remains an unidentified aerial vehicle."

Muskegon is a city in Muskegon County, Michigan, population 38,401..

MARCH 3

Triangle UFO 'glides' over UAB campus

An Alabama witness at Birmingham reported watching a white, triangle-shaped object "gliding over the University of Alabama at Birmingham (UAB) campus," according to testimony in Case 90540.

The witness was walking down 13th Street on the UAB campus at 5:35 p.m. on March 3, 2018.

"I observed a white triangular craft moving at a strange pace at high altitude," the witness stated. "I watched it head west, then abruptly southwest. I watched until it was out of vision."

Alabama Michigan CAG Field Investigators

Calvin Owens and Mary Owens closed this case as an Unknown Aerial Vehicle.

"Due to the lack of a witness interview, my conclusion is based on the original information provided," Owens and Owens stated in their report. "The object was described as a white triangular object travelling west and then abruptly turning southwest before disappearing out of sight. The wind direction was north-northeast, which means the object was travelling contrary to the prevailing winds and also made a change of direction."

The University of Alabama at Birmingham is a public research university in Birmingham, Alabama, with a student population of 19,656 located in the southside neighborhood of downtown Birmingham, Jefferson County, spanning about 83 blocks.

Nebraska witness reports missing time after UFO encounter

A Nebraska witness at Elkhorn reported watching a "disc of light," followed by their vehicle being engulfed in light and a possible alien encounter, according to testimony in Case 90584.

The witness was out driving in search of UFOs at 11:30 p.m. on March 3, 2018.

"This was probably about my hundredth search for UFOs," the witness stated. "Since about 2001, I have gone out driving near my home every once in a while. I have never, before this, encountered anything more than a probably misidentified ball of light. Needless to say, I succeeded last Saturday night."

The witness was driving in a remote area of rural Douglas County, somewhere to the north of Elkhorn.

"When I first noticed the object, it was a disc of light in the sky off to the west. It disappeared after approximately five seconds. Approximately 30 seconds later, my car was

engulfed in light. Almost immediately afterward, a large-ish (18-wheeler size?) disc of light similar to incandescent bulb warm light had landed in front of me. After about a minute, a bright blue ball (then varying shape) of light (entity?) appeared in my car on the passenger's seat next to me. It was about six feet tall and an irregular shape. The being(?) constantly varied in shape, although more or less taking the shape of the seat it was on. However, it never was anything other than a blue light. About 30 seconds later, my car overheated, stopped, and nearly injured me. As soon as the car began to become insanely hot, the aliens and light disappeared. The temperature, according to the meter in the car, reached 114 degrees. I needed to open the door, which was now possible with the lack of aliens. I cannot remember one hour before the incident. I am not available for contact."

Nebraska MUFON Assistant State Director Kyle Finley closed this case as an Unknown Aerial Vehicle.

"Very interesting case with no hard evidence," Finley wrote in his report. "Witness doesn't wish to be contacted for additional information."

Elkhorn is a neighborhood on the western edge of the city of Omaha, Nebraska, population 6,062.

MARCH 5

NC witness reports 'fog' around UFO

A North Carolina witness at Webster reported a low-flying, square-shaped object that moved directly overhead, according to testimony in Case 91103.

The witness was driving to work at 11:14 p.m. on March 5, 2018, when bright lights were first noticed.

"I first thought it was a house someone just moved into on a mountain," the witness stated. "As I got closer, I then noticed there was separation between the lights and the mountain. I drove just a little farther and noticed how slow it was moving. I stopped in the middle of the road and looked to see what time it was, and it was 11:17 then. This is a very windy road. I turned my radio off and rolled the windows down and got my phone to take a picture. I didn't have any data on it, so I couldn't take a picture. It was very low and didn't make a bit of noise. It was wide 'cause there was a light on each end and also about six to eight in the middle. I couldn't tell if it was long 'cause there were no lights. It wasn't foggy but this was really weird."

The witness then noticed something unusual around the object.

"When it was almost above me there was fog in the immediate area, mostly around the object. Not on the ground or close to me. I say fog because I couldn't smell any smoke. It wasn't thick and I could see the lights clearly. It floated in a straight line from when I first noticed it and where I stopped, it floated right over me. I say floated because it was moving so slow. I looked out of my passenger window and it went on its way. I couldn't believe it and wanted to call the sheriff's office, but thought they might think I was crazy. There is a very small airport that it was headed toward, but would have had to ascend to get that high to land. I never heard it accelerate. I called the airport the next day to see if anything had landed there the night before, and they said no. I was amazed that I saw it and that it was so low. I told some of my co-workers about it and asked if anyone else had seen it. None did."

North Carolina MUFON State Director David Glidewell closed this case as an Unknown-Other.

"Witness was on his way to work on a very windy mountain road about 11:17 p.m. and noticed some bright lights," Glidewell wrote in his report. "At first, he thought they might be house lights, but he noticed there was separation of the lights from the mountain. He noticed there were two bright lights on each end and multiple lights between them. He was unable to see if there was any height to what he was observing—only the width. Witness reported fog around the lights and that the lights floated over his vehicle.

"Witness reports two main lights were about 90 feet apart. The witness was unable to determine any height to the lights. The lights 'floated' low in the sky from north to south and over the witness location on Little Savannah Road toward the Jackson County Airport.

"Based on the information provided by the witness, the best fit case disposition would be Unknown-Other (odd-moving lights near the ground, strange floating objects)."

Webster is a town in Jackson County, North Carolina, population 363.

MARCH 6

Utah UFO described as 'size of a stadium'

A Utah witness at West Jordan reported watching a "white ship the size of a stadium," according to testimony in Case 93750.

The witness was at a park flying a drone at 10:42 a.m. on March 6, 2018.

"I noticed a huge, white mother ship flat like a Frisbee shape," the witness stated. "It had a com trail spreading out from behind it as wide as a two-mile spread. As I was positioning my drone to film this thing, I noticed a little door open on the front of the white ship. This ship was about the size of a stadium. A smaller black ship flew out of the front of the mother ship. The black ship had blue and pink lights that did not flash.

"It appeared to have tail wings on it. It made no sound. It was moving about Mach 5. The small black ship flew down towards me and buzzed the cell towers on the south side of the park, on the right side of me. My drone was hit with some emp and crashed. But not before I was able to get some pictures of both of the ships.

"After buzzing around the cell towers, the small ship flew back up to the huge, white mother ship. Then I watched the white ship literally disappear up into the sky. I downloaded the SD card footage into my laptop so I could zoom. The pictures are up close."

Utah MUFON State Director Michael Barrette closed this case as an Unknown Aerial Vehicle.

"I spoke with the witness during the evening of August 1, 2018 about his sighting," Barrette stated in his report. "He was very glad that someone actually would talk to him about it. He stated that he saw a large, circular white craft, approximately the size of a football field, heading towards him while he was flying a drone that he had just gotten for his birthday. Witness stated that he saw a black, round (saucer-type) craft come out of the white object, come down to his position and fly around him and stop by some cell towers that were in the area. Like the black craft was searching for something. Witness stated that when the black craft came into his area, that the drone lost its flight characteristics and crash-landed. The craft then came back to the witness and flew over him approximately 100 feet at a speed approaching Mach 5. Witness stated that he did not hear any engine noises, only the rushing of the air as the craft flew past him.

"Witness stated he believed that the white craft was 15,000 to 30,000 feet above ground level. He went on to state that when the craft departed his area and went back to the white craft, a door of some type opened, and the black craft disappeared inside. Witness went on to say that the white object left the area and just disappeared as it was heading in a southerly direction. Witness stated that he did not have any loss of time."

West Jordan is a city in Salt Lake County, Utah, population 103,712.

Georgia witness says UFO 'came right at him'

A Georgia witness at Marietta reported watching a diamond-shaped object, when a smaller object moved quickly toward him, causing him to fear for his life, according to testimony in Case 90698.

The witness took his dog outside at 9:40 p.m. on March 6, 2018, when the incident began.

"By the time the dog was finished with its business, I was heading around the block," the witness stated. "Instead of turning around and heading back to the house, I decided to continue around the block since it wasn't much farther to head home at that point. It was a brisk evening. Both the dog and I had on our jackets. There wasn't any wind, so the walk wasn't uncomfortable. Although it was dark, it was a clear night. I remember thinking how quiet it was outside and how dark the neighborhood was. I did hear some sounds of some dogs barking from a house we had passed two houses back. At no time during the walk did I see anyone outside their homes and no cars were leaving or coming. The only signs of life were the lights on in the windows of various homes."

As the witness turned onto the next block, facing the street he lived on, he noticed bright, white lights above the treetops.

"The lights were slowly moving left. My first impression when I saw the lights was that it might have been an aircraft turned sideways about to crash. However, the lights stayed in a direct path, skimming above the treetops.

As I got closer, I could make out that there were four lights on each corner in a diamond pattern. They looked like stadium lights. The lights coasted in a sweeping motion. My next thought was—'I'm not surprised at why people think they witness UFOs in the sky.' Never once thinking that it was something I wouldn't be able to explain. I was excited and interested in what I was seeing. Never did I feel any fear. I was just trying to figure out what I was looking at with my eyes. As I turned the corner, it turned, and it followed the woodline along my street in the opposite direction I was walking. The trees were now denser, and I thought I was about to lose sight of the object. I felt a little disappointment that I had not figured out what I was looking at. At this point I was about four houses down from my home. We have an international airport and an air force base nearby. We always have a busy sky. The dog and I were both calm while we were seeing this. As soon as I thought I was going to lose sight of the object, a smaller object swooped down and came right at me. I could tell that it was approximately the size of a medium-sized sedan. It had grid, a pattern of shiny, silver metal-paned glass on top. It had a dim light emanating from the inside."

The witness said he could tell there was a figure inside.

"The head, neck and shoulders were of a larger proportion than a normal human shape. I felt like I could hear radio chatter from inside the craft, but I couldn't make out anything said. It was almost like a double-cockpit made out of glass panes and shiny, silver metal inserts. The craft itself was silent. The way it maneuvered in a fluid-like motion in such a small space was impressive to me. I remember feeling annoyed that government would test such a craft in my neighborhood, amongst houses with many people. I believe I looked up to my left to see where it had gone, when that diamond-shaped pattern over the skyline side-swept and was instantly hovering vertically, above two houses directly in front of me. It was tall. It was at least a hundred feet tall. The sides of the object were hard to make out against the night sky. Almost like it camouflaged itself. The most impressive feature of this craft was vertical, towering windows like a cigar-shaped pillar that ran from top to bottom, in the center of the craft. It was made out of the same, shiny silver and glass that I saw on the smaller object. I remember thinking to myself that Steven Spielberg couldn't have done a better job. I was mesmerized. A beautiful, warm aura of light was emanating out from the windows. At no time did I feel scared. I was actually thinking that this was the most beautiful thing I had ever seen. I remember feeling amazement, excitement, surprise. And then this larger craft made a very fast and extremely aggressive maneuver. It was too fast for my mind to process, heading in my direction. I then knew that I had to run as fast as I could to reach my house."

The witness said he feared for his life.

"I felt like it was going to try to capture me or run me over. I have never been so scared before. I barely made it past one house when I realized I wasn't going to make it in time and darted to my neighbor's yard, towards his front door. I was running behind the dog who took off ahead of me. I was in 'fight or flight' mode, and I chose flight. As it suddenly shot over my head, I could hear the roar. I didn't feel any breeze or air flow. I ran into my house as fast as I could after the dog and slammed the door. I was out of breath and in a state of shock and disbelief. I heard the sound of the object one more time, shortly after, but I was too scared to look outside to see if it was still there. I wasn't able to sleep the whole night. I didn't discuss anything with my family until the following evening. I'm not surprised that there are these things out there, I'm just surprised it happened to me and where I live."

Georgia MUFON Chief Investigator Jerry Carlson closed this case as an Unknown Aerial Vehicle.

"Initially, object #1 had bright, white lights, which were slowly moving from the witness's right to his left," Carlson stated in his report. "The object was 197 degrees south-southwest from the witness at an elevation of 12 degrees above the horizon, with an angular size of two hands wide and three hands high. He stated that it could be about half the width of a house. As the witness got closer to the craft, he could make out that there were four lights in a diamond pattern on each corner of the craft and were described as bright as stadium lights. The witness stated that he didn't remember if the bright lights cast shadows of objects on the street. A few minutes later after the witness had progressed farther down the street, he stated that this craft had moved and was hovering vertically, above two houses directly in front of him. He states that it was at least 100 feet tall and had vertical towering windows like a cigar-shaped pillar that ran from top to bottom in the center of the craft. A beautiful, warm aura of light was emanating out from the windows. The object then made a very fast and extremely aggressive maneuver and headed in the witness's direction. Witness states that the object was between him and the house behind it, which was about 100 feet away from him. He further states that the object was as close as 10 feet away from him. It then suddenly shot over his head with an audible roar similar to a jet plane.

"Object #2 was described as a smaller craft, which swooped down at the witness. The object was 196 degrees south-southwest from the witness at an elevation of 7 degrees above the horizon. It was described as the size of a medium-sized sedan and having a grid pattern of shiny, silver metal with paned glass on top. Inside the glass, the witness noticed a dim light emanating from the inside and stated that he could see the head, neck and shoulders of a figure inside. He stated that the being appeared to be much larger than a normal human shape. He also said that he could hear radio chatter from inside the craft, but couldn't

make out anything else. Except for the radio chatter, the craft itself was silent.

"It is clear the witness believes he saw something. His initial CMS report contained approximately 1,000 words and was very detailed. During the face-to-face interview, the field investigator was comparing the witness's oral story with his written account. The witness related the story in a manner that was very close to the original report. If this were a hoax, one would imagine that the witness's oral and written report would have several discrepancies.

"For such a significant sighting in the middle of a heavily populated urban area, at an early evening time, one would expect numerous witnesses to come forward. However, no other reports (as noted above) were filed.

"It is clear that no currently known military or civil aircraft exhibit the properties reported by the witness. Additionally, no other research has identified any natural or manmade object that could be confused for the objects seen by the witness."

Marietta is located in central Cobb County, Georgia, population 61,048.

MARCH 7

Cylinder-shaped UFOs reported over rural Texas

A Texas witness at Gonzales County reported watching a low-flying, cylinder-shaped object moving fast, according to testimony in Case 90628.

The witness was driving at 10:34 a.m. on March 7, 2018.

"Object appeared slightly east of Route 183, one mile north of Gonzales, traveling due west at a very high rate," the witness stated. "When I crested the hill and was able to see the object again, I saw two of them, appeared to be in a formation where one was lower and to the right. They were completely out of sight in seconds. Talked to Ken at the San Antonio office. He told me to file this report. I first thought it was an ultra-light plane by our little airport, but quickly realized it was big. Then I thought... man is that thing booking across the sky. Then I saw the other one. No time to react...so fast."

Texas MUFON Chief Investigator Ken Jordan closed this case as an Other.

"This case is based on the written description of witness only, no pictures or video provided, and a long phone interview," Jordan wrote in his report. "Based on description from witness, weather conditions at time of sighting, this investigator concludes that the witness did not see an aircraft of any known configuration."

Gonzales is a county in Texas, population 19,807.

MARCH 10

Maryland witness videotapes triangular UFO

A Maryland witness at Manchester reported watching a low-flying, triangle-shaped object with a red blinking light in front and white lights at the back, bottom and sides, according to testimony in Case 90710.

The witness was sitting inside his house near a deck door at 11:57 p.m. on March 10, 2018.

"I noticed a light in the corner of my eye coming from outside through the trees," the witness stated. "I saw a flying object casting a bright light with smaller blinking lights around it. I thought it was just a plane, but as it approached, I knew if it was indeed a plane, it definitely wasn't an ordinary one. As it got closer, I was expecting to hear the sound of a regular plane engine and all that, but I wasn't hearing anything."

The witness decided to step outside on his deck to get a better view and listen closely.

"I still couldn't hear much. I didn't notice any noise until it was about 75–90 degrees over my head. It gave off a quiet hum/buzz that sounded like a plane engine, but it was extremely quiet and smooth. It continued flying in a straight line, coming from the northwest and continuing southeast, and as it was directly over me (a couple hundred feet at the most), I noticed two white lights to either side of it that weren't blinking, one red light on its front, and one white light on its back/bottom, and both the red and white light were alternating blinks. I could see the outline of it, and it was definitely a triangular shape. After researching a little, the only thing I found is a TR-3B or a B-2. It's just very unusual timing, and we've never had anything like this fly over before. We've actually seen some larger fighter jets fly over during the day once or twice, but nothing like this. And I'm not too sure of this, but having it coming from the northwest where I am located just seems different."

Maryland MUFON CAG Field Investigator Fred Kohler closed this case as an Unknown-Other.

From Kohler's report: "Cast light, pulsated, appeared solid, had outline. Surface: dark. Structural features: wings. Apparent size: larger. Actual size: 11-100 feet. Lights: white and red (exterior lights), brightened. Flashed: sequentially. Sound: hum/buzz. 90 degrees above the horizon. Lowest altitude: 500 feet or less. Distance from witness: 500 feet or less, straight-line path, northwest – southeast. No landing observed.

"The pictures are a little grainy, but you can see them well, the new video is well-taken.

"With the pictures attached and the evidence of another UFO sighting in the same town, I'm apt to agree that the witness saw something unique. Closing this down as Unknown/Other."

Manchester is in Carroll County, Maryland,

population 4,808.

NY witness describes hovering diamond-shaped UFO

A New York witness at Woodstock reported watching a silent, diamond-shaped object, according to testimony in Case 95178.

The witness was driving home from work at about 4 a.m. on March 10, 2018.

"I witnessed the object in the sky," the witness stated. "I stopped my vehicle and turned off all the lights, rolled my window down and watched it fly across the sky with Overlook Mountain to the north, and it flew from west to east direction and made no sound. It was diamond-shaped, headlights at each point. Made no sound whatsoever and the lights blinked regularly like an airplane. The photo shows a sketch of what I saw and the exact direction I was looking, with the field in the foreground and over the mountain in the background."

New York MUFON Chief Investigator Christopher DePerno closed this case as an Unknown Aerial Vehicle.

"The witness said the object was approximately 400 feet away from him and was approximately 300 feet or higher off the ground," DePerno wrote in his report. "The elevation was estimated to be about 70 degrees. The witness said that this object was hovering, with its lighting continuing to pulsate at a regular interval. The object then moved from its northwest location and slowly traveled northeast, gaining altitude and then disappeared. At the time of the sighting nothing else was seen in the air. The witness said the sky was clear, and nothing was blocking his view as it rose towards the mountains. The witness said he continued driving as he was observing the object until it disappeared. The duration of the event was approximately five minutes. The witness arrived home and the object was gone. The witness sent a picture of the scene and a

hand-sketched drawing of the event, showing the object and where it was. Both the drawing and the picture are part of the investigation.

"The witness is the sole individual to this event. The witness, who is educated, can communicate well, describing this event consistently. There are no commercial airports or military bases in the general vicinity that would give a reasonable explanation to this event. The witness stated that the weather was clear and the object being viewed stationary, at around a distance of 400 feet away. Also having an estimated altitude of 300 feet, with no sound. This would most likely rule out a commercial plane or military flight. The witness was very consistent that this was a diamond-shaped object. The witness was driving a Toyota at the time of the event and nothing unusual happened to the vehicle.

"Based on the witness interview, pending further information on this event, I would say the witness is credible."

Woodstock is a town in Ulster County, New York, population 5,884.

'Half-moon' UFO reported over Delaware

A Delaware witness at Dover reported watching a large object "the shape of the bottom of a half-moon," according to testimony in Case 90968.

The witness was smoking a cigarette on a back porch at 9:30 p.m. on March 10, 2018.

"Looked up into the north-northwest portion of the sky," the witness stated. "I noticed what I first thought was a half-moon, until I realized that it was would have been the bottom half of the moon. That is a view that we do not see on this planet. Looking closer I saw that it had a silvery surface that seemed to give off its own light. Judging from where I was, the object looked as if it was directly over what would be the town of Marydel, DE, right on the Maryland/Delaware border."

The town is about 10–13 miles away from Dover.

"Next, I noticed several small, white lights, (maybe three or four), one of which was pulsating, maneuvering around the large, bowl-shaped object. They were moving quite slowly in all directions. They would move in one direction, then stop and suddenly move in another direction. I called my adult son outside, and we both remarked that it had to be a UFO."

The two watched the objects for about 15 minutes.

"I even went back inside the house, came back and it was still there. There was absolutely no noise from the objects. This became very obvious when we suddenly could see and hear a helicopter near the objects, but could not determine how close it was actually getting. We also witnessed a plane passing by the objects, but at a much greater distance past them. The plane was not anywhere near the objects, just passed by in the same line of sight. I'm certain that the pilots would have seen the objects. Neither my son nor I saw the objects shoot off, fly away or land. One moment they were there, the next moment I looked up and they were gone. Both of us were a bit nervous and confused. After talking about what manmade objects it could have been, we agreed that it did not look like anything we had ever witnessed before. I use a flip phone and did not take a picture. My son's phone was upstairs and, honestly, neither of us even thought about taking a picture at the time of the incident. Neither of us mentioned it to our spouses or to each other again until March 17, 2018, when my daughter and grandson came to visit. Something she said sparked the memory of the event, and I talked about it in detail to my wife, daughter and grandson. I still have no idea what it was but would like answers."

Thank you."

Delaware MUFON Field Investigator Erin Bagnatori closed this case as an Unknown Aerial Vehicle.

"I was able to reach the witness by phone and we spoke for about 20 minutes," Bagnatori stated in his report. "He recounted his story pretty much to the detail of his written report, and, considering his military experience and his current status of being a deacon at his local church, I consider him to be a credible witness and believe he saw something that he could not readily explain. With some additional information I was able to gather today (regarding locations, direction and inclination of event), I will begin contacting local authorities and our other resource tools to see if any known objects could be what was witnessed."

Dover is the capital of Delaware, and the county seat of Kent County, population 36,047.

MARCH 11, 2018

Ohio witness says triangle hovered under 500 feet

An Ohio witness at Munroe Falls reported watching a hovering, triangle-shaped object under 500 feet, according to testimony in Case 90789.

The witness was driving home from a friend's home along River Road about 10 p.m. on March 11, 2018.

"Nice narrow country road that has some houses and a metropark along the way," the witness stated. "A few tight turns as well, then running alongside railroad tracks and the Cuyahoga River. After the last tight turn, I saw a brightly lit object in the distance, off to the left slightly, right near where the metropark area would be."

The witness first thought the object was a

helicopter.

"Then as I got closer, the object had slowly moved over the road, and, as I went to drive under it, I noticed no sound. Stopped, turned down my radio and tried looking up through the windshield to see it. My driver's window is broken, so I opened the door, stuck my head out and looked up. A brightly lit object was overhead at maybe 400–500 feet. Three brilliant blue-white lights in a triangle. One corner also had a strobing reddish light."

The witness then stepped out of the car (still running, in park) and stood there for maybe another 10–15 seconds.

"It was so brightly lit I could see some details of what looked like a smooth-ish bottom, grayish-colored, with some type of geometric pattern covering the surface. The object then started to rotate in place and slowly started to move off the road and over the woods to the right, towards the railroad tracks and then the river. I thought then I would try to get a picture. I bent down, reached into the car and grabbed my cell phone from the passenger seat. I was in the car no more than five seconds and was swiping the screen as I stood back up to get the camera on. I looked up, and the object was nowhere to be seen. Stood there another five minutes or more, dumbstruck. Perfectly clear night sky. In just a few minutes I had seen numerous high-altitude planes flying in the area as well. Am pissed off that I took my eye off it and did not see it go away. It had to either have blinked off or shot away, as it was moving very slowly when I last saw it, and should have been no more than another few hundred feet away by the time I got the camera app ready. Anyways...that's what I saw last Sunday night. A brightly lit triangle, right near the city."

Ohio MUFON Field Investigator Joseph Pavlansky closed this case as an Unknown Aerial Vehicle.

"While speaking to the reporting witness, the FI verified the name, address, and email address provided on the initial report," Pavlansky wrote in his report. "The witness seemed sincere about the sighting and was very helpful throughout the investigation. The FI has not found a reason to believe the witness is untruthful in his sighting or reporting. Google Earth was used to locate the sighting area and any locations pertinent to the case. The object observed seems to correlate with black triangular objects under the TR-3 project of secret government crafts. Most of the TR-3 objects had a red light in the center belly of the craft."

Munroe Falls is a city in the east-central portion of Summit County, Ohio, population 5,012.

MARCH 14

Michigan witness videotapes low-flying rectangle

A Michigan witness at Port Huron reported a low-flying, rectangle-shaped object the size of car crossing the sky, according to testimony in Case 90776.

The incident occurred at 5:38 p.m. on March 14, 2018.

"Hovered over center of St. Clair River at about the same height of the bridges," the witness stated. "Constantly changing reflective colors. As it flew east to Canada, it gained altitude and hid in clouds. I was fishing the St. Clair River at the north end of the water treatment plant. I started fishing around 5:15 p.m. I was sitting there waiting for a bite when I heard a man yelling very loud from the parking lot at the police department, which is next to the water treatment plant on the north side. He yelled, 'Oh wow. Wow.' Then he kinda laughed excitedly. I immediately looked to the north and saw a silver and gold reflecting object hovering very slowly over the St. Clair River."

The witness said the object looked like a rippling, rectangular mirror.

"It was about the height of the bridges from the water. The object was moving slowly from west to east, which is from Port Huron, Michigan, to Sarnia, Ontario. The object started flashing very reflective colors that kept changing. It was like a gyroscope of colored mirrors, for lack of better words. The object was about the size of a car, but was more of a rectangle shape. As it neared the Canadian shoreline, it started to ascend and flew around faster, but went towards the clouds. It was very reflective the entire time I observed it. When I first saw it, I tried to make sense of it. I tried to say it's a plane, a helicopter, a helium balloon, a jet, a drone, but it wasn't. It didn't make any sounds, and the way it was hovering and flying was very unique. By the time I realized I was looking at a UFO, it was up over Sarnia, flying around and into the clouds. I got a small video clip, but that doesn't do it justice. I couldn't see the screen on my phone very well because of a glare. I lost sight of the object when it flew in a cloud high up in the sky.

"Might be irrelevant, but I saw a U.S. Coast Guard boat heading out into Lake Huron about 20 minutes before I witnessed it. About 30–40 minutes after I lost sight of the object, that same Coast Guard boat was heading back in the river. I don't know where the object came from, I first saw it over the river."

Port Huron is a city in Michigan and the county seat of St. Clair County, population 30,184.

MARCH 15

Alabama witness describes low-flying triangle

An Alabama witness at Holly Pond reported watching a low-flying, triangle-shaped object, according to testimony in Case 97506.

The witness was standing on his back porch drinking a cup of coffee at 4:30 a.m. on March 15, 2018.

"It flew directly into my field of sight," the witness stated. "I was looking towards the south and it flew directly in front of me. It had three round balls glowing, not casting light, and it was triangular in shape, and on the very back on the top of the craft was a little blinking red light. It was completely silent and black, not regular black, but so black I couldn't see details of its bottom. And on the back of it were two panels that looked like closed blinds."

Alabama MUFON CAG Investigator William Morse closed this case as an Unknown Aerial Vehicle.

"The witness had gone to bed early at 8:30 or 9 the night before," Morse wrote in his report. "He arose early, made himself a cup of coffee, and went out on his back porch to smoke a cigarette at about 4:30 a.m. His back porch looks to the south. While he was standing there, an object in the shape of a perfect triangle appeared at treetop level and flew slowly from north to south over his field. He describes the object as solid black in color and about as thick as his house. At the points of the triangle were spheres that glowed in an unusual way. They emitted light, yet projected no light from them, as they did not light up the trees below. At the top of the object was a red light that he said looked to be in the shape of an old-time police light that we used to call a 'gum ball.' Behind the red light were two square flaps at the back of the object, which appeared to be closed. The object emitted no sound at all. He said he could still hear the crickets chirping. The object moved steadily at about one mph, never changing speed or course. It was a clear night and he could see the stars, but as the object moved it blocked the stars from view. He was frozen in fear, but after it passed, he went inside and told his wife. In January 2019, some 10 months later, he was watching a show on History and there was a reference to MUFON. This motivated him to report the sighting on the MUFON website."

Holly Pond is a town in Cullman County, Alabama, population 798.

Canadian witness encounters UFO hovering over roadway

A Canadian witness at Abbotsford, British Columbia, reported an object hovering over the roadway about the width of the two-lane road, according to testimony in Case 90803.

The witness was driving down a "poorly lit road" at 8:40 p.m. (already dark) on March 15, 2018.

"I had another person with me at the time," the witness stated. "At first I didn't really pay much attention to the craft as I assumed it was an airplane in a distance. I started taking more notice as I continued driving as the aircraft seemed to be quite low and seemed to be slow-moving. However, as I neared the aircraft, it was not moving at all. It was hovering in one spot directly over the road. It was hovering in one spot, probably above the power lines (distance wise). I kept driving, but I slowed down as I was driving under it (directly under it). I told my companion, 'that is no plane.'"

The witness described the object.

"It was a black color with lights (lights flashing like an airplane as that was the deception in the start). It was loud-sounding as I passed under it (loud engine). It was a long-ish kind of shape in width that was about the same size as the width of the road (double lane road). It had some kind of strips of material fluttering off it. It was not a drone. I drove under it, but, to be honest, I was tripping out a little bit in the moment as normally I am a very skeptical person. I drove up to the next street crossing (approximately a city block and a half) and did a U-turn as I was going to take pictures or a video, etc. I sped back down the road, but, as I neared it again, it left. It just seemed to look like just any other light in the sky within seconds. I don't know for sure what it was. When I

was under it, it was really the only time I could hear its engine. I couldn't hear what it sounded like when it took off as I was speeding back toward it to take some pictures. All that I could really hear was my own engine speeding back towards it. I don't know what it was, but it was not a drone or an airplane."

Canada MUFON Field Investigator Carl Peterson closed this case as an Unknown Aerial Vehicle.

"My investigation indicates that the witness has seen a very real UFO," Peterson wrote in his report. "We have received many reports from the lower mainland and Vancouver Island. The sightings have increased since North Korea has started testing long range missiles. We think the increased sightings are because that in the Hood Canal near the town of Bangor, WA, this U.S. naval base is the home of the Ohio-class Trident fleet ballistic missile submarines. This base provides maintenance, calibration, missile assembly/test, spare parts, and spare nuclear warhead storage for the Trident II ballistic missiles that are carried by the nuclear submarines. Hood Canal is only 140 km from this location. On Vancouver Island there is a submarine base called Nanoose Bay, site of a joint operation of the Canadian Navy and the U.S. Navy. This submarine base and a maritime test facility are known in the area as Whiskey Golf. This facility tests equipment and a variety of devices, including Sonobuoys, sonar systems, torpedoes and the repair and overhaul of the dipping sonar used on Canada's Sea King helicopter fleet. There have been as many as three Trident submarines at this base at one time. This base is only 164 km away."

Abbotsford is a city located in British Columbia, population 141,397.

MARCH 16

Indiana UFO described as lights in V-formation

An Indiana witness at Attica reported watching a V-shaped light pattern crossing the sky, according to testimony in Case 90816.

The witness was outside on a friend's roof taking measurements at 9:48 p.m. on March 16, 2018.

"Was looking up counting the number of siding strips up the side of the house when I noticed four lights in a V-formation," the witness stated. "Even though five lights would make it a symmetrical V, I only observed four—two on the left wing, one on the right, and one on the point.

"It was dark and there was a haze of cloud cover. The lights weren't very bright, but they were definitely illuminated. It was flying north-northeast, then took a significant turn to the southeast. These four lights didn't seem like they were part of one object, but looked like they did their own thing, but still flew in formation. The two lights on the left wing seem to dance around each other. While the front and right light just followed a weird path.

"This sighting lasted for five to 10 seconds. I don't know what to make of it. This was just my observation. There was nothing I can think of that I would have been mistaken for."

Indiana MUFON Field Investigator Jeremy Efroymson closed this case as an Unknown Aerial Vehicle.

"Witness said he was out on the roof of his friend's house when he saw lights travelling from the south to the north-northeast and then turning south-southeast," Efroymson stated in his report. "They were in a V formation with one light missing from the end of one side of the V. He did not think they were a single object because two of the lights circled around one another. The sighting lasted for five to 10 seconds. The lights were white in color and no sound was heard. He stated they travelled faster than an airliner. Since the objects were moving in formation and changing directions,

they were most likely intelligently controlled."

Attica is a city in Logan Township, Fountain County, Indiana, population 3,245.

MARCH 22

Georgia witness describes large triangular UFO

A Georgia witness at Chatsworth reported watching a triangle-shaped UFO hovering in the darkness and under 500 feet, according to testimony in Case 90959.

The witness was returning home after a trip to a McDonald's restaurant at 10:37 p.m. on March 22, 2018.

"I noticed to my left what first looked like an airplane flying low," the witness stated. "I almost thought it was an enormous drone, but it was way too big. Once I got closer, I could see in more detail that it was flying too slow to be a plane and saw its triangular shape. It had a red light on one side, a blue on another, and a flashing white one at the possible tip. It also had a sound. It had a bit of engine noise like a big engine. Amazed by the interesting sighting, I stopped dead in the middle of the road. Looked at it for a few more seconds and then pulled into a nearby parking lot to see it outside of the car. Unfortunately, when I got out it was already leaving. I can't explain exactly how it left because there are no human words for it, but I can try. When it left, it looked like it was moving at the same speed as before it stopped. (When I got a chance to see it.) But in a matter of seconds with it going that same slow speed it was already miles away. I searched for it afterwards, but I couldn't find it. I do remember hearing strange noises in the car engine, but that could have been paranoia. Other cars drove past but no one else seemed to notice."

Georgia MUFON CAG Field Investigators Mary Owens and Calvin Owens closed this case as an Unknown Aerial Vehicle.

"The witness included a drawing of the object showing a triangular object with blue, red, and white lights," Owens and Owens stated in their report. "He had no video or photos of the object. Based on his statement and the diagram this case is closed."

Chatsworth is a city in Murray County, Georgia, population 4,299.

Canadian witness says UFO was size of semi-truck

A Canadian witness at Coquitlam, British Columbia, reported watching a large, rectangle-shaped object the size of a semi-trailer, according to testimony in Case 91005.

The witness was driving home from work eastbound along Mary Hill at 11:45 p.m. on March 22, 2018.

"I suddenly saw a large rectangle object," the witness stated. "By large I mean like a semi-trailer, 53-foot, that looked very low and about to crash. As I got closer, it moved upwards like a roller coaster and then back down the same path and went west over the water. I was nervous, excited and scared. I rolled down my window to see what I could see and hear, and it sounded like a hover buzzing. It moved towards the water and now behind me. I pulled over as soon as was safe to get a picture, but now was too far away. It had lights that were very bright, like a solid rail underneath bright white. Also lights in front that I saw on and then went off. This object did not move like a helicopter or plane as I work near an airport and have never seen anything like this. When I got home I searched to see for any reports, as a few cars were around, but nothing. There was a similar report a week ago about 45 minutes south of here describing almost exact same thing as I saw. Not sure what I saw that night, but, boy, it was something I will never forget."

Canadian MUFON Field Investigator Carl Peterson closed this case as Info Only.

MARCH 26
Boomerang UFO reported low over Pennsylvania

A Pennsylvania witness at Bridgeville reported watching a boomerang-shaped object flying overhead 200 feet above the treetops, according to testimony in Case 91194.

The witness was sitting in a hot tub at 3:15 a.m. March 26, 2018.

"Noticed movement above," the witness stated. "V-shaped craft glided above my head heading west over trees. About the size of a 737 and no more than 200 feet above treetops. No lights. Probably wouldn't have seen it if it hadn't been for the ambient light from the large parking lot next door. Appeared dark brown but that could be the low light level. It glided smoothly above my head at less than 200 knots. There were regularly spaced artifacts on the underside, but couldn't say what they were. The pumps in the tub were off so I can say the craft made no sound. Got a very clear look at it, but for only three seconds or so."

Pennsylvania MUFON State Section Director Sam Colosimo Jr. closed this case as an Unknown Aerial Vehicle.

"Basically it was a V-shaped aircraft," Colosimo stated in his report. "It had a wing span of 150 feet or so and was the size of a small 737. Was moving much faster that a blimp, less than 200 knots, totally silent and was 200 feet or so above the trees. The color was dark, black or brown, and there appeared to be markings, but no lights on the underside. The underside of the aircraft did not have the tell-tale circle of a standard TR-3B. The aircraft was moving from east to west."

Bridgeville is a borough in Allegheny County, Pennsylvania, population 5,148.

MARCH 28

Fast-moving triangle reported low over New Hampshire

A New Hampshire witness at Brookline reported watching a triangle-shaped UFO at the tree line that quickly moved away, according to testimony in Case 91075.

The incident occurred at 3:15 a.m. on March 28, 2018.

"Hovering just above the trees in backyard, then quickly moved off to the east," the witness stated. "Trees moved, window shook. Awoke from sleeping and went to the bathroom facing back yard on second floor. Saw directly out the window above trees in the back yard a black triangle with three white lights, one at each tip and a red light in the middle. I saw it immediately upon getting to the window. All were unusually bright, but not blinding. Then heard a hum and the object moved off to the east quickly. The trees below where it was were moved, and the window I was looking out of shook.

"When I first saw it, I figured it was a plane, but then realized it was hovering and much lower than a plane would be. The lights were strange. Can't really describe why except they were bright, but not like landing lights or navigation lights and the color was wrong. When it started to move, I actually said out loud, 'What the hell is that?'

"The sighting didn't last long, probably a minute. It was just weird."

New Hampshire MUFON State Director Valerie C. Schultz closed this case as an Unknown Aerial Vehicle.

"The witness described this triangular craft as hovering and with a hum similar to being near a power plant," Schultz stated in her report. "As a private pilot, the witness was surprised to see this craft hover and stated that no plane can hover."

Brookline is a town in Hillsborough County, New Hampshire, population 4,991.

MARCH 29

Irish witness says craft body 'seemed to breathe'

A United Kingdom witness at Dublin reported watching a low-flying triangle where the object's body seemed to be breathing, according to testimony in Case 92167.

The witness was taking his dog for a walk at 5:30 p.m. on March 29, 2018.

"I decided to take the dog for a walk around to the local football pitches," the witness stated. "I put my phone on charge and left the house at approximately 5:20 and brought the dog to the field. I was bent at one knee about to take the dog off the leash when I looked up and saw a large black craft pass over silently above my head from behind. It did not fly normally. It sailed or glided. There was no sound, not even a break of air. This craft was well below the cloud level to a point I could almost reach out and touch it."

The witness said the object was captivating.

"I don't remember standing, but I must have done so as I followed it, directly underneath it. It was triangular in shape. There were zero edges on the craft. Its side and form were perfectly smooth and precision perfect. I could see patterns in it, like the skin of a reptile or something. It's hard to describe, but it looked like it was plated except without rivets or any noticeable joints. It was perfectly smooth in all directions. Like a layer of black skin. There were three orbs at each point of the craft. The forward orb and the right orb were static and did not pulse. The orb on the left was pulsing, not rapid like we see on a regular craft. It was like it was breathing is the only way I can describe it, slow, deep breaths. If you try it yourself, you will get the idea.

"The lights were a mix tint of white, green and blue. It sailed above my head, and I followed beneath it looking to get as much detail as I could. The bottom section contained a large, black orb which I could not make out. It appeared empty and hollow, but what drew my attention were the lines that ran along the base. They were angular and symmetrical and ran along the underside of the craft. It was these lines that helped me discern the hollow black center. I can draw them. The vision is so embedded in my mind. Again, there was zero sound. I watched as the craft crept away from me and saw at its rear two red lights at the back, like car lights; I could see indents in them. Three separate blocks of red light together to make one at each side. The center in between had what appeared to be pipes, or valves. If you can imagine, then look at Star Trek: The Next Generation. They have those containers in them. The center looked something like that, except again it was smooth, like it all joined together as one.

"The craft continued away from me and entered a thin cloud. I followed it through on its path until it emerged from the other side and slowly banked to the right. It continued to move over some houses. It could have been farther, but from my vantage point it looked like it was over houses where it stopped and began to pulse several times before blinking out of existence. Approximately three weeks prior, I heard trumpet noises mixed with metal work noises coming from the sky. Then to see this craft after, there is something going on."

United Kingdom MUFON National Director closed this case as Info Only.

Dublin is the capital and largest city of Ireland, population 1,173,179.

MARCH 30

Missouri triangle was size of football field

A Missouri witness at Excelsior Springs reported watching a silent, low-flying, white triangle, according to testimony in Case 91184.

The incident occurred at 4:30 a.m. on March 30, 2018.

"My friend and I watched a bright white flying object," the witness stated. "We watched it until it was no longer visible. The object flew in a straight path. It had white lights on each side of the craft. The whole event took no more than three to four minutes. It was quiet. I didn't hear it moving over, but it was very low. The craft was triangular in shape and lit up; bright, white lights are what made it so memorable."

Missouri MUFON Field Investigator Lawrence Tyree closed this case as an Unknown Aerial Vehicle.

"According to the first witness, he and his friend slowed their motorcycles so that they could observe the bright white flying object," Tyree stated in his report. "All told it lasted about three minutes. The first witness described it as a triangular-shaped craft with the leading point of the triangle in the direction of travel. The back two points were lit up with flashing white lights that blinked in unison.

"The second witness only recalled the craft being in one location while it was seen, and that it had no particular shape that he recalled. After losing sight of it when approaching town, it had vanished after they arrived in Excelsior Springs.

"Both witnesses believed the craft to be between them and Excelsior Springs, was approximately 300 to 500 feet high, and about the size of a football field. As they approached, the craft grew larger. The first witness stated that they were being rained on as they travelled, and that the craft was clearly under the clouds (under 6,000 feet). The craft was at about 20 degrees of elevation from the horizon. The angle of elevation could have risen closer to about 30 to 40 degrees as they approached it.

"As they approached the outskirts of Excelsior Springs, the road diverged to the left and the road became steeper, and they were surrounded by homes and trees, and thus they lost sight of the craft. When they arrived in town, it had disappeared."

Excelsior Springs is a city in Clay and Ray Counties, Missouri, population 11,084.

MARCH 31

South Carolina UFO disappeared into 'portal'

A South Carolina witness at Aiken reported watching a red, circular object that seemed to disappear by moving into a portal, according to testimony in Case 91151.

The witness was sitting on his front porch at 9:55 p.m. on March 31, 2018.

"Noticed a really bright, red light coming from the south headed north," the witness stated. "I was looking for blinking lights to identify it as a plane or helicopter, but this object was round, solid red in the middle, with short gold rays coming out of it all around the circle. It was perfectly silent and moving along about as fast as a little Cessna plane would. As it moved directly in front of me, it was only about 700 to 800 feet from me. The front two-thirds of the object disappeared and then a split second later the rest disappeared also. It kind of looked like it was moving into another dimension or something, the way the front part seemed to go through, then the back of it

a split second later. I did not see it after that. After the incident, two words have been stuck in my head, alpha and belvedere. Don't know what it means, if anything, but wanted to let you know."

South Carolina State Director Cheryl Ann Gilmore closed this case as an Unknown-Other.

"The witness is a 58-year-old builder," Gilmore stated in her report. "He stated he was on his front porch petting a pet cat when he noticed a very bright, red light coming out from the south of his location. He said it was an intense red with a fringe of yellow lights coming off the edges. He compared it to a drawing a child might make of the sun with lines coming off it. The center being red, not yellow. His wife was on the porch with him, but became afraid and went into the house. He stated the object passed directly in front of him at a distance of between 700 to 800 feet. The front two-thirds of the object disappeared, then the last part of the object disappeared, as if going into another dimension or through a portal. There was no sound nor did the object change trajectory at any time during the sighting.

"He stated he grew up in Nevada not far from Nellis Air Force Base outside of Las Vegas. He said he was used to seeing all types of aircraft. He said they would put a report from the base in the local paper when they would be test-flying a new craft, so they wouldn't be inundated with calls to the base from the local residents. He said he used to go to the air shows that were held at the base and got to see many types of aircraft on the ground and in the air.

"The object he saw did not resemble anything he has ever seen before.

"He said he had two words stuck in his head for several days after the sighting. They were alpha and belvedere. The one word, belvedere, was unusual; even though he is a builder he had not ever heard of it before. This caused him to look up the two words. Alpha meaning first or number one and also the first letter of the Greek alphabet. It is used in military communication as well as amateur radio transmissions and also in the Bible in the Book of Revelation. God saying, 'I am the Alpha and the Omega, the beginning and the end.' The definition for belvedere is a structure built on a high place to command a view.

"He interpreted the meaning in relation to his sighting. He had a number one sighting from a high place. His home is built on a tall hill with an unobstructed view for miles. There are several airports, one in Augusta, 20 miles by air to the south, and Columbia Regional Airport about 55 miles north of Aiken. He is used to seeing the regular air traffic and stated what he saw was not like anything he had ever seen before.

"He said he had seen three weeks earlier an orb that was like a pearl, also almost translucent, but did not report it. He said it wasn't until this sighting that he thought something unusual was happening and should file a report. I told him if he sees anything else unusual to please report it to us. He said he would be more vigilant and would keep a camera handy to see if he could get some photos. His geographic location might have some bearing on what he is seeing, not known to this investigator at this time. We will just have to see if anything else of importance transpires."

Aiken is the largest city in and the county seat of Aiken County, South Carolina, population 30,296.

APRIL 2018

Case 96086 witness illustration. April 7, 2018.

APRIL 1

Flying disc reported over Florida skies

A Florida witness at New Port Richey reported watching a "non-reflective, flying black disc moving overhead," according to testimony in Case 91199.

The witness was talking to a friend on the telephone at 6:02 p.m. on April 1, 2018.

"It was still blue skies with no clouds when I looked up and saw a black disc flying from the north coming over my house as it was flying," the witness stated. "It turned over and over from left to right about three times in a second, maybe a second-and-a-half, and did the same thing going the other direction. It hovered in one place just south of the house for about 10 seconds and then continued south. There was no vapor trail, no lights that I could see of any kind except for a glow of a turquoise-orange that I could see when the object was flipping over left to right and right to left."

The witness did not believe any known craft could complete maneuvers like that.

"An aircraft doing tight turns like that would probably make the pilot pass out from the G-forces and the plane would probably fall apart if it was a normal airplane. I was wondering if maybe the government has an experimental craft. I have seen a stealth bomber and fighter flying overhead. This did not look anything like that. I lost sight of the object as it went over some trees headed southeast. Maybe the Tampa Airport saw something on their radar. If it's not an airplane, then I think I just saw my proof that we are not alone in the universe—even though I am intelligent enough to know that the percentages are high enough to know that we probably aren't alone anyway."

Florida MUFON CAG Investigator James Horne closed this case as an Unknown Aerial Vehicle.

"The witness said the object had a turquoise-orange glow," Horne wrote in his report. "Turquoise and orange are on different parts of the color wheel. The witness said that the object was not moving that fast and described a rotation or oscillation left to right and then comments that a pilot would pass out from the G-forces. This subject was also explored. The witness provided plausible clarification to both in the opinion of this investigator. Flightradar24 did not show any likely commercial aircraft as being the source of the observation. Examination of MUFON CMS showed no corresponding cases."

New Port Richey is a city in Pasco County, Florida, population 14,903.

APRIL 2

Bosnia witness describes hovering disc

A Bosnian witness at Banja Luka reported watching a disc-shaped object hovering over a small forest, according to testimony in Case 91182.

The witness was driving a car leading to his home at 10:27 p.m. on April 2, 2018.

"It hovered over a small forest near the road," the witness stated. "I was shocked, didn't know what to make of it. Then I stopped, took a breath and realized that I was witnessing a UFO sighting. It was hovering over the small forest. It was very dark and dim in color, a disc shape as I could have seen because of the external lights, which it emitted from the bottom. First it was hovering, stationary, for

three to four minutes, then it just disappeared in the night. I was shocked, amazed and scared—didn't know what to do for first two minutes and my phone battery was dead at the moment. After it disappeared, I got afraid even more, and I rushed back home and told this to my wife. It just disappeared in the night by motion, and it was moving very fast."

CAG International Investigator Madgalena Biziuk closed this case as Info Only.

Banja Luka, Bosnia, is the second largest city in Bosnia and Herzegovina, population 138,963.

APRIL 4

Rectangular object described over Alabama

An Alabama witness at Fort Payne reported a black, rectangular-shaped object moving overhead, according to testimony in Case 91224.

The event occurred at 9:20 p.m. on April 4, 2018.

"As husband and I were driving home from his place of work, after 9 p.m., we saw in the sky directly over and in front of our car a black rectangular object with red glowing bars of light on the short sides of the rectangular shape," the witness stated. "Also, there was a blinking red light following. It was silently gliding across the sky—no noise at all. We pulled over to get out and look, but being in the middle of downtown it disappeared behind some buildings, as if it had descended straight down. My husband's cell phone was not working properly afterwards. I don't currently have one so nothing else to report other than I woke continuously from my sleep throughout the night with nausea and still felt the same the next morning and throughout the earlier part of the day."

Alabama CAG Investigator Sue Gerberding

closed this case as an Unknown Aerial Vehicle.

"Occam's Rule, a principal of logic and science, states that the simplest of two or more competing theories is preferable and an explanation for unknown phenomena should first be attempted in terms of what is already known," Gerberding wrote in her report. "However, the visual characteristics and flight path are among the characteristics of the sighting and object that indicate that this event was stimulated by an unknown object, which had a detrimental effect on the witness."

Fort Payne is a city in and county seat of DeKalb County, Alabama, population 14,012.

APRIL 5

Rectangular UFO reported at Tennessee tree line

A Tennessee witness at Reliance reported watching a rectangular-shaped object at the tree line that emitted a humming sound, according to testimony in Case 91263.

The reporting witness was up late with her fiancé about 11:30 p.m. on April 5, 2018, when they noticed both their television and Internet going out.

"Both of us decided to take a break and go outside to have a cigarette," the witness stated. "We no sooner had lit up our smokes, when we saw really bright lights suddenly dim and start pulsating, and coming at us, from the southeast side of the property over the woodlands. I stood transfixed as it literally came out of nowhere, going suddenly up and then down at a terrific speed, over the tree line."

The witness also noticed a sound with the object.

"There was a sound with it, that was a deep, low thrumming hum, which really hurt our ears. Fiancé actually had to cover his; it was painful to him. But then the sound eased up as it then halted, hovering above us for a few seconds, tilted to its side and then zoomed off straight to the north, so low that I watched it, till it rose up and then dipped back down. As low as it was, I was sure it was going to crash or something. I was shaking when we came back in, and this is not the first incident we have had since moving here these last four years. I only lost sight of the thing when it vanished into the north."

Tennessee MUFON State Director Angelia Sheer closed this case as an Unknown-Other.

"Reliance is a small town in the Appalachian Mountains near the Alcoa and Hiawassee Rivers," Sheer wrote in her report. "The object was at the top of a magnolia tree. There was a low strumming feeling. Her partly deaf partner said he could actually hear it. Thought it was a drone at first, but the lights were not just right. Too many lights, etc. Just wasn't normal and lights rotated in color, flashed very quickly and there was no pattern to the changes. Evidence—physical: Her chickens lost a lot of feathers and her chickens stopped laying and in one brood only one chick hatched. High EM readings at the site investigations. There is no natural explanation for the high EM readings at this time."

Reliance is an unincorporated community in Polk County, Tennessee.

APRIL 7

Australian reports disc hovering over rural property

An Australian witness at Warracknabeal reported watching a hovering "golden disc" above his property, according to testimony in Case 96086.

The witness had stepped outside at 1:30 a.m. on April 7, 2018.

"I live in country Victoria," The witness stated. "I usually go outside at night for a pee as I like looking at the stars. I was standing at the back gate just finishing and turned around and looked up as there was a golden disk hovering above me. I panicked and ducked heading to the back door of the house. It took off almost immediately. Reason I hadn't noticed it, there was no sound, no light shed on ground, glowing brightly without casting light on anything else. Speed was instant, blink of an eye. My feelings were fear at first, then curiosity. Reason I have left it this long, I was the only witness and I don't like being called a liar, but felt guilty I had not told anyone except family."

Australian MUFON Provincial Director Mike Robinson closed this case as an Unknown Aerial Vehicle.

"Witness was outside his house taking a comfort stop in his yard when he observed the UAV just above him, as per the photograph," Robinson stated in his report. "Where this occurred is a small country town of about 200 people. The informant's house has another house beside it. The informant panicked, was scared and went inside, but before he did the UAV shot off at an incredible speed. The UAV was only stationary for a matter of seconds over the informant at 21 to 100 feet.

"The informant, who has mechanical knowledge, stated that he was so close to the UAV that he could clearly see that it was seamless with no rivets. He couldn't believe that they had the technology to do that. The informant commented that we don't have the technology to do that—meaning seamless with no rivets on such a craft. Doctor Stephen Greer explains how this is done with multi-dimensional E. T. manufacturing technology. The informant did not state that he was familiar with Doctor Greer's explanation of this manufacturing technology.

"The informant advised that the UAV disk shape, metallic with a very sharp edge around its circumference was extremely bright—and this at 1.30 a.m.—but did not cast light on the ground nor on top of the informant's shed. This ability of UAVs to shine light not all the way to the ground has been reported in other cases (not related to this one). I can't explain how this occurs.

"The informant advised that in the seven months or so since this incident on 7 April 2018, the informant has felt a burning on the top of his head attributable to this incident. This burning sensation still persists to this day. The informant's wife has had a look at the informant's head and can see no abnormality. The informant has not advised me about any medical examination of the top of his head, so it is my understanding that none has been done. The informant attributes this burning sensation to the UAV incident.

"Color of UAV was yellow. Top side of UAV not visible to informant, who was pretty much underneath the UAV. I could detect no evidence of any embellishment, nor exaggeration. The sighting was at such close range (20 to 100 feet) that it is 100 percent certain it was a UAV and could not have been anything else. Further, it is also certain that it was not an alien reproduction vehicle but a manufactured off-world vehicle. Reason: Definitely no rivets.

"The informant was of the view that the UAV did not know he was there and when the informant's presence became apparent to whomever or whatever was in control of this intelligently piloted vehicle, the UAV left immediately and a great rate of knots."

Warracknabeal is a wheatbelt town in the Australian state of Victoria, population 2,745.

APRIL 10

British witness says object followed vehicle

A British witness at Bromsgrove reported

an unknown object with four pulsing lights approached his vehicle and directed a bright light into the vehicle, according to testimony in Case 96307.

The witness and his partner were driving from Redditch through Hanbury and were about on Astwood Lane at 2:30 a.m. on April 10, 2018.

"We usually do go for a drive on the night and listen to music and get some fast food at the 24-hour drive-through," the witness stated. "As we got onto Astwood Lane, I noticed in my rearview mirror four separate dim lights, which at first I thought was a car on the road behind us. This was until I looked again in my mirror and saw that the four lights started to pulsate off and then on. Imagine car headlights with the fog lights on also, the shape would almost be a rectangle with four lights. When the lights started to pulsate, the two top lights on the left and the right pulsated and joined together with the two lower pulsating lights. And when this happened, I stopped the car immediately and said to my partner, 'What the hell was that?'"

The witness then stopped his car and the lights behind vanished.

"My car is still in stationary, and as me and my partner went to go again, into my car the brightest white light pierced through my back window and illuminated the whole of my car inside, to the point where even when my partner and I were looking straight ahead, we couldn't see anything apart from white light. I couldn't even see my dashboard or any of my lights—it was that intense. Then my partner and I screamed our heads off, saying I love you, etc. and almost crying. I put my car in first gear and put my foot down, and we got to a speed of 60 to 70 mph with the light dimming as we were getting farther away. And then I looked in my rearview mirror, and a huge face in a grayscale effect along with the white light seemed to be pressed against or in the boot of my car. I looked at my partner to say, 'Did you see that?' and she screamed so loud and started to cry, so we carried on driving so fast on a country lane to save our lives. . . .".

Very shortly the face was gone.

"As we drove so fast whilst screaming and shaking with bodies full of goosebumps, the face just vanished. I was so scared for my life. We came to a left turn at the end of Astwood Lane and took the turn, and I cannot remember exactly the road, as I was too frightened to take notice. As we got away from the light as I was coming around a bend in the road, we checked the rearview mirror again to notice orange lights in a similar shape to the first four lights at the start, but hovering along the road behind us and pulsating brighter and brighter, until we came to a building with a few street lights to the left of us. I stopped the car and my partner and I got out of the car so I could check the boot of my car to see if what we had seen was inside the car or against it whilst I was driving at 60-70 mph."

The witness was convinced something was inside the vehicle.

"I opened the boot and then realized nothing was there. We jumped back in the car and drove to Redditch without any hesitation to get out of Hanbury. As I got back home, I dropped my partner off at hers, and I was so scared and excited that I woke my mom up to tell her my experience."

United Kingdom MUFON Field Investigator James Dallas closed this case as an Unknown Aerial Vehicle.

Bromsgrove is a town in Worcestershire, England, population 29,237.

Streetlights flicker as UFO moves over Utah

A Utah witness at Heber City reported a low flying, dark triangle UFO, according to testimony in Case 91382.

The witness was outside at midnight on April 10, 2018.

"I looked up because I saw a darker triangle shape in the sky very low," the witness stated. "I knew it was a UFO and I didn't want it to notice me. So, I just sat there and smoked my smoke. I then heard birds going 'crazy' chirping like fighting. It was 12 a.m. and that was late for birds to be out. The street light flickered, and I felt uneasy and put my smoke out and went inside. It was unbelievable. I wanted to report this somewhere and so glad I found this site."

Utah MUFON Field Investigator Michael Barrette closed this case as an Unknown Aerial Vehicle.

"During questioning, the witness did mention a couple of facts that I found very interesting," Barrette stated in his report. "First, she said that immediately after the sighting and for a short time period after, her son (four years old) stated to her that he was telling her that 'they' were coming, but couldn't get him to describe to her who or what they were. Secondly, she stated that when she has her bedroom window cracked open, she can hear wind like an object is flying by her house, that there would be no wind blowing when all of a sudden, she would hear this wind like noise."

Heber City is a city in northwestern Wasatch County, Utah.

Thailand witness says UFO was series of refrigerator boxes

A Thai witness at Nakhon Nayok reported watching a rectangular object that look like "seven or eight refrigerator boxes glued together" crossing the sky, according to testimony in Case 93224.

The witness stepped outside to a vehicle about noon on April 10, 2018.

"This was my first UFO sighting, but my father, who was an amateur pilot, saw one when I was young— the standard silver disk," the witness stated. "This was a couple of months ago in Nakhon Nayok, Thailand. I often observe aircraft as they fly over. I saw a commercial airliner flying over from south to north at about 7,000 or 8,000 feet. As I tracked it, I saw this elongated, box-type object flying in the opposite direction, which I then tracked until it was almost out of sight toward the northern sky."

The witness stared intently at the object trying to figure what it was.

"It looked like seven or eight refrigerator boxes glued together, dark brown, with a couple of angular surfaces, one at the front and two toward the rear and on the side. It also rotated slowly two or maybe three times on its long axis as I watched go over. It must have been about 5,000 feet in the air and about 30 to 40 feet in length—so somewhat bigger than a single-engine aircraft. It made no sound at all, had no jet or propeller engines, and had no wings. Actually, I could see the whole craft as it rotated, which gave me a clear view of its surface features—well, what there was of them. I know civilian and military aircraft and keep up with the advanced prototypes or secret designs. I have never seen anything like this object, on any media, in my 62 years on the planet. It may not have had anyone inside it, but it was definitely being controlled and its flight was in an absolute linear arc across the sky. Someone asked if I thought it was a drone—not a bad idea, but I've never seen any drone that looked like this, with no visible power source. I feel privileged to have experienced this event and have sort of been waiting all my life to finally see a UFO like my dad. The engineer and scientist inside me is searching for a logical explanation; the boy is thrilled. Thank you for giving me an opportunity to share this experience. I want to know if anyone else has seen such an object."

MUFON International Director of Investigations Steve Hudgeons closed this case as an

Unknown Aerial Vehicle.

"Possibly a balloon, but have not heard of one with this description." Hudgeons stated in his report.

Nakhon Nayok is one of the central provinces of Thailand.

APRIL 15

'Tic Tac'-shaped object reported over Australia

An Australian witness at Arncliffe reported watching a white, Tic Tac-shaped object moving quickly across the sky, according to testimony in Case 94668.

The witness was in a vehicle waiting at an off-ramp red light at 1 p.m. on April 15, 2018.

"Odd shape, trajectory and speed," the witness stated. "Thought it was perhaps a balloon (like a party balloon) but there was only one. It wasn't the correct shape (more like a tic tac or egg) and was not ascending (like a balloon with helium would), rather it was moving horizontally across the sky, far quicker than a balloon would be moving."

The witness was surprised that an object like that would be in the sky so close to the airport.

"Went outside of my field of view."

Australia MUFON Provincial Director Mike Robinson closed this case as an Unknown Aerial Vehicle.

"Object not a weather balloon," Robinson stated in his report. "Movements not consistent with a balloon. Object not an aircraft—no wings, fin, or tail. Daytime sighting 501 to 1,000 feet, so relatively close."

Arncliffe is a suburb in southern Sydney, in the state of New South Wales, Australia.

APRIL 17

UFO reported hovering over Florida power plant

A Florida witness at Lakeland reported watching an orb hovering over a local power plant, according to testimony in Case 91498.

The witness and his fiancé were walking dogs near Lake Parker at 9 p.m. on April 17, 2018.

"I noticed what looked like an orange orb stationary in the sky," the witness stated. "The craft seemed to be hovering above the C.D. Mcintosh Jr. Power Plant from my perspective. I stood and watched it for a few minutes and pointed it out to my fiancé to confirm I wasn't seeing things."

The fiancé confirmed that she could see it too and that it was not moving.

"After watching it for a couple minutes, the glowing orange orb emitted a bright white light (resembling a spotlight from a distance) for approximately 10 to 15 seconds before changing back to an orange-amber glow. My fiancé and I brought our dogs into our house and I went to the window to keep watching it. By the time I got to the window, the object was travelling west at what looked like the speed of a commercial airplane. No blinking lights on wings or anything that would identify the object as an airplane or helicopter could be seen on the object."

Florida MUFON Field Investigator Marc D. Barbieri closed this case as an Unknown-Other.

"Upon interviewing the witness, it was determined that the witness and his fiancé were in agreement that they did see something unusual (a yellow/orange orb); however, the second witness did wish to remain anonymous, and was not interviewed by this investigator. Having not been able to glean any additional information from the interview with the primary witness, and the fact that the weather was completely clear and calm the evening of the sighting, this cased is closed with a disposition of Unknown-Other."

Lakeland is a city in Polk County, Florida, population 100,710.

Cylindrical UFO seen at Indiana treetop level

An Indiana witness at Osceola spotted a large, cylinder-shaped object at treetop level and multiple orbs flying nearby, according to testimony in Case 91485.

The witness was outside with dogs at 10:45 p.m. on April 17, 2018.

"Noticed a gold-colored, huge object flying just above the trees just a block away, flying up and down the road like it was looking for something," the witness stated. "As I was watching it, the object started to come closer. Whatever it was they must have spotted me because all of a sudden it stopped and zipped south about a mile towards Lincoln Way. At that second, I heard what I thought was a jet, but it was flying low and wasn't moving very fast. As I was watching the object, I observed three orbs fly into it. As the object flew south, I saw what looked like three jet engines blowing fire out the rear of the object. All of a sudden, the object changed its appearance to a triangle and flew straight up right after a jet flew by. There were orbs everywhere just above the trees like it was looking for something. Then the big object zipped up as it was going south at a high rate of speed."

Indiana MUFON State Director Jeremy Efroymson closed this case as Unknown Aerial Vehicle.

"Original object was just over the trees in her backyard and was the size of a bus but cylindrically-shaped," Efroymson stated in his report. "The triangular craft, which it turned into after shooting off a mile away, was huge. The size of a football field.

"Witness's story was similar to her statement. She saw a bus-sized, cylindrical object hovering over the trees in her backyard. It shot off to a mile away where she saw it absorb three orbs. It then turned into a triangular craft and disappeared. There was no noise. She felt like it was searching for something."

Osceola is a town in Penn Township, St. Joseph County, population 2,463.

APRIL 19

British witness describes low-flying triangular UFO

A United Kingdom witness at Stonehouse reported watching a large black triangle "with six dim lights," according to testimony in Case 91752.

The witness was on a roof stargazing on a clear night at 10:30 p.m. on April 19, 2018.

"I'd been up there maybe 20 minutes when suddenly I noticed a black triangle moving slowly across the sky, southwest, in a straight line," the witness stated. "It was travelling at a steady pace, no faster or slower than you'd expect from a commercial aircraft. I stargaze frequently in the summer, and I am familiar with planes, satellites, blimps, etc. This was unlike anything I have ever seen in the sky."

The witness described the object.

"The craft was clearly a solid and a complete triangle, or at least very close to being complete as it blocked out the stars. It had six white lights around the edge, evenly spaced. The lights were very dim and stayed solid the whole time. There were no flashing lights, only the six solid, white lights. Other than this, I couldn't see any other detail on the craft."

The witness tried to get a closer look with binoculars but had trouble focusing.

"Or the lenses were misted up—either

way, the event only lasted approximately 30 seconds, so I didn't have time to figure out the problem. I can't say for sure if it was making noise or not. I live near a relatively busy road so there was car noise, which made it harder to determine. Also, I was so excited by what I was seeing that I was just trying to focus my binoculars to get a closer look and wasn't concentrating on sound. I'm a keen stargazer, but it's hard for me to say exactly what the altitude was—if I had to guess I would say somewhere between 8,000–15,000 feet. But as the event was so quick and because I couldn't make out details on the craft to give me a sense of scale, it was difficult to gauge."

The craft kept moving at the same pace until it went beyond the witness's view.

"My initial thought was that it must be a B-2 from RAF Fairford. The next day I contacted a friend who is one of the founders of RAF Fairford Air Day—a very popular aircraft show held at RAF Fairford. RAF Fairford is the closest military base that has a variety of aircraft, and I believe the only one that might have aircraft that could offer a possible explanation. I explained what I saw to my friend and he couldn't tell me what it was. He said that RAF Fairford was at that time closed and didn't think any aircraft would be flying in or out of there. Also, it seemed unusual as the lights were unlike ones I've seen on a B-2 (however, I am not an aviation expert or even an aviation enthusiast so there may well be other light configurations that I am not aware of). He couldn't give me an explanation, so I am trying to seek out others who might have seen it that night."

United Kingdom MUFON Field Investigator Lee George Strydom closed this case as Info Only.

"The object was possibly a TR-3B."

Stonehouse s a town in the Stroud District of Gloucestershire in southwestern England, population approximately 8,000.

APRIL 21

Slow-moving triangular UFO described over Maine

A Maine witness at Orrington reported watching a silent, black triangular UFO with lights at each of the three corners, according to testimony in Case 91553.

The event occurred at 9:55 p.m. on April 21, 2018.

"Viewed through 10x50 binoculars for duration," the witness stated. "First viewed exactly west from my position; travelling from southwest to northeast, losing sight just past north due to building and tree obstruction, taking just under 10 minutes from first being observed to last. Moved very slowly, absolutely no sound, never going above 20 degrees above horizon."

The witness described the object.

"Had three brilliant-white static lights in each of the three corners with one strobing red light centered on the underside hull. There was also a less-bright fourth light seemingly on the aft part of the fuselage, centered between (but higher than) the two rear lights. With binoculars, the fuselage against the background sky was clearly visible: a literal triangle, slightly longer than wide (i.e., not equilateral), and relative to commercial aircraft, very dark. I've seen quite a few of these now, all following the same relative paths; southwest to northeast or northeast to southwest, in exactly the same two paths, i.e.: directly east or west, which is so common I keep an eye out on either path."

The witness described the object's lighting.

"Interestingly, the light-strobe pattern and colors were somewhat different with this: The red-strobe flashed more frequently than others in the past, and was exactly opposite a strobing white light, seemingly from the aft-starboard white light. They never went out of sync, compared to commercial aircraft. Also compared to previous sightings, when at its most southern position (front hull most visible), there were no red/green, port/starboard winglet lights, which until now have always been visible from the front (not from the rear ever 100 percent). Anyways, nothing special, but I figured I'd report it for posterity. I would draw it, but other than flashers and attitude indicator lights, it's the same basic vehicle people see daily. Lastly, I must emphasize 'no-sound.' There were commercial aircraft much higher and farther away that were distinctly audible, whereas this/these craft was/were not."

Maine MUFON Field Investigator Fred Richards closed this case as an Unknown-Other.

"The location of this event is close to military activity so it is possible there could be a military connection since there is a Military Operations Area nearby and it is close to the Army/Air National Guard bases."

Orrington is a town in Penobscot County, Maine, population 3,733.

NY Navy veteran describes chevron-shaped UFO

A New York witness at Irondequoit reported watching a chevron-shaped object that may have been as large as "two or three football fields," according to testimony in Case 91559.

The event occurred at 10:20 p.m. on April 21, 2018.

"I'm a 65-year-old retired Navy vet and have viewed a lot in the night skies over many years, both out at sea and living on a high tundra ranch in Colorado, west of NORAD," the witness stated. "Have never seen so much activity as last night and early this morning. Making ready to see the Lyrid meteor shower peak before dawn, I was out around 10 p.m. on the back deck and front porch before bed thinking there may be some stray meteors around then already. But looking west, noticed to my

right the moving V-formation of six to eight, dimmish-green tinted lights (like sodium street lamps) against a faint dark, chevron silhouette moving silently in a straight course due west a bit north of us, maybe along the Lake Ontario shoreline. Couldn't really judge altitude at the angle because not a good reference to size. Could have been as large across as two or three football fields, slow enough for me to keep in sight maybe 20 seconds before it faded into the western rooftops in the distance. Focusing on every detail I could and grasping the fact I'm not seeing something normal, not meteors, landing pattern aircraft, or even a reflective chevron flock of geese crossed my mind since it seemed ghostly and distant. But very distinct and unwavering. My feelings were like when I've witnessed similar things in the past, awe, excitement, but even more so that I'm not in an isolated area alone. I immediately told my longtime mate, who'd already retired to bed reading and knew I didn't have time to call her out to see it, but is equally excited—we're both sky watchers.

"The secondary event to this: I went to bed excited, then we got up at 4 a.m. today to watch perhaps the meteors peak on the back deck, and at 4:20 a.m. saw three bright, white lights in chevron formation streak downward low, it seemed out of the southwest, over the top of the house, banking in a curve to the northeast and disappearing behind the tall trees. It was quick, in sight about two to three seconds, recognizable enough to realize it wasn't meteors, and I told my mate something like, 'That was them again, this is really happening!' She hadn't seen that. So, we moved around watching every part of the sky we could cover. In a bit she said, 'That was it. I saw it go along there.' It was 4:40 a.m. She described three lights travelling so low to the horizon, so fast, it was only a couple seconds before they were lost behind the front of the house, facing south, so travelling a straight line west to east. The last I saw after she went back in was at 5 a.m., when the same or a similar

V-formation of three lights moved silently and straight northwest to southeast (towards NYC). They seemed to be moving slower than before because I could track them from over the lake to the southeast horizon for all of six to seven seconds. I stayed around till 5:30 a.m. when the sky was getting bright."

New York MUFON Field Investigator Chuck Streb closed this case as an Unknown Aerial Vehicle.

"The witness seemed very creditable with a lot of naval experience," Streb stated in his report. "It is clear he saw something. We have a lot of activity in this area along the lake as we have Griffith Air Force Base and a military zone over our lake. Not sure what was seen. Case is unidentified object."

Irondequoit is a town in Monroe County, New York, population 51,692.

APRIL 22

UFO reported hovering over Pennsylvania interstate

A Pennsylvania witness at Manheim who works in law enforcement reported watching an object that looked like the "lunar lander" hovering over a major highway, according to testimony in Case 91575.

The witness was traveling southbound along Interstate 81 toward Harrisburg near Lavelle Mountain at 5:14 p.m. on April 22, 2018.

"Just all of a sudden this object appeared over the interstate and appeared to hover stationary for like 20 seconds and quickly went into the trees on my right at a high rate of speed," the witness stated. "Object appeared quite large. At first, I thought it was some type of drone, but it moved too fast to be one. Kind of looked like a lunar lander in my opinion. I was shocked by what I saw and got emotional. When I had passed the spot where I thought

the object would be, found nothing."

Pennsylvania MUFON Field Investigator Larry Shaak closed this case as an Unknown-Other.

"Witness stated he saw an object that appeared to look like the lunar lander in the center of the highway," Shaak stated in his report. "The object appeared and moved very fast across Route 81 and disappeared into some trees to his right side of the road. Witness stated that others must have seen it also, because it was daylight and there was a fair amount of traffic at the time of the event. When questioned, he said no one stopped at the time to observe. The site is five miles away from Harrisburg International Airport.

"The witness works in law enforcement. I believe the witness saw some kind of strange object fly over I-81, south of Harrisburg. Since he is in the field of law enforcement, he has most likely had some past training in observation for his present job."

Manheim is a borough in Lancaster County, Pennsylvania, population 4,858.

Silver disc-shaped UFO reported over Brooklyn

A New York witness at Brooklyn reported watching a silver disc with golden lights, according to testimony in Case 91572.

The witness was smoking a cigarette in a friend's backyard and watching planes fly by at 5:20 p.m. on April 22, 2018.

"I saw what I thought was a very reflective helicopter and began watching it out of curiosity," the witness stated. "It made no noise and had a somewhat wobbly flight path at a fairly (but not completely) constant slow to medium speed, moving unlike what a helicopter is capable of. I saw it at a low angle coming from behind the house blocking the sky (perspective), looking north towards Gowanus and Park

Slope from my location in Kensington. It began in the north sky and moved west, then north-west, away from me. I clearly observed a large metallic, reflective silver disc with moving/pulsating golden lights. The most prominent light was circling the disc as it was moving from the top to the bottom and back again like a helix, making me think the object may be spherical, even though the structure was clearly a disc. This main light appeared to move from above the structure to below the structure, with an observable air gap between said light and structure when it reached its apex. Other lights observed on the object seemed as if reflections of sunlight upon a moving sphere, moving flashes, which were golden yellow in color. By the time I was certain this was not a helicopter, plane, or other known aircraft, and overcame my sense of absolute wonder, I called out to the person nearest to me, but it was flying lower in the sky, and was blocked by a fence on the north side of the backyard, which said person was leaning up against and they did not observe it. The sighting lasted approximately 15–30 seconds and I did not have time to take a photo or video with my phone. Approximate flight path was heading north-northwest over west Brooklyn, passing over Prospect Park, Gowanus, Park Slope, and Red Hook."

New York MUFON Field Investigator Keith Conroy closed this case as an Unknown Aerial Vehicle.

"I feel confident the witness is capable of eliminating IFOs, and his description is unique," Conroy stated in his report. "Also, the wobbly behavior is a known UFO characteristic. The spiral light is very unusual and consistent with something unidentified. Looking forward to a drawing from witness."

Brooklyn is the most populous borough of New York City, population 2,648,771.

Large triangular UFO reported over Edmonton

A Canadian witness at Edmonton reported seeing "a large, black triangle with four underside lights," according to testimony in Case 91570.

The witness and friends were smoking cigars on a 10th floor balcony on April 22, 2018.

"It was a nice clear night and we could see a few stars in the distance," the witness stated. "Our conversation was interrupted by a pulsing sound and we all looked up to see a large, black triangle flying overhead at a pretty fast rate. It had four large, silvery lights on the bottom of the triangle, with one light in the center and the other three at the corners. There was also a strange, dark green aura around the front of the craft, which outlined the front two edges and seemed to glow. It took about five or six seconds for the craft to fly overhead and out of sight from our balcony. It seemed to be fairly close to us, or just very large. All three of us heard and saw the craft."

Canada MUFON Field Investigator Ryan Stacey closed this case as Info Only.

"I have reached out to the witness numerous times and have yet to establish a connection," Stacey wrote in his report. "Case closed as Info Only."

Edmonton is the capital city of the Canadian province of Alberta, population 932,546.

APRIL 25

Texas witness describes silent 'silvery object'

A Texas witness at Webster reported watching a "round, silvery object "moving into a cloud and then reversing direction, according to testimony in Case 91628.

The witness was driving south of Houston

eastbound toward Clear Lake on FM528 from Friendswood and approaching the I-45 south underpass at 2:30 p.m. on April 25, 2018.

"While stopped at a red light just before the I-45 intersection and looking upward at the light, a bright flash of light caught my eye," the witness stated. "Looking upward I saw a round, highly reflective object streak southbound through the air and into a cloud. I had only a second or two to view the object and noted that it was round but slightly flattened on top and bottom, much like a very fat football. It had a center line from the nose to the rear along its horizontal axis. I could not tell if it was a marking or a part of the structure of the craft. It was fast, much faster than any conventional low altitude aircraft would be flying under this circumstance, and over a populated area. From my vantage point, in size the craft could be roughly compared to a dime, or slightly smaller, held out to my windshield in front of me. I estimate my position of observation to be approximately one mile from the cloud into which it disappeared."

The witness could hear no sound.

"After only another second or two, the craft (or another just like it) came out of the cloud just above where the first had entered but headed back the opposite direction (northward) towards another cloud. It seemed to be going even faster than the first, and quickly just dissolved into a streak of reflective light about halfway to the second cloud. The second cloud (to the left-north) was separated from the first cloud by a space roughly the size of the first cloud. The left cloud was about 25 percent larger than the right. I checked with the Galveston Scholes Flight Service Station, and scattered cloud ceiling altitude was around 2,500 feet, with scattered cloud height varying from 4,000-6,000 feet."

The witness reported the weather was predominately clear, with a temperature of about 83 degrees.

"No other aircraft was seen, but my travel dictated that I leave the scene for an appointment. I did get a short, but accurate view of the craft. It was clearly not a conventional aircraft. I estimate the clouds and activity were maybe a mile from my street location, but these things are difficult to estimate without a known object at a known location for reference. My guess, based on the FSS report of the 2,500-foot ceiling of the clouds, is that the UFOs were approximately the size of a normal small aircraft at maybe 25–40 feet in length. I am 73 years old and have significant experience as an aircrewman in the Navy during the Vietnam war. I also obtained my private pilot's license after the Navy tour and owned my own aircraft. I am not presently an active flyer, but am not easily fooled by what I observe in the skies. This is the only UFO sighting I have had in my lifetime. NASA and Ellington AFB are located within a couple miles of this location. The Ellington facility is frequently open to the public and does not seem like it would be a special place of interest for the UFO. However, I have heard stories of occasional UFO sightings in the corridor from Galveston to the top of Galveston Bay. Also, there are rumors of black choppers seen at the base."

Texas MUFON Field Investigator James Donald Gilchrist closed this case as an Unknown Aerial Vehicle.

"I checked weather conditions, and what flight information I could get from the Ellis Air Force Base PR officer of any unusual activity in the area," Gilchrist stated in his report. "NASA was not forthcoming with any information. As a Field Investigator, I cannot definitely say that the object observed was manmade or other. Given the background of the witness, something was seen, it was intelligently controlled, and, based on the movements observed, it probably was not piloted."

Webster is a city Texas located in Harris County, population 10,684.

APRIL 28

Houston witness videotapes 'tall structure' UFO

A Texas witness at Houston reports watching and videotaping a "tall structure moving northwest" that emitted no light, according to testimony in Case 91666.

The event occurred at 10:20 p.m. on April 28, 2018.

"Never thought I'd have something to add," the witness stated. "Just observed this in Houston, near Memorial Drive and Shepard. Object was moving north-northwest. Was keeping the same elevation and didn't move like balloons. Much larger, vertical structure like a floating tower with a pointed tip at the top. Don't know what the hell that was. Freaking out a bit."

Texas MUFON State Director Steven Bates closed this case as an Unknown Aerial Vehicle.

"The witness observed the object moving silently across the sky and was able to capture video," Bates wrote in his report. "Basic video analysis seems to indicate that the video is original and has not been manipulated. The object has a vertical 'tower' shape, appears to be black and emits no light and does not seem to have any reflective surfaces and was silent. This does not conform to any known conventional aircraft or drone. The direction and speed of movement during the video seem consistent with the direction and speed of the wind at the time of the sighting, suggesting that the object was 'floating on the wind.'

"Using landmarks and frame grabs from the video and Google maps and wind speed and direction data, the object can be estimated to be about 33 feet tall and about 11 feet wide (three stories tall and one freeway lane wide) and approximately 2,500 feet or one-half mile from the witness. From witness testimony the object was more like 1,000 feet away and about the size of a car. Given the geometric analysis from photos, frame grabs and known landmarks, if the object was 1,000 feet away from the observer, it would be approximately 13 feet tall and 4.4 feet wide and moving at about 3.24 mph.

"To the eye of the Field Investigator, the object in the video looks like some sort of string of balloons drifting on the wind. However, this is not consistent with the analysis of the estimated size of the object. Further, the witness has an extensive professional background in aviation and UAVs and had a much longer view of the object than just the video clip and is quite sure the object was not balloons."

Houston is the most populous city in Texas, population 2.312 million.

MAY 2018

Case 92029 witness illustration. May 15, 2018.

MAY 1

Black triangle UFO over London has 'digital glitch'

A British witness at London reported watching a black, triangle-shaped object "about two to three times the size of an A380 passenger jet" moving overhead, according to testimony in Case 92298.

The witness and his wife were standing in their backyard having a cigarette at 11:30 p.m. on May 1, 2018.

"Jupiter was very low in the sky and we were wondering what it was," the witness stated. "We got out my phone and used the Skyview app to work it out. We both commented on the fact that we hadn't ever remembered seeing Jupiter, or if we had, we didn't know that's what it was. London skies are always full of passenger aircraft coming in to land at Heathrow and we are on one of the flight paths they use. The planes come in from the east over

our house and then head out west before they turn north towards Heathrow airport. You can always hear them. This black triangle object with round lights on each of its three corners and one central light that was reddish orange in color appeared in the west."

The witness said the object was about two to three times the size of an A380 passenger jet.

"It flew right over us in one fluid motion, in a slight arch. It rotated slowly as it moved across the sky. It probably made one full rotation in the time we witnessed it. It flew from the west horizon to the northeast horizon in about 8-10 seconds. It was completely silent. The sky was completely clear. There were no clouds and the stars were very visible. We both watched this object come in and pass right over us both. We both knew exactly what we had both seen. It was like watching a silent fiction movie or one of those UFO TV shows, but real life. We both just watched it until it wasn't visible anymore, then looked at each other both with shocked but excited faces and said, 'what was that?'

Then we both said together, 'that was a UFO for sure.' We both knew exactly what we had seen. We are in the photography/film industry. We use our eyes for our job. This object was so clearly a solid structure, but it also had a film static kind of shimmer to the underside of it, a bit like digital glitch. I know it sounds ridiculous, but it was like its cloaking device was switching on or switching off. This was so incredibly strange and overwhelming it has most definitely changed our view on UFOs."

United Kingdom MUFON Field Investigator Karl Webb closed this case as an Unknown Aerial Vehicle.

"The description is of course becoming a familiar sight in our skies; however, the distinction between what is ours and what is theirs is becoming more of a gray area due to unknown knowledge of reverse engineering and the continuing disinformation from all major governments," Webb wrote in his report. "That said, the description above bares an uncanny resemblance to the triangle in the Belgium wave back in the 90s, that being with the white lights towards each corner and the reddish/orange light to the center. The problem is that there appears to be many subtle permutations on a theme, when it comes to black triangles. From the description alone and the fact that this witness has been bothered to contact and make the report, tells me that what he saw was very likely real. That said, the reason for the distinct lack of independent witnesses always eludes me, particularly in a large populated area such as London. On the basis of the report I would have to conclude that this was an unknown UAV even if it was human in construct; the technology is very likely alien anyway."

London is the capital and largest city of both England and the United Kingdom, population 8,787,892.

Alabama witness says UFO hovered 200 feet overhead

An Alabama witness at Loxley reported watching a "glowing orange light" that approached and hovered before moving away quickly, according to testimony in Case 91829.

The witness was outside near a barn sitting by a small fire, watching the sky on May 1, 2018.

"Had just gone back in house for a few minutes," the witness stated, "when I started walking back towards the barn and noticed a bright orange light coming over the treetops about 500 meters to the northwest. Grew larger as it came closer until it was almost directly over me. Hovered above a few seconds before shooting off to the south and out of sight. While above, maybe 200 feet or so, it appeared reddish-orange and circular, but with three slightly brighter spots around the edges. Overall, a round, glowing object, but with three brighter spots that would seem to have made it triangular, although too luminescent to distinguish a triangular shape."

Alabama MUFON CAG Field Investigator Mary Owens closed this case as an Unknown-Other.

Loxley is a town in Baldwin County, Alabama, population 1,632.

MAY 3

'Mist' surrounded Missouri UFO 'string of lights'

A Missouri witness at Caverna reported watching a string of lights surrounded in a mist and at treetop level, according to testimony in Case 91773.

The witness was driving south on I-9 roughly three miles north of the Arkansas and Missouri border at 10:28 p.m. on May 3, 2018.

"I noticed what I initially thought was a helicopter," the witness stated. "Once I noticed it, I realized that it was ringed in brilliant white light like over-powered LEDs or (very) bright halogens. I watched it approach from the southeast moving northwest at a very gradual angle as it crossed the highway at treetop height. I noticed that the light was swirling in a light mist that seemed to surround the object. It continued up traveling across the road, and, as it reached the top of the next hill, a brilliant light was emitted from the bottom of the craft almost like a really bright aura. At that time the lights on the side of the craft began to strobe multiple colors and then just winked out all at the same time leaving a void in the sky. I couldn't watch any longer as the area that the object went to went past my point of view. Had I not had my family in the car, I would have investigated further."

Missouri MUFON Field Investigator Britt Faaborg closed this case as an Unknown Aerial Vehicle.

"White-bluish light from ground illuminated the bottom side of the craft just before he lost sight of it," Faaborg stated in the report. "The white light ring changed to multi-colored at that time. The witness seems very credible. There were other occupants in the vehicle at the time of the sighting, but they were all asleep (his family)."

Caverna is an unincorporated community in southern McDonald County, Missouri.

MAY 4

Utah witness says UFO followed her home

A Utah witness at Enterprise reported encountering and photographing an object with two green lights that followed her home, according to testimony in Case 91780.

The witness was driving home from St. George to Enterprise heading northwest on Highway

18 at approximately 2:45 a.m. on May 4, 2018.

"At approximately mile marker 38, I saw two green lights to the southwest of me," the witness stated. "As I drove through the canyon, the lights came closer towards me and were descending from the dark sky. My initial thought was, 'what a weird place to see a drone,' but as I thought through it I realized nobody would be flying a drone in this area at this time of morning.

"Then as the lights got closer, I realized this was a bigger object than I thought, and it began hovering next to me as I drove. I reached for my phone to take a picture and the object hovered above me then hovered just ahead of me, hugged up to the mountainside. I wondered if it was going to land because it was so low. Then it hovered up and over the mountain, keeping close to the treetops and then out of sight in a northern direction. As I came out of the canyon, I scanned the dark sky looking for the green lights again, but I didn't see anything but stars. As I continued driving home, I was questioning what I saw and my own sanity. Then as I turned right down my street, there were the two green lights again, about 150 yards in front of me and approximately 20 feet above the ground, coming at me, so I turned my lights off and grabbed my phone. As I snapped two pictures, the object just hovered in place for about 15 seconds. This is when I noticed the green lights spinning into and out of sight and the first time, I saw an orange-ish red light blinking below the green lights; then it floated away in a southwest direction."

When the witness got home, the green and red lights were still seen in the distance.

"I was so creeped out and was afraid of abduction because of the object 'following' and 'watching' me that I sat in my car with the lights and engine off for five minutes before running in my house and locking all the doors and shutting all the blinds. I could not hear anything, and I could not make out a formation with my naked vision. But, when I looked at the pictures I had taken, I then saw the formation of the object, the windows in the object and some sort of blue glow at the top of the formation. None of those visible to the naked eye in the dark. I continue to now hear a 'hovering' sound over my house come and go as I type this—four times in the last hour, but when I look outside there is nothing to be seen. Then the sound just disappears. I'm not 100 percent sure this is related, but we do not have known flying objects such as helicopters flying around Enterprise, and the sound is not that of an airplane."

Utah MUFON Assistant State Director Stephen Walker closed this case as an Unknown Aerial Vehicle.

"The witness had a close encounter with an unknown air vehicle," Walker wrote in his report. "It played a form of tag with her while she was driving. She stated she was fearful of a possible abduction due to the closeness of the object, especially when it was traveling on top of her car. She also noted that it pulled in front of her while she was in the canyon and she thought it might try to land. She stated that it seemed to have difficulty while inside the canyon, and it climbed up over the mountainside and vanished. The darker side of this sighting occurred when she arrived home. The witness stated as she turned onto the street before her house, the object reappeared, rising up from the cemetery across the street, and floated toward her and blocked the intersection, hovering less than 20 feet above the ground. She stopped the car, turned off the headlights and snapped two photos. The witness believes that the object had landed in the cemetery and was waiting for her with some type of intent. I found the witness to be intelligent and highly credible in this event."

Robert Spearing conducted a photo analysis: "Object had a row of solid green lights across its middle with a red-orange blinking light on the lower left side. Object had a blue glow on top not visible to the naked eye. This lighting configuration is not standard on aircraft. Blue lighting is unheard of apart from U.S. military refueling aircraft, and those blue lights are on the underside of the tankers not on top. Witness was very close to object and the photo suggests the craft was far bigger than a drone, being possibly close to 50 feet long. It is doubtful it was a helicopter, but it had the ability to hover like one. Object was also exhibiting dangerous maneuvers close to highway. Concurring with field investigator that this is an unknown aerial object."

Enterprise is a city in northwestern Washington County, Utah, population 1,711.

MAY 11

Canadian witness describes two cigar-shaped pods

A Canadian witness at Esquimalt reported watching two cigar-shaped pods moving southbound in a straight line under 500 feet, according to testimony in Case 91939.

The witness was on a work break at about 10:20 a.m. on May 11, 2018.

"Looked up in the sky and noticed a blue/gray, wingless, soundless pod fly over top of us heading southbound in a descending straight line," the witness stated, "whilst we were looking in a southerly direction. It made no noise and it wasn't an airplane. Looked like a cigar-shaped pod, no wings. Then a second one followed a couple minutes later. Then about a minute later, the coast search and rescue airplane flew over top of us in a couple of circles and flew off. We wondered if it was a missile or drone. It didn't have wings. Later on in the day airplanes flew over and you could definitely tell the difference. You could see a contrail and big wings. This area is near a naval base. Thought I'd see if you could help explain what I 'maybe' saw. Thanks. Both of them just kept flying until we couldn't see anymore."

Canada MUFON Field Investigator Carl Peterson closed this case as Info Only.

The Township of Esquimalt is a municipality in British Columbia, Canada, population 17,655.

New Jersey witness reports Object with 'fuzzy edges'

A New Jersey witness at North Plainfield reported watching a hovering object with "fuzzy edges," according to testimony in Case 91968.

The witness was driving a friend home at 11:45 p.m. on May 11, 2018.

"Saw a star and another object below it that caught my eye," the witness stated. "At first, I thought it was possibly a house with weird lights up in the wooded area, but, after it disappeared, I realized there was no wooded area up there. And even if there was, it was way too high to be a house. For the whole time I saw it, it was hovering in the same place. There were a lot of blueish-white lights turning on and off, so that it looked like it was shimmering. And I couldn't make out the shape of it. We stared at it about 30 seconds while waiting to turn onto the highway while the light was red until it straight up disappeared. My friend and I were both trying to come up with explanations until it disappeared. And after about two minutes of going back and forth for a rational explanation, it disappeared."

New Jersey MUFON State Section Director Robert Spearing closed this case as an Unknown-Other.

"Witness saw hundreds of shimmering, star-like, blue lights in a thumb-sized, rectangular area over North Plainfield, New Jersey, until lights suddenly went out," Spearing stated in his report. "Saw this while at stop light. Altitude and distance could not be defined. However, a check of flightradar24.com showed no objects over North Plainfield from 11:30 to midnight. So, object was anomalous. Unknown-Other as there is no positive proof it was an object. Cloud ceiling was 1,962 feet so object may have been below radar."

North Plainfield is a borough in Somerset County, New Jersey, population 21,936.

MAY 13

Indiana witness says UFO had 'windows'

An Indiana witness at Garrett reported watching a slow-moving, cigar-shaped object with windows, according to testimony in Case 92110.

The witness was outside having coffee at 5:05 p.m. on May 13, 2018.

"I spotted something to my left in the sky," the witness stated. "I was looking to the south. It looked like it had windows and was shining, moving slowly. It looked like it was turning, but that was just the shape of the object. It was going straight. No noise. No wings. When it got more in front of us, it was either glowing from sunshine or flame. It must have been as big as a Greyhound bus. I have seen objects before, but never this close. It seems it is just now sinking in what we saw.

Indiana MUFON Field Investigator Patrick O'Brien closed this case as an Unknown Aerial Vehicle.

"More information needed on the case," O'Brien wrote in his report. "Very limited information, unless further information given by witness."

Garrett is a city in Keyser Township, DeKalb County, Indiana, population 6,286.

MAY 15

Oregon witness videotapes black cylindrical UFO

An Oregon witness at the Medford Airport reported watching a hovering object that began to move and eventually completed a 90-degree turn, according to testimony in Case 92030.

The witness and four others were sitting outside at work watching a thunderstorm pass by at 4:45 p.m. on May 15, 2018.

"One guy said, 'what is that?' the witness stated. "We looked up and saw a black cylinder hovering above us to the northwest about 1,000 to 2,000 feet. It hovered there for a minute or so. I ran and grabbed my phone and started to video record it. It flew in a level path to the north-northeast, I am guessing about one-half mile, and came to a hover while maintaining the same altitude. Hovered for a second (when I zoomed in on the video recording, I noticed a flash of red on top—very faint)."

The object then made a 90-degree turn and flew to the northwest.

"Once on the northwest path you could see it accelerate while maintaining the same altitude, and it flew out of my sight. I recorded it for three minutes. It was black and did not make any sound that I could hear. There was an airplane running on the ground so I could not hear much. It was a great sighting, and I am glad I was able to record it. I was very excited to witness this amazing sight. I am a firm believer and believe we are not alone. I am a helicopter pilot and know about flight. I was very excited to share this experience with my friends and colleagues. I even shared it with my wife (who is not a believer) and she couldn't explain it. Always keep your eyes up!"

Oregon MUFON State Director Thomas Bowden and CAG Investigator Susan Gerberding closed this case as an Unknown Aerial Vehicle.

"The witness provided a video," Bowden and Gerberding wrote in their report. "The object was clearly visible in the video. All video metadata was consistent with witness statements. Video taken with Apple iPhone 8 Plus. The video shows the object moving back and forth under a dark thunderstorm cloud. The object appears to 'hug' the underside of the cloud. Though not mentioned by the witness, at times there appears to be a white aura around the object. The object in the actual video does appear longer than wide with rounded edges, matching the witness description. Enlargements of photos taken from the video show it appears to be more rectangular, and even square. However, this may be the result of an effect of enlargement and light in digital video.

"Historically there have been 55 reported sightings for Oregon in the MUFON database for cylindrical objects. This is the fourth such reported case for Jackson County, which previously has had cylinder/cigar-shaped sighting events reported for 2007 and 2009.

"Occam's Rule, a principal of logic and science, states that the simplest of two or more competing theories is preferable, and an explanation for unknown phenomena should first be attempted in terms of what is already known. The visual characteristics, flight path, travel speed and object shape indicate that this event was stimulated by one of two things. The first, a rectangular military object, or secondly, by an unknown object. For the reasons given above, it is unlikely this object belongs to the military; the object in this case has been determined to an unknown. The final disposition in this case is that of an Unknown Aerial Vehicle, observed in a maneuver encounter of the first kind."

Medord is a city in, and the county seat of, Jackson County, Oregon, population 81,780.

New York witness describes two glowing orbs

A New York witness at Bay Shore reported watching two silent, glowing orbs, according to testimony in Case 92029.

The witness and her boyfriend were sitting in a parked car at 9 p.m. on May 15, 2018.

"I was looking one direction and he was facing the other," the witness stated. "Suddenly I see two orbs coming at us fast, like a car, with an almost blinding, ball-lightning-like light, connected by red in the center. My boyfriend sees three distinct flashes of light, which he says resemble a camera. I thought it was a cop car until it disappeared without a sound, never passing our car."

New York MUFON Field Investigator Mary Fancher closed this case as an Unknown-Other.

"The witness was an intelligent young woman who felt she saw something truly bizarre in the few seconds it lasted," Fancher wrote in her report. "What at first appeared to be car headlights approaching the car she and her boyfriend were parked in were instead two large orbs, each the size of her torso. They moved extremely rapidly toward her, then stopped before reaching their car. Immediately there was a flash of brilliant light, similar to a camera flash, during which the witness saw a red light connecting the two orbs, almost like the aftereffect of having a brilliant light flash before your eyes. The object disappeared.

"After speaking with the witness, I believe she saw something out of the ordinary. I have tried to come up with something prosaic that might have produced the same effects—speed, flashes of brilliant light, lack of sound, red connecting the orbs, disappearance—but have been unable to."

Bay Shore is a hamlet in the Town of Islip, Suffolk County, New York, population 26,337.

Silent triangular UFO reported over Lisbon

A Portuguese witness at Lisbon reported watching a silent, triangle-shaped object that was "completely silent," according to Case 93352.

The witness and a daughter were outside stargazing on May 15, 2018.

"We usually spend an hour or so looking for something in the skies," the witness stated. "Having had our first sighting in 2012, we experienced many more since then. Most of the times, the only 'things' we get to observe are orbs of light though. Around midnight and out of the blue, I saw a black triangle flying above us. It made no sound at all and it had three lights, one in each corner. I only had time to say, 'Look at that.' It flew in a straight line and suddenly changed direction and disappeared. We could not believe what we had seen. As soon as we got home, I went online to check if anyone had seen the same thing. That's when I found out something weird. The exact same UFO had been seen flying above my old house, where I had lived for 15 years."

CAG International Investigator Ken Pfeifer closed this case as Info Only.

Lisbon is the capital and the largest city of Portugal, 505,526.

MAY 16

Triangular UFO with red lights moves under 500 feet

A California witness at Salinas reported watching a triangular object moving under 500 feet with "between seven and nine red lights" along the edges, according to testimony in Case 92036.

The witness was outside smoking a cigarette at midnight on May 16, 2018.

"I noticed a triangular shape flying not too far away with red lights," the witness stated. "It was flying on a straight line, no noises at all. I really couldn't believe what I was seeing. I could see it perfectly. Somehow it disappeared about 40 seconds later going north. A triangular shape with between 7 and 9 red lights over the edges."

Northern California MUFON State Director Ruben Uriarte closed this case as an Unknown Aerial Vehicle.

"The reporting witness did not respond to the three emails sent. Did not include his home address or phone numbers. However, did leave enough information including a sketch of the object to conclude the case as an Unknown Aerial Vehicle."

Salinas is the county seat and largest municipality of Monterey County, California, population 157,218.

MAY 18

Irish witness describes morphing-hovering object

An Ireland witness at Ballymahon, County Longford, reported watching a glowing object that morphed into a "large, silver star shape" before quickly disappearing, according to testimony in Case 98601.

The witness was home and up late at 4:25 a.m. on May 18, 2018.

"I went to the window seat to get my laptop and as I live on the fourth floor and have no covering at all over the windows," the witness stated, "I glanced out over at the forest across the river and noticed a large glowing red/pinky orange object just sitting in the sky above the treetops. At first glance it looked just like the sun, but it was already daylight and the sun had risen. I quickly realized this was no sun or fallen planet, which was what I first thought,

and which made me really take note."

The witness could not understand what the object was after watching it for 15 minutes.

"This object was sort of glowing, shimmering but was clearly round and was very sun/planet-looking, but was obviously way too low in the sky to be the sun or moon or any other planet. I had to walk away and go back to the window, as I couldn't believe what I was seeing, nor work out what it was. After realizing this thing was still there after a five-minute break, I was just totally gobsmacked, speechless and stunned, as I stood staring. After about 10 minutes this object suddenly changed shape/morphed into a large silver star shape and just disappeared before my eyes. As it vanished, it made a weird light in the sky that sort of looked like the light the old TVs used to make when they were turned off, and a thin white line stayed in the sky for a while after."

The witness was shocked.

"I'm still speechless and dumbfounded at what I saw. A friend who lives miles away who rises early for work told me two weeks later that he had seen this with a couple of differences. This was before I'd said a word to him, so I know I'm not alone and can't believe I'm the only local who saw this, as lots of people here rise early to work at the local factory. I've never before seen anything of this nature and would love to find out more if possible as there was nothing in the media as I thought there would be."

Ireland CAG MUFON Field Investigator Linda Dungan closed this case as an Unknown-Other.

"The photo evidence was inconclusive and looks like a contrail," Dungan wrote in her report. "Sighting time was reported at 4:25 a.m. when she first saw the object. Civil twilight was 4:43 a.m. and witness claims it was daylight when she saw the planet-like object morph into a star-like object and disappear.

Photo evidence suggests the sun had risen. Unknown if any drones were in the area. Object was too low in the sky for a satellite and there were no reports of lightning in the area.

"Based on witness interview, I believe the witness saw a UAP. She doesn't want to remain anonymous and appeared genuine. I'm classifying this case as Unknown-Other due to the lack of structure observed."

Ballymahon is a town in the southern part of County Longford, Ireland.

MAY 21

Oklahoma witness says triangular UFO hovered over trees

An Oklahoma witness at Arkoma reported watching a triangular object hovering just over the tree tops and moving slowly, according to testimony in Case 92164.

The witness and her children had left a friend's house in Arkoma after a birthday party at 9:59 p.m. on May 21, 2018.

"Initially, I dismissed the craft, seeing it vaguely through trees on Celia, but when I got onto Main Street in Arkoma, I realized its lights weren't blinking and it was hovering over trees, moving slowly," the witness stated. "I pulled into the parking lot of Maverick Loans in an attempt to get the kids out to watch while I took pictures, but it shot southward. Spent 20 minutes driving up and down State Line Road trying to find some sign of it. No evidence. Moved too fast and can't focus on the skies while driving on that torn-up street. I was excited at first, wanting to share the experience with my kids (cried out 'no, don't leave until my kids see you.') and disappointed that I am the only person on that street that night willing to admit what I saw, evidence or not."

Oklahoma MUFON Field Investigator Steven Cates closed this case as an Unknown Aerial Vehicle.

"Witness was well able to articulate what she saw, evidencing much presence of mind in her event," Cates stated in his report. "She has convinced herself that what she saw was a TR-3A Black Manta of a new model as this one did not have the exposed canopies of the TR-3A and the circle on the ventral side said to be the mercury plasma accelerator of the TR-3A. These points noted as based on her Googling black, triangular UFOs. I have not been able to find any other witnesses. There are no photographs. There were no other reports of the sighting of a UFO (black triangle or otherwise) on the night in question with MUFON, API, or NUFORC, and I could not find a report in either the local paper or TV stations on the following day. There have been reports historically of black triangles seen over Ft. Smith, AR, and I have no reason to think the witness was hoaxing. The witness was too near, and the activity too vehicular in manner, to think it was misrecognized planets, stars, space debris, etc., and the sky too clear. However, since the USA does not acknowledge having a TR-3 of any model (or any other government) I cannot call this an IFO. Consequently, this is a UAV."

Arkoma is a town in Le Flore County, Oklahoma, population 1,989.

MAY 22

UFO reported hovering over Illinois lake

An Illinois witness at Hudson reported watching two lights "attached to something" hovering over a lake, according to testimony in Case 92950.

The witness and three friends were watching the sunset on Evergreen Lake in Comlara Park in Hudson, about 10 miles away from their college campus at 8:12 p.m. on May 22, 2018.

"As the sky was getting darker, two lights

appeared out of nowhere (literally in the blink of an eye) directly above the lake," the witness stated. "The red light was above the green light and they were obviously attached to something in which the outline slightly resembled a human with his arms a bit out. It flew towards us, evident by how the lights were getting larger as it flew closer, flew backwards (without the lights turning away from us) and then disappeared just as fast as it appeared. The lights did not blink once. We immediately left."

Illinois MUFON Assistant State Director Roger Laurella and Chief Investigator Daniel Snow closed this case as an Unknown-Other.

"This is a location where we had reports submitted from, and east of this location is where we have had multiple night watches with some success," Laurella and Snow stated in their report.

Hudson is a village in McLean County, Illinois, population 1,838.

MAY 24

Vermont witness describes low-flying triangle

A Vermont witness at Saint Albans reported watching a triangular object under 500 feet that appeared to be 10 feet x 10 feet in size, according to testimony in Case 92228.

The witness was traveling northbound along I-89 at 11:45 p.m. on May 24, 2018.

"My girlfriend and I were remarking on the lights that at the time became more apparently a triangle formation," the witness stated. "Because of the distance we had traveled, the UFO's actual area in the sky became very apparent. As we continued closer and closer our angle to look at the lights got steeper and steeper. From what I saw, it was very capable at flying at low heights and could change

direction easily. It was over 10 feet by 10 feet. Possibly had thermal imaging as it moved away as we started taking pictures. It made no sound and had a range over 15 miles."

Vermont MUFON State Director Ken Pfeifer closed this case as Info Only.

"No response from the witness," Pfeifer wrote in his report.

St. Albans is the county seat of Franklin County, population 6,918.

MAY 25

Washington UFO described as 'submarine with rectangular edges'

A Washington witness at Poulsbo reported watching a "brown metal object" that looked like a submarine with rectangular edges, according to testimony in Case 94857.

The witness was outside "enjoying the beautiful orange cast of a colorful sunset" at 8:30 p.m. on May 25, 2018.

"The tree line starts 200 to 400 yards away," the witness stated. "I was seated on my deck facing east. A quiet time since there is very little traffic on our road and the birds were settling in for night. A fast-moving object caught my eye above the trees headed directly west into the sun. It was a beautiful brown metallic structure. The intensity of sunlight made it shine and revealed shadows indicating layers of metal. It was submarine-shaped only with sharper, rectangular edges defining its exterior. It did not have an intake opening for a jet engine. It did not have a propeller. It made no noise. Silent and fast."

The witness did not have time to grab a camera.

"My cellphone was in the house as I like to enjoy nature without electronics. Just prior to this sighting, a bald eagle flew directly over the open part of the yard, heading northeast almost at eye level since our house is on an elevated part of the property. This was the first UFO sighting of my life of 63 years. The naval base at Keyport, WA, was lowering their flag just prior to the sighting. The retreat music is heard during this time throughout the neighborhood. Afterward I felt that I had been visited by an old friend now deceased. He was a retired submariner."

Washington MUFON State Section Director Zach Royer closed this case as an Unknown Aerial Vehicle.

"I interviewed the witness at her home and found her and her husband to be very credible and reliable witnesses," Royer wrote in his report. "They are both professionals who work in the area. I conclude the witness saw an unknown hexagonal, cigar-shaped craft."

Poulsbo is a city on Liberty Bay in Kitsap County, Washington, population 9,200.

MAY 29

German witness photographs hovering disc-shaped UFO

A German witness at Kronberg im Taunus reported watching and photographing a hovering disc-shaped object, according to testimony in Case 92387.

The witness was looking out a window at 8:50 p.m. on May 29, 2018.

"Saw some kind of a disc/oval-shaped object on the left side (northwest) of the building," the witness stated. "I was excited and decided to record the event. When I came back with my mobile phone, I spotted the object at some distance and took some pictures. On the pictures it looks like it could be a bird of some kind, but it was a hovering object—stationary—at about one km distance. I recorded the event and caught the object coming out of the thun-

derstorm clouds, and it fell about 300 meters in about half a second—then hovered and remained stationary again. I recorded about 1:30 mins. The whole sighting was approximately three minutes."

Germany MUFON Field Investigator Andreas Schönhofen closed this case as an Unknown Aerial Vehicle.

"I examined the pictures and they look authentic in forencially.com [site no longer accessible at this URL; now located at https://29a.ch/photo-forensics/]," Schönhofen stated in his report. "The information in the EXIF data are identical to the information in the witness report. Note: Hoaxers can edit pictures in such a way that they are not recognizable as hoaxes. This risk exists always.

"I checked all possible man-made objects like drones, weather balloons, etc., and natural phenomena like birds, etc. I can't find any explanation. The shape does not fit a drone, weather balloon, bird or something else. This object is unknown."

Kronberg im Taunus is a town in the Hochtaunuskreis district, Hesse, Germany.

JUNE 2018

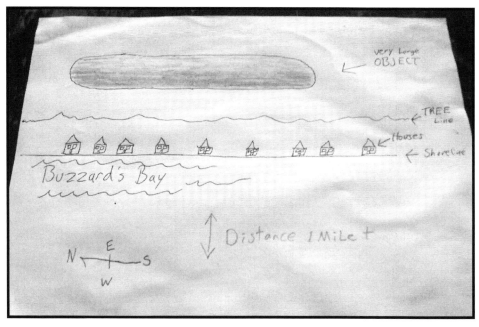

Case 97168 witness illustration. June 6, 2018.

JUNE 1

Brazilian witness says triangle appeared after seeing fireball

A Brazilian witness at Sao Jose dos Pinhais reported watching a "large fireball in the sky" and then immediately seeing a black triangle UFO, according to testimony in Case 92432.

The event occurred at 7:41 p.m. on June 1, 2018.

"A large fireball in the sky," the witness stated. "After this went away, a black triangle appeared. The sightings of these objects are becoming more frequent, becoming almost daily."

Brazil MUFON Assistant National Director Thiago Luiz Ticchetti and International Director of Investigations Steve Hudgeons closed this case as Info Only.

"I got in touch with the witness," Ticchetti and Hudgeons wrote in their report. "Waiting for feedback with more information. Witness responded to the email and said he is only reporting on his sightings. I asked him to try to register the objects using a digital machine, camera or cell phone."

Sao Jose dos Pinhais is a city in Paraná, Brazil, part of the Metropolitan Region of Curitiba.

Silent UFO reported over Czech Republic

A Czech Republic witness at Novy Jicin reported a silent, triangular-shaped object moving under 500 feet, according to testimony in Case 93565.

The witness was in a swimming pool at 11:01 p.m. on June 1, 2018.

"Above the nearby town of Pribor was a large thunderstorm and flashes at around 11 p.m.," the witness stated. "And suddenly, a three-helical, triangular-shaped object appeared on the ground above my house and sailed across the sky toward the southwest. When he was at my level, he did a little maneuver and leaned at a distance of about 20 degrees to me and continued on the flight without noise and lighting. I was quite impressed when he appeared so close to me completely silent, and I saw the contours and the hemisphere, and I watched in amazement as he went on to the neighboring houses and disappeared on the horizon. I lost sight at the last house in our street."

Czech Republic MUFON Field Investigator Magdalena Biziuk closed this case as Info Only.

Novy Jicin is a town in the Moravian-Silesian Region of the Czech Republic, population approximately 26,500.

Airline passenger photographs UFO

A Missouri witness on a fight from Houston to Chicago photographed a triangle-shaped UFO, according to testimony in Case 92483.

The witness was flying on American Airlines flight 3996 Houston to Chicago at 2:30 p.m. on June 1, 2018.

"About halfway through the flight (over Missouri) I was photographing storm anvils for use as desktop wallpaper," the witness stated. "Our flight was at about 36,000 to 38,000 feet. Immediately after taking three pictures in about 10 seconds, the craft appeared suddenly to the east of the flight path at about 50,000 feet from nowhere, as if in some Star Trek 'de-cloaking' scene."

The witness immediately took another photo of the craft.

"Three seconds later the craft went ballistic to the south and ascending. So fast that the track was almost imperceptible. From stationary to like light speed disappearance at an angle up and reverse of our flight path, which would be south. Sun was west of our airplane and so was not causing a reflection or spot on window or lens of camera phone. Craft had a triangular shape to it, and must have been very large as I had been watching out the window and observing airliners crossing our flight path for about an hour, so was used to what winged planes looked like and how fast they would become visible and then pass out of view. Got used to the shape and look of normal airliners and this one that suddenly appeared in an area I had just been watching and photographing for the last few minutes. It had no time to have made its way into my field of view at normal speeds of 300 to 500 mph. Just appeared, and, after shooting it, I lowered the camera phone to observe with just my eyes and it suddenly went light speed ballistic at an angle that could only be up and reverse of our path. Was there for about three seconds and then shot out of the scene in less than a second."

The witness has an aircraft background.

"I was a small craft pilot in my youth and worked at NASA for many years at JSC in Houston so have a fairly good experience base with things that fly and what looks materially manifest versus what is ghost imaging or reflective anomalies. Never saw or heard of anything like this in shape or performance. And, I knew many astronauts and test pilots during my tenure at NASA. As with many of these occurrences, it happened so fast that I was lucky to capture anything at all, and the picture is too blurry for me to accentuate it with Photoshop, so I am including the raw shot off my camera unadulterated by me in any way. All of this happened in blue clear sky above cumulus clouds far below both craft."

Missouri MUFON State Director Debbie Ziegelmeyer closed this case as an Unknown Aerial Vehicle.

"From the submitted picture of the craft, I believe the craft could not have been an additional 11,000 feet higher," Ziegelmeyer stated in her report. "From the window angle the picture was taken through, the craft was most likely flying at approximately the same altitude as the AA flight or maybe 2,000 feet higher. Aircraft generally do not fly above 40,000 feet. Whiteman AFB and Scott AFB are both in close proximity of this AA flight path. The witness is a small craft pilot and retired from NASA. He seemed to know how aircraft generally perform (except for altitude) and reported that at least one other passenger witnessed the same craft and its out of the ordinary flight maneuvers. The witness waited to speak to the pilot for a few minutes after the flight had landed, but the cabin door was closed, and the pilot did not come out. I fly American airlines quite a bit and this is unusual, the cabin door is always open and the pilots in open view after the flight has landed. I also watch for aircraft outside my window seat when I fly, and submitted a picture of what is normally seen. This picture and described movement were different. Flight paths are normally straight-line. The flight was in the vicinity of both Scott AFB and Whiteman AFB. There is a possibility this was a secret military experimental aircraft; however, this would still be an Unknown Aerial Vehicle—which is my final conclusion."

JUNE 2

British witness videotapes disc-shaped UFO

A British witness at Crieff, Perthshire, Scotland, reported watching and videotaping a disc-shaped object, according to testimony in Case 92499.

The incident occurred at 3:10 p.m. on June 2, 2018.

"There was an approaching thunderstorm from the southeast," the witness stated. "I looked out of a window as I was at home. I noticed an object in the distance that did not look like a bird, drifting in the sky. I then went and grabbed my camcorder—Panasonic HC-V250, 10.0 mega pixels, 90x zoom—to see if I could zoom in on it to see what it was."

When the witness returned with the camera the object had moved some distance in the sky.

"My view of it was blocked as it had passed the town clock and I lost sight of it as it passed behind a rooftop. I then ran to another window in my house so I could see it again. I opened the window as I did not want to film it through glass. I managed to film it for about 30 seconds, maybe actually only 20 by the time I focused in."

The witness described the object.

"Puck-shaped, or a disc with an edge. I was viewing it moving from my left to right. It does appear cigar-shaped as it moved horizontally. There were clouds above it and below it. It approached some lower level clouds, then banked. As it did this, you could clearly see it was circular when viewed from underneath. In brief, it traveled at a constant speed, approached a cloud formation and then banked and went into the cloud and that is when I lost sight of it. I have only basic computing equipment, so have not had the chance yet to try and enhance the images in Photoshop. The film is a bit shaky, but when slowed down and screenshots taken, you get some better images. I only noticed afterwards looking at screen shots that as it approaches the cloud to descend into it, there appears a green doughnut-shaped light underneath it. Have attached the film clip and a couple of screen shots, and hopefully someone out there may be able to enhance them a bit more than I can. Was filmed in Crieff, Perthshire, Scotland. View for yourself."

Robert Young for UK MUFON closed this case as an Unknown Aerial Vehicle. The witness provided four still images and one video with the report, which was filed on June 5, 2018.

"The only possible rational explanation that could account for the video is that it is either hoaxed or the object may be some sort of drone, but seems unlikely," Young stated in his report. "My own conclusion is that it is a real object and not a hoax, an unidentified flying object whatever it may be."

Crieff is a market town in Perth and Kinross, Scotland.

NJ photo shows multiple UFOs in formation

A New Jersey witness at Salem reported a string of objects in formation that were discovered in a photograph, according to testimony in Case 92481.

The witness was driving to work about 5:30 p.m. on June 2, 2018.

"Watching a storm close in over the area," the witness stated. "Something out of place caught my eye and I slowed my vehicle, took a couple of pictures and continued on my way to work. I reviewed the pictures yesterday afternoon and found the objects in question then."

New Jersey MUFON Assistant State Director Ken Pfeifer closed this case as Info Only.

"Camera capture only," Pfeifer wrote in his report. "Witness saw the objects on the photo and not in the sky."

Salem is a city in Salem County, New Jersey, population 5,146.

Canadian witness reports triangular UFO moving overhead

A Canadian witness at London reported watching a triangular-shaped object moving overhead, according to testimony in Case 92445.

The witness was at the University of Western Ontario Cronyn Observatory for an open public summer night at 10:05 p.m. on June 2, 2018.

"I was out on the balcony waiting for my turn to use the telescope," the witness stated. "I was looking straight up to see if I could see any stars as it was getting much cloudier. I noticed the object fly right into my sightline and I froze. I just felt really numb, stunned. It was definitely a ship of some sort, and so black it stood out from the night sky. It had lights on the bottom of it, along the edges—I think seven in total. One at the peak and three down each side. They were not obviously bright but, casting a white glow, seemed to be dome-shaped almost, rather than flush against the surface. I immediately thought it was a UFO. It was flying really low, right over our heads. Perhaps 50 feet up. It was moving rather slow, totally smooth, and was completely silent. It had a solid outline and distinct triangle shape, but the body was also moving. Its body reminded me of a Rubik's Cube with the square parts rotating forward in some sort of perpetual kinetic motion. I was so shocked I couldn't speak. I did look around me and could not process no one else was seeing it. Everyone was talking, or on their phones, or looking through the telescopes at Jupiter. I wanted to say something but felt frozen. I looked back up and it just continued moving along until it disappeared into the distance. I felt like talking to someone, but I couldn't. Just felt really surreal. I remember thinking, 'wait, come back,' but it was gone."

Canada MUFON Field Investigator Dan Jones closed this case as Unknown Aerial Vehicle.

"Witness is credible," Jones stated in his report. "I exchanged email with the witness as well as a lengthy telephone interview. The witness promptly provided additional information when requested throughout the investigation. The witness has a PhD and is an educator at a university in Ontario. On June 2nd, 2018, the witness was star-gazing at the observatory on the university campus. At approximately 10 p.m., while taking a break outside of the observatory, she witnessed a triangle craft pass over her at a distance of approximately 50 feet. The craft appeared to be approximately 30 feet wide. It had seven white lights along the edges and made no sound. The craft was black. The witness describes the surface texture as being made up of squares, which appeared to be rotating forward as the craft moved slowly overhead. The duration of the event was approximately 20 seconds. The craft traveled in a straight path from east to west as it moved out of sight. The witness provided a sketch, which I have attached to this report.

"I believe the witness did, indeed, observe some type of triangle craft."

London is a city in Southwestern Ontario, Canada, population 383,822.

JUNE 3

Radio, cell phone stopped during NY UFO encounter

A New York witness at Springville reported watching a black metallic object with a dome on top that may have caused her car radio and cell phone to stop working, according to testimony in Case 92447.

The events occurred beginning at 1:20 a.m. on June 3, 2018.

"Initially thought lights were dim stars or stars covered with clouds," the witness stated. "Realized lights were too close to ground. Lights pulsated and appeared to be on the outside of a saucer-like flying object. Radio cut out as I was driving in the direction of object and got closer. Made me fearful. Thankfully, I had to turn to get home, which took me away from where the object was hovering. I turned and did not look back."

New York MUFON Chief Investigator Christo-

pher DePerno closed this case as an Unknown Aerial Vehicle.

"The witness said that about 1:20 a.m. she had just passed the Springville exit on 219 South, when she noticed through the windshield of the vehicle a cluster of what she believed to be stars in the southern sky in front of her," DePerno stated in his report. "The witness said the weather was warm, not raining and the sky was clear of cloud cover, where she could notice several stars in the sky. The witness then took a closer look at this particular cluster of stars and noticed that this particular cluster was in line and was lower than the other stars in the sky. The witness said from her point of view, from in her car, she believed the elevation was about 45 to 50 degrees. As she was driving and getting closer, she noticed this cluster was not stars, but a round object, with a single row of horizontal lights that were attached to a round-shaped object. The witness described the object as follows:

"Round, black metallic object, with a dome on top, with one row of five to six horizontal white lights, Saturn shape. Size: approximately the size of an acre.

"The witness described the object as being 'Huge,' about the size of an acre. The witness then said the object's lights began pulsating as if to get her attention. The witness then said her car radio stopped working. She explained that this has never happened before. She did explain that the rest of the vehicle's functions continued working.

"The witness became gripped with fear; she explained she was extremely frightened as the lights now began pulsating, changing color from white to red. The pulsating lights were moving from front to back. The witness continued driving, approaching the intersection of 219 South and Peters Road.

"The witness then noticed from the windshield of her vehicle the object rapidly move a very short distance from west to east. The object then started moving south away from her. At the same time the witness turned onto Peters Road and attempted to use her cell phone to call her brother. She discovered that her cell phone had no service. The witness continued driving and after a couple of minutes the cell phone service returned. The witness said she has traveled this road several times and knows where the dead spots are and that is area is not one of them.

"After completing the interview with the witness and further investigation, I have come to the following conclusion.

"I believe that the witness interview was credible. The witness said during the interview she had always ridiculed her brother. When questioned why, the witness stated that her brother had explained that he had seen a 'UFO' and she always criticized him for talking about it. The witness said she didn't really believe in her brother's sighting, until she had her sighting. The witness spoke as though she had genuine fear in her voice about the time of the sighting.

"The witness also noted that as the event was going on, her car radio stopped working. The witness stated that has never happened before. Also, her cell phone would not work, showing no service. The witness said she has driven that same route several times and she knows where the dead zone areas are and that area is not one.

"The witness was consistent in her interview and never changed her story. She was confident in her interview in what she saw and how it reacted. The weather at the time of the incident was clear and nothing interfered with the sighting. No airports are within 30 miles of the area of the incident. No military bases in the area."

Springville is a village in the southeast part of the town of Concord, Erie County, New York, population 4,596.

Mississippi witness reports low-flying cylindrical UFO

A Mississippi witness at Panola County reported watching a cylinder-shaped object hovering over a local church, according to testimony in Case 92469.

The event occurred at 6:45 a.m. on June 3, 2018.

"I was heading to pick up my girlfriend from work," the witness stated. "I was taking the back way through town to avoid red lights. On my way I passed by a church. I saw it in the sky above the church and thought it was my eyes at first because it was early in the morning. But I stopped at a nearby stop sign and looked back to make sure it wasn't my eyes. And it was still there hovering over the church."

The witness described the movement of the object.

"It shifted slightly to the side and then shot straight up with more speed than anything I've ever seen. There was cloud cover, but it made no disturbance to the clouds as it vanished into them afterwards."

The witness experienced an illness following the event.

"I have been having unusual ringing in my ears and sickness to my stomach."

Mississippi MUFON CAG Investigator Thomas Wertman investigated this case and closed it as an Unknown Aerial Vehicle.

"The object hovered for a total time of one-to-two minutes before moving away vertically at a high rate of speed," Wertman stated in his report. "As it left, the object did not disturb the cloud cover. There were no apparent lights on the object.

"The witness observed a single, cylindrical-shaped, dark object with no apparent light, large in apparent size, between 31 and 100 feet in actual size and less than 500 feet away. The object hovered for between one-to-two minutes before moving vertically at a high rate of speed. The witness could not identify elevation in degrees, only that the object appeared to be 200 feet above the ground. He was also unsure of direction first and last observed.

"During the interview the witness was excited about what he had seen. The witness appeared credible and stated the event as it was perceived. Flightradar24 indicated there were no low-flying aircraft in the region (plus/minus one hour) at the time of the sighting, even though the witness reported seeing an aircraft. The closest airport is Panola County Airport, approximately four miles from the sighting location. Skyvector indicates approximately 16 single and multiengine aircraft are at the airport. No records of helicopters.

"FAA records indicate Columbus 3 MOA is four miles to the east. Exercises were conducted on June 5, but the Field Investigator could find no scheduled exercises for the day of the event. The hovering of the object was similar to a helicopter. There is no evidence to support a man-made explanation.

"The witness was from a family with very rigid religious beliefs. The event appeared to create emotional turmoil. The unusual ringing in the ears and sickness to the stomach may be side effects of these feelings. The Field Investigator did not get any indication they were related to actual physical effects of the object."

Panola County, Mississippi, has a population was 34,707.

British witness describes 'horseshoe-shaped' UFO

A British witness at Dartford reported watching and videotaping a horseshoe-shaped object that moved around before fading away, according to testimony in Case 93607.

The witness was outside sitting in a garden in southeast London near the M25 at 7:49 p.m. on June 3, 2018.

"I noticed a light in the sky," the witness stated. "I initially thought it was a star but after looking at it through my binoculars I realized this wasn't the case. Through my binoculars I saw the object close up and it was a distinctive horseshoe shape. While looking through the binoculars I saw the object twisting and turning, plus I'm convinced I saw two red lights at the end of each 'arm' whilst it was turning."

Unfortunately, the observed lights did not show in the pictures.

"The end of the 'arms' just appears black. There is a strand that shows up on the right of the object that appears in all of the pictures and video, which may be connected to the magnetic field. Or maybe the craft's energy is reacting with the atmosphere, which the sun is highlighting? I wasn't on my own. I was with my friend and she saw it too. I was able to take the pictures and video with my Nikon P900. I was about 80 percent zoomed out on the optical zoom, so before this the object appeared as a white light to the naked eye, and as I said before it just looked like a star. After viewing the object for at least 10 minutes, the object started to go in and out of the atmosphere, with the light fading and reappearing. Eventually it faded out completely and disappeared. I was so overwhelmed after seeing the object that I said 'thank you' afterwards. I had my awakening in early 2017, and I feel so privileged to have had this encounter."

United Kingdom MUFON Field Investigator James Dallas closed this case as an Unknown Aerial Vehicle.

"He first notices what he describes as a bright star in the sky, but he thought it was moving, so called his girlfriend to get his binoculars, so he could see it more closely," Dallas wrote in his report. "To his astonishment it now resembled a horseshoe and asked his girlfriend to look and verify what he was seeing. Having a new camera, he was able to use an optical zoom to take photos; the images we have on file. The more they looked, the more it seemed to morph, and he was sure that it was either morphing or tumbling. It appeared to have two appendages or arms, which he believed were black in color with red lights on the tips. He has since been on the Internet to see if there were any more like this and uncovered a sighting in France. I believe this to be a positive sighting."

Dartford is the principal town in the Borough of Dartford, Kent, England.

California witness says 'disco ball' UFOs frequent property

A California witness at Flournoy reported watching and videotaping "orb-like disco balls" that appear at and near the property and have followed the witness, according to testimony in Case 92452.

The current sighting occurred on June 3, 2018.

"These things have been around here for months, maybe even longer," the witness stated. "I noticed them because it became impossible not to. My niece and I have even witnessed them very low (like a foot or two off the ground) and I don't believe they are much higher than the length of a football field. At first, they appeared to just act like stars but were bigger, but as time has progressed, they have been known to follow us around our property (100 acres) and even in our car. And as of this date the only time we lose sight of these objects is when the sun comes up, but they are the first to come back in the evenings (nightly). Originally, I just called these 'not stars,' but in a state of panic because I was driving right into a type of cluster of them, I called my mom and to calm me she suggested they were drones."

California MUFON Field Investigator Hady Felfly closed this case as an Unknown-Other.

"Five of the videos show the object from afar, and it appears small, like an object that seems round, but changes shape a little as it is moving, sometimes appearing as if it is two or more roundish objects, or maybe the object has a different shape from each angle and that's what we are seeing," Felfly stated in her report. "The movements are quite irregular back and forth movements. The movements are not like any plane or drone, very strange and sudden changes in direction. In the remaining three videos, the filming seems a close-up, and the object appears as a very bright, white sphere of light displaying same movements and sometimes zapping in one direction.

"Using MPC-HC software, I was able to detect metadata for all the videos.

"We can hear the 'night noise' in the background, indicating the video was genuinely taken outdoors and sometimes we hear what could be the witness talking and commenting on the object. She mentions treetops but the sky was too dark, and I could not see treetops on the video.

"Related case: MUFON CMS Case #92472 reports white spots seen in the day in the sky, with pictures; they are a bit similar in shape and size to the object reported here in #92452. NUFORC: None reported on June 3, 2018.

"While the videos show a bright light/object, the fact that it is always near the witness's house can also indicate the possibility of some light effects installed in her area that she is not aware of. Alternately, it may be some orb. Without further evidence, it is hard to conclude with more precision. Therefore, it is my recommendation to close this case as Unknown, Other."

Flournoy is a census-designated place in Tehama County, California, population 101.

JUNE 4

Virginia witness describes three 'silver orbs'

A Virginia witness at Leesburg reported watching three "silver orbs" moving at a high rate of speed and shooting off in different directions, according to testimony in Case 97913.

The witness was on a back deck watching air traffic on June 4, 2018.

"First, I am a retired police officer who spent 24 years on patrol and never observed anything like this before," the witness stated. "My wife and I were enjoying a beautiful sunny afternoon on our back deck looking at the regular planes coming and going when I noticed and pointed out a silver orb cutting through white, puffy clouds flying left to right to my wife. She is a skeptic through and through, so I was very happy she witnessed what I observed. As the orb flew at a high rate of speed, it stopped and then changed direction. A second orb appeared and went left to right as well. They shot across the sky around the planes entering and exiting Dulles airport. We watched for a couple of minutes and a third orb shot like a light into the oncoming path of a large airplane. Then they crossed each other's paths several times and shot off in different directions. Two shot off southeast and one ascended straight up into the sky, cutting through white puffy clouds. They appeared to be silver metallic and the size of golf balls, at least half the size of large commuter planes, distance unknown. However, they circled the planes as if they were standing still. The exterior of the orbs reflected light, blue skies and white clouds. My wife was forced to admit she witnessed three UFOs, which it killed her to admit. We were not scared, we didn't have crazy nightmares or piss ourselves while using our microwave afterwards. But it was an incredible experience,

and I felt very honored to have witnessed them. That's it. The experience, however, made me understand we are not alone."

Virginia MUFON Field Investigator Victor Rodriguez closed this case as an Unknown Aerial Vehicle.

"Both witnesses were cooperative and willing to share their experience," Rodriguez stated in his report. "Unfortunately, the event occurred over six months ago, making it close to impossible to verify weather and other pertinent facts. The date itself is approximate, which is unfortunate as the event involves air traffic from nearby Dulles International Airport. This does not take away from the credibility of the witnesses or their vivid description of a very unusual event. Added to the description is that one of the orbs approached a small cloud and punched a hole in it as it traversed it.

"The witness's background makes him a very discerning witness. When questioned why he waited to report, he stated that he saw a similar report on the web and decided to come forward. He and his wife have become believers."

Leesburg is the county seat of Loudoun County, Virginia, population 52,607.

JUNE 6

Massachusetts UFO described as hovering 'huge cigar'

A Massachusetts witness at Plymouth reported watching a "huge cigar-shaped object" hovering nearby that eventually moved out over the Atlantic Ocean, according to testimony in Case 97168.

The witness was outside at Buzzards Bay with a friend at 1 p.m. on June 6, 2018.

"It was a very clear, beautiful day as you can see clear across the bay, which is more than a mile to the other side, which is Cape Cod," the witness stated. "As I was scanning the shoreline across the bay just looking at the sites, I noticed a huge, blimp-like object, gray with no colors, just hovering in the distance over the land. It appeared to be gigantic compared to houses on the ground beneath it. Almost could have been a mile long. It was slowly moving back and forth for a couple minutes as I was still trying to figure out if I was watching some gigantic blimp or something, and then it began to get what looked to be smaller, but then I realized it was just turning left about 90 degrees facing down the ocean on the other side. And at that moment I realized it wasn't a giant flying saucer, but a giant cigar-shaped aircraft of some sort, and then it sort of got smaller as it went away from us towards the Atlantic Ocean. And it got smaller quite fast so almost represent that it was going a pretty good clip. There were no other witnesses on the beach that day, and after the sighting we're trying to figure out what exactly we had seen. Looked like something out of the Independence Day film, and I was quite blown away to have seen something like that in my lifetime. We literally left after the incident, and I have been trying to find out if there was any kind of air show that day because there is Otis Air Force Base right in that vicinity or some kind of blimp thing going on, but everything that I look into says nothing and with no other witnesses, and it's pretty astonishing to me how no one could have seen this gigantic object just over their heads. And that's probably why it had that hazy look to it, because it was using some kind of active camouflage. I didn't know what to do so I didn't report it for a while. But I feel like people need to know what I've seen, and I can't believe what I have seen."

Massachusetts MUFON State Director Eric Hartwig closed this case as Info Only.

"Witness has not replied to email or text messages requesting an interview," Hartwig stated in his report. "Because there is no exact address to this beach, I am very limited to what I can check on."

Plymouth is a town in Plymouth County, Massachusetts, population 58,271.

JUNE 7

Rectangular UFO spotted moving over Oregon

An Oregon witness at Dallas reported watching a large, gray, rectangular-shaped object reminiscent of an aircraft carrier moving overhead, according to testimony in Case 92560.

The witness was sitting outside after dark on a lawn chair watching a movie on a laptop at 10:05 p.m. on June 7, 2018.

"I was aware of a noise like a plane, but it wasn't until it was right overhead that I looked up to see a large gray object flying north to south," the witness stated. "It seemed to be flying rather low for a jet liner, but still several thousand feet up. It had two white lights in the front and two red lights in the rear. It appeared to have no wings and a flat bottom. Its rectangular shape reminded me of a barge or aircraft carrier. Its corners did not appear to be rounded, but more squared off, hence the resemblance to a barge. It continued from over my head south until it was out of sight. It was not quite as loud as a jet plane but made a noise very similar. I continued to watch it and noticed the light pattern did not change as if it was two separate planes flying together. It flew south over the nearby town of Dallas until it was out of sight."

Oregon MUFON State Director Tom Bowden closed this case as an Unknown Aerial Vehicle.

"There is no simple explanation for this sighting," Bowden wrote in his report. "The object described does not fit any known conventional aircraft, blimp or balloon. The lighting configuration of two white lights in front and two red lights in the rear does not conform to standard aircraft lighting configurations. The object having an apparent size of a golf ball held at arm's length and taking about three minutes to fly overhead, the witness would have had a really good look at it. In my opinion, this sighting cannot be explained as any known conventional aircraft or lighter-than-air craft, nor can it be explained as any kind of natural phenomenon."

Dallas is the county seat of Polk County, Oregon, population 14,583.

Five UFOs reported hovering low over Colorado town

A Colorado witness at Colorado Springs reported watching five low-flying objects hover and move around their home for more than an hour, according to testimony in Case 92568.

The incident began about 10:30 p.m. on June 7, 2018.

"My daughter and I went outside to smoke a cigarette, and we like to look at the night sky anyway," the reporting witness stated. "We have seen objects in the sky off and on for months now anyway."

The two were standing by a back door when they looked to their right and noticed a larger and brighter light hovering over the treetops across the street, and then another one that was not as bright higher and to the right of the first.

"Then we saw another one start moving right over us in a straight line, no noise, and in a complete straight line until it stopped over by our back yard, where it stopped, and hovered. There was also one that stopped over our heads, made no noise, and hovered there. And one more that was a little distance away from the one hovering over us and it also sat in the sky."

The crafts each had a small extension on the bottom.

"But only two shone brighter, and one was giving off red and white colors. We watched for about 15 minutes, put the dog inside, and watched for a few more minutes, and then went in our home."

The two stepped back outside about 45 minutes later and three of the objects were still there.

"My daughter tried to video, but when it didn't come out very well as it was so dark outside, she deleted it before I could stop her. We were not afraid and did not feel threatened. We were also not surprised, as I have seen craft since I was a kid. And since moving from Denver to Pueblo a couple of years ago, we have seen craft numerous times, especially when we lived in Pueblo West. We saw craft all the time over the reservoir."

Colorado Field Investigators Richard Evans and Deborah Evans closed this case as an Unknown Aerial Vehicle.

"The five objects were observed initially for about 15 minutes and then the witnesses went inside the house," the Evanses stated in their report. "Several objects were barbell-shaped in a vertical direction, had an apparent size of two fingers, and an estimated size of up to 'as big as a house.' No sounds were heard from the objects. The first object was seen just above tree level to the west and was flashing a bright white light; a definitive shape could not be observed, and the object may have been more than a mile away. The second object was seen higher in the western sky (60 degrees?) and was not as bright. It glowed and looked a bit like a barbell in a vertical position, with the top being much larger than the bottom. It was stationary in the sky. The third object came from the west over the 40-foot tree across the street and moved directly overhead before continuing east. With its bright white light, its shape could not be determined. A fourth glowing orb-like object was seen, and a needle-like protrusion hung down. The fifth object observed was to the south towards the backyard. It had very bright, white lights that would stay on for a couple seconds and then be replaced with bright red lights for a couple seconds and then the pattern would repeat. The witnesses went inside the house for 45–60 minutes, and, when they returned outside, objects one and two were gone. Object three was a little higher than treetop level and details could not be seen. Objects four and five could not be seen.

"The primary witness provided a detailed account of her sighting and she appears credible. It is noted that the primary witness has had experience with similar objects personally in the past as has her family. Other natural and man-made objects meeting the witness's description have been ruled out."

Colorado Springs is the largest city by area in Colorado as well as the county seat of El Paso County, Colorado, population of 465,101.

JUNE 9

Iowa witness describes circular object at treetop level

An Iowa witness at Oelwein reported watching a black object with red lights at treetop level, according to testimony in Case 92591.

The witness was outside having a cigarette about 1:15 a.m. on June 9, 2018.

"I happened to be looking at the sky because I heard like a helicopter noise and I saw a circular-shaped object that had red lights that was flying behind a tree in a straight line," the witness stated. "I really didn't have any necessarily feelings about it. Just kind of odd, I guess. I mean I watch UFO shows with that type of thing so I kind of look for the stuff to begin with, which is why I'm writing this. But in a way it kind of looked like it could have been a drone or something like that. But I've never seen one around here, and I've never seen one fly at night or quite look that way.

Iowa MUFON Field Investigator David Kreiter closed this case as an Unknown Aerial Vehicle.

"Much of this case was dependent upon eyewitness testimony as many cases are," Kreiter stated in his notes. "Taking account of the witness's testimony and using measurements from the Google Earth's ruler tool, it was possible to measure the distance the object traveled from its initial position, where he first saw the object, to its last observed position. The object traveled across 72 degrees of space and 328 feet in 10 seconds, or 22 mph.

"According to testimony, the object went behind the tops of a cluster of 50-foot-high trees approximately 300 feet in distance, located diagonally across the street from his position. He believed that the object was only a few yards beyond the trees. Using this information, it was possible to calculate the object's altitude above the horizon (less than 1 degree), and the air distance (about 305 feet). The apparent size of the object was about that of the full moon or one-half degree of arc. Since the air distance and separation angle were known, it was then possible to calculate the actual size of the object (about 3 feet in length). Of course, if the witness underestimated the distance of the object, its size and speed would be larger. The object could not have been a wind-driven balloon or Chinese lantern for a couple of reasons: First, the wind was from the east-northeast and the object was moving north, perpendicular to the wind direction. Second, the wind speed was only 7 mph, too slow to propel an object going 22 miles per hour. It is possible it could have been a drone, but in my opinion, this is unlikely as well. The witness agreed with this supposition. As a result of my investigation, I have given this case a disposition of Unknown-UAV."

Oelwein is a city in Fayette County, Iowa, population 6,415.

UFO flying 50 feet over Maryland bridge

A Maryland witness at Alexandria reported watching a self-illuminated, missile-shaped object moving rapidly 50 feet over a bridge, according to testimony in Case 92619.

The witness and his wife were traveling home southbound along I-95 at about 8:32 p.m. on June 9, 2018.

"The weather was clear, with very little haze in the air," the witness stated. "The sun had pretty much set to the west and the sky was lit slightly as dusk had settled in. At the time of the sighting, we were traveling due west as we crossed the Potomac River on the Woodrow Wilson Bridge. We were moving at about 60 mph. At the time I noticed the object, we were about one-third of the way across the bridge, and within three-to-four seconds, the object was out of our field of view. I had a full and clear view of the Alexandria, Virginia, shoreline when I noticed a long, flat, white, self-illuminating object above the water to my right. It was moving to the south at what appeared to be a very high rate of speed. It was almost dead center of the river, going from the north to the south. It maintained the same altitude the entire time we viewed the object. I pointed at the object and asked my wife, 'What is that?' repeatedly. The object looked almost perfectly flat, kind of like a missile, but had a bright white glow to it. No wings or tail/rudder assembly was visible. The object was about 50 feet above the height of the bridge as it crossed over and seemed to be going in a perfectly straight-line travel. As it crossed the bridge, I noticed that it was about the width of two lanes of traffic, which would make this about 30 feet wide. I'd estimate the height of the object to be about four to five feet, compared to the width. About once per second, there appeared to be a larger amount of light about that would ripple down the length of the object, similar to the flapping on a bird's wing, but the entire length. We

have lived in this area for over 30 years and are very used to the passenger aircraft that fly over the Potomac River to land at National Airport. We often see planes on final approach over this bridge. This object was far too low in altitude and was moving at a speed five to six times faster than an aircraft on final approach."

Maryland MUFON CAG Investigator Tom Wertman closed this case as an Unknown Aerial Vehicle.

"The witness stated the weather was clear with little haze," Wertman stated in his report. "Wunderground indicated there were thunderstorms in the region. The FI used Flightradar24 to search for local air traffic. Monitored air traffic at the time of the sighting was moving the opposite direction from south to north. This does not rule out air traffic as being a possible explanation. There still may have been untracked air traffic in the region. The slender body without wings is the appearance of an aircraft tilted at a proper angle, the glowing a reflection from sunlight. The other possibility is wildlife such as a gull. There were no other reports from the region."

Alexandria is a city in Virginia, population 139,966.

Florida witness sees UFO twice in one night

A Florida witness at Daytona Beach reported watching a "brilliant, pulsing orb" in the night sky, according to testimony in Case 92639.

The witness was outside walking dogs at 9:15 p.m. on June 9, 2018.

"Something caught my eye from the west," the witness stated. "I looked up and observed a bright, circular object just hovering in the sky. It was in size slightly smaller than a golf ball and was also a reddish-orange in color. The object was slowly pulsing. It remained stationary for approximately 30 seconds. It then slowly started to move closer to my position, when it suddenly made a right angle turn and began heading north. At first it was moving slowly and then it accelerated at an unbelievable rate and just disappeared. This event is not over yet. At approximately 9:45 p.m. that same night, the exact same thing happened again. Needless to say, I'm totally freaked out. I am really hoping someone else saw what I saw."

Florida MUFON State Section Director Orlando Rodriguez and CAG Director John A. Gagnon closed this case as an Unknown Aerial Vehicle.

"At 11:15 p.m. the wind was from the east-southeast at five mph," Rodriguez and Gagnon wrote in their report. "At 11:45 p.m., it was from the south at five mph. The object was first observed to the west, then last seen heading north, with a wind from either the south or east-southeast. The witness describes that the object accelerated at an unbelievable rate of speed. Furthermore, the witness later observed the object for a second time."

Daytona Beach is a city in Volusia County, Florida, population 61,005.

JUNE 10

Witness says helicopter followed three UFOs

A Massachusetts witness at Blackstone reported watching a low-flying helicopter following three objects, each with a dim, greenish light, flying in formation, according to testimony in Case 92653.

The witness was home watching television at 10:27 p.m. on June 10, 2018.

"Heard a low-flying helicopter approaching from the southeast," the witness stated. "Went out into pool area and watched three objects in formation with dull green cockpit lights fly

overhead with the helicopter following closely. Objects made no sound and could not make out a shape. They were very dark other than the dim green light. Watched as they flew over and until they flew past. Objects were not traveling super fast or high."

Massachusetts MUFON State Director Eric Hartwig closed this case as an Unknown Aerial Vehicle.

"This directly relates to Case 92641 with a similar description, which took place a few towns away, three minutes later. Having interviewed both the Attleboro and Blackstone witnesses, I'm confident the two cases are related: helicopter following three UFOs.

Blackstone is a town in Worcester County, Massachusetts, population 9,026.

Second witness reports helicopter following UFOs

A Massachusetts witness at Attleboro reported watching three orange lights followed by a helicopter, according to testimony in Case 92641.

The witness was in his living room at 10:30 p.m. on June 10, 2108.

"I heard a very strange noise," the witness stated. "I went out on my front porch to see what it was. I observed at first a helicopter through the trees coming from a northwest direction. As soon as it came over the tree line, I noticed it was tailing three extremely dim orange lights. They didn't seem connected. As in, it didn't seem as one object. But maybe three separate objects. The sound was extremely powerful. I could hear the helicopter, but could not distinguish the sounds emitting from the other objects. I could see an outline of the chopper. But no outlines of the other three, just the dim orange glow."

Massachusetts MUFON State Director Eric Hartwig closed this case as an Unknown

Aerial Vehicle.

"Taking the witness at his word," Hartwig wrote in his report. "This is three mysterious orange lights followed by a black helicopter. Corroborating Case: 92653."

Attleboro is a city in Bristol County, Massachusetts, population 43,593.

JUNE 11

Multiple objects reported over North Las Vegas

A Nevada witness at North Las Vegas reported watching multiple objects moving overhead at different altitudes, according to testimony in Case 92673.

The event began about 2:11 a.m. on June 11, 2018, when the witness and a girlfriend stepped out onto a porch to smoke.

"Hovering about 500 feet high and one-quarter mile down range," the witness stated. "No clouds or wind. The object rotated about two or three revolutions per minute. On one axis the object was diamond-shaped with a cross inside the diamond. Both the diamond and cross radiated red, green and white light. On the other axis it appeared as a solid white line. No audial sound."

About a minute later, the witness spotted another identical object at the same altitude but three to five miles away.

"At this point a private Cessna-style plane flew behind the closest object and I could hear the motor noise from the plane. Then out of the corner of my eye a third object, in the shape of a sergeant's stripe with five circular, red lights, flew a straight line path across the whole Vegas valley at the same altitude as the first two in three to five seconds and passed between me and the first object spotted. The valley spans 25 miles."

Both witnesses got into a vehicle to get a closer look.

"I decided to run down the farther object because of its proximity to the western mountain range and unobstructed view of the valley. As we moved along Highway 215 from Decatur heading west at 90 mph, the first-spotted object paralleled my route, randomly changing altitude. During our 15-minute ride I spotted an extremely solid white fourth object descend from the sky at a high rate of speed. I only saw it momentarily because of the highway sound barrier wall. We both tried to approximate the location and came up with the McCarran International Airport area, approximately 18 miles as the crow flies. About a minute farther down the road our sight became unobstructed and witnessed the object coming directly at me and in an instant was gone. No noise. The light was extremely bright."

The witness and three additional cars all stopped in the middle of the highway to try and process what they were seeing.

"We continued for three miles and pulled off on Sahara, got to a side street, got out and we stood on the roof of my minivan. We were now miles from city lights with a completely unobstructed view of the entire valley. The object that had followed me was now stationary, roughly one-quarter mile downrange west, but changed its altitude from 1000 feet to a mile high at a slow rate of speed, and the second object spotted seemed to keep its original distance when first spotted. The west mountain range was approximately two miles from our location."

The witness said the object population increased dramatically at this point.

"We started to see more and more (approximately 40 objects) of the same type of objects as a star size at first, with a blue hue, but as they descended around the whole valley at each mountain range peak, they became recognizable as the first type of object spotted at the beginning of this encounter. I would say there were two to three miles of separation between each of the objects bordering Vegas. Then two objects, one on the north end, the other to the south, seemed to appear out of nowhere approximately 100-200 feet off the deck and hovered motionlessly for 30 minutes. Both of these were identical, upside-down, acorn-shaped, giving off pure pulsating, white light and nowhere as bright as the one on the highway."

The witnesses then lay down on the roof of the vehicle and began to notice more of the first type of objects in triangular formations at a much greater altitude, approximately 10 miles away, crisscrossing the valley.

"In one of the formations the lead ship changes direction 180 degrees instantly and the two on the trailing edge jump to light speed and shoot straight up. Gone! At three different times we saw police cruisers pulled over with their heads out the window looking at what we were seeing. The morning light was appearing, and the objects seemed to just fade away, so we decided to call it a night. The drive home was only 10 minutes but halfway home I looked up out the sunroof and the object that had been trailing me was still there. We pulled into the garage in complete stunned silence. I immediately went back to the porch where it all started and sure enough—there it was! Finally, with the first light I was able to see some outline to the object, which was white in color. Before I could really tell what shape it was, it ascended up into the sky and faded away."

Nevada State Director Sue Countiss closed this case as an Unknown Aerial Vehicle.

"Multi craft sighting," Countiss stated in her report, "with no defined shapes, changed directions, turned abruptly, changed shapes, light hovered, descended, ascended, fluttered, spun, pulsated, varied surfaces, larger than basketball, structural features unknown, 101–300 feet, white exterior, lights red, white, green, no emissions, no sound, airplane in vicinity during sighting. About 65 degrees above witness, lowest altitude of about 500 feet or less."

North Las Vegas is a city in Clark County, Nevada, population 216,961.

JUNE 16

Low-flying triangular UFO reported over Texas

A Texas witness at Sour Lake reported watching a fast, triangular-shaped object moving less than 500 feet overhead, according to testimony in Case 92750.

The event occurred at 11:30 p.m. on Jun 16, 2018.

"A large black craft flew right over my head, somewhere between 500–1000 feet above," the witness stated. "It made a sudden right angle turn. Too fast for any known plane. No lights and no sound, other than what I can best describe as the hum emitted from a low bass speaker."

Texas MUFON Chief Investigator Kenneth Jordan closed this case as an Unknown Aerial Vehicle.

"This Field Investigator feels he saw a typical black triangle craft of unknown origin."

Sour Lake is a city in Hardin County, Texas, population 1,813.

JUNE 17

UFO seen while witness photographs moon

An Oregon witness at Portland reported unknown objects while photographing the moon, according to testimony in Case 92817.

The witness described two photo sessions on May 22 and June 17, 2018:

"1st UFO on 05-22-18 @ 6:18 PM, was photographing the moon with 800mm lens, saw a flash reflection. UFO lasted about 25 seconds. 2nd UFO on 06-17-18 @ 3:49:41 PM was photographed with a 300mm lens, same, saw a flash reflection, UFO lasted about 30 seconds."

Oregon MUFON State Director Tom Bowden closed this case as an Unknown Aerial Vehicle.

"This report addresses two separate incidents," Bowden stated in his report. "In each case, the witness noticed only a bright flash and then began taking photos in rapid succession with his digital SLR camera. The objects were too far away for most people to see with the unaided eye, and besides, the witness has glaucoma and would not have been able to visually observe the objects; thus the photographic evidence is all we have to work with so far as what was provided by the witness.

"Incident One—May 22, 2018: Twenty photos were taken showing a bright object passing close to the moon in the sky. An 800mm telephoto lens was being used, which provides 16X magnification. The object appears in most frames as just a bright dot, probably due to reflected sunlight. The photos were taken at 4:24 to 4:25 p.m. facing east so that the sun would be behind the photographer. The photos were all taken within one minute, and during that time the object moved from just right of the moon to the upper left, farther above the moon. My Starry Night astronomy simulator does not show any objects that might have been spotted near the moon at that time. The asteroid Aegina with a magnitude of 12.71 would not have been bright enough, and its orbital movement does not at all match the observed object. No known artificial satellite

was shown in the area of the sighting. If this object was an artificial satellite, then it was an untracked, derelict satellite or other space debris equipped with solar arrays that reflected the sun to make it shine so brightly. It is possible that this object is a high-flying aircraft that is too far away to be clearly seen; however, it seems the telephoto lens with 16X magnification would have been able to resolve the shape of the aircraft. After a lot of time spent examining these photos, I cannot see how this object could be seen as a man-made aircraft. Based on the apparent diameter of the Moon (one-half degree of arc), the object moved approximately 1.5 degrees in 55 seconds. This is actually quite slow and would be too slow for an object in a low Earth orbit, or on a reentry trajectory. (For example, the ISS travels over 140 degrees in 2.5 to 3 minutes.) It is also much too slow for a meteor. I also considered if the object could have been a clump of mylar balloons, but upon careful examination, I don't think this explanation holds up. Having ruled out a conventional aircraft, a meteor, a space junk reentry, a satellite or other orbiting body, I have to say that I consider this object to be unknown.

"Incident Two—June 17, 2018: Fifteen photos were taken showing an elongated object with a reflective gold metallic appearance that seemed to reflect the sunlight. The photos were all taken at 3:20 p.m. and camera was pointed toward the east, so that the sun was behind the camera. The exposures were taken at varying time intervals, and the object appears to be in different orientations, as if rotating or tumbling continuously. The telephoto lens was 300mm, giving a magnification of 6X. The shape and other features of this object suggest that it might be a rocket body in reentry. There had been a Russian satellite launch of Cosmos 2527 on a Soyuz 2-1b rocket from Plesetsk Cosmodrome on June 16, 2018, at 9:46 p.m. UTC, about 28.5 hours prior to this sighting time. However, I have a problem with this explanation. Based on the clouds in the background of the photos, the object appears to be moving slowly in the sky, unlike a reentering object such as a spent rocket body. Also, there is no sign of the object burning up due to reentering the atmosphere. Another possible explanation might be a large Mylar balloon, or a large cluster of Mylar balloons; however, a close examination of the photos does not support this explanation very well. The rotating or tumbling motion of the object would rule out a conventional aircraft in controlled flight. Also, the shape of the object in the photo does not really look like a known manmade aircraft. In conclusion, I really cannot identify the object with any reasonable level of confidence; therefore, my conclusion remains that it is an unknown object with an apparent structure."

Idaho witness reports cube-shaped UFO

An Idaho witness at Ada County reported watching a cube-shaped object with spinning lights, according to testimony in Case 92802.

The witness was looking at the sky before going to bed at 11:30 p.m. on June 17, 2018.

"I saw a large UFO that was swirling and darting up and down and from side-to-side," the witness stated. "This occurred low over a mountainside located one to one-and-a-half miles from my cabin. I took several videos of the UFO between 11:30 p.m. and 2:40 a.m. The video I'm submitting is nine minutes long."

This was not the first time the witness saw a UFO.

"I've lived at this cabin for nearly nine years. During that time, on clear nights, star-like UFOs can be seen, numbering from two to seven. I have been told such activity is unlikely, but it's what I've seen and there have been neighbors, friends and family who've witnessed them as well. They hover, rather than remain stationary, and can sometimes be seen moving slowly across the night sky. Several times I have seen them drop down to the mountainside, and on occasion, dart back and forth across the night sky. They flash and swirl blue, green and red in the middle and display white, brilliant light on the top and bottom.

"Recently activity at this location has increased. I became aware of it when videoing the sunset on April 24, 2018. When I watched the video, there were three orbs: one large, one directly below it, which was smaller, and the last orb, which was smaller yet. They moved in synchronicity, as if tethered together. I was certain it was a fluke; that maybe my camera was defective. It's what I wanted to believe. But the following night at dusk, I took another video and caught several black discs and more orbs, which are gray in color and appear to be nearly transparent. I have been filming nightly at dusk since April 24, and in all but one video, black discs, gray orbs, or both, are caught on video. I have also captured video of black shape-changing UFOs on three separate occasions. I have video and pictures of them. Over the past two weeks, I viewed another UFO that was triangular with red glowing lights along the top and bottom edges on two separate occasions. It was too dark to get a video of it, but I did get a photo of the object.

"If someone had told me what I've written to you here, I'd have a hard time believing it. However, I've taken videos each night at dusk, and each time, the objects are there. I would be happy to send you what I have—both videos and pictures. What's most important is to have someone investigate (at least the videos and pictures) of what I'm seeing and to receive an investigator's opinion, no matter the outcome. The videos range from 5 minutes to 20 minutes in length. I am not technically savvy enough to edit them into shorter videos, and have tried to capture stills, but was not successful. I would need to download them to a flash drive to get them to you."

Idaho MUFON State Director James Millard closed this case as an Unknown Aerial Vehicle.

"Video provided shows a cube with lights spinning," Millard wrote in his report. "The witness stated the object was 501 feet to one mile away."

Ada County is a county in the southwestern part of Idaho, population 392,365.

JUNE 19

Canadian witness says UFO hovered and disappeared

A Canadian witness at Joliette reported watching a "non-symmetrical" object that hovered, turned and disappeared, according to testimony in Case 92792.

The witness was driving to work at 7:10 a.m. on June 19, 2018, when the event occurred.

"Really blue sky, not a single cloud," the witness stated. "I checked the sky thinking it was a plane, but it was stationary. It was metallic and very reflective. It had a weird shape, asymmetrical. I thought to myself: 'What is that?' And then it made a tight spin on itself and then it vanished, like when it was turning itself on, the movement was like facing a piece of paper, and then when you turn it, you don't see it 'cause it's so flat. It was a bit like that. It was bigger than a small plane and very stationary, very metallic."

When turning, the object disappeared.

"I was checking the sky two or three minutes in that area after, and never saw it again. It's impossible. It really was a solid object in the sky, solid, reflective, a bit like a plane, but planes don't disappear like that. I made a drawing of the shape and size in the sky. It's really hard to explain the shape. It was standing straight, right side was flat, and the left side was curvy a bit like the number three

in reverse."

Canadian Field Investigator Allen Des Roches closed this case as an Unknown Aerial Vehicle.

"The staff of the Joliette Airport (northwest and clear sky) confirms to me that it could have had landings or takeoffs at the time of the observation. Is not a plane or a drone. The object looks flat and is silvery and transparent in color, stationary and reflecting, then turns abruptly and disappears."

Joliette is a city in southwest Quebec, Canada.

'Blimp' UFO photographed low over Missouri

A Missouri witness at Warrenton reported watching and photographing a "blimp-like" object near the tree line, according to testimony in Case 92800.

The witness was traveling northbound along Stracks Church Road in Warren County at 11:15 a.m. on June 19, 2018.

"My business partner (driver) and I (passenger) were heading to our shop, when I caught a quick glimpse of a rather large, blimp-like object, over the tree line to the west-northwest at an estimated distance of about 1.5 miles," the witness stated. "I asked aloud if he had seen it and his response was no. Upon reaching the next hill we slowed to get a better look, again a brief glimpse before a nearby tree line obstructed view."

The business partner agreed he saw the object as well.

"We both agreed it appeared to be in the area of the baseball fields to our northwest. Upon agreement to give chase toward ball fields, as our elevation would allow, we maintained brief visuals of the object. It appeared as a dull metallic color, with a rather reflective area in the center to the rear. Our estimation of size was very large, approximately 400-

600 feet long and 75-100 tall with a tapering aft."

As they pursued the object, they noticed the object had put significant distance between them in a matter of minutes.

"He and I also noticed it now appeared more north than west, so we assumed it had traveled north in that time. When we reached the ball fields, our view was now unobstructed. We located the object, which was now due west and a considerable distance from us. My business partner was able to zoom in maximum with his phone's camera and got one photo just prior to the object pitching to about 40 degrees and disappearing behind the tree line a few hundred yards out in front of us. The object was never more than slightly above the tree line on the horizon of our view, so I have to assume it was less than 500 feet off the ground. Also, the profile never changed despite the noticeable changes in direction of travel. At the time of the photo, the skies were clear, and the object was at what we believe to be max visibility at the time. The distance it was covering was remarkable. It disappeared from view, and never returned. The entire event lasted four to five minutes."

Missouri MUFON Chief Investigator Joe Palermo and State Director Debbie Ziegelmeyer closed this case as an Unknown Aerial Object.

"The photo is taken from a vantage point of lying in the grass with no mention of such in the narrative," Palermo and Ziegelmeyer wrote in their notes. "Spoke with witness on the phone. Very sincere. Explained the picture (grass looking foreground; actually corn field in the distance); he and business partner will try to make it to tonight's MUFON meeting. Also uncovered two historic cases he and partner will be reporting on."

Warrenton is a city in Warren County, Missouri, population 7,880.

Pennsylvania witness photographs orb UFOs

A Pennsylvania witness at Lower Burrell reported watching and photographing two orbs in sky doing maneuvers near the moon, according to testimony in Case 92803.

The incident occurred at 7:30 p.m. on June 19, 2018.

"We were swimming in our pool when our oldest noticed what he thought was a plane near the moon," the witness stated. "We all looked and realized there were two orbs separated by some distance. Over time they came closer together. One disappeared. Through binoculars, I saw triple bright, white lights but through the telescope you could see more of a long maybe cylinder-like structure (black) with some gaps. Once the one disappeared maybe 45 minutes later, 20 minutes later the other disappeared and through the telescope the cylinder seemed to expand as it did. I did try to take some pictures and video but so far, the quality isn't that great. I may have more on another camera and can share as well."

Pennsylvania MUFON Field Investigator John Carano and State Section Director Sam Colosimo Jr. closed this case as an Unknown Aerial Vehicle.

"Based on the telephone interview with the witness, we have found that the witness was able to fully and verbally explain his observations in a very coherent manner and was verbally expressive based on having a degree in physics," Carano and Colosimo stated in their report. "The attached photograph in CMS and associated video of the objects clearly are an expression of something that is unknown at this point. The weather conditions during the event were favorable and there was no rain in the area, and it was before dark and civil twilight. The witness indicated that the full timing of the event was just short of an hour, which allowed for time of the witness to take photographs and the video. No sound was observed during the event. No high strangeness right-angle turns were seen. However, the object did appear to break apart and reconstitute itself into both a circular and at times a cigar-shaped object. Based on the attached photographs in the CMS and the witness testimony during our interview, we can find no reasonable explanation as to what the objects are. Therefore, we're going to find as unknown."

Lower Burrell is a city in Westmoreland County, Pennsylvania, population 11,761.

JUNE 20

New Jersey witness captures four spheres in photo

A New Jersey witness at Egg Harbor Township reported watching four spheres hovering in a "square formation" near an airborne black crow, according to testimony in Case 92849.

The witness had just gotten into a vehicle in the Home Depot parking lot at 3:15 p.m. on June 20, 2018.

"A black crow caught my eye," the witness stated. "It was about 150 feet or less from me and about 50–75 feet off the ground. I then realized there were four black spheres or orbs around the crow. I then quickly glanced around for a camera that I keep in the car and remembered I had left my camera at home. I then focused my attention on the spheres that had now formed a square formation and moved higher into the sky and were heading northwest."

The witness recalled he had a camera on his cell phone.

"I then quickly grabbed my cell phone and snapped a picture, thinking I wouldn't capture them because they were so far away by now. But I can see them in the picture. I watched them until they were out of sight and they stayed in the same formation the whole time."

New Jersey MUFON State Section Director Robert Spearing closed this case as an Unknown Aerial Vehicle.

"This is an excellent case with photographic evidence," Spearing wrote in his report. "What is unique about this case is that the entities were not interested in humans but with a bird. Objects apparently surrounded a bird in flight in an attempt to analyze it. Bird exhibited no adverse symptoms and was unharmed. Objects took off flying higher and higher. Remaining in formation of a square.

"One can ask if these were scientific drones of some sort observing natural animals. Photographic evidence is exceptional. Closing case as four unknown aerial objects."

Egg Harbor Township is a township in Atlantic County, New Jersey, population 43,323.

Washington UFO described as 'black ball'

A Washington witness at Pasco reported watching a black sphere that appeared, hovered and disappeared, according to testimony in Case 92828.

The witness was sitting outside on a deck watching storm clouds at 8:20 p.m. on June 20, 2018.

"A black ball appeared to the northeast at the base of a cloud," the witness stated. "It remained for about 10 seconds and disappeared. It was very dark and had defined edges. Not like its surroundings. It didn't move that I could tell, just vanished. I estimate the size at that distance to be quite large, maybe 100–300 feet. I was not able to retrieve my phone in time to get a photo. I am prior military and law enforcement."

Washington MUFON Chief Investigator Daniel Nims closed this case as an Unknown Aerial Vehicle.

"The witness was sitting on his back deck watching a thunderstorm, hoping to see some lightning," Nims wrote in report. "He was looking north-northeast about 10–20 degrees above the horizon. While looking at the clouds, a black ball appeared beneath and in front of the clouds. He watched for a few seconds and then went to get his phone to take a picture. When he returned and was pointing the camera at the ball, it disappeared. He estimated the distance to be 5–10 miles. The ball appeared dark black with clearly defined edges. He said it was clearly not just a dark cloud. It had no perceptible appendages or features. He said it was much smaller than a full moon but was clearly a ball, not a dot. He estimated the size to be 100–300 feet in diameter. He said the ball appeared and did not come out of the clouds. It disappeared and was not enshrouded by the clouds. At that direction and distance, the object would have been near the Hanford Nuclear complex, a former major nuclear weapons site, which made plutonium. An object even one-fifth the size of the full moon, at five miles, would be nearly 1,500 feet in diameter. The experience and objectivity of the witness give strong credence to his testimony."

Pasco is a city in, and the county seat of, Franklin County, Washington, population 59,781.

JUNE 21

Minnesota witness describes hovering disc-shaped UFO

A Minnesota witness at New Brighton reported watching a hovering disc-shaped object less than 500 feet away, according to testimony in Case 92852.

The witness had just left a restaurant with friends and was in an adjacent parking lot at 10:58 p.m. on June 21, 2018.

"I looked up and saw this object just above the buildings," the witness stated. 'It was hovering with red lights all in one area and two white lights in front. Then the colors changed to blue and green blinking. Then the red lights came on in the middle of the space-ship. I could then see the shape of the craft."

The object then began to move.

"It moved up and down. Then sideways. By the time I got my cell phone, it was already leaving. I only got a picture of if leaving. It had gone higher as it was leaving and then I lost sight of it."

The witness supplied several illustrations of the object and one image with the case, which was filed on June 22, 2018. Minnesota MUFON Field Investigator Stephen Hero closed this case as an Unknown Aerial Vehicle.

"Witness describes the object as disc-like, with red lights around the perimeter," Hero stated in his report. "It was first seen over a building only a few hundred yards away. Approximate size is hard to determine, but it is estimated to be approximately 40–60 feet in diameter. She made some drawings of what the craft looked like at different times during the sighting. There is also a cell phone photo, which shows a (blurred) red image of the object. This was taken as the object was leaving.

"The witness description of the shape of the craft and the lighting pattern on the craft leads me to believe that this is not any type of conventional aircraft. At that time, the sky was clear."

New Brighton is a city in Ramsey County, Minnesota, population 21,456.

Mexican witness describes low, fast-moving sphere

A Mexican witness at San Felipe Baja Norte

reported watching a sphere-shaped object moving along at "tremendous speed" near treetop level along a remote road, according to testimony in Case 92994.

The witness was outside in the El Dorado Ranch area watching stars from a rooftop location on June 21, 2018.

"I am very remotely located," the witness stated. "This particular evening was perfectly dark (no street lights or nearby houses), lit by a waxing full moon. I have a great view of the mountains, the Sea of Cortez, and roads leading throughout the ranch. A brilliant white light (as bright as the full moon) traveling north very fast caught my eye in the distance as I was looking west towards the mountains. I knew the road well and thought how unusually fast the 'car' was going for time of night and condition of road.

"A few seconds later, when the globe was parallel to where I was standing (still at a distance), it abruptly disappeared. I reflected upon what I had just seen and noted then that there had been no head beams. That the short bushes in the desert and occasional Ocotillo trees never seemed to impede the light—as is usually found when cars pass behind shrubbery. If the car had been traveling down the road, I would have seen it continue instead of disappearing since there were no cross roads.

"A few days later I had a friend drive along this route at night going at least 50 mph. The speed limit for the ranch is 20–35 mph because the roads are sandy and unlit. People often get lost up here. Based on the comparison of my friend's speed, an estimate of speed the globe was traveling, the globe would have exceeded 100 mph. I watch cars all the time when I am on the roof and their headlights are always dim; there are always headlights and reflections in the passing vegetation; and occasionally they disappear as the cars meander around curves. There is hardly any car traffic up here. With my friend duplicating

the same route for this experiment, I watched from the roof and noted several discrepancies: Firstly, I always saw a red tail-light and dim headlight from her car. There were car beams that reflected in the vegetation; the car lights flickered as it passed behind vegetation and trees; and the speed seemed very slow compared to what I had witnessed with the round, glowing, white light. The white light was as bright as the moon.

"Also, in passing, we have frequent ATV and stock car races (the Baja 500 and the Baja 250) in this area, which I can view from my roof. I can see the racing cars, which periodically race in Baja along the mountain passes, looking towards the west from my roof. They are much farther away (almost several miles from my house) and I can still make out clearly their head beams. I have seen other unusual activity in Baja Norte as do some of my friends."

Mexico MUFON CAG Investigators Chase Kloetzke and Mary Owens closed this case as an Unknown-Other.

"Witness supplied a written diagram of area where sphere was seen. Corroborating cases: None. Disposition: Witness is very familiar with the surrounding area near her home. She has seen vehicle traffic in the desert at night and described the light as being a single white sphere travelling in excess of 100 mph."

San Felipe is a town on the bay of San Felipe in the Gulf of California (Sea of Cortez) in the Mexican state of Baja California, population 17,708.

JUNE 22

Rural Missouri community watching for more UFOs

A Missouri witness at Farmington reported watching a triangular-shaped craft with lights through binoculars, according to testimony in Case 93841.

The witness and a grandchild were outside watching the stars at 8 a.m. on June 22, 2018.

"An object appeared over the house across the street at a high altitude," the witness stated. "At first, we thought it was an airplane, so my grandchild started looking through binoculars and realized it was the shape of a triangle. It was traveling from the northeast to the southwest at a pretty good pace. This was the same direction we had seen a fireball a few nights before. My grandchild was so impressed by what they saw that they sent me a drawing after they went home."

Missouri MUFON State Section Director Lynne E. Mann closed this case as an Unknown Aerial Vehicle.

"After having gone to the residence it was confirmed that the primary witness was credible, and though the secondary witness was not present having gone back to their residence, both were credible witnesses. Shape and lights on the craft were seen through binoculars first by secondary witness (their drawing supplied), thereafter primary witness saw through the binoculars. The primary witness after having seen the triangle in question had, however, mistaken several planets for a return of the craft. This was due, I think, to an expected reaction to its return, which is a perfectly normal reaction to having seen the craft and an orange fireball from the same direction as the craft. The primary witness is staying in touch in case the triangle returns or any other fireballs, etc. are seen. Several of the neighbors on that street were present for the night watch and confirmed that that street had been a very busy area of late with the sighting of a huge orange ball next to a tree several days after the craft appeared. It hasn't been determined exactly what the attraction is in that area. Primary witness and the neighborhood are keeping their eyes to the skies for any new events and have my information and instructions on how to report in case of new sightings.

Farmington is a city in St. Francois County, population 16,240.

JUNE 23

California witness says 'ball of flame' stopped to hover

A California witness at Oakdale reported watching a "large ball of flame" that stopped and hovered before moving away, according to testimony in Case 92947.

The witness was sitting outside by a pool at 11:45 p.m. on June 23, 2018.

"A large ball of flame came rocketing through the sky at high speed and then it came to a complete stop instantly," the witness stated. "After that, it started hovering slowly over my ridgetop. After it passed behind my chimney it moved down towards the Earth and disappeared. The video I recorded from my iPhone isn't the best quality—it was a lot larger in person. I was hoping you guys could enhance the video quality. To me it appeared to be within 500 feet, but I was hoping maybe you could analyze the video and let me know what you guys think. I know for sure it wasn't a shooting star or rocket or any kind of airplane."

California MUFON Field Investigator Jerry Gerow closed this case as an Unknown Aerial Vehicle.

"Actual size unknown; appeared size of basketball," Gerow stated in his report. "Distance was one-half mile away, though he said 100–500 feet in CMS report. He was facing south, and it came from east to west. It did not change shape or have any dome or structural features, though he said it did in his report. It appeared as a glowing red, orange and yellow ball with what appeared to be flames around it.

"The reporting witness was sitting in his pool when an object seemed to move quickly toward him, not more than 100 feet away, hover almost overhead, and then drifted away slowly until it went out of sight behind his chimney. I asked about the two pictures and video attached to the CMS report. The first two photos were as the object was hovering overhead and the video shows the object drifting away behind the chimney. I asked why the video showed a white object leaving, and he said it just sort of turned white after it started drifting away. Witness had no animals and said he did not feel ill or notice any paranormal activity.

"I checked with MUFON and NUFORC and found nothing. I checked with the Modesto Bee online and found nothing. Stellarium shows Mars and the meteor shower Piscis Austrinids to the southeast. Saturn and the dark nebula Ophiuchus at 45 degrees south. Space Archives showed a Falcon 9 launch from Vandenberg on the 22nd of June. My evidence is the witness's word and cell phone video/pictures. And the witness's believability. In this case I am focusing on reliability. The witness spoke well and seemed sincere, has some college and a technical background."

Oakdale is a city in the San Joaquin Valley and Stanislaus County, California, population 20,675.

JUNE 24

Columbia witness describes two tic tac-shaped UFOs

A Columbian witness at Medellin reported watching and videotaping two black, tic tac-shaped objects, according to testimony in Case 95063.

The witness was on vacation in Medellin and was on the second floor of a building and was looking out a window on June 24, 2018.

"I saw a black, oval, tic tac-shaped object floating in the sky," the witness stated. "It was difficult to judge the distance. I immediately got my Samsung S9+ smartphone and began videotaping the object. The object simply hovered in place. The object was pitch black, but there was a glow outlining the object. After about four minutes, the object started to fade behind clouds that moved in front of it. The clouds were large and far away, but the clouds were in front of the object. This leads me to believe the object was relatively large given the distance from which it was viewable with the naked eye. Almost as soon as the first object was blocked by the clouds, I noticed a second object rise from below.

"In the video, you can see the second object rise before I actually noticed it with my eyesight. The second object was more of a diamond shape. It moved slowly upward and wobbled/pulsated as it slowly ascended. This object also had a glow around it. At times, the second object had a shimmer. At this point, due to the five-minute video duration limit on the phone, I stopped recording momentarily. I then re-initiated the video recording of the second object. I continued to record the second object for an additional three minutes and 26 seconds before it moved out of view behind an adjacent building. I have the videos posted to YouTube and I can provide that to you if requested. For some reason, my copy of the second video is corrupted and won't play on a computer. It does play on my phone. When I try to transfer it from my phone to my computer, the 1.81 GB file on my phone will only transfer 446 MB to my computer. These objects appear to be remarkably similar to the craft captured by F-18 gun cameras and released by the Department of Defense in December of 2017."

Columbia MUFON CAG Director John A. Gagnon closed this case as an Unknown Aerial Vehicle.

"The witness provided two video clips from his phone," Gagnon stated in his report. "One clip is corrupt and will not play. The other clip shows an object very slowly moving from right to left over a mountain range. Near the end of the video, the object appears to hover.

Then a second object appears below and to the right of the first. Both objects are too far away to identify. The object first seen appears to be under intelligent control. It disappears behind some clouds near the end of the video. The witness then provided a link to a YouTube video of the second video clip. Both clips show an object moving slowing and hovering.

"When asked, the witness stated he believed the objects were, 'Two black craft powered by some sort of antigravity.' Based on the videos, that is going to be the best conclusion."

Medellin is the second-largest city in Colombia and the capital of the department of Antioquia, population 2.5 million.

Alaska security cam picks up spherical UFO

An Alaskan witness in Anchorage County reported watching a sphere-shaped object on a video security camera, according to testimony in Case 92893.

The witness lives near an airport and the garage security camera picked up the images beginning at 1:51 a.m. on June 24, 2018.

"At the beginning of the video you can see what airplanes look like taking off from our house right to left of the screen," the witness stated. "The other runway is shut down for repairs. This white light shows up, going from south to north across the flight path, which I've never seen. Then it disappears into the sky. Looked like it was revving up before takeoff."

Alaska MUFON CAG Investigator Michael Barrette closed this case as an Unknown Aerial Vehicle.

"Size—unknown—object was only seen on video," Barrette stated in his report. "Distance is approximately two miles to airport; direction of travel: south to north; elevation is unknown, as is angular size.

"I found the video very interesting. Did not see any type of strobe lights, which would be indicative of airplane lights. As the object got closer to witness's home, the object appeared to take on an oval shape and the light was a brighter intensity. Spoke with witness, she stated the only thing that she knows about the object is what is in the home security video."

Anchorage is a unified home rule municipality in Alaska, population 298,192.

JUNE 26

Wisconsin UFO puts witness into 'trance-like' state

A Wisconsin witness at Madison reported watching a hovering, triangular-shaped object that seemed to put the witness into a trance, according to testimony in Case 92954.

The witness, awakened by a child in the middle of the night, went to a balcony to have a cigarette at 2:41 a.m. on June 26, 2018.

"I was gazing into the sky when I saw a light that got closer," the witness stated. "It appeared to be triangular-shaped like I thought maybe a helicopter or some military plane or something. When it appeared closer, it was not that of the likes of what I saw before. The object began to descend a little bit, but I wasn't able to move as if I was in some kind of a trance. There was a beam that was near me. It slowly ascended to the sky and traveled toward the northwest."

Wisconsin MUFON Field Investigator Donna Fink closed this case as an Unknown Aerial Vehicle.

"The witness reported that the object descended to treetop level," Fink stated in her report. "That would mean the object was 12 feet away. It emitted a blue beam. The witness put his hand in the beam and then he was in a trance-like state and became paralyzed. After the event was over, the witness described some muscular aches and pain. He asked about time travel."

Madison is the capital of Wisconsin and the seat of Dane County, population 255,214.

Triangular UFO reported over Oregon skies

An Oregon witness at McMinnville reported watching three flashing, glowing red lights in a triangle formation moving slowly across the sky, according to testimony in Case 92936.

The witness had just returned home from shopping at 10:04 p.m. on June 26.

"Put solar light in front yard while my room-mate came out front door," the witness stated. "I walked towards her and glanced up and immediately saw three flashing, glowing, red lights in a strange triangle-like formation all going same direction but keeping same slow speed. Wasn't an airplane and heard no noise in sky. We observed it speechless for about two minutes and five seconds. Then it was out of our view. I immediately knew it was a UFO because I have seen them my whole life, but this one was unique from all rest. It was moving so slowly but perfectly in sync with all three. It was too big to be anything else but also way high in sky. It was red and lighter orange pulsing and flashing light at random intervals. I was excited but in awe, speech-less and stunned, frozen. Forgot to grab my camera."

Oregon MUFON Field Investigator Kellie Graham and State Director Thomas Bowden closed this case as an Unknown-Other.

"The Field Investigator was not able to inter-view this witness but found other similar cases in NUFORC on the next day, June 27, 2018. Both cases had three red lights high in the sky, lined up. This report stated that red lights were in a triangle shape, but that could be the

difference in the angle of the sightings.

"Red lights are required on airplanes, but so are green and white. All three reports only note the red lights, so FI rules out a plane since the witness had already identified a plane in the area before the sighting. FI ruled out a Mars sighting as there were three red lights that moved together, unlike Mars, a single red light that is stationary in the sky.

"FI found a report to the American Meteor Society of a fireball in Keizer, OR, on the next day also, but it was only about 12 feet above street light and only lasted 1.5 seconds. I do not think this sighting is a fireball based on the difference in the time observed and the slow movement of the sighting compared to the quick movement of a meteor/fireball.

"FI will conclude that no other known sky anomalies were found; the witness did not state that the red lights looked like a craft. Since FI could not interview the witness to acquire more info, this case is closed with the disposition of Unknown-Other."

McMinnville is the county seat of and largest city in Yamhill County, Oregon, population 32,187.

Minnesota witness says helicopter chased UFOs

A Minnesota witness at Fridley reported watching two sphere-shaped red lights in the sky and a helicopter that moved into the same airspace to intercept them, according to testimony in Case 92957.

The incident occurred at 10:30 p.m. on June 26, 2018.

"My wife had left some things on the clothes-line and it was forecast to rain late evening," the witness stated. "I work nights and had been up about an hour. I took the clothes down and put the basket on the patio. I usually al-ways have a smoke and walk around the yard, check out the sky. The far side of the yard is pretty clear with a good view west. As soon as I looked up, I noticed two very bright red lights. Had no idea what this was.

"Both were motionless, one was much larger than the other. From my vantage point one was about the size of the moon, the smaller one about the size of a very bright star. I stood staring at them for about a minute or so, and the small light was at about 11 o'clock in relation to the large light and maybe what looked to be about six inches between them. The small light slowly moved right above the large light, keeping what looked to be the same distance. It again was motionless for maybe 20–30 seconds and returned to the 11 o'clock position. Within about 30 seconds it slowly went straight up into the cloud cover.

"The large red light this whole time had not moved or changed the intensity of its red color. The small red light was not visible through the clouds. About 10–20 seconds it became visible again and was descending until it was nearly out of sight because of the tree line. Just before it left sight, the large red light flashed very bright; in fact, enough to create a quick red glow on the clouds above. It then started to descend.

"With the small light now no longer visible and the large one nearing the tree line, I could hear a helicopter not far away east of my location. Just as the large light dropped out of my line of sight, I could see the helicopter, because it had a very powerful spotlight on the front. It travelled nearly over my house at a very high rate of speed—at least I've never seen a helicopter at that speed at treetop level in a residential area before.

"In fact, I was quite surprised because we have high tension power lines very near us, and they are up much higher than the tree level. At this point both objects/red lights are totally out of my view and the helicopter also left my sight in the same vicinity as the lights.

I'm guessing the distance was maybe a quarter mile or just slightly more, which puts two major freeways, 94/694 West and 252 going north and south nearly right underneath where I saw the lights. I didn't know what to think when I first saw the lights, but the movement and flash of light were spectacular, most likely a once-in-a-lifetime observance. The helicopter with the searchlight sealed my thoughts and confirmed it was most likely something more than just red lights. This whole episode was less than five minutes and it has definitely changed my perspective on UFOs."

Minnesota MUFON Field Investigator William Odden closed this case as an Unknown-Other.

"This helicopter is flying treetop height at high speed," Odden stated in his report. "It had a very bright spotlight and was headed in the direction of the orbs. This entire happening took about five minutes. The orb size for the distance would make it over 100 feet across. The light it emitted was so bright it lit up the clouds before descending. The size and the way it lit up the sky would mean it was not a drone, and the way it hovered and slowly descended with no noise means it was not a plane. The two would have gone down somewhere close to the river. Then he heard a helicopter, which was flying at treetop level and went to where the lights went down. I think this was a good sighting."

Fridley is a city in Anoka County, Minnesota, population 27,208.

Montana witness describes disc-shaped UFO and creatures

A Montana witness at Noxon reported watching disc-shaped lights in the sky and creatures, according to testimony in Case 95960.

The witness was outside on a porch on June 26, 2018, between midnight and 2:30 a.m.

"I saw the lights and took video," the witness

stated. "On occasion my phone would shut off, then I was able to turn it back on and record more. I have video and pictures of the creatures and events that evening and the following evening as well."

Montana MUFON State Director William R. Puckett closed this case as an Unknown-Other.

"Discussed photos with witness," Puckett stated in his report. "Witness has taken videos but cannot transmit at this time. The photos show strange shapes. Witness says that he has seen these lights on several nights between midnight and 2:30 a.m. He never sees anything unusual during daylight hours. The photos sent were taken on July 30, 2018. He listed the report date as June 26, 2018. Apparently, that was the first date that he saw the lights. I can't determine if the photos have been fabricated as there is no metadata in the photo files. The photos were taken with an inexpensive Android phone purchased at Walmart."

Noxon is a census-designated place in Sanders County, Montana, population 218.

JUNE 27

Silent Nevada UFO described with windows

A Nevada witness at Mesquite reported watching a cigar-shaped object with apparent windows moving under the light of a full moon, according to testimony in Case 92964.

The witness stepped outside to look at the full moon on June 27, 2018.

"It was a clear night with no cloud cover," the witness stated. "Then I saw this object flying by going east to west, and south of me. This was around 10 p.m. It wasn't going real fast, just moving along. Had no idea what this object was."

The witness described the object.

"The object itself was dark in color and was cylinder in shape. It had two what looked like oval windows that had an amber glow shining out of them. The glow was beautiful in the color of amber. It also had white running lights. As the object got farther away, I could see what I think was the exhaust of the engine, but it was pulsating. This object was close, no more than a mile from me. There was no sound at all. I knew this was something out of the ordinary. The object flew over the horizon to the east of me. Then I started looking for jets, because they fly over all the time heading to Las Vegas. Ten minutes went by before I spotted the lights for a jet. I thought it was an awesome experience."

Nevada MUFON Field Investigator Donna Rothenbaum closed this case as an Unknown Aerial Vehicle.

"Based on submitted report and witness drawing, object was not an airplane or other standard aerial vehicle," Rothenbaum stated in her report. "My determination is that this object is a UAV."

Mesquite is in Clark County, Nevada, population 18,541.

JUNE 28

Military veteran describes circular UFO

An Arizona witness at Buckeye reported watching a circle-shaped object moving under 1,000 feet at high velocity with no noise, according to testimony in Case 93454.

The incident occurred when the reporting witness and his wife were setting up a telescope in a local park on the night of a full moon at 11:15 p.m. on June 28, 2018.

"Before the telescope was fully set up, a

vertically-aligned, donut-ringed object with yellow-orange light/surface appeared below the moon traveling from southeast to north-west at extremely high velocity and low altitude, roughly 500–1000 feet AGL," the witness stated. "The object made absolutely no sound but at closest approach was within one mile of our vantage point/location."

The witness is a United States Air Force veteran and Special Operations intelligence analyst who previously held a top-secret with caveats clearance.

"I can say I witnessed a craft to which I have no explanation or knowledge of existing, yet can't explain what my wife and I saw that night. It traveled approximately 50 miles across the sky at low altitude within 15 seconds and yet made no noise. I tried to capture the object on my phone that was in my pocket, but was unable to do so in the five seconds it took me to grab my phone due to the object's extremely high velocity and short observation time."

Arizona Field Investigator Lisa Carol Bradford closed this case as an Unknown Aerial Vehicle.

"This reporting witness has an extensive military background in the Air Force," Bradford stated in her report. "His experience includes Special Operations and Operations Command Intelligence. I feel the information he has provided was credible, as well as the information given from his wife. Both parties seem levelheaded and intelligent. No photos or evidence was provided; however, the descriptions provided were clear. A jet engine flare was considered as a possible explanation for this sighting; however, the speed of this object was reported to be 12,000 mph and it was silent. The object appeared out of nowhere, traveled horizontally, then disappeared instantly. Although Luke AFB is 17 miles away, the object's maneuvers and appearance reported would not be consistent with that of military training or military aircraft."

Buckeye is a city in Maricopa County, Arizona, population 62,582.

JUNE 29

North Carolina witness describes lights in vertical pattern

A North Carolina witness at Carolina Beach reported watching "five to seven white lights" in a vertical pattern hovering over the ocean, according to testimony in Case 93050.

The incident occurred at 9:30 p.m. on June 29, 2018.

"It was the night of the blood moon and I had noticed the beauty of this moon earlier in the evening," the witness stated. "Later I went back out on my balcony, which is across the street from the ocean, with taller buildings obscuring some of my direct view of the ocean. I saw a bright, orange/yellow sphere comparable in size to the blood moon I had seen earlier. It was between the two buildings across the street, giving me a direct view. When I spotted it, it started to move upward, and my first thought was why is the full moon moving up and so quickly? It was then that I noticed the small white lights on it in a haphazard vertical pattern. There were five to seven small lights and they were solid, not blinking. It ascended into the sky still over the ocean and high enough that I could visually follow its path without the oceanfront buildings blocking it. The object travelled north over the ocean at a fairly fast speed, and then may have taken a turn west, where my view would be blocked by buildings, or it disappeared, for I couldn't see it anymore. This observance did not last long, about a minute, but it was incredible."

North Carolina MUFON Field Investigator Linda Larsen closed this case as an Unknown-Other.

"Lights do not appear to be from any known aircraft in those colors or movement," Larsen wrote in her report. The witness made a drawing of what she saw, and it is uploaded to this report. I reported this as 'Other' instead of 'UAV' because no solid type object was seen by witness, only lights. Also, it did not appear to be the Moon (in the southeast at a low altitude) because of the white lights seen with it in proximity and movement with object."

Carolina Beach is a town in New Hanover County, North Carolina, population 5,706.

JULY 2018

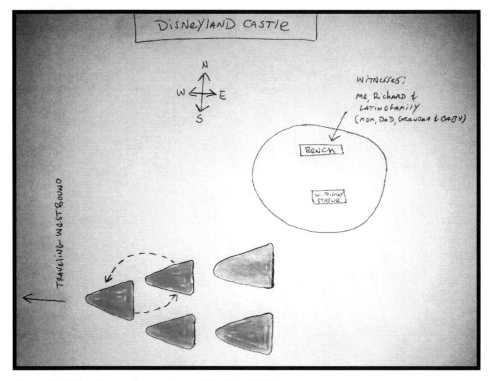

Case 93687 witness illustration. July 22, 2018.

JULY 1

North Dakota witness felt watched by UFO

A North Dakota witness at West Fargo reported watching a "metal orb" hovering over a nearby power line, according to testimony in Case 93045.

The witness was getting out of a car to open a garage door at 9:23 p.m. on July 1, 2018.

"I looked up and saw a metal orb floating in the air just over the power lines across the street," the witness stated. "Seconds after I saw the object it started to move northeast towards a storm cloud. When I first saw it, I was very shocked. I walked towards it to get a better view and pulled out my phone to take a

video of it. When I first saw the object, it was about 500 feet away from me, give or take 50 feet. It was able to move very rapidly without giving the appearance of it moving fast, if that makes any sense. I had a feeling that it was watching me and left because I noticed it. The way it moved was strange. It floated but not like the way a balloon would float, more like it was moving without being affected by the air around it. It was able to float over a mile in under a minute. It floated into a storm cloud and that's when I lost sight of it. I have the tail end of the experience on camera before it got into the cloud."

North Dakota MUFON CAG Director John A. Gagnon investigated this case and closed it as an Unknown-Other.

"One would think that if the object sighted was a hobby drone, the witness would hear the motors," Gagnon stated in his report. "It also would not disappear into a storm cloud."

West Fargo is a city in Cass County, North Dakota, population 35,708.

JULY 2

California UFO described as 'semi-invisible'

A California witness at Gustine reported watching a "triangular, stealth-like craft" that was semi-invisible, according to testimony in Case 93418.

The witness was videotaping smog and contrails in the early morning on July 2, 2018.

"Happened to notice that the trails were being cut in half but could not see what was doing it," the witness stated. "I then started to feel a faint vibration like the same kind of sound and vibration a dishwasher makes when its starts to wash dishes. [I noticed a] triangular, stealth-like craft that appeared to be moving; the skin on the frame of the aircraft appeared to be moving. It was very hard to see, and I was staring at the sun. I was at this point still taking video while battling the sun. It was semi-invisible, but at certain times it was possible to make out edges. There was a window I could see. It had a red shine to it. The window was the only thing that didn't appear to move but it was able to become transparent. The window was how I was able to keep my phone on it somewhat."

The witness described the object's movements.

"It didn't fly like birds fly or airplanes. It kind of skipped. It would be in a spot for a split second and jump a little farther ahead. It was the strangest thing I've ever seen in my life. When I got home from work, I was able to get some better frames where it was a lot easier to make out."

California MUFON Field Investigator Jerry Gerow closed this case as an Unknown Aerial Vehicle.

"I believe this witness to be sincere and passionate about what he saw," Gerow stated in his report. "I know of no craft that resembles what he saw, but have read in other cases of similar type sightings. The translucent skin, very minor sound and no apparent propulsion have been well documented. I checked with NUFORC and MUFON and found nothing on that date. I surfed the net and found no activity in that area."

Gustine is a city in Merced County, California, population 5,520.

Cigar-shaped UFO reported under 200 feet over Indiana

An Indiana witness at Carmel reported watching a "bright, glowing object" that moved 200 feet overhead, according to testimony in Case 94741.

The witness was outside walking a dog on a "perfectly clear night" at 9:55 p.m. on July 2, 2018.

"I observed an orange glowing object traveling in a straight line in a northeast to southeast direction," the witness stated. "At first I thought it was fireworks since it was July 2. Then I thought it was a drone. But the object did not fizzle out like fireworks and there was no sound like a drone or erratic flight. The object was cigar-shaped. No flashing lights but gave off a bright orange glow. I followed the flight of the object for several hundred feet before I lost sight of it over some trees. I captured a poor image of the object due to the time of day. It was getting dark and the object was moving at a pretty good speed before I was able to take the picture. I walk the dog at this spot at least three times a day and have not observed a similar incident. As an avid sky watcher, I can honestly say this was not anything normal, such as a drone or fireworks."

Indiana MUFON Field Investigator Patrick O'Brien closed this case as an Unknown-Other.

"The witness had no further information on the object," O'Brien stated in his report.

Carmel is a city in Clay Township, Hamilton County, Indiana, population 92,198.

JULY 3

British witness says UFOs appeared overhead

Two United Kingdom witnesses at Wrexham reported watching three unusual craft from a distance that quickly moved to treetop level and less than 20 feet away, according to testimony in Case 93128.

The events began at 1:30 a.m. on July 3, 2018.

"Observed a star-like object in sky over a farmer's field approaching from right," the reporting witness stated. "Believed it to be the ISS until it suddenly curved in direction and started to descend. Another object of identical appearance then appeared on far left of sky and accelerated to the first object. They avoided each other and continued hovering and moving in severe, yet smooth movements."

The witness observed these for two to three minutes.

"An orb of light then materialized approximately 12 feet above us and fired diagonally towards the objects. Orb appeared like a mini explosion of light and approximately the size of a baseball. Orb consisted of a solid white light yet dim in center and a beige sandy X-shaped object in its core. No sound. Two witnesses - one experiencing severe terror and evacuated

field immediately. Objects no longer visible after exiting field."

MUFON United Kingdom Field Investigator Karl Webb investigated and closed this case as an Unknown Aerial Vehicle.

"After obtaining a statement from both witnesses, it became clear that an encounter had likely taken place in the early hours of the July 3, 2018, in Wrexham, North Wales, UK. The behavior of the initial lights was in itself strange and certainly not that of any known terrestrial craft, particularly in the dead of night at that hour. We know scientifically that satellites and other man-made objects put into our orbit cannot perform the maneuvers that were witnessed, and as such we are starting to limit the known possibilities. The lights were, according to the witnesses, executing both smooth and sharp movements at an unknown altitude. In addition to the lights, there was clearly another and more intimate element to the sighting that involved an orb of some kind getting close above both witnesses and certainly seen by the male. He describes an orb-like object that came so low that he described that he could have reached up and touched it. He states an orb the size of a ball, consisting of an outer ring, a darker, inner ring and some kind of 'X' shape spinning mechanical device within the center was above him for several seconds.

"We are clearly dealing with something of unknown technology, considering the speed of descent and ascent and extreme maneuverability. The speed at which the orb left upwards and diagonally clearly frightened the female witness; though she did not see the orb, she clearly felt its velocity at it shot upwards.

"I have to conclude that this is a very interesting encounter and certainly one of note, as we have a reasonably good description of the small craft that ventured down to earth. Neither witness was hurt, and I have no reason to think that the objects were anything other than inquisitive. That said, I do believe based on the witness testimony that this was likely extraterrestrial in origin."

Wrexham is the largest town in the north of Wales and an administrative, commercial, retail and educational center, population 61,603.

JULY 9

Three 'meteor-like' UFOs reported over Texas

A Texas witness at San Antonio reported watching a triangular-shaped object that was "burning white" and "falling like a feather," according to testimony in Case 96065.

The event took place on July 9, 2018.

"I was looking at the southern sky," the witness stated. "I turned around to look north and noticed three meteors falling like a feather. It was an angular fall. I began to wonder what it was. I was on my driveway. It was heading to the center of the city as it continued to fall. The tips of the triangle were burning hot, bright, white yellow. Just as I thought it was going to crash-land, it pulled up ventral side up. I noticed the pink burning atmosphere around the sides. It had three bright, green lights on its sides. It looked as large as a jet airliner. As it pulled up to avoid a crash, it flew over the area; it appeared to head to the downtown area or a base, following parallel to Fredericksburg Road. I did not hear a sound. There were no planes, helicopters or jets before or after. It was a very quiet night. As I stood there focusing on it, it became more clear it was a triangle with big bright, green lights burning through the atmosphere just as I was losing sight over neighbor's roof. I knew what I saw. My hairs all over rose up. My eyes opened wider and I said, 'oh my God.' No one was awake at the time or on the street."

Texas MUFON Chief Investigator Ken Jordan

closed this case as Info Only.

"No contact with this witness to date. Witness is a USAF vet with a responsible job with a good work history. However, the written statement and the color painting submitted do not track with any craft or craft characteristics in any database."

San Antonio is a city in Texas, population 1,327,407.

JULY 10

Florida UFO described as 'pattern of black dots'

A Florida witness at Deland reported watching a diamond-shaped object defined in a "pattern of black dots," according to testimony in Case 93256.

The witness was about to leave his development for work at 7:35 a.m. on July 10, 2018.

"I noticed what seemed like a flock of birds in a strange pattern," the witness stated. "I slowed the car to a stop and studied the object for several seconds. I could then determine that the object was staying still and was translucent with black dots forming a triangle/diamond pattern. It almost looked like a blue kite with black dots forming a perfect pattern similar to bowling pins. The larger part of the object was at least 30 of these dots on the front triangle and 10 dots on the back triangle. It seemed to be at least one to two miles away with very clear blues skies. I continued to stare until a driver behind me beeped and started to leave. I then could not find the object once I drove away."

Florida MUFON Field Investigator David Toon closed this case as an Unknown Aerial Vehicle.

"The witness lives in a suburb of a small town in a neighborhood with high vegetation growth and tree height," the witness stated. "The road he was on during the sighting offered a small path of visibility to the north that would not allow for observation of aircraft traffic from a small airport eight miles away. The skyline from his point of view also included powerlines near tree level to the north and east. Data from FlightRadar24 did not show any helicopter or aircraft in the area during that time. No other reports of similar objects were discovered in the MUFON or National UFO Reporting Center. Given the witness's high level of education, the sighting was significant enough to warrant reporting regardless of the lack of evidence obtained."

Deland is a city in and the county seat of Volusia County, Florida, population 27,031.

Low-flying cylindrical UFO spotted over Canada

A Canadian witness at Newmarket, Ontario, reported watching a cylinder-shaped object where the body was slowly rotating, according to testimony in Case 93369.

The witness was facing the eastern sky near Yonge Street and Mulock Avenue at 8:50 p.m. on July 10, 2018.

"This craft was traveling in a south-to-north direction," the witness stated. "On closer examination, the body of this craft appears to be rotating slowly as it moves though the sky. The video was recorded on an iPhone 6."

Canada MUFON Field Investigator Dan Jones closed this case as an Unknown Aerial Vehicle.

"The witness is credible," Jones wrote in his report. "The witness had good recall of the event. I discussed the event with the witness via telephone for over an hour. The witness also submitted good quality video of the object being reported. Most of my investigation hinged on analysis of the video. The object is travelling on a straight path from south to north. It appears to be ellipsoidal in shape. I could not see any evidence of a propulsion

system. I could not see an engine, exhaust, wings, propellers or anything that would suggest it was a conventional man-made aerial vehicle. On close examination of the object, it also appears to be rotating as it travels. It is white in color and does not appear to have any visible windows or exterior lights or markings. The witness reports the object making no sound."

Newmarket is a town and regional seat of the Regional Municipality of York in the Canadian province of Ontario, population 84,224.

Canadian witness describes seven UFOs in triangular formation

A Canadian witness at Toronto reported watching "seven bright lights loosely in triangle formation," according to testimony in Case 97688.

The witness and his wife were on a balcony at 10 p.m. on July 10, 2018.

"It was night at that time of the year, but there was lots of glow from the city lights as usual," the witness stated. "The sky was cloudy but not completely overcast. We saw seven bright, green lights flying roughly from the lakeside in an approximate southeast-northwest path. For those familiar with Toronto, it looked like it was flying over Spadina or University Avenue. To be honest, it looked like a flock of geese, but they seemed to be flying unusually high. After a few seconds, the formation disappeared above a gray cloud, never to be seen by us again. Also, it seemed to me very odd that geese can reflect that much greenish light at night from that distance. It might have been a group of drones? It made no sound, but on the other hand it looked very far high in the sky, probably as high as Piper aircrafts fly."

Canada MUFON Chief Investigator Ryan Stacey closed this case as an Unknown-Other.

"Based on the image and the description, I no

longer believe the objects to be birds," Stacey wrote in his report. "Because the type of birds that have green feathers within Ontario are quite small. And because the light is not orange or red, I do not suspect sky lanterns."

Toronto is the provincial capital of Ontario and the most populous city in Canada, population of 2,731,571.

JULY 11

Oregon witnesses watch UFO hover 45 minutes

An Oregon witness at Pendleton reported watching a hovering white, metallic object, according to testimony in Case 93427.

The witness was outside at 9 a.m. on July 11, 2018.

"We were waiting to tear up a street and rebuild it," the witness stated, "and we noticed something flashing way up in the distance. Kind of looked and carried on our talking with a veteran that lives on the street. I looked back up and it was still in the same spot, so I took my smartphone out and zoomed in and noticed it was just hovering. We all started looking then; it didn't float around like a bag or a balloon but stayed in one place. The color was white and glimmered in the sun. The newspaper came up because I sent video to their Facebook messenger, photographer came up and took pictures. He was extremely excited as we all were. Another one just appeared out of nowhere, like coming out of light speed, and slowly descended beside it for a few minutes. It slowly faded and went north, then the one we were watching took off in a straight line for a few miles, didn't speed up or slow down, but considering the distance it was from us, it was still very visible. It kind of faded away. One witness is a Vietnam vet. He flew planes and choppers. He had big binoculars and we all took turns looking. Photographer took a

picture and it had a big shadow underneath. He judged it at 250-300 feet in length."

Oregon MUFOFN Field Investigator Kellie Graham and State Director Thomas Bowden closed this case as an Unknown Aerial Vehicle.

"Based on witness interview, background, and the news article, Field Investigator found the witness credible.

"The object(s) were seen by at least three witnesses who could see them with the naked eye, before using high powered binoculars. Through the binoculars, the witness could see that the object was solid and had a shape. The witness described the object as 'shimmering' and had a dome on the top. In the article, it was noted that the Pendleton Airport, which is home to Pendleton UAS Range, did not have anything in the air of significance at the time of sighting. The article also states that the National Weather Service near the airport was contacted and was told that no balloons (pibals) had been set off that day, and that they usually were red in color. The witness was convinced that he was seeing a craft that hung in the air with no sound for at least 45 minutes, before slowly heading west across the sky after it had some sort of interaction with another identical object. FI cannot find any other sky anomalies."

Pendleton is a city in Umatilla County, Oregon, population 16,612.

News photographer confirms Oregon UFO sighting

An Oregon news photographer witness at Pendleton reported watching a hovering white object, according to testimony in Case 93419.

The witness approached the scene after his newspaper was contacted through their Facebook page that a white object was seen hovering over the town for the past hour at 10:45 a.m. on July 11, 2018.

"My editor told me about it when I came in to work about an hour later (so other witnesses had been watching the one object for two hours before I headed to their location)," the witness stated. "Upon arriving at the scene, I began talking to the witnesses and they pointed out the object to me. I began taking photos of the object with a 300mm lens (the object was so high up it looks like a white semi-translucent dot) when we noticed another similar object appear. The two objects appeared to merge before moving apart from each other and eventually it either disappeared, or we lost track of it. A few minutes later we saw another, lower object. I began taking photos of that object as well. I quickly looked at the images I had taken, and my first thought was it was a plastic bag flying through the air. The object was again a white, semi-translucent object that seemed to be changing its shape. But as myself and multiple other witnesses watched, we saw this object traverse a distance of around 10 miles in the span of a minute's time. While watching I had called another friend of mine who happened to be working in the area that the object took off in. He was literally right under the object when we were talking. He found it with binoculars and watch as the objected climbed up to 10,000 feet in the air before vanished before our eyes. Around this time, the original object vanished too.

Oregon MUFON Field Investigator Kellie Graham and State Director Thomas Bowden closed this case as an Unknown Aerial Vehicle.

"Field Investigator feels that based on witness interview, background and news article, the witness is credible," Graham and Bowden stated in their report. "The object(s) were seen by at least three witnesses who could see them with the naked eye, and with the help of a 300 mm camera lens and powerful binoculars could make out a defined shape, although each witness describes object differently. The witness described the object as 'globular' and 'cloud like.' When the first object slowly moved lower, the witness thought that the object was 'rolling' or 'morphing' into other shapes, like a cloud might do. The witness noted the research done in the area by the East Oregonian, along with his ability to identify other objects in photos (pelicans, and planes), indicates that this was not a known object in the Pendleton area.

"In the article, it was noted that the Pendleton Airport, which is home to Pendleton UAS Range, did not have anything in the air of significance at the time of sighting. The article also states that the National weather service near the airport was contacted and was told that no balloons (pibals) had been set off that day, and that they usually were red in color. This FI is ruling out a plastic bag (object seemed too large), a balloon (first object stationary for three hours; second object moved east too quickly for the 3 mph varied winds in area), or a known craft."

Pendleton is a city in Umatilla County, Oregon, population 16,612.

JULY 13

Indiana UFOs described as 20 feet off ground

An Indiana witness at Alexandria reported watching a group of lights moving at high speed just 20 feet off the ground, according to testimony in Case 93410.

The witness was northbound along County Road 400 East in Madison County at 9:30 p.m. on July 13, 2018.

"Just after crossing 1250 North we passed a house and observed off to the left lights flying across a bean field at a high rate of speed," the witness stated. "The lights were somewhat shielded from our view by a row of trees along a ditch line on the southeast corner of the field. My initial thought was, 'Why would they be crop dusting at night with lights on the plane?' Then I remembered it was a bean field and they are not usually dusted by plane. Just before reaching a small bridge where the ditch crosses the road, the lights were at the east edge of the field just before reaching the edge of the road. I noticed then that the lights appeared to be a bright sphere, but then it turned slightly to the road and I could see five or six spheres in a straight line equally spaced apart, and they seemed to nearly stop at the edge of the road. Then the farthest one away turned back west and up at about a 45-degree angle and the rest followed as if tied together and then just vanished. My wife was with me, and she saw the same thing, only she described it as similar to a row of very bright streetlights. She also said she thought it moved more like a fighter jet flying at very low altitude across the field, before she realized it was a row of lighted orbs. The spheres were not more than 15–20 feet above the ground and were around 10–12 feet in diameter."

Indiana MUFON State Section Director James Wolford closed this case as an Unknown-Other.

"This sighting originally looked like an open and shut case of farm machinery moving across an agricultural field, in this case soy beans," Wolford wrote in his report. "After reviewing the details with the witness during the interview it became clear that the lights' speed and altitude during the event were not consistent with plows, harvesters, crop dusters and the like. Drones and radio-controlled model aircraft are also a poor fit. Extreme speed and ability to leave the ground at a respectable angle of ascent and in an astonishingly short period of time leave little doubt that this is something else. Some of the heights above ground are too low to be any type of aircraft normally seen near Alexandria, IN. Although we basically have only the reporting witness's word for all of this, the story basically holds together pretty well."

Alexandria is a city in Monroe Township, Madison County, Indiana, population 5,145.

JULY 15

Multiple orb UFOs form triangle over Niagara Falls

A Canadian witness at Niagara Falls reported watching a hovering ball of light that produced two additional balls of light to form a triangle that quickly moved away, according to testimony in Case 93445.

The witness was not far from the Canadian side of the falls at 8:06 p.m. on July 15, 2018.

"I noticed a low-flying ball of light, orb-shaped, that was traveling very fast," the witness stated. "Under 500 feet on a clear night. The orb-shaped ball of light was changing colors from red to orange. It abruptly stopped and another orb-shaped ball of light came from the orb that abruptly stopped and then another until there were three orbs of the same shape and size in a straight line. 1-2-3. The first orb that stopped, suddenly moved to the front of the line, and the middle orb moved directly above the two other orbs, to form a triangle of three lights. The three orbs then moved in a sideways pattern (altogether in a triangle) slowed, stopped and pulsated and then faster than any jet I've seen moved directly up and were gone. I'm not a fanatic but since seeing this have seen similar sights. If anything, I'd still say I'm a skeptic, but the night I saw this and the others after my blood runs cold. Almost like you can feel electricity in the air. I wasn't the only one to see it or the lights after, but I'm hoping there's an answer or truth to be found. Maybe this helps that come to light. Thanks."

Canada MUFON Field Investigator Dan Jones closed this case as an Unknown-Other.

"The witness seems credible," Jones stated in his report. "She had good recall, and consistently described the event details. Initially, I had good communication with the witness. She answered my questions and provided additional information via email. The witness is reporting seeing three orbs that changed color from red to orange. They were seen close to the Canadian side of Niagara Falls. I initially thought that the witness may have been seeing large moisture particles rising up from the falls. These particles can be illuminated by light and look very anomalous. The witness maintains that the orbs traveled in a controlled path. First in a straight line and then in a triangle formation. Based on all the information provided, I believe what the witness is reporting are mechanical or biological orbs."

Niagara Falls is a city in Ontario, Canada, population 88,071.

JULY 17

Illinois witness says UFO came to ground level

An Illinois witness at Brookport reported watching a bright light that moved to ground level, according to testimony in Case 93540.

The witness had just come home at 10:40 p.m. on July 17, 2018.

"Looked above my house at 45-degree elevation and saw bright light in the sky," the witness stated. "Saw light move a little. It made me pay closer attention. As I watched the light it started descending. I thought was airplane crashing at first. As it came down it was like a leaf falling from sky fast. Halfway down, the light went out. Next thing I know spacecraft was hovering right in front of me. No sound. Stayed hovering for one minute then started moving away from me. No sound. Banked to the right. Made start-up sound swish noise. Took off so fast. Was gone out sight fast."

A second witness filed as Case 93541.

"The time I got home around 10:40 p.m., I turned into my driveway with my boyfriend," the witness stated. "I looked in the sky and saw the object. I said to him, 'what is that?' He said the same. I said maybe it's a satellite.

I parked. He got out to look at the sky. I stayed at truck getting stuff out. I heard him yelling 'UFO!' It startled me. I said, 'what?' about that time. I heard a noise like an engine starting. Ran beside the garage. That's when I saw the object with the lights and the swoosh noise. Went above the trees and out of sight. I could feel the hair stand up on my neck. Scared me like I've never been scared before. It was hard to sleep that night. I'm scared to go outside at night by myself. It was life-changing."

Illinois MUFON Field Investigators Barry Gaunt and Bill Kidd and State Director Sam Maranto closed this case as an Unknown Aerial Vehicle.

"Note that there were multiple interviews made by two State Directors, including recorded interviews," Gaunt, Kidd and Maranto stated in their report. "The following is a short summary of events by Sam Maranto.

"As noted in the witness statement, they had noticed an unusually brilliant and large light in the sky and then another, smaller illumination departs from the larger, descending in a falling leaf motion until lost from view behind the roof of the house. He exits the truck and proceeds to go behind the house to see if it is still visible.

"To his surprise, the large illumination folds in on itself and moves off instantaneously. Once behind the house and next to a field, he notices a dark object with precisely the same type of illumination hovering above the trees north of his property. The object begins to descend in his direction above the field to his left and relatively close. The object clearly has three lights affixed to its exterior – two red and one green. The brilliant white light is located on the bottom of what appears to be a large craft.

"A flat black shape elongated with what appear to be four windows, one large and three smaller along the port side. It's in the larger window that he detects motion of something or someone inside.

"Curiosity got the better of his apprehension. He walked closer to examine the object some more. Then he turned around and ran to get his lady friend.

"The object begins to move downfield, so they have to go behind the garage to catch up to it. There he gets a better view of the beings in the craft through the window, even being able to detect some detail, which appears to be skin coloration and head shape. Now at least two clearly visible beings are seen through the window. One bent forward as if engaging the power source of the craft. It was only at that time he heard a sound. Prior to that, there was only silence. The object veered up and out to the west in a fluid-like motion similar to a centipede making an abrupt turn. Another sound is noted much like a 'whoosh.' In seconds, it is out of sight.

"Disposition: Based solely on: 1) The veracity of the witnesses' account/statements. 2) Their information supplied in this report, both phone and in-person interviews. 3) Their ability to observe, then convey relevant information. 4) Other, a) supporting witness account; b) photos; c) videos; d) possible trace evidence; e) other.

"No reasons have been discovered to call into question the genuine nature of this account. More information to be entered."

Brookport is a city in Massac County, Illinois, population 1,054.

JULY 18

Two cigar-shaped UFOs described over Oregon

An Oregon witness at Hood River reported watching two cigar-shaped objects that stopped and hovered, according to testimony in Case 93708.

The witness was a passenger in a vehicle driven by her mother at 2:06 p.m. on July 18, 2018.

"I was in the passenger seat," the witness stated. "My mom then pointed out two white lines in the sky. They were far off and too big to be an airplane. The lines were definitely not airplanes because there was no tail or wings. On a regular airplane you can make out the shape of it, but these were just straight white, cigar-shaped lines in the sky. They appeared to be headed eastward in a straight path before they stopped and started hovering. One of the cigar lines appeared to be flying below the higher-up cigar line and a distance back from it. Then after the higher-up white line stopped, the lower white line caught up underneath the higher-up white line and then ascended upwards to merge with the higher-up white line. At the time in my confusion, and while I was trying to figure out what the cigar-like objects were, I did not think to record. After the two objects merged, they moved northward, disappearing into a thundercloud, in which an airplane would not go. Also, I noticed the two objects were flying in close vicinity of each other, and I know commercial airliners do not do that. I guess I would describe the way that the objects were flying was as if they were formation flying. I witnessed this event in Hood River, Oregon, and the objects seemed to be flying over the Washington side of the water from where I was at the time."

The witness did not feel like the objects were posing a threat in anyway.

"People in movies tend to make UFOs seem like these dangerous beings that come to Earth to solely kill humans. But these objects only appeared to be investigating the Earth below. I was not frightened by these objects, but instead I was left with many questions. What were they here for? Did anyone else see them? And what was the sole purpose of them coming to Earth? When my mom and I came home we told my dad and brother about the bizarre event. They did not believe us though. And because we don't have any pictures or videos, this event will be nodded off as another illusion, human imagination, or for entertainment. And though I do accept that not everything on the Internet is real, I know what I saw, and UFOs are real. The UFOs that I saw were real."

Oregon MUFON Field Investigator Kellie Graham and State Director Thomas Bowden closed this case as an Unknown Aerial Vehicle.

"The Field Investigator found the adult witness #2 very credible, a career military person until 4 years ago," Graham and Bowden wrote in their report. "The adult witness #2 was very sure of what they saw, and said it was like nothing she had ever seen in her military career in the Navy. The size of the object described is much larger than known aircraft (three times the size of a 737, of which the witness is very familiar), moved slower than ordinary aircraft, and hovered while the objects appeared to dock to each other. FI asked the adult witness if objects could have been military helicopters, and witness was positive they were not. FI searched for other sightings, called Ken Jernstedt Airfield-4S2 for any unusual aircraft in the area, and found nothing out of the ordinary.

This cased is closed based on the background and credibility of the adult witness, that there were two witnesses, and that no other known objects that look like flying tubes are known in the area or to this FI."

Hood River is the seat of Hood River County, Oregon, population 7,167.

Las Vegas pilot sees UFO trailed by jet

A Nevada witness at North Las Vegas reported watching an orb-like UFO followed by a high-speed traditional aircraft, according to testimony in Case 93459.

The witness and his wife were sitting in their backyard at 9 p.m. on July 18, 2018.

"We noticed a solid orange, orb-like object moving at 300–400 mph at approximately 10,000 feet in a northeast direction almost directly above the I-15 freeway leaving the Las Vegas Strip area," the witness stated. "This object was trailed by a high-speed aircraft with traditional aircraft night lighting, which was trailing the object by about three-quarters of a mile, with red/green on wingtips clearly visible as opposed to the solid orange orb. I'm a pilot and this was no aircraft I've seen. This was witnessed also by my wife. I attempted some video, too much surrounding light for my shots to come out."

Nevada MUFON State Director Sue Countiss closed this case as an Unknown-Other.

North Las Vegas is a city in Clark County, Nevada, population 216,961.

JULY 19

Kentucky witness says UFO was 'glass-like globe'

A Kentucky witness at Mount Washington reported watching a "large, glass-like globe" that floated over her home, according to testimony in Case 97557.

The witness was standing in her front yard with her dog at 9:30 p.m. on July 19, 2018.

"I thought I saw, off in the distance, an airplane on fire," the witness stated. "It slowly descended for a few seconds and then it was immediately hovering over the roof of my house. It appeared to be a large, glass-like globe about 30 to 35 feet in diameter. It was clear like glass. Inside was a large flame approximately 15 feet tall. I stood there and watched in amazement. It was totally silent. Then it floated over my house slowly and was gone. It was totally silent and emitted no heat. Strangely, my dog did not seem to notice it. Since that time, I have looked for pictures for something similar to this and have not found anything. I am on no medication. I have never had hallucinations. I still feel a certain sense of disbelief, but I swear I saw this thing. Even stranger, I asked them to visit me. No, I swear I am not crazy. I sit on my patio each night and gaze at the stars looking for constellations. Just for the heck of it, I asked them to show themselves to me if they were really up there. And boy did I get results within a couple of weeks. If necessary, I would be willing to pay for and take a polygraph test to prove that I saw this. I do not tell friends and family as they think I am crazy. I continue to ask but I have not seen anything like this since that date. Please let me know if other people have seen anything similar to this so I will know that I am not losing my mind. Thank you so much for all the good work you do."

Kentucky MUFON State Section Director Bill Kidd closed this case as an Unknown-Other.

"Unfortunately, I could not find any corroboration of this event," Kidd wrote in his report. "The local police department was genuinely interested, but none of their officers have received reports such as this. A review of other UFO reporting sites did not reveal similar reports either. I think it is possible that the duration of the event was mistakenly entered as 9 hours 25 minutes when it was actually 9 minutes 25 seconds. My thinking is that surely an event lasting 9-plus hours would have been seen and reported by others. I sent a second email questioning the duration time and to ask a couple other questions. No response. I do believe the witness saw something. Her description most resembles an orb, but I cannot identify what it was."

Mount Washington is a home rule-class city in Bullitt County, Kentucky, population 9,117.

JULY 22

Washington witness captures photo of disc-shaped UFO

A Washington witness at Darrington reported discovering a UFO in a photo taken of White Horse Mountain and meadow, according to testimony in Case 93732.

The incident occurred at 1:42 p.m. on July 22, 2018.

"Didn't see the object in the photo until I went to crop and color correct it after a number of days," the witness stated. "At the time, I was facing into the sun and had to cover up the top of the camera to prevent lens flare. I don't recall any planes or helicopters in the area at the time, but it was hot and windy with many cars on the road, so I didn't linger and quickly took the photo and moved on. I don't live in the area, so not certain if that area has any regular commercial air traffic. Either way, it was very interesting to find it in the photo."

Washington MUFON Chief Investigator Daniel Nims closed this case as an Unknown Aerial Vehicle.

"The witness seemed very credible," Nims wrote in his report. "The witness was returning from a day trip to the mountains when he stopped to take a picture of White Horse Mountain. He says that he did not notice anything in the sky at the time he took the picture. He didn't hear anything. Except for cars driving by, it was a very quiet rural location. He says he would have heard a low-flying aircraft or a drone. When he got home and went to crop and print the picture, he noticed the object in the photo. The object in the photo does not look like a lens flare. The witness is experienced enough and said he intentionally shadowed the camera with his hand to avoid a lens flare. Also, the object shown is not the normal light orb shape you normally get from a lens flare. When you blow up the picture and look at the object in detail, you see it clearly has shape and detail. However, it does not show wings or a tail that you would expect for an aircraft. It also does not have the square, four-propeller look of a drone. It has what appears to be a disk-shaped lower section and a fuselage-shaped upper section. At the very top there seems to be a tail fin. Several observers have commented it looks like a space shuttle. There is a small airport four miles to the east. FlightRadar24 showed no aircraft in the vicinity; however, it does not show private aircraft without an ADS-B transponder. The appearance of the object is not of a small light aircraft. Also, the object does not give the appearance of a large bird, or some sort of cloud. Finally, the picture clearly shows the variation from the clear and distinct objects in the foreground to the hazy appearance of the mountains four miles in the distance. The object does not have the hazy appearance of being in the distance. This is a very crude measure of distance, but based on it, the object would appear to be more likely a mile or two away and not four miles away or more like the mountains. Sizewise, it is comparable to the truck shown parked in the lower portion of the picture. The picture of the object does not show the characteristics of common daytime flying objects like birds or aircraft or the look of a model airplane or drone; also the witness did not hear any sound associated with these types of objects, the disposition of the case is Unknown-UAV."

Darrington is a town in Snohomish County, Washington, population 1,347.

Five triangular UFOs observed over Disneyland

A California witness at Anaheim reported watching "five glowing triangles flying in formation," according to testimony in Case 93687.

The witness and his nephew were at Disneyland about 10 p.m. on July 22, 2018.

"We were sitting on a bench located at the dead center of the park," the witness stated. "We observed five soft, glowing triangle-shaped objects traveling in formation westbound at about 500 feet up. They made no sound. And as they were directly over us, the lead triangle switched places with the triangle that was behind it on the right-hand side. After that happened, within seconds they all disappeared. A Latino family consisting of a mother, father, baby and grandmother also witnessed the event."

California MUFON Field Investigator Earl Grey Anderson closed this case as an Unknown Aerial Vehicle.

"I interviewed both witnesses separately, two times each," Anderson stated in his report. "They both recounted the exact same details, except for a visual detail that differed between the two of them (the main witness believed the objects to be featureless gold triangles with blunt leading edges, whereas his nephew believed them to be elongated horseshoe-shaped. Both saw the lead object switch spaces with the one behind itself, which the witness shows in the diagram in attachments.

"I was impressed by both witnesses' 'matter of fact' description of the objects. I did mention that Disneyland sometimes has balloon releases and laser effects, and both witnesses stated emphatically that that was the first thing they had wondered. But being plane spotters, and used to seeing all manner of flying objects, both conventional and experimental, neither witness has ever seen anything that looked like that which they observed on July 22, 2018.

"I asked both witnesses if they could've just seen a group of balloons that had gotten away. Both had similar reactions, with laughter, and the main witness stated, 'No, balloons couldn't do that. They moved in tandem, then there was that maneuver where the lead object switched.'

"As both witnesses were credible, with no reason to manufacture a story like this 'whole cloth,' both being seasoned observers of aircraft—vintage, contemporary, and experimental—yet they were equally baffled by what they had observed.

"I'm going to log this in as Unknown/UAV, as both witnesses are seasoned observers of aircraft, both told the exact story during their various interviews, without embellishment. And neither could identify what they had seen, and neither can this FI. Both witnesses seemed a little shaken by what they had seen."

Anaheim is a city in Orange County, California, population 336,265.

JULY 23

Blue UFO over Seattle splits and merges again

A Washington witness at Seattle reported that a "blue object rose up, split into two pieces, and merged again," according to testimony in Case 93587.

The witness was working near the top of Columbia Tower at 6:30 p.m. on July 23, 2018.

"Several tourists, myself and the bartender saw a blue thing rise up from either Ballard or Magnolia heading south, split into two pieces, rise up over the water and merge back together again," the witness stated. "It kind of looked like it was tumbling upwards up until it merged again. It went towards SeaTac and then after a while we couldn't see it anymore. I told the tourists it was probably a giant thing of blue balloons, but it honestly could have been anything. I was a little freaked out by it, thought it was a nearby drone at first as it came up, but then it split into two pieces and it was a lot farther away than I initially thought. I watched it until it was very high and probably past SeaTac airport, then I couldn't see it anymore. I lost track of it a few times, but found it

again pretty easily until it got too small for me to see. It was also blue, so it blended in a bit with the sky, there was a bit of a black outline though. I was working so I was unable to take a photo of it."

Washington MUFON Field Investigator Anthony Nugent closed this case as an Unknown-Other.

"Being that the primary witness seems to be quite familiar with aircraft that she sees on a daily basis in the course of her work at the Columbia Tower," Nugent stated in his report, "that this phenomenon struck her as weird, that there were a total of five witnesses, that she felt compelled to report this to MUFON (and Reddit) a few minutes after her sighting, and that this object cannot be identifiable as any known natural phenomenon or man-made object, I am classifying this case as Unknown-Other."

Seattle is the seat of King County, Washington, population 730,000.

JULY 24

Triangular UFO described with 'red glowing band'

A Washington witness at Winlock reported watching a triangle-shaped object with a "red glowing band" for five to six seconds before it moved out of sight, according to testimony in Case 93703.

The 69-year-old witness woke up at 2:30 a.m. on July 24, 2018, and looked out a bedroom window.

"I have a great view of the sky," the witness stated. "Pine trees to the left and the right and a low row of trees on the bottom frame the window. I was staring out at the sky when this craft rolled into view from the left side, north."

The witness said he was looking at a "complete triangle."

"I say it 'rolled into view' because it slowly turned in a clockwise direction while slowly moving south in a straight-line motion. It looked to me like a pool rack triangle on its side. There was a wide, red glowing band that ran around the perimeter of the craft. There also was a red circle at each corner. The red glow was very bright and slowly pulsed as it turned. The red light clearly showed the outline of this object. I was fixated on the light trying to set this picture in my mind."

The witness described the object's color.

"The body of the object could have been anywhere from light gray to black. The light defined the edges but obscured the color of the body. I viewed the craft for about five to six seconds total. After this experience I got up and made a quick sketch. Later, I drew it up on a CAD system. I don't really believe that this craft was trying to be stealthy in any shape or form. It was so clear and so defined I believe it could have been seen from miles away. I don't feel the need to have someone justify this sighting, but it would be nice to know someone else had this great experience.'"

Washington MUFON Chief Investigator Daniel Nims closed this case as an Unknown Aerial Vehicle.

"The witness said the outline of the craft was very discernable, a rounded triangle," Nims wrote in his report. "The craft was not oriented horizontally as is commonly described but on edge, vertically. There were three red lights at the corners and a perimeter strip of light on the same surface as the lights, near the edge of the craft. The perimeter strip was not on the edge of the craft. The craft was rotating and made one-and-a-half to two clockwise revolutions during the few seconds it was in view. Both the lights and peripheral band were the same red color. The witness was uncertain of the color of the surface of the craft but felt it was dark gray or black.

"The shape and lighting of the craft are dissimilar to that of any aircraft or helicopter. The lighting did not match any common aircraft lighting. It was larger and slower than a meteor, although it made a straight path. The slowly rotating motion of the craft is unlike any motion an aircraft would make.

"Based on the size, lighting and motion of the object the disposition of the case is Unknown-UAV."

Winlock is a city in Lewis County, Washington, population 1,339.

JULY 29

Low-flying Kansas triangle caught on camera

A Kansas witness at Hesston reported watching a silent, triangle-shaped object just above 500 feet, with three white lights at its points and one red light centered on its bottom, according to testimony in Case 93741.

The witness was sitting in his company parking lot watching cloud lightning as a storm passed at 5:35 a.m. on July 29, 2018.

"Noticed lights coming into view out of driver window above car," the witness stated. "Spent a few minutes trying to make out what it was. Traveling roughly at 5 knots. A couple flashes of cloud lightning in the distance showed the shape of the triangle with no facets or edge differences of any of the three sides, three straight lines only. Continued to follow storm until view was obstructed by parking lot lights. Moved slow and in a perfect straight line. I had no assumption of what it was, thought possibly a Life Watch helicopter until the rest of the lights came into view. No sound that I heard."

MUFON Kansas State Director Stan Seba closed this case as an Unknown Aerial Vehicle.

"Dark triangular object that reflected light, appeared solid, and had an outline," Seba wrote in his report. "The surface was dark, with no structural features. Actual size is indeterminate. The object had white lights with one red light in the center with dark surfaces. The exterior lights were unwavering. The elevation of the object was above 500 feet. The object was at least 501 feet away to one mile away from the witness. Object flew in a straight-line path. Object was first and last seen in the northeast by east direction."

Hesston is a city in Harvey County, Kansas, population 3,709.

JULY 31

Ohio witness reports 'humanoid-like creature'

An Ohio witness at Mount Vernon reported watching a "skinny, humanoid-like creature" crossing a road, according to testimony in Case 93831.

The witness was driving home at 1:43 a.m. on July 31, 2018, along State Route 13 north of Mount Vernon.

"A seven- to eight-foot-tall, skinny, humanoid-like creature ran across the road out of a cornfield across into a soybean field moving from east to west," the witness stated. "I noticed the creature in my headlights from 50 to 75 feet away as I was traveling at a rate of 55-60 mph. As it came out of the cornfield, I immediately let off the accelerator at first thinking it was a deer, but then saw the creature walked upright. It was seven- to eight-feet in height, tall slender body, arms and legs small in diameter, hands and feet looked oversized for its body proportion, small neck with oval, elongated head; being had dark tan to light brown skin tone and had no body hair. The creature slightly turned its head towards my vehicle's headlights, and I saw the creature's black eyes and small mouth just open slightly as it continued to run across the road.

It barely took two to three steps and it was across the road at a tremendous rate of speed. I was in total shock and thought I should check it out at first, but then thought for a second and, being uncertain of what I may have just seen, decided I had better get out of the area. I lost sight of the entity due to darkness."

Ohio MUFON Chief Investigator Ron McGlone closed this case as an Unknown-Other.

"I found the witness to be well grounded, sincere, and somewhat concerned by what he saw and said it changed his whole way of thinking about such things like entities and such," McGlone stated in his report. "The witness is in good health (under no medications or use of drugs/alcohol), and others have described him as being honest, and if he said he saw something, then he did.

"Although I found no sign of footprints, crop damage, or trace evidence, and based on my conversation with cryptid expert Fred Saluga about not finding such things in his cases, I do believe the witness had seen something as described. With the lack of physical evidence, I contacted the local newspaper about the story and sought for anyone with information to contact our office. I received dozens of emails, finding several with stories of having seen such a creature/entity before. It seems this 'Rake-type' creature has been seen in many places. I even had two reports of it passing through basement walls as if in a different reality of sorts, not paying attention to its surroundings."

Mount Vernon is a city in Knox County, Ohio, population 16,990.

AUGUST 2018

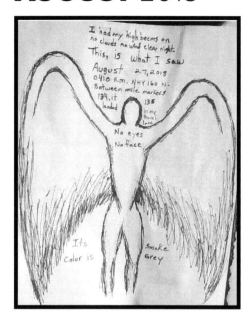

*Case 97499 witness illustration.
August 27, 2018.*

AUGUST 1

Oregon camper reports interacting with UFO

An Oregon witness at Breitenbush Hot Springs reported watching and interacting with a hovering UFO over a campsite, according to testimony in Case 97862.

The 50-year-old witness and avid outdoorsman was on a camping trip with his grandson at 9:02 p.m. on August 1, 2018.

"I experienced something truly bizarre and life changing," the witness stated. "This is my story.

"We arrived at the lower lake trailhead in the late morning of July 31st, 2018, and backpacked about two miles to our usual camping spot at the west end of the lake. We set up camp and had a great but uneventful day. The following day, August 1, 2018, we ventured out hiking and fishing at several other small lakes

in the area. We returned to camp an hour or so before sunset to eat and settle in for the night.

"We were both pretty tired as we had hiked about eight to 10 miles of very rugged country. My grandson was tired and went to bed about a half-hour after eating dinner. I started a small fire and stayed up to watch the stars.

"The weather was perfect, and the skies were crystal clear. While sitting in my camping chair I began meditating, which is a normal practice for me. I began a simple Vedic meditation practice focusing my thoughts and intentions on kindness, compassion, love and curiosity as to what or who may be out there amongst a sea of stars. I also flashed a very bright LED pulse light directly overhead for two or three minutes. After about 15 minutes or so of meditation I opened my eyes. Much to my surprise, a black triangle-shaped object had appeared seemingly out of nowhere. It was a very, very flat black color and several shades darker than the night sky background. It had a small white light in each corner for a total of three lights. It was approximately 50 to 75 feet above the trees and about 50 to 60 feet to the east of our camp. It was between 25 to 35 feet in length. At this point I was still uncertain as to what I was seeing and remained in my chair with my eyes fixed on it for maybe 30 minutes. After this period of observation, I began to get a little rattled because this thing did not move, and it blocked out the stars as they moved behind it. It was then that I knew it was something of substance, capable of blocking the light of the stars behind it. I then aimed my LED light directly at it and nothing happened. It seemed to absorb the light and not reflect it in any way. I found this to be quite odd as this particular light was very powerful and would easily light up trees 100-plus yards across the lake. At this point I got up out of my chair and began walking 30 or so feet toward the object. I remained standing for the rest of the experience (approximately 2.5 hours). I base this timeline by the amount and type of wood I had placed on the fire. As I got closer to the craft it emitted a quick flash of very white light from all three sides (it had a very slight blueish hue in with the white). It was about as bright as a large camera flash, but, oddly, it did not project light outward onto the trees or anywhere else. This flashing happened two more times at seemingly irregular intervals. Things really got weird as I got closer to the object. I will try to describe it to the best of my ability using what I know to try and explain what I don't know. I walked directly underneath the object, and immediately began to experience a very powerful vibration-type feeling deep within the core of my body. It was similar to standing directly in front of a giant wall of studio monitor speakers at a Metallica concert, except without the sound. This object made no sound whatsoever. The feeling was similar but much, much more intense and different. It wasn't a deep bass-type feeling but much higher in frequency. It was unbearable to stand under it for more than three or four seconds at a time. My excitement had turned to fear by now. It took all my willpower and a lot of deep yoga-type breathing to keep myself together. It felt like all my internal organs were being shaken in a very strange way. After two or three passes underneath this thing, I almost lost control of my urine and bowels. I stepped back about 20 feet or so and dropped my pants and emptied the contents of my bladder and bowels. I never took my eyes off the object for the next two-plus hours. I walked in circles around the object and underneath it very briefly countless times for the rest of the experience. I was kind of like a madman by this point, trying to communicate with this thing with sign language and my flashlight and even my thoughts, but nothing changed. The object never moved or made any noise. At one point I took out my pistol and thought about shooting at it just to get its attention or get some kind of reaction, but I quickly got a feeling that that was a terrible idea. I put my gun back in the holster and kept walking around and near it.

I was also afraid to wake my grandson up to this craziness. After what I estimate to be three hours, I was mentally, physically and emotionally exhausted. The object never moved or flashed again. The campfire was out and relatively cold. I was more tired than I have ever been. I determined that whatever this was it had no intentions on harming us or it would have done so by now. The experience ended with me yelling at it, 'show yourself, communicate, move, leave, do something,' followed by a verbal 'f--- you, I'm done.' I checked on my grandson who was sound asleep. I got into my tent and literally passed out within a minute or two. We woke up the next day, did a little fishing and went home. In hindsight, I think the most surprising thing about this experience was that this thing, whatever it was, tuned into my consciousness or thoughts in some manner. I think it appeared as a result of my thought processes and also influenced me not to shoot at it. That's pure speculation, however, and is based only on my feelings."

Oregon MUFON State Director Thomas Bowden closed this case as an Unknown Aerial Vehicle.

"The witness in this case seemed very credible," Bowden stated in his report. "I spent just over one hour on the telephone with the witness, and I am convinced that he is sincere. No evidence was provided beyond the testimony given. Based on information provided by the witness, I have changed the event data in the CMS report from July 31 to August 1, 2018. The original detailed statement he entered into CMS was lacking in detail, so I asked him to write a complete narrative of the event in his own words. This narrative was sent to me via email, and I have included it here. This statement includes a number of noteworthy details about the experience: Close encounter lasting for an estimated three hours; black triangular object with a surface that did not reflect a very bright LED flashlight; black triangle had three white lights, one at each corner; object emitted flashes of blue-white light around its edges; when directly beneath the object, witness experienced an energetic vibration inside his body; witness considered firing a pistol at the object, but got the feeling that this was a terrible idea; grandson was sleeping nearby, did not wake up; witness did not see the object depart; instead, he finally went to bed and fell asleep while the object was still present.

"Although this experience was a close encounter in which the witness experienced a sense of reality transformation, there does not seem to be an abduction component to this story. Even so, it is obvious that the witness experienced a profound experience that must be described as a reality transformation."

"In my opinion, this witness is sincere. I find no reason to suspect deception. Because this is a very close encounter with reality transformation, I think it is safe to discount any known manmade aircraft or natural phenomenon as the cause of this experience."

Breitenbush is an unincorporated community in Marion County, Oregon.

AUGUST 3

Bell-shaped UFO described over Oregon

An Oregon witness at Newport reported watching an "orange, bell-shaped, rounded saucer" crossing the sky, according to testimony in Case 94007.

The events occurred beginning after 11 p.m. on August 3, 2018, while the witness and her husband were vacationing in Newport.

"He was asleep, and I suddenly awoke for no reason between the hour of 11 p.m. and midnight," the witness stated. "Since it was an ocean view room, we left the drapes and the windows open. Upon wakening, I propped myself up on my elbow to peer out the window. Just as I did this, I saw a well-lit, glowing orange, bell-shaped, rounded saucer. It crossed

the window, making no sound, and maintained a straight trajectory, moving from north to south. It was traveling at a pace that took two to three seconds for it to cross the frame of the hotel window. I knew immediately what it was, but I was in shock and fearful. I froze and checked in with myself about what it was that I saw. I pondered for about 20 seconds before getting up to run to the window, which faced west towards the ocean, but I could no longer see it. I looked down to the right and noticed a couple at a bonfire lighting firecrackers intermittently. They seemed to not notice. We were on the third floor of a hotel that is located on a bluff overlooking the ocean. The craft was relatively close to the window; so close, I could see the outline of its shape clearly, for it emanated a strong light, much like how the moon glows. It cast no rays or beams of light and did not have any lights on it. After I determined it was gone, I still sat vigil for an hour hoping to see it return. I was rattled and knew I wouldn't be able to sleep. I did, however, allow my husband to remain sleeping. After an hour of no further sightings, I went to bed. The next morning, I told my husband and scoured the Internet for any reports but found none."

Oregon MUFON Field Investigator Brogan Callahan and State Director Thomas Bowden closed this case as an Unknown Aerial Vehicle.

"Initially, I had suspected that what the witness described was a Chinese sky lantern, and her seemingly sudden awakening was due to the sound of the fireworks being set off outside," Callahan and Bowden stated in their report. "However, when the phone interview was conducted, we found that she has experience with observing Chinese sky lanterns and what she observed did not match that description. Furthermore, she explained that she could not have woken up to the sound of firecrackers due to the ambient ocean noise."

Newport is a city in Lincoln County, Oregon, population 9,989.

AUGUST 5

Fast-moving triangle reported over Oregon

An Oregon witness at Florence reported watching a fast-moving, triangular-shaped object, according to testimony in Case 95040.

The witness and his wife were walking on the beach at 3 p.m. on August 5, 2018.

"Huge roar overhead," the witness stated. "Looked up to see triangle-shaped shadow in overcast sky shooting west at Mach 5."

Oregon MUFON State Director Thomas Bowden closed this case as an Unknown Aerial Vehicle.

"This was a close encounter case," Bowden stated in his report, "CE1, based on witness estimate that the object passed over at less than 500 feet. Because the date given was approximate, the weather data cannot be reliably established. The witness estimated the cloud cover to be at 500 feet, but he does not have any special qualifications to make this estimate.

"The witness described a roaring sound with a sudden onset that appeared to come from the dark triangular object in the clouds. One explanation for this is that a delta-wing jet approached at or near the speed of sound. I asked if there was a sonic boom, but the witness said there was none.

"The witness described the object as a triangle with rounded corners, which agrees with one of the often-reported shapes of black triangle UFOs; however, these objects are not usually reported as making a loud roaring sound. There is still a strong possibility that what the witness saw was a military type delta-wing aircraft, such as an F-14 or F-22; but without any confirming information, I cannot establish this explanation.

"Based on the witness's estimate, he was within 500 feet of the object, giving him a close enough look at the object. His estimate of apparent size was similar to a playing card held at arm's length. I am closing this case as an Unknown, UAV, based on the witness perception of a dark triangular object with rounded corners."

Florence is a coastal city in Lane County, Oregon, population 8,466.

AUGUST 6

Iowa witness reports 'glowing, saucer shape'

An Iowa witness at Waterloo reported watching a glowing, saucer-shaped object, according to testimony in Case 93940.

The witness was walking her dog at 10:15 p.m. on August 6, 2018, and approaching a car sales lot.

"I usually look up at night to view the stars," the witness stated. "When I looked up, a round, glowing object was in the sky to the left of the car place and high in the sky. I thought it was a flying saucer. I watched and couldn't believe what I was seeing. So, I got my friends to come with me to look at it and they verified what I saw. I tried to take a picture of it with my phone and it went up and away with no noise. I was surprised at what I was seeing. My friends verified it did look like a flying saucer. When I raised my cell phone to take a picture of it, it went up and away, but there was no noise at all."

Iowa MUFON Field Investigator David Kreiter closed this case as an Unknown Aerial Vehicle.

In addition to Investigator Kreiter's interaction with the reporting witness regarding her sighting of August 6, 2018, Iowa MUFON Chief Investigator, Beverly Trout, interviewed the reporting witness by telephone for 45 minutes on August 10, 2018.

"This phone interview took place because she had referred to childhood experiences indicative of alien-human interaction," Kreiter stated in his report. "Suffice it to say, that she has memories of aerial traveling, 'seeing different beings,' and being told, 'time to go back now,' meaning to return her to her home. And there are other markers pointing to her involvement with the UFO phenomenon, which, by her preference, need not be covered here. This witness also has paranormal events in her life, as does Beverly Trout, so there was considerable dialogue on that subject. Investigator Trout considers this witness as very credible; she did not over-conclude, and sensibly related her experiences. She indicated that she 'felt better' for having shared the information with someone who could listen. Investigator Trout always tells such witnesses to feel free to call at any time they may feel a need to further explore the subject of UFOs and/or their own experiences, and so further communication does frequently occur.

"This was an intriguing case because of the credibility of the witness and the circumstances that allowed me to calculate the size and distance of the object. Of course, calculations are only as reliable as the input data. My first task was to find the altitude of the object. The witness stated that the object she saw appeared about three times higher in the sky than some very tall lights (100 feet) adjacent to Interstate 380. I found that she was approximately 660 feet from those lights, so that altitude figured to be 24 degrees. Next, I wanted to find the distance and size of the object, if possible. She described the object as being just below the cloud cover, as if the object had punched a hole in the clouds. I found that the cloud ceiling on that evening was 1,117 feet. This gave me two pieces of information, the degrees above the horizon (24 degrees) and the actual height of the object (1,117 feet). From that information, I was able to establish the ground distance to the object as 2,508 feet, the air distance as 2,744 feet,

and the actual size of the object as 46 feet in diameter. Unfortunately for this case, the secondary witness, the primary witness's friend, did not want to be interviewed. She said that he did not want to entertain the idea of extraterrestrial life visiting our planet even though he concluded that the object he saw in the sky looked like a 'UFO.' I found the dog's behavior to be intriguing as well. She said that the dog was old and rarely got excited, yet it barked during the sighting and continued to be agitated after they got home."

Waterloo is a city in and the county seat of Black Hawk County, Iowa, population 68,406.

AUGUST 8

Missouri UFO had different levels of transparency

A Missouri witness at Sunset Hills reported watching a diamond-shaped object with white lights, according to testimony in Case 94049.

The witness was stopped at a stoplight along westbound Highway 30 and 270, on the east side of 270, at 9:45 a.m. on August 8, 2018.

"I was watching stoplight and noticed the object just above the stoplight," the witness stated. "Object was moving north. I first thought it was an airplane and then noticed it had a steady bright, white light in front and back. In between was a silver color that seemed transparent. It was moving at a constant speed similar to a small propeller aircraft, but the shape looked diamond but slightly flatter on the bottom. I lost sight behind trees after the light changed to green and headed down the hill. I also had a hard time determining how far away it was because of the shape. Seeing and experiencing this did not bother me. I also know that what I saw is what I described, as I have waited a few days to think of what it could have been before doing this report."

Missouri MUFON State Section Director

Dana Simpson West closed this case as an Unknown Aerial Vehicle.

"The UAV was like a squashed diamond that he approximated at 8–10 feet thick, depending on how far away it was," West stated in her report. "He had a hard time determining how big it was because he wasn't sure how far away it was. He estimated it to be about a half-mile (close to the stoplight at the Life Christian Church just down the hill) or a mile away (close to the bridge that crosses over the Meramec River before the Fenton exit). He estimated it to be moving about the speed of a Cessna. There was a bright light emitting from the south and north ends of the craft (which was traveling south to north, parallel to I-270). The lights weren't real intense, but they were round and brighter. They were either really big or brighter than anything around it and brighter than the craft. The lights didn't pulse or change colors. The lights emitting from each end were the same size and brightness. Although the witness thought the craft was either silver or chrome because of the reflection that caught his eye, the oddest thing was that the body of craft pulsated and assumed various levels of transparency. Sometimes you could see through it and sometimes you could see through it less. The craft didn't change shape, it changed density and looked kind of like a plane flying through clouds, but it wasn't. He indicated the craft got fairly close to completely transparent, but the lights never changed regardless of what the body was doing. It never did get completely crispy clear. There were no contrails or emissions and no loud sounds, not even the usual jet sound. There were no other crafts in the vicinity because he was looking for something to establish scale.

"He described the bottom of the craft as a slight curve, and where it met each light was almost a point, although the ends were interrupted by the lights. The top was more like the top of a diamond with slanted sides. The craft never changed shape, speed, direction, or altitude throughout the two-minute sighting.

Once the light changed, he drove west on Highway 30, which involves traveling down a big hill, and so he lost sight of the craft as his elevation changed and trees blocked his view. As he traveled down the highway, he looked for any unusual events—firetrucks, police cars—but everything was normal. There were no technological effects and no missing time, and it didn't bother him physically or psychologically. It just didn't make sense and he couldn't find a reasonable explanation, so he decided to report it.

"Based on the description of the UAV and the details the witness provided of its unusual characteristics, such as its pulsating transparency, I do not think that this is a UAV that can be definitely identified and, therefore, I am classifying it as an Unknown-UAV."

Sunset Hills is a city in south St. Louis County, Missouri, population 8,496.

AUGUST 9

Witness watches UFO take 15,000-foot dive

A California witness at San Diego reported watching a hovering, oval-shaped object at 20,000 feet that dove toward the ground and stopped at 5,000 feet, according to testimony in Case 94827.

The witness was eastbound along Freeway 8 at 2:45 p.m. on August 9, 2018.

"I was approaching the College Avenue exit and I noticed a large white object in the sky at about 20,000 feet," the witness stated. "It was just staying still. Then I noticed to the left end of it there was a black fin standing pretty tall. Trying to get an idea how big this thing was, I was looking around and saw an airplane coming into San Diego airport to the south of me. It was much closer to me, so I looked at its size and then looked back at the object and the object was much farther away, but it was four to five times bigger than the airplane."

The object then quickly moved.

"Then, the object made a 45-degree dive toward the ground in a blink of an eye and stopped at about 5,000 feet. At the same time it made the move, it always stayed level. It was unbelievable how fast it moved. I have never seen anything move that fast. After that I was trying to watch it, but I was also driving down the freeway. The object hovered for a bit, then it started to move slowly to the south. I then pulled off the freeway in La Mesa. Got out of the car, but at that time I could not see it anymore."

California MUFON Field Investigator Earl Grey Anderson closed this case as an Unknown Aerial Vehicle.

"The witness was lucid, sober, and eloquent in his description of the event, and I have no reason to believe that he was fabricating a story, or had mistaken a prosaic object for a UAP," Anderson stated in his report. "The witness is not looking for fame, as he wishes to remain anonymous. The witness allowed this Field Investigator to examine his work badge during our Skype interview, and his badge is consistent with his story. Because the witness was able to recall his story without even the slightest deviation from his first and second interviews, I'm deeming that he was recalling an actual event, and not fabricating a story. The object described does not resemble any known conventional craft, nor do the flight characteristics described match any known craft."

San Diego is a city in San Diego County, California, population 1,419,516.

AUGUST 10

Indiana witness describes dull gray UFO

An Indiana witness at Hammond reported a flat, dull gray object that hovered and made small turns, according to testimony in Case 94038.

The witness was driving eastbound along Route 80/94 at the state line between Illinois and Indiana at 7:19 p.m. on August 10, 2018.

"This is a route that I take every Friday at approximately the same time," the witness stated. "I noticed to the north of my location a couple of miles earlier the rain clouds in the sky and how they were breaking apart and the evening sun was poking through the clouds. Conditions to the east were mostly cloudy. As I glanced to the north, I noticed the strange object from its broad side. It was approximately a half-mile away from my location and appeared to be turning to its left, heading east. The broad side of the object had approximately three different sections along its otherwise flat, dull gray exterior. I was traveling at approximately 50 mph through this stretch of the interstate and the object remained in view for approximately two minutes, so it moved from my left to in front of me, then to my right and eventually out of my range of sight. The object never got any closer to me than a half-mile and moved under the cloud cover. It would hover and then make small turns to the right or left, showing its broad side and its narrow side, which looked like the letter I. It would stay vertical the entire time I viewed it.

"If you travel this corridor you know that cell phone usage while driving in Illinois is illegal, but not in Indiana. I was getting my phone to check my messages when the sighting occurred. I took a few photos through a dirty and cracked windshield—sorry. I did catch something when I zoomed in on the photos. Take a look at them and come to your own conclusions. I cannot explain it."

Indiana MUFON State Section Director James Wolford closed this case as an Unknown Aerial Vehicle.

"If the object was a light-weight, wind-blown

item, such as a garbage bag or kite, its orientation should have been random and ever-changing," the witness stated. "Also, the path it took would have been uneven. Instead the object maintained a constant upright stance and moved in a perfectly straight line. Its elevation was close to constant as well. The witness had the impression that purposeful motion was involved. The box outline observed is a regular geometric shape and some surface detail was visible, although it was not a typical blimp shape. Since the object moved from northwest to southeast, but the wind was from the north and only 7 mph, it seems likely that powered flight was in use. A drone might be an explanation for the sighting except that no propeller blades or other common means of propulsion were visible. No noise was heard, so it must not have been loud enough for an individual inside of a car to hear it. Although there is still a chance that this was a common imposter, the evidence, for the moment, does not support it. It would help if a little bit more information were available."

Hammond is a city in Lake County, Indiana, population 80,830.

Multiple witnesses watch red lights hovering over Illinois

An Illinois witness at Tinley Park reported watching two red lights that hovered while one of the lights released five smaller, white orbs, according to testimony in Case 94525.

The witness received a phone call from a brother three miles west at 9:50 p.m. on August 10, 2018, asking him to look west for two red orbs hovering in the sky.

"I stepped out of my front door and there were the two red orbs hovering in the sky around airplane elevation," the witness stated. "At this time, I ran back inside my home and told my wife and kids to come outside so all six of us could witness orbs. We took pictures and tried to take video, but the orbs did not show up

very well on videos. My kids and I sat outside for about 30 minutes observing the UFOs. The UFOs just hovered in the sky while the air traffic continued in the area. It did appear as if at least one plane noticed the light because a plane changed course as it approached the area where the UFOs hovered. At about the 20-minute mark we noticed the lower UFO ejected about five small, white orbs (much smaller than the UFOs) that just disappeared after being ejected. After 10 more minutes, the higher UFO light faded out and about two minutes later the other UFO faded out and vanished."

Illinois MUFON State Director Sam Maranto and Assistant State Director Roger Laurella closed this case as an Unknown Aerial Vehicle.

"I find it difficult to imagine that only three reports appear anywhere regarding this event in an area known for some of the best UAP mass sightings of all time," Maranto and Laurella wrote in their report. "To highlight some of the observations noted beyond the obvious display of two red, illuminated objects in the sky:

"Moved very slowly without noise, though depending on the location of the witness to the subject, there may not be any discernible sound. I do think the Mokena witnesses were closer to the object(s) and yet they heard nothing.

"The wind direction was north by northeast turning easterly by northeast. Wind speed during this time period was six mph, and yet it appeared at times they hovered.

"Sparks-like material dropped from trailing light in western sky, then light went out, then came back on for a while. Flickering or dimming down was said to have happened at least four times. This is characteristic of CSLs and flares. White object can also be like slag from a safety flare."

Tinley Park is a village located in Cook County, Illinois, population 56,703.

AUGUST 12

Multiple witnesses affected by hovering 'cruise ship' UFO

An Illinois witness at Godfrey reported watching a cigar-shaped UFO the "size of a cruise ship," according to testimony in Case 94081.

The witness was watching a meteor shower with seven other friends around 2:10 a.m. on August 12, 2018.

"After seeing several meteors, one friend pointed toward the northern sky and showed everyone what appeared to be two stars moving in synchronicity," the witness stated. "They stayed the same distance, and we then noticed they were connected by something, which appeared to be transparent, but made the sky look different. It seemed to be a cigar-shaped craft about as large as a cruise ship around the same height as a private airplane. It was heading southeast from the north. It turned slightly toward the tree line, dimmed its lights and hovered. Before we saw the craft, there was the sound of coyotes from approximately three different locations west, south and northwest of us. They increased in volume until we sighted the craft. At that point, every sound from the nearby forest ceased. At that point, I stood from a sitting position and requested everyone leave and head toward my father's home, which was approximately 300-500 yards from where we were sitting. Everyone resisted, saying they wanted to see where it was going. Five of the eight of us heard a sound sort of like a mechanical trumpet, or as one witness described it, 'an auto-tuned semi-truck horn.' It was coming from the east-southeast and echoed from the vicinity of Beltrees Road. Right around then, my cousin and I had an overwhelming feeling of calm and restraint, which felt unnatural. She reported feeling dizzy and I felt absolute panic and a heaviness associated with the silence of the woodland creatures. Another witness reported feeling unbridled rage followed by silent cry-

ing. A fourth witness said she had a feeling of missing time, and a fifth said he felt followed as he left the property until he reached the nearby town of Alton, Illinois, which is approximately 10 minutes away. All eight witnesses saw the craft. Six reported noticing the animal silence. Five heard the sounds. Four were emotionally affected. Two, including myself, felt contacted telepathically."

Illinois MUFON Field Investigator James Wolford closed this case as an Unknown Aerial Vehicle.

"I phoned local area police departments to see if a police report had been turned in by anyone," Wolford stated in his report. "Alton Police Department, Madison County Police, Illinois State Police: None of these organizations said that they had any reports from local residents for the sighting date and time or at any time on the following morning. Blimp schedules were sought out and I could only find that for the Goodyear Blimp. It was not in the area at the time. Either these lights are due to some problem with perception or they are associated with an unusual object. They are clearly not meteors and are difficult to attribute to air traffic. The silence of animals in the vicinity during the transit of the lights and the alleged psychological effects may indicate a powerful electromagnetic field that has been 'sensed.' Attempts to get contact information for the remaining seven witnesses have not been successful so far, but I will keep trying. Updates can be made after those witnesses have been interviewed. So far, I have sent one email and made two phone calls in pursuit of this."

Godfrey is a village in Madison County, Illinois, population 17,982.

Colorado witness describes 'orb-like' object following jet

A Colorado witness at Parker reported watching "a UFO orb-type object with reflective qualities," according to testimony in Case 94086.

The witness was on a flight home from Tucson, AZ, to Denver, CO, at 5:06 p.m. on August 12, 2018.

"I saw out of the window of the plane an orb-like object hovering beside the wing of the plane," the witness stated. "I first thought it was something on the window, but the UFO moved up and down in the same position. This made me curious about what this object really is. The object flew past the wing and I never saw it again."

Colorado MUFON Field Investigator Jeffrey Hastings closed this case as an Unknown Aerial Vehicle.

"The witness provided two photos and one video," Hastings stated in his report. "Photo #1 (Snapchat): I ran this photo through Fotoforensics. The ELA showed where the circle had been drawn by the witness, the JPEG quality was 95 percent. There were no hidden pixels but there were no 'dates' associated with the photos. I've not reviewed Snapchat photos in which someone has circled a portion of the image, so I'm not really sure what I should see. However, there was no reference to the use of additional photo editing software being used.

"Photo #2: I ran this photo through Fotoforensics. The ELA did not highlight any anomalies, the JPEG quality was 96 percent. There were no hidden pixels and all of the dates matched. There was no reference to any photo editing software being used.

"Video: Only reviewed it two dozen times. I simply don't have the tools necessary to determine if a video has been altered. However, since the photos did not appear altered, I will place the video in the same category. I found the video to be very interesting. The witness felt the object was small; however, I disagree. I believe the object to be as large as an aircraft and much farther away than what the witness believed.

"During the first part of the video, I saw what

at first I thought to be contrails; however, the color was darker instead of lighter, which is what I would be expect when a condensation trail is created. After a few more viewings, I became convinced that what I was seeing were not contrails, but a disturbance in the top boundary layer of the cloud below.

"The video moved around, and the focus came and went. This actually helped. When the focus went from outside to the window, that allowed me to determine that what was being videoed was not something as simple as something on the window. When the witness zoomed in, you can see lighter colors on the top and bottom. These are either wings from a standard man-made aircraft or an energy source emanating from both above and below the craft."

Parker is a home rule municipality in Douglas County, Colorado, population 45,297.

New Mexico UFO described as donut-shaped

A New Mexico witness at Los Lunas reported watching a "giant, metal, donut-shaped" object moving overhead, according to testimony in Case 94105.

The witness was in the backyard facing south on August 12, 2018.

"A shiny, donut-shaped object appeared from the tree line," the witness stated. "I have never seen anything like it before. I was a little scared at first. It seemed to flip and spin at random. Gained altitude, then passed almost overhead. Its motions smoothed out as it headed north. Sometimes it appeared shiny, and reflected the sunlight, other times it appeared black or dark. It moved north from south of my house until it disappeared into clouds north over Albuquerque. I would guess it covered about 20 miles in two minutes, until we lost sight. My 10-year-old daughter also witnessed the object."

New Mexico MUFON Assistant State Director John Fegel closed this case as an Unknown-Other.

"Some inconsistencies, object not described as high-altitude but said sometimes to reflect sunlight at midnight."

Los Lunas is a village in Valencia County, New Mexico, population 14,835.

South Carolina witness: UFO twice moved to ground level

A South Carolina witness at Ridgeville reported watching an "egg-shaped object" that moved quickly to ground level twice before shooting away, according to testimony in Case 97164.

The witness and friends were returning home at 12:15 a.m. on August 12, 2018.

"I noticed (what I believe is a military, stationary drone that flashes all kinds of colors) a stationary object that I've noticed for the past few months. But it was really active and bright and flashing very fast and with different colors. So, I stopped and at this time I was in my brother's yard—he lives a few hundred yards from me. When I stopped, I could feel a presence and noticed something just above the illuminated yard from the yard light. It was making quick and short lines and turns and then it came down into the illuminated yard. And about three feet from hitting the ground, it slowed just enough for me to get a permanent illustration in my head of the shape and the same feel and visualization as a live object with a clear outline of it before shooting straight back up. And once above the illuminated yard it disappeared. I asked my friend, who was in the passenger seat, 'did you see that?' He said, 'see what?' and I said nothing. So, after a few seconds of gathering control of myself, we proceeded to my house and when we got out and started walking towards my house, it came down again. And so quickly we both ducked at the same time, because we thought

we were going to be hit by it. But it changed direction and shot straight back up into the sky. This thing was about five to six feet long and two to three feet wide and had a dull, white glow and made no sounds and had no visual propulsion. And the second time, it came down between a palm tree and an oak tree that are nearly touching. I do not believe anyone can maneuver something that fast in such a tight area by remote control, and it wasn't big enough for a man to be in it. I ran inside my house and told my wife what I saw and the next day I told my sister and her boyfriend. And described it as an egg or teardrop shape and I googled UFO on the Internet. And that's when we saw the Navy jet encounter with the UFO and that's exactly what it looks like."

South Carolina MUFON Field Investigator Steven Schumpert and State Director Cheryl Ann Gilmore closed this case as an Unknown-Other.

"This was a unique case from the standpoint of the reporting witness's vantage point, and the fact that he discusses two separate events," Schumpert and Gilmore wrote in their report. "Initially, he mentions what he describes as a 'stationary drone,' which has colored lights, near his residence. This investigator noted the parameters and specifics of military drones when researching this case. Second, the witness goes on to describe an 'egg-shaped' object that gave off no visible propulsion and made no noise. The witness did not believe the object to be a drone, but could not be certain. From the description of the object's movements, they seemed consistent with a possible civilian drone. This cannot be verified due to being unable to verbally speak with this witness. The area in which the witness lives is near several military installations, including Charleston Air Force Base, Marine Corps Air Station Beaufort, and a Coast Guard station. In addition, there are several civilian airports within a 10-mile radius. The area immediately surrounding the residence is wooded, with a few scattered homes and a high-tension powerline. These circumstances led to the conclusion of Unknown-Other."

Ridgeville is a town in Dorchester County, South Carolina, population 1,979.

AUGUST 14

Norwegian witness encounters gray humanoid creature

A Norwegian witness at Elverum reported watching a gray, humanoid creature, according to testimony in Case 94117.

The witness was standing near a window and looking into the woods below at 1:07 a.m. on August 14, 2018.

"And there it was standing," the witness stated. "A tall, humanoid creature, with long legs and arms, and a color of gray. The creature was making noise and I immediately went to the window. It was walking, or stalking me. It stared at me for some time, and after approximately 30 seconds, I was feeling a weirdness in my head, almost as if it was trying to get in my head. After 10 minutes, it went into the woods and disappeared. I hope my description is good enough. My English is a bit bad, 'cause my language is originally Norwegian."

Norway MUFON CAG Investigator Sue Gerberding closed this case as Info Only.

"This case involves an entity only," Gerberding stated in her report. "As described by the witness in CMS, the entity appears to be similar to the group of entities commonly known as Greys. Therefore, this case, a close encounter by the witness of the Third Kind, is being closed as Info Only."

Elverum is a city and municipality in Hedmark County, Norway.

AUGUST 15

Missile-shaped object reported over Florida building

A Florida witness at Pensacola reported watching a missile-shaped object moving slowly at the rooftop level, according to testimony in Case 94170.

The witness was driving home from work through downtown Pensacola on at 3:45 p.m. on August 15, 2018.

"I stopped for a traffic light and something off to my left caught my eye," the witness stated. "I turned my attention towards the movement and witnessed what appeared to be an 18- to 24-inch long, silver dart-shaped object moving slowly just above the rooftop of a building. I know it was just above the roof because the object was between me and the taller building behind it. As I watched, it slowly began to accelerate while gradually gaining altitude. It looked more like a rocket from an old science fiction movie than an airplane but there was no exhaust or propellers that were visible. If it had wings, they were very stubby. I really can't say that I saw any wings. The object continued to gain altitude and accelerate off towards the north, but suddenly made a left 180-degree turn and headed south (back towards me) at a slower pace. The traffic light changed, and I had to move, but I glanced up at it twice more as I crossed the intersection, and it appeared to have slowed or perhaps to have come to a stop about 500 feet up in the air. This was not a drone. Well, not any kind of drone I have ever seen, and I do a lot of research on a lot of things and I have never seen anything this small with these characteristics."

Florida MUFON Field Investigator David Toon closed this case as an Unknown Aerial Vehicle.

"After a telephone interview, a better understanding of the object was realized in that it was a solid, seamless, chrome-looking tube with stubby rounded ends no more than three to four inches in diameter, and about two feet long," Toon stated in his report. "It had no structural appendages or characteristics other than a rod or thick tube. It lifted from the building top next to the left side of the witness and began a steady, slow climb perpendicular to the road at about 25-degree elevation and increased its altitude on a 20-degree slope from the building top. It continued to climb as it crossed the street from left to right at about 20 mph and after 100 feet past the street heading east, it made a slow 180-degree turn to the right and flew back 50 feet, stopped and hovered at approximately 500 feet above the ground, just barely still visible. The street light turned green and the witness drove beyond the object as it remained hovering, and then drove out of sight of the object. The witness is an RC enthusiast and is extremely familiar with RC drones/quadcopters. His education level and experience helped him determine this object was not executing anything comparable to normal flight and had no identifiable aircraft features. He researched the shape and size on the Internet and found nothing like it except for reported 'rods.'"

Pensacola is the county seat of Escambia County, Florida, population 51,923.

New York house lights dim as UFOs hover outside

A New York witness at Staten Island reported the house lights dimmed, an electrical explosion or buzzing sound was heard, and two, black, disc-shaped objects were seen hovering nearby, according to testimony in Case 94184.

The witness was sitting in his living room at 10:30 p.m. on August 15, 2018.

"My daughter was in her room right next to me," the witness stated. "My brother lives in the apartment upstairs from me. We own the house and property. My daughter's boyfriend was sitting outside in the car with one of his friends. I was watching TV with the lights on, when out of nowhere the lights dimmed to

almost turning off. They stayed that way for about two seconds and then came back up. The TV picture only flickered. Right after the lights came up, this loud sound was heard outside. It sounded like an electrical transformer started buzzing, but extremely loud. My daughter came into my room and asked if I heard that. I told her, yeah, I think it was outside. With that my brother and his daughter and son came out into the hall and confirmed that his lights did the same thing and heard the same noise. My daughter's boyfriend came in the house and asked if we all heard it. He said he was sitting in the car and was looking behind my house and looked up in the sky and saw a black object just sitting there. He said out loud, what the hell is that?, and his friend said, you see it, too? He said, yeah, only his friend was looking in the other direction. So, there were two. He said it was huge, bigger than a plane and round. He said as he was looking at it he heard the loud buzzing. He said it sounded like a power surge. When he heard it, the object lit up around it in a bright light and they both took off and nothing after that. Neighbors came out of their houses also."

New York MUFON Field Investigator Jonathan Schwartz closed this case as an Unknown-Other.

"The object described by the witness's daughter's boyfriend does not seem to fit anything conventional," Schwartz stated in his report. "The sound of an explosion that he described that was coming from it was corroborated by the witness who filed the report."

Staten Island is one of the five boroughs of New York City, population 479,458.

AUGUST 16

Triangular UFO reported hovering over Washington town

A Washington witness at Gig Harbor reported watching "three red lights configured in a triangle hovering above the neighborhood," according to testimony in Case 95179.

The witness was driving from his home to a neighborhood convenience store on August 16, 2018.

"The store is located on top of a hill, my house on the bottom of the hill," the witness stated. "Going down the hill headed north I noticed three red lights forming an isosceles triangle (no light being reflected in between the lights, it was nighttime, clear weather but a dark night). The lights were hovering above my neighborhood, seemingly stationed in between my house and the neighbor's. As I approached down the hill, I thought the lights were drones so I turned off my car's radio and stuck my head out the window, but no unusual sounds were noticed. I parked my car and stood at the driveway observing the lights, trying to rationalize or legitimize what I was seeing. Upon closer examination on the light's charac- teristics while I was in the driveway, I noticed that they did not resemble any electronic light I am familiar with. They seemed to move like a stationary flame, but while maintaining a color of red darker than fire, and it moved more slowly while in place than fire as well. I walked into the backyard of my home, and the lights were in the same place they were in the drive- way. (The lights seemed unaffected by the low wind.) Upon further examination of the lights from my backyard, they seemed to move slow- ly to the southwest, but I noticed that while the spaces in between the lights were the same black as that night (nothing in between them), I noticed that the flame-like light of the light closest to me (being closer to it in the back- yard) reflected a slight silvery surface directly behind it from my perspective. The lights then moved in the same direction past some trees and out of my view. I ran inside to a fellow oc- cupant of the house, saying something starting with, 'I know how this is going to sound.' The occupant declined coming to the front yard to look at the lights. I was in the house for about 30 seconds when I came out of the house in

the front yard and the lights were gone. The thoughts that went through my head were, 'holy **** don't take a picture.' That was a weird recurring thought that I had the whole time. In hindsight, I really should have taken one. The lights stayed in the same triangular shape the whole time. I first noticed the lights a half-mile away. I watched the lights from my house as they appeared very close, 30–40 feet away. The triangle was large. I'm not sure of distance between lights. It emitted no sound. I felt no change in anything standing under them. After, I thought they were flying lanterns like you see people make in places like Japan, but the whole experience has stayed with me, enough that I wanted to see if I could research the strange lights. The only information I can come up with research is UFO phenomena."

Washington MUFON Zach Royer closed this case as an Unknown Aerial Vehicle.

"This case seems to fit into the Unknown UAV category for the following reasons," Royer stated in his report. "The witness indicated the object had moved out of view after appearing to hover directly above him for four min- utes, indicating some sort of flying craft and movement under intelligent control. The object gave off no noise and the lights observed were noticeably different than any usual aircraft lighting, a red glow. The witness indicated he stood for a short period of time trying to figure out what it could have been, indicating some- thing unusual, which is usually a first indicator. The witness claims to have been so intrigued by the sighting that he went into his home to tell another person, who did not seem interest- ed. When the witness came back outside, the object was gone.

"Historical weather data would indicate a clear night with 0% chance of precipitation."

Gig Harbor is the name of both a bay on Puget Sound and a city on its shore in Pierce County, Washington, population 7,126.

AUGUST 17

Key West witness describes 'darting balls of light'

A Florida witness at Key West reported "two balls of light darting in and out of the water," according to testimony in Case 97678.

The witness was on the balcony of a cruise ship cabin at 1:30 a.m. on August 17, 2018.

"Noticed a helicopter, then birds," the witness stated. "We then saw these white balls of light zigzagging in sky, sometimes together in unison, other times separately in different directions. They went straight from sky into water and would just reappear back in sky even though we watched for them to come out. At one point they came together less than 100 feet in front of us, together side-by-side, still not moving, facing us. We felt they were looking at us. Then together they started slowly moving in straight line toward us. They came so close, we ran into the cabin, pulled the curtain and turned the lights out. We later found the courage to peep out of the sliding glass door but saw nothing. It was so scary. We were the only people we could see who were on the balcony because it was so late. We thought they would take us, and no one would know what had happened to us, or would have thought we fell overboard as we were on floor seven, I think. I later looked into how many people went missing on cruise ships and found it has happened many times."

Florida MUFON Field Investigator David Toon closed this case as an Unknown-Other.

"This witness corroborates another MUFON case, # 97233, from another cruise ship passenger relating the same sighting," Toon stated in his report. "To date, no report is visible on the Internet apart from the two witnesses to this case, who were on the same cruise ship. The witness provided a near mirror report of details of this encounter, also found in case #97233 as described in the 'Witness-es' Original CMS report statement' above. The best-detailed description of the objects was simply noiseless orbs; however, due to their persistent observation, the orbs did get close enough for the witness to offer a size of five feet in diameter. By giving elevation, size and impossible maneuvering characteristics both in the air and the water, there is enough information conveyed to confidently conclude this investigation."

Key West is an island and city in the Straits of Florida, population 25,478.

Second witness files Florida orb case

A Florida witness at Key West reported two white orbs flying in formation that descended into and ascended out of water, according to testimony in Case 97233. A second report is in Case 97678.

The witness and a friend were on a cruise heading back to Florida from the Bahamas on August 17, 2018.

"Late on the last night of the trip we stood on our balcony for a long time looking out at the sea and talking," the witness stated. "The balcony faced north as the ship was traveling west. We passed by an island, we saw other cruise ships, a plane, a helicopter, birds, and stars. We were the only people on a balcony at that hour. Our whole side of the ship was dark except for our room. We suddenly noticed two white balls of light (orbs) flying toward the ship from the distance. At first, they were flying in perfect formation in a straight line. We thought the appearance of the two objects—spheres of white light with no wings and no sound - was unusual. How could they be flying? We commented on how perfect the formation was, and we wondered what could fly like that. The two orbs were coming closer to the ship, and they started flying separately in random directions and at impossible angles. We kept asking ourselves, 'What were they?' Because we had already seen other objects, we knew they were not planes, not birds, not helicopters, and not anything else we could imagine. We both do not drink or anything so that was not an issue. Then we saw the orbs enter the water easily. They went from flying in the air to directly entering the sea with no slowing down. We couldn't believe what we were seeing. After a few minutes submerged, the two orbs came up almost vertically out of the sea. They flew closer to the ship and up to about 45 degrees high and about 200 feet away. I'm estimating they were each about five feet in diameter. They both came to a complete stop and hovered there. Our eyes were locked on them. We were captivated and had a long look at them. Then they suddenly moved directly toward us, fast, as if they had seen us. We each recognized this as an act of intelligence, that we had been seen and that the orbs now knew they were being watched, so we ran screaming and terrified into the room and hid behind the couch. We both had this fight or flight response at the same time. We spent the rest of the night processing this event. I haven't been able to forget this experience so I thought documenting it with MUFON would help. FYI, I am an engineer with a PhD. I have wondered if these orbs were balls of plasma under remote control by the military, but then I cannot imagine how they would be able to see us and scare us like they did (no apparent camera). I have also not been able to reconcile the objects entering and leaving the water at full speed and at sharp angles and traveling in random directions without wings and without noise. There are just too many unbelievable facts for me to understand. I wish I'd had the initiative to take a photo."

Florida MUFON Field Investigator David Toon closed this case as an Unknown-Other.

"Given the unknown location of the ship at the time of the sighting, corroboration would need to come from an aircraft pilot report if flying in the same area, at the same time or from other ship passengers," Toon wrote in his report. "To date, no report is visible on the Internet. The witness is a highly educated professional working at the university level and offered enough detail in the report to follow the events smoothly through the encounter. As a commercial rated pilot myself, I know the current aircraft capability to transition from air to water back to air does not exist. The best-detailed description of the objects was simply noiseless orbs; however, due to their persistent observation, the orbs did get close enough for the witness to offer a size of five feet in diameter. By giving elevation, size and impossible maneuvering characteristics both in the air and the water, there is enough information conveyed to confidently conclude this investigation."

Key West is an island and city in the Straits of Florida, population 25,478.

Indiana witness reports low-flying triangle

An Indiana witness at Portage reported watching "two bright lights that were connected to a triangle shape," according to testimony in Case 94217.

The witness was driving eastbound along Route 20 towards Chesterton at 10:30 p.m. on August 17, 2018.

"I noticed the object was far too low to be a plane and too big to be a drone," the witness stated. "I thought it was a plane first until I got closer. The object was a bright, white light with a triangle body. It hovered for about two minutes above a local park, then effortlessly glided west to the next town of Lake Station. I was feeling very nervous and curious along with my girlfriend and mother. I started to drive slowly to keep an eye on it and see what it did. Then it started moving slowly and then vanished. Never saw anything like that."

Indiana MUFON State Director Jeremy Efroymson closed this case as an Unknown Aerial

Vehicle.

"Witness clearly stated he saw a triangular craft with lights hovering over a park," Efroymson stated in his report. "Craft was at 100 feet above the tree line, hovering over a local park. Witness described object as a triangle, about 40 feet from front to back and 20-30 feet across. Witness's interview was consistent with his initial statement."

Portage is a city in Portage Township, Porter County, Indiana, population 36,828.

AUGUST 18

New Jersey witness sees saucer-like UFO near skyscraper

A New Jersey witness at Jersey City reported a black, saucer-shaped object flying around a large skyscraper, according to testimony in Case 94231.

The witness was standing near a busy train station in Jersey City at 5:15 p.m. on August 18, 2018.

"I noticed what appeared to be a black, saucer-shaped disc flying slowly around the Goldman Sachs building on the Hudson River," the witness stated. "At first, the two people I was with saw the object also. They believed it was just a drone. I decided to walk a little closer to observe the object more, and left my friends behind. The plaza I was standing in was packed with people. It's a Saturday afternoon and we are standing across the river from the World Trade Center. Lots of helicopters and commercial aircraft flying into nearby Newark Airport. A storm was also blowing in at the time with dark clouds and gusty winds. Anyway, after some time, I watched the object slowly ascend up into the clouds and disappear. Please note that this object was flying around a large area. I observed it fly over the Hudson and back over Jersey City. It just appeared to be too high in the sky to be a drone,

but also, it wasn't affected by the wind either."

New Jersey MUFON Assistant State Director Ken Pfeifer closed this case as an Unknown Aerial Vehicle.

"The area is within the flight path of Newark Airport," Pfeifer stated in his report. "After a 30-minute conversation with the witness, I will classify this one as an Unknown. Witness was in the military and is very credible with attention to details. No drone or helicopter. No noise."

Jersey City is the seat of Hudson County, New Jersey, population 270,753.

Multiple cylindrical UFOs spotted over Texas

A Texas witness at Flint reported a "highly reflective" cylinder-shaped object flying at high speed and followed by two other objects, according to testimony in Case 94292.

The witness and his wife were outside at a swimming pool with a clear sky and no clouds at 6:35 p.m. on August 18, 2018.

"I noticed a bright, cylindrical object directly overhead at a very high altitude," the witness stated. "Which is normal for commercial flights in our area, which we see occasionally. However, this object had no wings and was travelling at a high rate of speed. My wife and I watched the object as it passed and moved away. The sun was lower on the horizon and was reflecting extremely brightly off the side of the object. As we watched the object move away, we saw it change from a smooth, cylindrical shape to look more like four interconnected spheres appearing like a caterpillar or pearl necklace. The object disappeared from sight moments later. Scanning the sky, we saw one and then another object of similar shape, but smaller, travelling in the same direction, at a similar speed and altitude as the first object. At that point I started thinking something really strange was happening.

"We observed the two smaller objects until they appeared like bright stars seen during daylight, then they faded from view.

"Moments later we saw two aircraft at what appeared to be the same altitude flying in the same direction as the objects. The aircraft were travelling much slower than we would expect from the normal flights we see. The aircraft were unusual. One was a large, four-engine, all white bomber-looking type aircraft. The other was orange or red and looked more like a commercial aircraft-type plane. As they passed overhead they followed the same flight path as the objects, as if they were in pursuit. They had no chance of catching them.

"I stayed watching the sky for a time (15 to 20 minutes) when I suddenly saw the two aircraft return. They performed a circle and then split up. One on the same flight path as the objects, the other on a more westerly heading. This action in and of itself is very unusual for our skies as we've never seen aircraft of that type turn around. I had my phone camera ready, but only managed to get a telephoto shot of the white bomber-looking plane.

"My wife and I are convinced we saw something very unusual. The objects we saw were not normal aircraft and most certainly did not have any wings. I actually felt a sense of fear when I saw the objects. I checked the local news for any reports but found nothing. The entire incident happened fairly quickly.

"The incident was such that I feel compelled to share my experience here in the hope that perhaps someone else might do the same to corroborate our sighting."

Texas MUFON State Director Gary A. Neitzel closed this case as an Unknown Aerial Vehicle.

"The witness provided a fairly detailed description of what he saw," Neitzel wrote in his report. "This may have been some unknown

military testing unknown aircraft; however, since this is not known for sure, the case is completed as an Unknown UAV. Balloons are ruled out since the craft was traveling faster than normal aircraft the witness could observe. The object had no wings but was interconnected by four spheres."

Flint is the county seat of Smith County, Texas.

Malta witness describes 'huge' UFO with dome

A Malta witness at Cospicua reported watching "a huge, oval-shaped object with central dome hiding above clouds," according to testimony in Case 96784.

The incident occurred at 9:40 p.m. on August 18, 2018.

"Huge oval-shaped object with central spherical dome hiding above clouds at east-northeast caught my eye from rooftop," the witness stated. "Observed for around seven minutes at 30-degrees elevation, around three kms away from witness and at around 300 meters above ground. Estimated size of oval is about 250 meters in length and around 150 meters in width. Central spherical dome with a diameter of around 30 meters. Object's thickness from dome to tip was tapered, starting from around 10 meters to a slim edge. It made a whitish glow on the clouds beneath it, which reflected its shape. Then the glow went off and the object disappeared. Three bright point sources followed later on in the night sky the same night in a south to north direction."

MUFON International CAG Investigator Steve Hudgeons closed this case as an Unknown-Other.

Cospicua is a harbor city in the southeastern region of Malta, population 5,395.

AUGUST 19

Missouri UFO described as cloaking itself

A Missouri witness at El Dorado Springs reported watching a saucer-shaped object "as blue as sky background" that crossed the sky just before a storm, according to testimony in Case 94262.

The sighting occurred at 8 p.m. on August 19, 2018.

"I saw the strange object while driving home from in-law's house after a wall of torna-do-producing storms passed through our town," the witness stated. "Earlier, the tornado sirens and phone's emergency system had alerted me that we were under a tornado warning. My fear of storms is compounded when I'm alone (husband at work), so my dog and I went to their place for shelter. A tornado popped up south of us, but we were fine. About 30-45 minutes after the storm had passed and the clouds were moving out, we headed home. On our short drive back, around 7:50 to 8 p.m. as the sun was about ready to wear out its welcome for the day, I spotted movement in the sky. It was a saucer-shaped object as though seen from the side, where the middle appeared fatter than either edge. It floated steadily high in the sky, moving approximately northeast, as though trailing after the tail of the storms. It was difficult to gauge the distance, due to there being little near it to use for scale or knowing how big the object was. I didn't hear anything, like the distinct rumble of a helicopter or the engines of a plane, though my windows were up. Generally, if it were either machine, the distance would have been close enough to warrant some sound or vibration, regardless of window placement. It moved too slow and steady for it to be a plane. The color was the first thing that really struck me as strange, though. It was distinctly an object in the sky, but the color was as though it were reflecting or absorbing and mimicking the color of the sky around it. It was like an invisibility cloak, but with a clear border that indicates the presence of an object. Then the whole thing shone white. It was a quick gloss-over of the object, like it reflected the sunlight before disappearing behind something else, but there was nothing between it and the sun the whole time. Then it shone white again, and then back to its cloaked state. I thought it had to be something like a helicopter. The hospital in town gets them all the time, taking patients to a larger, better equipped facility outside of town. It flew in the air like a helicopter, steadily and smoothly. But there was no sound, no vibration, and I saw no blades. The shape was clearly like a classic UFO saucer (seen from the side). There were no lights or any other distinctive patterns or writing on it. I thought about pulling over to observe it better and to keep from being distracted while driving, but I thought, 'Don't be silly.' I approached the stoplight and slowed down, hoping it would turn red so I could watch it some more. It did! I thought, 'Could it be a balloon? A storm just rolled through, so maybe it let one loose somewhere?' It was just too odd how it reflected the color of the sky and did the weird illumination at seemingly random intervals. It wasn't a reflection of something in or near the car, because as I sat still, it still moved. I was curious and interested. But when the light turned green, I turned and kept moving. Once I got home, I stood outside and searched the sky in the place where I had seen it, but it was gone by then. I felt nothing differently, just piqued my natural curiosity, and the anoma-lous qualities of the object drew me to it. Had I not been already scanning the skies (as I do post-storms, looking for any more ominous clouds or admiring the scene of a stirred atmo-sphere), it would have blended in really well and escaped my attention. I looked up pictures of weather balloons, just in case, and what I saw on a cursory Google search was definitely not what I witnessed. I searched for helicop-ters in sky and the pictures confirmed my conviction that it was not a helicopter. I have no clue what it was, and it makes my insides ache to know that I'll probably never know what this thing was."

Missouri MUFON Field Investigator Britt Faaborg closed this case as an Unknown Aerial Vehicle.

"Witness is very credible and recalls detailed information about sighting," Faaborg stated in the case report. "This report seems to correspond with other reports of UFOs after severe storms have been experienced. The craft matching the color of the sky behind it may point to a cloaking device of some kind. The storms could have disrupted this cloaking or shielding technology."

El Dorado Springs is the largest city in Cedar County, Missouri, population 3,593.

British witness reports silent black triangle

A British witness at Port Talbot reported watching a silent, black triangular UFO moving overhead, according to testimony in Case 98200.

The witness and a friend were sitting in a garden on August 19, 2018.

"We noticed what we thought was a plane," the witness stated, "with a light on each point heading directly towards us at approximately 200-300 feet, but as it got directly above us, we could clearly see this was not a plane or drone. It looked similar to a B-2 stealth bomber but more triangular in shape, flying in a reverse position and flying extremely slowly and dead silent. This took place at 10 p.m. and the camera on my phone hasn't picked anything up. Another local had seen it a couple miles away from me, and he said he thought it was a drone when he first saw it, but when it got closer, he said it was too big and looked like nothing he had ever seen. There must be more witnesses, he said, as

he was stuck in traffic when he noticed it and others stuck in the traffic must have witnessed it. He last saw it heading east over the Bristol Channel."

British MUFON National Director Jack Turnbull closed this case as Info Only.

Port Talbot is a town in the county borough of Neath Port Talbot, Wales, population 37,276.

AUGUST 21

Wisconsin witness reports hovering shape-changing UFO

A Wisconsin witness at Farmington reported watching a "reflective silver" object that seemed to change shape, according to testimony in Case 94322.

The witness was driving northbound along Highway D about two miles south of Highway B just west of Farmington in Jefferson County at 2:30 p.m. on August 21, 2018.

"I observed what at first I thought was a drone," the witness stated. "It at first appeared to be hovering, but as it became closer it seemed to be traversing in a north to southwest general direction. As it became closer it appeared to be a solid, reflective object, trapezoidal in shape with no indication of propellers or any drone features. The sun was to my rear left, so the object was very bright from reflection. The object slightly changed to a more of direct southerly path, and as it changed direction, the shape seemed to change, but still trapezoidal. It passed overhead and I tried to locate it in my rear-view mirror. Unable to see it, I pulled over immediately and tracked it traveling in a southern trajectory. There was no sound from it. And it did not appear shiny anymore, as it was now in between the sun and myself. I observed it until it was out of my sight, and from start to finish the entire event was barely 10 to 15 seconds. On my return travels following the same route, I measured the distance from where I first saw it to the point it was out of sight to be approximately one-quarter to one-third mile. The object was higher than the power lines, but underneath the cloud cover on a partly cloudy day. I stopped to take a picture of the clouds to try to reference the cloud height."

Wisconsin MUFON State Director Zelia Edgar and Field Investigator Susan Birttnen closed this case as an Unknown Aerial Vehicle.

"At 2:30 in the afternoon of August 21, 2018, a man was driving to one of his jobs," Edgar and Birttnen stated in their report. "He was traveling on Highway D headed north onto Highway B near Farmington when he saw an object that appeared to be a drone. Upon closer inspection, it was not a drone but a reflective, solid, trapezoidal object that hovered before moving in a southwesterly direction. The object moved in a jumpy motion and appeared to change shape when it made a directional change to the south. The witness got out of his car and watched as it moved farther and farther south, no longer shiny and reflective, but a dull, black color. The whole length of the sighting was between 10 to 15 seconds. A dump truck was suddenly on the road, so he got back in his car and drove off. When he made the return trip an hour or two later, he took a picture of the clouds for reference and measured the distance the object traversed to be about a quarter-mile. He later made a sketch of the object.

"After contacting MUFON, the witness experienced computer issues. During the interview he hesitated when asked about missing time or abnormal occurrences. Because of the detailed description of the sighting, as well as the witness sketch, it is my conclusion that the witness did observe an unidentified aerial object."

Farmington is a town in Jefferson County, Wisconsin, population 1,380.

Nevada witness describes entity as 'wings and no face'

A Nevada witness at Pahrump reported swerving around a "human-like entity with wings and no face" that landed in the travel lane ahead, according to testimony in Case 97499.

The witness was northbound along Highway 160 between mile markers 134 and 135 at 4:10 a.m. on August 27, 2018.

"I saw this thing land in front of my car in the street in my travel lane," the witness stated. "I didn't know what it was when I saw it and I still don't. I don't know how to feel about it. I have no answers. It was about 4:10 a.m. It was a clear sky. No wind. No clouds. I was a little behind my schedule, so I was going fast—85 mph. I did have my bright lights on. This event lasted about four or five seconds. I had just finished a small snack. I was listening to some music and then suddenly this thing came from up high and landed in my travel lane on the street. Very tall, seven feet or more, very large wings, smoke gray in color. I couldn't see any eyes. No face. As it was landing the wings were out to each side of it. Once it was on the ground, it wrapped its wings around itself as if it was bracing for an impact. The wings were wrapped around its front. It put its head down slightly and just stood there. It would not move as I approached it. The only thing I could think is, what is that? I cannot crash my car. I cannot hit this thing. It will destroy my car and put me in the hospital. So I said no and turned my wheel slightly to the left. I did this four times as I took my foot off the accelerator to slow my speed as I passed the thing. I did look in my rearview mirror, but it was too dark to see anything. I didn't stop because I didn't know what it was, and I didn't want it to come after me. I just kept saying out loud, what was that, what was that, what was that? Over and over. Where did it come from? What is it? Its body was like a human. Its wings and arms were one unit. There was a car in front by about a half-mile and behind me by about a half-mile. I don't know if anyone else saw it or not. I would like to know if anyone else has seen it. I look for it every day and wonder where it came from."

Nevada MUFON State Director Sue Countiss and CAG Investigator Dinah Lechner closed this case as Info Only.

"Witness was cooperative in reliving the event," Countiss and Lechner wrote in their report. "The witness was unable to understand the sighting and filled out a MUFON report in hopes of finding some answers. The witness was ex-army, plus presently works in law enforcement outside of Las Vegas. Witness makes the drive daily to work on Highway 160, turning onto I-95. Attached to CMS is location sketch plus on-site photos taken by Nevada SD, who feels witness is credible and has no interest in fame or fortune. This is an entity case and may relate to CMS case 94461."

Pahrump is an unincorporated town in Nye County, Nevada, population 36,441.

Military helicopter appears 'escorting' three orb UFOs

A Washington witness at Eatonville reported watching two Chinook helicopters apparently "escorting" three orange orbs in a tight formation, according to testimony in Case 94482.

The event occurred at 11:05 p.m. on August 27, 2018.

"I heard two helicopters flying over Eatonville and it sounded very low," the witness stated. "But this sounded really loud and it shook the house. I ran outside and saw two Chinook helicopters in a staggered formation with an orange orb flying side-by-side with the first helicopter. The second helicopter

was very close behind and it had the second orb between the first and second helicopter. The third orb was flying next to the second helicopter. They were all flying in a tight formation. As they flew over me, I could see the helicopter navigation strobe light flash and that's when I saw the shape of the helicopter and I knew I was looking at a Chinook helicopter. I could see the blades rotating. The orbs looked reddish-orange in color and were a solid color. They flew over me and I watched them heading west until they disappeared. It looked as if the helicopters were escorting the orbs."

Washington MUFON State Section Director Allen Thompson closed this case as an Unknown-Other.

"This Field Investigator finds the report very detailed as to the altitude of the sighting, between 400 and 500 feet, and the identification of the flying aircraft," Thompson stated in his report. "Due to the time of night there were not identifying marks visible on the helicopters other than the nav lights. The close proximity of the orbs to the helicopters never changed, giving the witness the impression that they were flying in formation. Who was leading? The witness has made one other MUFON report and is an avid observer of things flying around his house, particularly when they are close enough to shake the ground. The witness has other corroborating individuals, as the Facebook posting called 'Eatonville Heads Up' had two other posts reporting the same configuration of flying objects at the same time. His discussion with one of the reporters revealed that they had seen the same formation flying in the same direction. Further research shows that there were no other activities associated with JBLM (Joint Base Lewis-McChord) as the most recent 'Rainier War' exercise was conducted in June of this year. Due to the unidentifiable nature of the orbs in this instance the conclusion of this FI is the sighting was Other."

Eatonville is a town in Pierce County, Washington, population 2,758.

Las Vegas the county seat of Clark County, Nevada, population 648,224.

AUGUST 28

Nevada witness describes 'giant moth' moving nearby

A Nevada witness at Las Vegas reported watching a "giant moth" moving at a constant speed under 50 feet, according to testimony in Case 94461.

The witness was in a front yard at 4:15 a.m. on August 28, 2018.

"Directly across the street I saw a dark, triangular object illuminated by moonlight and streetlight gliding in the air just behind and as high as the streetlight, which would be about 30–40 feet high," the witness stated. "It was shaped like a giant moth. It was about three feet in diameter. It maintained a constant speed of about 20 mph. I could see the silhouette of it silently gliding in a straight path heading southwest for about 1,000 yards before losing sight of it, and it did not flap any wings. I have searched the Internet for night-flying insects or birds that may have fit the description of this thing, but there are none that size. It was a spooky thing to witness."

Nevada MUFON State Director Sue Countiss closed this case as an Unknown-Other.

"Witness was outside at night when he saw the features of this odd creation," Countiss stated in her report. "Unknown whether it is machine or alive. He tended towards it being alive. Talked extensively with witness about this and a previously closed case. He was very startled and thought this was a living creature. He did not think about it being either an owl or large hawk. He said it was not a drone, either."

AUGUST 29

Witness says UFO hovered near naval base

A California witness at Jamul reported watching "a craft twice the size of an aircraft carrier" approach and hover near an air base for 18 minutes, according to testimony in Case 97227.

The event occurred at 8:15 p.m. on August 29, 2018.

"We live on a large, 250-acre ranch 25 miles from the harbor in San Diego at an altitude of 3,000 feet," the witness stated. "We have a large concrete observation deck where we can see Mexico, part of the San Diego Harbor, Point Loma and up to Oceanside. On August 29th, 2018, my son and I were at the lookout point at around 8:15 p.m. and saw this huge UFO come across the Mexican border and stop near the navy base in San Diego, about 600 feet above the land surface, and it stayed there for about 18 minutes gathering information of some kind. During the UFO stop (18-minute stay) an F-18 Navy jet was dispatched to intercept the UFO, but as the jet approached, a small UFO fighter came out of the UFO mothership and stopped between the mothership and the F-18, and when the F-18 pilot saw the UFO fighter, the F-18 pilot turned 180 degrees and returned to the Coronado Navy Base. There are many YouTube videos of the August 29th sighting in both Rosarito, Mexico, and San Diego. Just type in Google: 'Lights over San Diego and Rosarito August 29th, 2018.' After the UFO turned off its lights and went north, the admiral at the navy base in San Diego ordered a helicopter to drop flares where the UFO was and ordered the navy press office to state that the incident was a never-before-conducted navy training event. This was a complete and total misrepresentation of the facts. Just look at the videos and you can clearly see the navy is lying to cover up the fact that UFOs have been visiting our world since the beginning of time. This is the third UFO I have seen at my ranch and was by far the largest."

California MUFON Field Investigator William Crowley closed this case as an Unknown Aerial Vehicle.

"Witness very credible background with unwavering details," Crowley wrote in his report. "Ruled out possibility of squid lights on fishing boats as these UAV lights were far too high in the sky."

Jamul is a census-designated place in San Diego County, California, population 6,163.

AUGUST 30

Triangular UFO reported in Portuguese skies

A Portuguese witness at Funchal reported watching "three lights that formed a triangle," according to testimony in Case 94524.

The event occurred at 9:30 p.m. on August 30, 2018.

"I was looking at the sea from my house, when suddenly on the horizon I saw three white lights forming a triangle in ascending path from south to north," the witness stated. "The separation of the lights was like the size of more than one coin. The three lights rotated together slowly as if they were a single, triangular object until reaching almost above my city. The triangle became smaller and smaller, rotating and becoming a unique object light above the clouds until it was totally covered, and I stopped seeing it."

MUFON CAG Investigator for Portugal, Ken

Pfeifer, closed this case as an Unknown Aerial Vehicle.

"This is an island west of Portugal," Pfeifer stated in his report. "Made contact with the witness. I am classifying this case as Unknown Aerial Object. Witness is a professional. Objects witnessed were not Chinese lanterns, drones or satellites."

Funchal is the largest city, the municipal seat and the capital of Portugal's Autonomous Region of Madeira, population 111,892.

AUGUST 31

Texas witness videotapes triangular-shaped UFO

A Texas witness at El Paso reported watching "strange lights in a triangular shape toward the horizon," according to testimony in Case 94699.

The witness was driving to work at 6:35 a.m. on August 31, 2018.

"I stared at the sunrise as usual because I have to stop at a damn red light right before I get on the freeway to work," the witness stated. "After a few minutes I glanced to the right and saw a glowing triangle and thought it was weird. So, I took several pictures and a short video with my Samsung Galaxy S8. It's still new to me and noticed afterwards that the phone does an amazing thing automatically. It stabilized the video on its own. Yes, I did zoom in on the object and luckily it worked perfectly. Even if it's explainable, it is an interesting video and pictures."

Texas MUFON State Section Director Melanie Young and Field Investigator Ray Young closed this case as an Unknown Aerial Vehicle.

"Witness states that he saw a triangle-shaped object in the eastern sky while driving to work," Young and Young stated in their report. "The object appeared to hover in the sky and reflected the sunshine. The object appears to be solid. After interviewing witness and researching triangle-shaped airplanes, the pictures do not look like any known aircraft."

El Paso is a city in and the county seat of El Paso County, Texas, population 683,577.

SEPTEMBER 2018

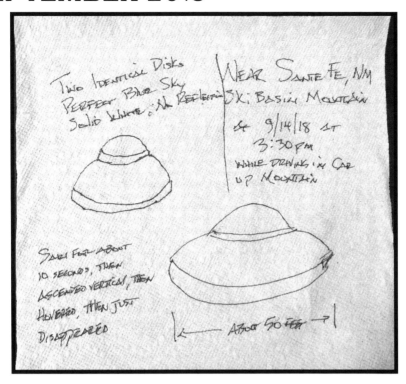

Case 84892 witness illustration. September 3, 2018.

SEPTEMBER 1

Boomerang-shaped UFO reported over Texas

A Texas witness at Porter reported that a boomerang-shaped object with no lights moved over his workplace, according to testimony in Case 94960.

The witness was at work and getting ready to leave at 4:20 a.m. on September 1, 2018.

"I was loading up my car close to 4:30 a.m.," the witness stated. "As I was heading back into the shop to shut off the machines and turn out the lights something caught my attention. I saw an aircraft flying by my workplace. It was the shape of a V. It had no lights and didn't make a sound. It was gray-colored, a little over 1,000 feet in altitude. It looked as if this object didn't want to be seen or was in some kind of stealth mode. The only reason I saw it is because the moon was kind of bright that night and reflected off the object. It came in from the north heading south along loop 494. It wasn't moving too fast. It was just cruising through the sky. The sighting only lasted for around 10 seconds, but it felt like five minutes. After it flew out of my sight range, it had really sunk in what I saw and I started shaking, so I rushed back into the shop. I was scared and kind of freaked out by what I saw so I waited about 20 minutes to summon up the courage to go back outside to get to my car and leave. It's something I will never forget."

Texas MUFON Chief Investigator Ken Jordan closed this case as an Unknown Aerial Vehicle.

"Witness saw a large, metallic object above his work place at 4:30 a.m.," Jordan wrote in his report. "It was illuminated by a very bright moon and was a dull gray, boomerang-shaped craft with no lights or no sound. Witness provided a YouTube video that closely resembled what he saw. The object in the YouTube video was three separate objects, moving randomly. The object the witness saw was a single, solid object."

Porter is an unincorporated community in Montgomery County, Texas, population 25,769.

SEPTEMBER 3

UFO appears in Ohio drilling site photo

An Ohio witness at Perrysville reported discovering a UFO in a photograph taken of an old drilling site, according to testimony in Case 95976.

The event occurred at 4:07 p.m. on September 3, 2018, when the witness was taking pictures with his father.

"We did not notice anything strange," the reporting witness stated. "We also did not hear a jet engine or anything to indicate a craft was nearby. Before leaving the site, I took a series of two or three photos and then rolled up the windows and left the site. After looking back at the pictures obtained, we noticed a symmetrical craft extremely detailed in the photo. My dad is a private pilot and former Army and I am retired from the Marine Corps and we both have never seen a delta-shaped craft like this. My dad has reached out to other pilots to help identify, without any help. It is odd, however, because when he forwards the photo, the craft is distorted in some fashion."

"Again, there was absolutely no noise or any

indication that there was a jet or some UAV above us. In one photo it is way off in the distance, and, within one to two seconds, the next photo in the quick click series has the craft much closer and very detailed. We cannot figure out if the craft is descending towards us or ascending away from us. The vector the craft was on puts it towards Mansfield Lahm Regional Airport where the 179th Air Wing is located. My dad has asked 10-15 airmen from the wing and none have confirmed knowing anything unusual about that day or have a clue as to what the craft may be. It looked just like a stingray and was all black. I have the original two photos of the craft as well as zoomed screen shots that show the craft in very plain view."

Ohio MUFON Field Investigator Scott Miller closed this case as an Unknown Aerial Vehicle.

"I found the witnesses to be credible and reported as they remembered the event," Miller stated in his report. "After looking at the photos using photo-forensics software, I believe the photos to be authentic in nature, and while I believe the object to be manmade, I am not sure what the photo represents. I have not been able to tie it to a specific aircraft based on the shape."

Perrysville is a village in Ashland County, Ohio, population 735.

SEPTEMBER 7

Ex-military witness reports chevron-shaped objecct

A Greek witness at Kos Town reported watching a chevron-shaped object move overhead with a soft orange glow, according to testimony in Case 94837.

The witness and a friend were staying in the rooftop apartment in Kos Perdis Family Resort in Kos Town between September 6 to 10,

2018. The incident occurred at approximately 1:30 a.m. on the 7th.

"We had made the bed outside so we could sleep under the stars as the weather was especially warm, something we did every night of our stay," the witness stated. "We had a clear view of the sky and part of the horizon from our bed where we were chatting. The strange thing is that before the sighting I said, 'Would you come with me if aliens would beam us up?' Completely in jest/joking, and we both said in a heartbeat as long as we were together, both genuine about it, but still a little tongue in cheek. We'd seen four to five streaks of light above us, which were a red/orange glow. These moved very fast and would tail off in different directions, so these weren't shooting stars, maybe too fast for fireflies or possibly bats. They seemed too fast for either: possible reflections off the bat wings? Bird wings? We're not too sure (but trying to find logical solutions for it). At approximately 1:30 a.m. plus or minus a few minutes, we then saw a delta/chevron black craft fly over us. The rear of the craft was harder to define (kind of blurry). It was moving south-southeast over the building/resort from north-northwest direction (nearly from north to south). It was very easy to define the front edge of the craft, having a triangle/swept wing front, and it was completely silent, steady and constant in motion. As it was dark, we could see a faint orange glow on the underbelly of the craft in various locations (lights of sort, but hard to make out a defined shape/source, and because it was dark, to allow yourself to get detail we had to look slightly off to one side of the actual craft, due to night vision). The craft moved right over us, and looking at the rear of the craft once it had passed us, it didn't seem to have anything that resembled a conventional engine, i.e., like a normal aircraft would have, or flashing lights. The craft then went out of sight across the mountain range. My girlfriend said it was an eagle—something I found very hard to believe at the time. It was 1:30 a.m., and she was now in complete denial about it. I

said, did you see that? And she said, yes, I did. I thought I was seeing things, but this was witnessed by both of us. It left me feeling as if this was presented to us for a reason, something maybe connected to our consciousness; seeing that craft having had the conversation we did was not a coincidence. I feel it was to let us know they're here and they can sense us and are connected through consciousness. Maybe the red/orange streaks were connected, and prompted us to have the conversation we'd had before seeing the actual craft. Either that or a major coincidental encounter with a stealth-like craft, the technology of which is beyond our wildest dreams. I, myself, have had a major experience separate from this some years ago, and I'm ex-reconnaissance in the British Army, having served over 10 years on operations in the Middle East and various other countries around the world, so I appreciate how crazy this sounds, but nevertheless we saw it."

MUFON International Director of Investigations for Greece, Steve Hudgeons, closed this case as an Unknown Aerial Vehicle.

SEPTEMBER 8

UFO reported over battleship reunion ceremony

A North Carolina witness at Wilmington reported watching and photographing a bright, blue sphere crossing the sky and that momentarily hovered near the battleship North Carolina, according to testimony in Case 96379.

The witness was attending a military reunion on September 8, 2018.

"We were having our memorial meal on the fantail of the battleship North Carolina," the witness stated. "The weather was warm with no wind. The battleship sits in a small inlet off the Cape Fear River. The tide was in and the ship had no movement. We had approximately 150 marines and their wives on board and ages were late-60s to late-70s. After dinner we were listing to our speakers when I noticed a bright blue orb moving into view from my right. It moved across my view to my left and then came to a stop in an instant like it hit a wall. After a few minutes, it continued its silent path to a position just forward of the ship, where it stopped again and sat there for some time. It then reversed its path, staying at the same height and same position from the ship. As the orb passed in front of me the second time it seemed to grow brighter or intensify. As the orb continued on its path above Wilmington, it went out to what I figured was over the Atlantic, where it went down below my sight line. It was not gone for long when it tracked back over to Wilmington to approximately the left of the ship and then vanished."

Colorado MUFON Field Investigator Jeffrey Hastings closed this case as an Unknown-Other. The witness was from Colorado.

"I talked to two different professional drone operators in the locale area," Hastings wrote in his report. "Both agreed that it was not their equipment and doubted that it was a land-based drone as the witness stated, 'I figured it was over the Atlantic.' Both also stated concerns about any professional operator flying at night with the airport less than three miles away.

"The witness seemed reasonable and provided unaltered photos. Due to the blue color and the fact this was a war memorial ceremony, this may fall more into the paranormal category than UFO category."

Wilmington is a port city and the county seat of New Hanover County, North Carolina, population 119,045.

SEPTEMBER 10

Wisconsin witness reports sphere hovering over shed

A Wisconsin witness at Colby reported watching an orange-red sphere hovering above a shed and then quickly moving away, according to testimony in Case 98808.

The witness was standing outside a camper at 10:30 p.m. on September 10, 2018.

"Upon exiting the camper, I saw this orange-red ball above my shed not moving," the witness stated. "I called into the camper to my wife that she needed to see this. I then said to hurry. As soon as she exited the camper, it moved very quickly behind the pine tree tops in a red streak, then disappeared. My wife only saw the red streak. I truly think it heard me call for my wife. I stayed outside for about the next 10 minutes but didn't see anything else. This is out in the country, clear sky, calm wind. There was no sound at all."

Wisconsin MUFON Field Investigator David Brown and State Director Zelia Edgar closed this case as an Unknown-Other.

"Witness has property in Colby and visits in the warm months (resident of Texas)," Brown and Edgar stated in their report. "Said he likes to 'go out and listen to the sky at night' just about every night and has never witnessed anything similar in those circumstances. He did, however, see a strand of light stretch across the sky while driving on the 4th of July a few years ago. Object described in this report was 'perfectly round,' made no audible sound, and it was illuminated, but the light did not appear to reflect off the metal roof of his shed. He also said he felt like it was watching him."

Colby is a city in Clark and Marathon Counties, Wisconsin, population 1,852.

SEPTEMBER 12

Spheres observed moving around West Virginia property

A West Virginia witness at Hurricane reported watching "three red balls stacked on top of each other," according to testimony in Case 94839.

The witness was on a back porch at 1:15 a.m. on September 12, 2018.

"It was very cloudy," the witness stated. "A cloud we noticed was bright orange, like fire. An object dropped from the cloud. It was like three pure, red balls stacked on top of each other. It moved slowly with no sound. It came across the length of our property slowly and then went completely to the left, without turning, slowly and then in a very fast, streaked movement went completely backwards to where it had appeared from. And it hung there still without movement for about two minutes, and then it started moving again. It traveled around the same area for about 10 minutes. We were standing off the porch on the patio and it started moving slowly towards us, and then it stopped completely still for a minute. Then went completely sideways to a sharp left and went out of sight. Then we spotted it through the trees very low. It looked like it was angling downward towards the ground. Then all of the sudden it was right back again where it had started. Came over the back yard again very slowly and shifted left, but this time instead of being upright, it sort of angled and then went out of sight. The color was the purest red I've ever seen. Solid red, but as it came over us you could see a solid black center in the middle of the red. Pure black. When it lay slightly in an angle when it left, we could see a small green light on the right side of it. It never had a glow. There was no sound. It was just solid, bright, pure red. Very bright."

West Virginia MUFON Assistant State Director Delmer Kelley closed this case as an Unknown Aerial Vehicle.

"Conducted in-person interview with witness on October 13, 2018," Kelley stated in his report. "Witness described the sighting much as reported in the initial report. She added that the object was first observed by her son while outside on the back porch. He then woke her up and they both watched the object during the time it was manifest. Additional information and clarification were provided indicating that the initial 'bright orange' color of the cloud was due to the presence of the object, which was enclosed in the cloud, and when the object 'dropped from the cloud,' the cloud then lost its color. We went outside to the actual location where the sighting took place, and the witness pointed out the location of the initial appearance and the trajectory, subsequent limits of motions, and locations of the stationary positions the object had maintained. The witness came across as totally credible and was very much interested in finding an explanation of the nature of the object.

"During the interview the witness's details of the sighting were impressive, and the fact that the object exhibited very fast (as in almost instantaneous) multiple movements at times suggests an object of definite anomalous characteristics. In addition, a solid black center was evident in the middle of the object, indicating that it was a craft and not simply another light in the sky. No known man-made or natural object seems to accommodate the appearance and motions observed."

Hurricane is a city in Putnam County, West Virginia, population 6,284.

Two triangular UFOs reported hovering over Canadian town

A Canadian witness at Ancaster reported watching two, triangular-shaped objects hovering overhead that quickly moved away, according to testimony in Case 95268.

The witness was sitting in a hot tub looking skyward on September 12, 2018.

"I observed overhead two triangular objects with round lights in each tip," the witness stated. "The two crafts appeared to hover momentarily and were gone in a flash. They were travelling from the northeast to the southwest. My guess is that they were at approximately 10,000 feet in relation to other aircraft overhead. The triangular shape seemed to be a shadow of the crafts and the lights in each tip had approximately eight or nine lights arranged in a circle. A diagram of the two crafts is attached."

Canada MUFON Chief Investigator Ryan Stacey closed this case as an Unknown Aerial Vehicle.

"I have spoken to the witness via telephone prior to this report," Stacey stated in his report. "I believe the witness to be credible. The drawing is interesting as there appear to be two objects in the sky and within close range of each other. They are not perfectly aligned, which could suggest that these are piloted. I could compare these to the TR-3B. Either way, these objects appear to be unknown."

Ancaster is a community in Hamilton, Ontario, Canada, population approximately 15,000.

SEPTEMBER 13

Idaho UFO was 300 feet off ground

An Idaho witness at Hailey reported a silent, rectangular-shaped object about 300 feet off the ground; it quickly disappeared, according to testimony in Case 94937.

The witness pulled into the Shell station at the corner of South Third and Main in Hailey at approximately 8:30 a.m. on September 13, 2018.

"I observed a solid, structured craft to the south at an altitude of what I estimated to be 300 feet above ground level and 100 yards to the south of my position," the witness stated. "It was not a conventional fixed or rotary wing aircraft. It was not a balloon or a conventional drone. It seemed in an odd location since it was in the proximity of the north end of the

runway at the Hailey airport. I observed this object for approximately 30 seconds until I moved around the car to get a better look. I took my eyes off the object for about 10-15 seconds. When I looked again, the object had completely disappeared from sight.

"At the time, visibility was greater than two miles with low clouds down to around 2,000 feet. My field of vision was clear from horizon to horizon. There were no sounds or emissions. The object appeared to be a tapered rectangle and I estimated the size to be around 6 feet by 6 feet (estimated). Surface color was dark, possibly gray/black. There appeared to be external apparatus on the surface closest to me. I couldn't determine which side was the 'front.' I first observed it when I was pulling into the gas station, looking out for traffic. My first impression was that it could have been a balloon or drone but rejected those possibilities after a few seconds of observation. What really struck me as odd was how quickly and completely it had disappeared. I didn't really have any feelings about it other than trying to identify it. Curiously, when I left the station and went about my business, I didn't have any thoughts or think about the incident until later that evening. I did make a rudimentary sketch of the object the following day. Note: I am a former U.S. Army Air Defense Artillery Officer and have had extensive training in Visual Aircraft Recognition. I also am very aware of the fact that there are many unusual things in the sky, especially in this region, that are not extraterrestrial."

Idaho MUFON State Director James Millard closed this case as an Unknown Aerial Vehicle.

"Airport did not respond," Millard wrote in his report. "Witness sounds credible."

Hailey is a city in and the county seat of Blaine County, Idaho, population 7,960.

Two triangular UFOs spotted over Indiana

An Indiana witness at Columbus reported watching two, triangular-shaped objects flying at low level, according to testimony in Case 94903.

The incident occurred at 9 p.m. on September 13, 2018.

"Saw two flying objects," the witness stated. "Lights showed triangle shape. No noise heard. Appeared the object was on its side. Triangle-shaped craft flying approximately 500 feet to the eastward direction."

Indiana MUFON Field Investigator Patrick O'Brien closed this case as an Unknown Aerial Vehicle.

"In parking lot at work, the witness saw two sets of lights forming a triangle," O'Brien stated in his report. "No sounds. Observing lights, it looked like craft was on its side and then righted. And witness noticed lights on the craft as green, orange, and white on tips of the craft. Traveling at a low altitude of 500 feet. Lights were solid. Crafts were moving slowly eastward."

Columbus is a city in and the county seat of Bartholomew County, Indiana, population 44,061.

SEPTEMBER 14

Two disc-shaped UFOs reported over Costa Rica

A Costa Rican witness at Santa Elena reported watching two small disc-shaped UFOs near a local mountain, according to testimony in Case 95265.

The incident at 8:15 a.m. on September 14, 2018.

"Two small discs seen from a distance just above the nearest hill/mountain," the witness stated. "They were moving farther into the southeast direction at high speed, slightly moving upwards towards the sky at the same time. An unnatural movement for a plane, drone or helicopter as they seemed to cover much distance in a matter of seconds. They disappeared into the sky before I could notify anyone. I saw these discs from the big window at hostel Que Tuanis, which is a very wide, large window, allowing one to see the entire valley and mountain area."

The MUFON International Director of Investigations for Costa Rica, Steve Hudgeons, closed this case as an Unknown Aerial Vehicle.

New Mexico witness describes two disc-shaped UFOs

A New Mexico witness at Sante Fe reported watching "two identical, white, non-reflective discs with domed tops," according to testimony in Case 94892.

The witness and his wife were driving up the Santa Fe Ski Basin mountain at 3:28 p.m. on September 14, 2018.

"On a curvy mountain road but generally headed northeast," the witness stated, "my wife looked up through the windshield at about 45 degrees and saw two identical, white, non-reflective discs of circular shape with domed tops. It was a perfect blue sky with zero clouds. The disks ascended rapidly and then stopped and hovered motionless for about five seconds and then simply just disappeared from view in an instant. The total sighting lasted approximately 10 seconds. There was no time to grab a cell phone or take a picture and my wife was so spellbound that she was motioning to me, the driver, but I did not look fast enough to see the disks. See attached crude sketch of the two discs."

New Mexico MUFON Assistant State Director John Fegel closed this case as Info Only.

SEPTEMBER 16

Witness describes six descending bright lights

A California witness at Kensington reported of watching a row of six, bright, white lights that descended into a nearby tree line, according to testimony in Case 94931.

The witness was outside at 1:15 a.m. on September 16, 2018.

"I took my dogs outside to the backyard and they ran very quickly to the south gate of the yard," the witness stated. "I looked to the south to see if there was an animal in the yard, such as a raccoon. That is when I noticed this wide set of six bright, white lights in a straight line descending. Much too wide to be an aircraft. The lights descended behind trees and I could no longer see them. I've never seen anything like this. Too large to be a conventional aircraft."

California MUFON Assistant State Director Devlin Rugne closed this case as an Unknown-Other.

"Based on his description of the six lights that were in a straight line and too wide to be an aircraft that was descending, I'm going to close this out as an Unknown-Other.

"Witness said the six bright, white lights were independent of each other, but attached to something, since they moved down at same speed and remained exactly separated. The witness was one-half to one mile away from the trees. At arm's length, the objects were the size of a salad plate."

Kensington is an unincorporated community in Contra Costa County, California, population 5,077.

SEPTEMBER 17

Conical UFO described under 300 feet over Colorado

A Colorado witness at Highlands Ranch reported watching a silent, cone-shaped object under 300 feet, according to testimony in Case 94983.

The witness was in the backyard with dogs at 9:42 p.m. on September 17, 2018.

"Noticed the object because its three lights faced straight down," the witness stated. "It had a dome/cylinder-shaped top with flat bottom and the flat bottom is where the lights were. It was so low that that is what first caught my attention. Then I realized it made no sound at all. It was way too big to be a drone and too small to be a plane/jet. Did not make noise at all so not a helicopter. I watched it fly northeast towards Denver and then it suddenly switched direction, moving up, then down. Then it just disappeared. Although there were clouds in the sky, there was nothing right above it or in front of it and I could see it really well because of the Denver lights lighting up the sky. It just disappeared. It was one of the scariest experiences and confusing experiences I've ever had."

Colorado MUFON Field Investigators Richard Evans and Deborah Evans closed this case as an Unknown Aerial Vehicle.

"The object observed was unique in its shape, lighting, and movement with a lack of sound and unknown propulsion," Evans and Evans stated in their report. "A balloon is ruled out because the object was traveling oppositely of prevailing winds."

Highlands Ranch is a census-designated place in Douglas County, Colorado, population 96,713.

SEPTEMBER 18

Washington witness videotapes flashing spherical objects

A Washington witness at Vancouver reported watching "pulsating, flashing, spherical objects" at about 3,500 feet, according to testimony in Case 94996.

The witness was out for a walk after lunch at 12:25 p.m. on September 18, 2018.

"I saw a bright, pulsating and flashing object traveling southwest to southeast at about 3,500 feet; maybe around 200 mph," the witness stated. "Really hard to tell just how high or fast it was since its size was unknown. Not an airplane or other known aircraft. I am a private pilot and I have more than 35 years' experience looking for aircraft while airborne. It appeared to increase altitude very rapidly as it moved away from me to the southwest. This was very unusual - in fact, unusual enough for me to post this to your site. It would be interesting if others had the same sighting."

Washington MUFON State Section Director James E. Clarkson closed this case as an Unknown Aerial Vehicle.

"The report to MUFON was made on the same day as the event occurred," Clarkson stated in his report. "The witness responded immediately to my inquiry. He was anxious to know what he observed or to communicate with any other witness. The witness has a highly technical background and is employed by a company that manufactures high-tech equipment. The witness is also an experienced small plane pilot and has flown in the same area where the UAV was seen on numerous occasions. The observation occurred while the witness was at work while taking a walk during lunch on September 18, 2018, at about 12:25 p.m. in Vancouver, WA, about two-and-a-half miles from the Portland Oregon International Airport across the Columbia River.

"I interviewed the witness by telephone, and we exchanged several emails. The witness had taken a short video with his cell phone. He had also reconstructed his position and the flight path of the unknown object on a map. He also obtained professional assistance with stabilizing the video and making the UAV slightly more visible.

"It should be noted this was a daylight sighting by an experienced pilot with photographic evidence.

"The weather conditions were clear in all directions. The witness was attracted by the random very bright flashes of light coming off the object. He stated that the flashes were bright like that of an arc welder.

"The object flew from the northwest to the southwest of the witness over an estimated distance of about 11 miles. It took about four minutes for the UAV to cover this distance. This equates to about 165 mph, which places it well within the performance of man-made aircraft, either piloted or a drone.

"The witness remained adamant that the object had a definite spherical shape and that it was not like any other aircraft he had observed in the sky. When the UAV was closest to him, he observed it at about a 60-degree angle, and he could have covered it with a 'BB' held at arm's length.

"The object did not engage in any unusual maneuvers that are often associated with UFO reports. However, the witness did point out that the object appeared to climb over 2,000 feet in about 10 seconds.

"We discussed the possibility that the UAV was a drone craft. If it was, it is not clear who was responsible. We talked about the company INSITU, which does manufacture drone aircraft for the military in Bingen, WA. Their plant is about 35 miles from Vancouver. There is no reason to believe they would test valuable drone craft over a highly populated area near the approaches to a major airport.

"The exhibits submitted by the witness are included with this report. There are no known additional witnesses to this event. The witness checked pilot radio traffic in the area at the date and time of his sighting. There was no mention of the UAV he observed.

"This is a high-quality event with a high credibility witness. This file is closed at this time as an Unknown Aerial Vehicle."

Vancouver is the county seat of Clark County, Washington, population 161,791.

SEPTEMBER 19

Philippines witness describes transparent triangular UFO

A witness in the Philippines reported a transparent, triangular-shaped object that quickly disappeared over the horizon, according to testimony in Case 94990.

The witness was stargazing on the roof of a house at 9 p.m. on September 19, 2018.

"I accidentally panned my head over the southeast corner of my view," the witness stated. "What I saw was a triangular-shaped craft and it was quite huge. It was gliding straight into the cloudiest part of the horizon. It revealed its transparent, triangular shape to me just before it disappeared over the horizon, where there were more clouds that were heavier and thicker. I think it went there to hide. I don't know if you guys know like in the movies how a stealth object has this transparent effect. It was like that just before it entered into a more cloudy area. I saw it like flicker a bit while keeping its transparency. But what surprised me was the thinner clouds helped exposed the object to me. I don't know if anyone in my country saw it just now. I'm not sure and I'm not really expecting that the Philippines will be visited a lot, but it's

an insane experience because I don't expect anything much from our boring sky at night. P.S. Do not tell me it's an airplane because I know what I saw."

Philippines MUFON Lee George Strydom closed this case as an Unknown Aerial Vehicle.

SEPTEMBER 20

British witness describes quickly descending disc

A British witness reported watching a silent, disc-shaped object that descended quickly and vanished, according to testimony in Case 95065.

The witness was a passenger driving home along a motorway at 7:45 p.m. on September 20, 2018.

"We were about five minutes from home," the witness stated. "There were three bright flashing lights to the left of us and my dad (who was driving) pointed it out. We didn't know what it was at first, so my mum and I continued to watch its movements, since we thought that it looked very strange. At first it was hovering quite far off the ground. And then the lights started flashing. It very quickly descended and stayed there for about 10 seconds before flying very quickly upwards, making no sound at all. At first my dad said to my mum and me, 'look, up there in the sky,' so we both looked and couldn't quite figure out what it was. We then decided to watch it, soon realizing that it was a disk shape and was tilted (we could tell by where the lights were). I then knew it was something much more than a helicopter or an airplane. It vanished suddenly."

United Kingdom MUFON Field Investigator James Dallas closed this case as an Unknown Aerial Vehicle.

"The witness stated in her report that they were leaving the M4 motorway at Junction 16, which is approximately 1.70 miles as the crow flies and around five minutes on the road," Dallas stated in his report. "This area is very rural farm land, though to the north there is Hullavington Airfield. This is an ex-RAF base, which was closed in 1992 but remains MoD property.

"I was unable to get any answers from either Lyneham or Buckley; in fact, the brush off from Lyneham was a bit harsh. Nothing from the local constabulary in Chippenham some 2.25 miles away. So once again I contacted my friends in N.A.T.S. (National Air Transport Service) to ask if they could shine a light on the subject for me. No. Not a surprise there. I have drawn a blank on this one, but I'm going with my gut and nearly 35 years of ufological study.

"Conclusion: I believe that the witnesses saw something that night. I wish others had come forward to verify the sighting."

SEPTEMBER 21

Amateur AZ astronomers report multiple UFOs

An Arizona witness at Sonoita reported a silver, teardrop-shaped object with five, large, white balls of light, according to testimony in Case 98732.

The witness and her husband were outside in front of their house looking through his William Optics 132 FLT telescope on their 25-acre ranch from 7:30 - 8:30 p.m. on September 21, 2018.

"We had looked at Jupiter before it set, Saturn, then Mars and far away Neptune, the Ring Nebula, the Dumbbell Nebula, plus the Hercules Cluster," the witness stated. "We noticed satellites, planes, and a drone coming from the south going north, watching us - possibly from Fort Huachuca as we briefly used lasers to point out things in the heavens to each other.

"At 8 p.m. my husband was wondering what

else we could look at through the telescope. I started looking at the moon (it was waxing toward full on Sept. 25th). Partial clouds crossed the moon and as I scanned the clouds near it, I saw a teardrop-shaped craft that was white/silver on the top facing the moon and dark charcoal/blackish on the sides away from the moon. It had a canopy. I kept the binoculars on it and said excitedly, 'J are you seeing this?' Me describing that it was to the right bottom of the moon, and not taking my eyes off it. J got his telescope on the moon and was trying to see the craft I saw, but didn't before it disappeared slowly like it was fading out into the clouds around it.

"J saw a large, white ball of light and at first thought it was a satellite, but it didn't move properly for a satellite and was too big. I found the ball of white light in my binoculars, and we both decided it wasn't a satellite, because it didn't move in the same quick continuous trajectory path. Then we both saw two balls of light, me using the binoculars and J, the telescope.

"I came over and looked in the telescope and another white ball of light came from the moon's direction. Now there were three in a triangular pattern as if flying in formation. J then looked in the telescope and there were four, then five, flying together in a V-shaped formation. The fourth and fifth ones would blink out, and then reappear, but always staying in formation. I didn't see them do this. J was extremely excited and said several times, 'They are between the clouds and us.' That confirming to him again that they weren't satellites (besides the fact the satellites don't fly in formation and make turns).

"We watched them from 8 to 8:30 p.m. Then the five balls of white light faded from view within the clouds at 8:30. We scanned around a few more minutes, but they weren't there. We covered the telescope and went in the house - and yes, we were freaked, excited and laughed a lot. "Ancient Aliens" and YouTube had exposed us to partial disclosure before we saw the six UFOs. It was incredible and we can't wait for our next sighting. My husband is an engineer and amateur astronomer. Our ranch is under a dark sky, that being his dream. I'm an author, illustrator and rancher. I've had other ET/UFO experiences but those are for another time."

Arizona MUFON Field Investigator Shane Hurd closed this case as an Unknown Aerial Vehicle.

"Based on the fact there were two witnesses, the credibility of those witnesses as amateur astronomers, one as an engineer with security clearances, the descriptions of performance and appearance, the logical process of elimination, I am assigning the disposition of Unknown-UAV," Hurd stated in his report. "The description of their flight performance (flying separately then in a formation) and visual appearance (metallic spheres) suggests craft of some sort as opposed to a light-like orb. Unfortunately, I was unable to confirm Border Patrol or Fort Huachuca were performing UAV training or testing to obtain a positive identification.

"Most importantly, this report deals with a controversial subject. The conclusion presented here is not the only possible interpretation; however, it is based on available supporting facts and evidence revealed in the course of this investigation. Viewers of this report are invited to make a judgment based on all available information and evidence, not by unsupported speculation. This case is subject to changes should future evidence suggest such a change."

Sonoita is a census-designated place in Santa Cruz County, Arizona, population 818.

SEPTEMBER 23

British witness videotapes glowing triangular UFO

A British witness at London reported watching and videotaping a triangular-shaped object, according to testimony in Case 95215.

The event occurred at 5:40 p.m. on September 23, 2018.

"The object was somewhere between three and five meters large," the witness stated. "Difficult to say. It was metallic and glowed a bright, blue color. Very visible because of the pulsating blue light. It was moving fast. The area in Herne Hill is very active in terms of UFOs, orbs, critters and anomalies."

United Kingdom MUFON National Director Jack Turnbull closed this case as an Unknown Aerial Vehicle.

"Spoke to the witness on October 1," Turnbull stated in his report. "Received a range of photographs portraying what appears to be a strange object. Unable to ascertain what they are other than they seem to be a bit surreal."

London is the capital and largest city of both England and the United Kingdom, population 8,787,892.

SEPTEMBER 24

Spherical UFOs captured in NY witness photo

A New York witness at Baldwinsville reported watching and photographing three UFOs over a five-second period, according to testimony in Case 95317.

The witness and his wife were shopping at Kohl's store on Rt. 31 near Clay, NY, at 6:45 p.m. on September 24, 2018.

"I was taking pictures of the sunset," the witness stated. "I was facing directly west. I took one picture, looked at it, noticed a glint of light so took the second picture in which the UFOs show up just above the horizon. Within a few seconds they were no longer visible."

New York MUFON Field Investigator Keith Conroy closed this case as an Unknown-Other.

"Reviewed the submitted photos and found the objects in question to be physically part of the original photograph," photo analyst Sam Falvo stated in his report. "File # F391C3CD-B0E8427B971AED2E9BBC1080.jpeg is sharp enough that the diamond shape of a four-blade iris is visible in one of the objects. Also, I superimposed one image on the other and matched the light poles and objects in the tree line. The result clearly showed the movement of the items in question. The approximate center of the grouping had moved approximately 609 pixels and changed altitude by 14 degrees of slope. This cannot be possible for a lens flare since the orientation of the camera has not been significantly altered between the two images. Also, the camera lens geometry with respect to the axis is not correct for a lens flare. The items seem to have moved either towards or away from the witness as well. This is indicated by the change in relative sizes of the individual items as well as the grouping size. Below is my working image."

"Based on witness testimony and cooperation and input from photo analyst Sam Falvo, I conclude this as Unknown-Other," Conroy stated in his report.

Baldwinsville is a village in Onondaga County, New York, population 7,378.

SEPTEMBER 25

Canadian witness describes disc crossing over roadway

A Canadian witness at Lachute reported driving at night with a colleague and seeing lights in a circle with a red light in the center that crossed the road at the treetop level, hovered and moved 90 degrees west, according to testimony in Case 95703.

The event occurred at 10:30 p.m. on September 25, 2018.

"No sound, no rotor downwash, silent with light all around," the witness stated. "Seemed to light downward."

Canada MUFON Alain Des Roches closed this case as an Unknown Aerial Vehicle.

"The story of the two witnesses," Roches wrote in the report. "Witness 1 and Witness 2 finish their work and take Route 329 north of Lac La Fontaine. They see in the distance a light that comes to them. Thinking of a truck, but they see the object above them—50 feet high, at treetop height—at a speed of about 10 km/h. Their car drives at 90 km/h, then Witness 1 idles the vehicle at 5 km/h to see better. They see a wide disk of 30 to 50 feet in diameter with about 15 lights below and with a red light in the center that rotates like a beacon. The object changes direction abruptly and then disappears towards the forest. The two witnesses have the same testimony except that Witness 1, the driver, has more details because the object was above the vehicle and the driver's side. While Witness 2 is the passenger and must bend over to see the object better.

"Witness 2 is 24 years old and Witness 1 is 58 years old and both are carpenters. Witness 1 has a plane and helicopter pilot license, so he knows aviation well. Witness 1 points out another observation during his adolescence. He thinks he was in Saint-Canut and observing the sky. He sees a luminous point of the size of a star that moves in a straight line and then changes direction often and goes away—disappears. This observation lasts about one minute.

"Conclusion: Witness 1 is credible and gives me a lot of details and has a pilot's license, so he knows how to differentiate between airplanes and helicopters. Witness 2, passenger of the car, confirms to me the story of Witness 1."

Lachute is a town in southwest Quebec, Canada, population approximately 12,000.

Black helicopter reported chasing egg-shaped UFO

A Washington witness at Silver Creek reported watching a black, egg-shaped object followed by a black helicopter, according to testimony in Case 95249.

The event occurred at 11:15 p.m. on September 25, 2018.

"I live in a semi-rural location on Lake Mayfield, in East Lewis County, Washington, in the Cowlitz River Valley," the witness stated. "I live alone in a trailer across the road from my parents' house. I was in my home watching TV at 11:15. I heard a helicopter coming down the valley. It was extremely loud, so I decide to walk out on my driveway to take a look. I saw a helicopter and its running lights. It was coming at me at a 45-degree angle, slightly to my left at approximately 500 feet. As I watched it approaching, I noticed the helicopter was following a black, egg-shaped object that was approximately 20 to 30 feet ahead of the helicopter and approximately 10 to 20 feet below the helicopter. It appeared like a black egg-shaped shadow. It was a clear evening and the helicopter and the object flew by me at a very brisk rate. I could see that there was actually an object in front and below the helicopter. As I watched, I could see that there was an object because it covered the stars that were directly behind it. I stood back and checked myself by asking if I was sure I was seeing what I had seen, and yes, I was absolutely positive. There was an egg-shaped shadow being followed by what appeared, at the time, to be a black helicopter. I continued to watch as long as I could, approximately three minutes in total, as the object and the helicopter flew out of my line of sight. I stood there for a few seconds putting it all together in my mind. I felt bewildered at the sight. I had never seen anything of that

nature before. I felt a little anxious as well, and because of the time of night I waited till the next morning to tell my parents what I had witnessed. I am convinced of what I saw."

Washington MUFON State Section Director James E. Clarkson closed this case as an Unknown Aerial Vehicle.

Clarkson provided additional details from the witness in his report: "The incident occurred on the evening of September 25th, at approximately 11:10 p.m. On that particular evening there was a full moon. The moon was in the southern sky to the location I was standing. As the helicopter approached, I visually picked it up east of my location. It was heading westbound. I picked up the running lights of the helicopter, and at this point I didn't see the object. As the helicopter approached, I picked up the black, egg-shaped object just in front and below the helicopter. The helicopter and object flanked me on my left, approximately 500 feet off the ground. The helicopter and object were approximately the size of a car. Fairly close to where I was standing. If you reference Google Earth and my location, I was standing across the street from my parents' home. There is a shop and residence there. I was standing in the open driveway. North of that location is a tree farm, with very small trees. The helicopter and object flew just north, heading in a westbound flight path.

"The helicopter appeared to be the size and shape of a Blackhawk. I say that because on occasion I do see military aircraft in my area since JBLM [Joint Base Lewis-McChord] is north of my location. I am uncertain of the helicopter color; it appeared to be of a dark color. I cannot tell you how many rotor blades the helicopter had.

"The helicopter and the object moved across my field of view at a rapid but constant speed.

"I would mention this. I might have missed the fact that there was an object at all. But as I watched the helicopter approach me, I noticed the black, egg-shaped object initially because I couldn't see the stars behind it. As it flew through the sky, it covered up the stars behind it. When I noticed that, I could see the outline of the object, and I realized that there were two crafts, the helicopter and the black, egg-shaped object.

"I have tried many times to think of a rational explanation to my experience, but I cannot. I am convinced that what I saw was unidentifiable regarding my experiences. My father spent 25 years in the navy. I spent a lot of my childhood on military bases. I've seen military aircraft, including the stealth fighter and bomber. I have to say this was nothing like those aircraft. In addition, the object had no (running) lights on it that I could observe. Also, I could not hear anything but the sounds of the helicopter itself. The object did not make any sounds that I could detect."

"I verified that the moon was full at the time and date of the sighting using the USNO database," Clarkson wrote in his report. "The weather was ideal for night visibility. I checked other UFO databases and found no other reports of this event.

"This file is closed at this time on the basis that a high credibility witness did observe a military helicopter escorting a dark, egg-shaped, round object flying through the air (UAV) by no known means of propulsion."

Silver Creek is an unincorporated community in Lewis County, Washington.

OCTOBER 2018

Case 95323 witness illustration. October 2, 2018.

OCTOBER 2

NJ orb UFO morphs into triangle shape

A New Jersey witness at Toms River reported watching a bright orb that morphed into a triangle shape, according to testimony in Case 95323.

The witness was walking to a friend's home at 8:25 p.m. on October 2, 2018.

"I looked up into the sky and noticed a very bright, glowing orb at a 60-degree viewing angle," the witness stated. "After moments of looking at the object for a minute or so the orb faded away completely. It then reappeared about 20 seconds later, at the time it was way below cloud cover, so it left no explanation of its vanishing. Over the next 15 minutes or so the object would reappear in different locations that were far distant, and not in a forward direction. The orb then was at a closer distance to me and was noticed to have shaped into a triangular craft with sequential flashing lights, with two brilliant, bright lights, that were somewhat cloaking the object I was trying to view. Noticeable was an infrared light that was emitting from the front of the craft that extended some large distance. This same thing had occurred multiple times during viewing it, as its most intriguing capability was its ability to go from a super bright orb and then completely vanish and appear in other parts of the sky, which it had done multiple times.

This is the second encounter I have had with this type of craft; however, last time was a much closer encounter that had psychological impacts on me for over six months. Feel free to contact me for more specific information pertinent to this report."

New Jersey MUFON Chief Investigator Glenn Green closed this case as an Unknown-Other.

"Here our observer shares with us a 'from the heart' story that is jaw-dropping," Green wrote in his report. "From intelligent movement, cloaking capabilities, and possible communication-based light show, this otherwordly green triangle had it all. Telepathy took place throughout the four-minute event. All this from about two miles away from where the observer first saw it. First seen at 60 degrees as a bright, white orb transforming into a multi-lit triangle. Predominately green, there were two front, white lights that shifted from bright to really bright, seemingly searching for something. Our observer noticed sequential and random patterns among the multi-colored canvas this species of ET painted that night. Please see the artist's amazing drawing of this event. A very special thank you to the artist for taking the time to sit down with the witness and paint this once in a lifetime event."

Toms River is a township in Ocean County, New Jersey, population 91,239.

OCTOBER 3

Triangular UFO hovered over NJ campground

A New Jersey witness at New Lisbon reported watching a silent, flying triangle just above the treetops, with bright, pulsing lights at each corner, according to testimony in Case 96637.

The witness had just arrived at the Brendan T. Byrne Campground after a 15-mile hike on the Batona Trail at 7:30 p.m. on October 3, 2018.

"It was a very dark night, the campground was completely dark, and I was hiking alone with no one else there," the witness stated. "As I was searching for a good camp spot, near sites 54/56, I happened to notice an odd and unique looking set of pulsating lights up in the sky to the northwest through a break in the forest canopy above the campground road. The lights pulsated very rapidly with various colors. I was fascinated by the appearance of these lights, which I have never seen before. (I grew up near Philadelphia International Airport and have witnessed many planes landing during the day and night.) The color of the lights very rapidly shifted. There were three lights forming a triangle, all moving at the same rate and velocity. I could not see any craft or solid object. The object made no apparent noise. Earlier and later airplanes in the sky made noises and looked completely different and farther away. I attempted to take a video of whatever it was on my iPhone, but it was too dark, and nothing showed up. (It was also difficult to aim the phone correctly, and the sighting didn't last long enough.) Listening to the video, I can hear crickets and very distant car sounds but nothing else. The object moved at a steady velocity and didn't change direction. It moved to the northwest until I couldn't see it anymore above the forest. It was definitely just above the forest canopy, but didn't appear more than approximately one to two miles or so away. It appeared so low that it was right above the forest northwest of my position."

New Jersey MUFON Assistant State Director Ken Pfeifer closed this case as an Unknown Aerial Vehicle.

"After a long telephone conversation, I will classify this as an Unknown. Witness is very credible and witnessed the event from the campground area."

New Lisbon is an unincorporated community within Pemberton Township in Burlington County, New Jersey.

Utah UFO seen during 'massive downpour'

A Utah witness at Orem reported watching a metallic, cigar-shaped object, according to testimony in Case 98214.

The event occurred at 9:40 p.m. on October 3, 2018.

"I saw something in the sky, and, quite honestly, I cannot identify what it was," the witness stated. "I was driving down a road in Utah County. I looked up and over to my left as I drove east towards the mountain and saw three lights in a perfect row, two red and one blue, all evenly spaced. It was off towards my right and was to the northeast of me, and about a mile-and-a-half away.

"The thing that really caught my eye was that we were in the middle of a massive pocket of downpour, with sheets of rain, and horrible winds. I could literally feel my smaller SUV being jostled by the winds. I grew up next to two airports; one being an air force base and the other being a modestly busy commercial airport, so I know planes. I also have lived in this area for five years and know that it's not a flight path.

"I immediately thought it was a drone, because: 1) no plane flies that close to the mountains and 2) helicopters don't take that path, and 3) who flies in that weather especially if it was a helicopter? So, our paths were on a fairly similar trajectory, and I could tell we'd intersect in a matter of a minute, so I kept a close eye on it, but that's all I could do as I was trying to drive safely in the rain.

"As I got closer and closer, I could tell it was relatively low, less than one-and-a-half football fields off the ground, but was moving in a perfectly straight line, despite being in winds of 21 mph. As I was about to pass under it, I got a semi-good look at the lights, and saw three evenly spaced lights – one red, another red and then blue on the tail end. I also could see a distinct outline, almost cigar-shaped and slightly metallic.

"I couldn't make out any form of propulsion or, even weirder to me, stabilization. I went back and saw, checked to see if this was even possible for me to see, but humidity was at 87 percent at this time, winds in a heavy 21 mph blowing west, meaning this was fighting and flying in a south-easterly direction, on straight line and dead even speed.

"Visibility was just about three miles and after it passed over my car, I could no longer see it. Also, as to how I could see it through such rain, I can also confirm my car windows were completely fog free, with windshield wipers going on max (the rain was insane), and I had had Lasik back in March, after which I have had perfect 20/10 vision in both eyes.

"This all being said, it may have been a mundane object, but to me I am added to the list of those who have seen something in the sky flying that they cannot comfortably identify. I saw a UFO."

Utah MUFON State Director Michael Barrette closed this case as an Unknown Aerial Vehicle.

"This Field Investigator had an opportunity to speak with the witness on February 1, 2019, about his sighting," Barrette stated in his report. "Witness stated that he first saw the object off to his left (about one-and-a-half miles away) and farther on down the road would intersect with the object. Witness further went on to state the object was in heavy downpouring rain and heavy winds, but was able to describe the object as a cigar shape with three lights going down the middle (in CMS was listed as two red lights and 1 blue light, but the witness stated to me that it was two blue lights and one red light).

"This incident was reported as occurring at approximately 9:40 p.m. during heavy rain and wind. The witness stated that he was going to intersect with the object, but then stated that he was traveling on a five-lane highway and was driving slow for safety reasons—that when the object went over his head it couldn't be seen and that it had disappeared from sight.

"The witness states the entire incident [i.e., the intersection portion only of the sighting—ed.] occurred in two to three seconds. In the initial statement in CMS, the witness described the object as being one-and-a-half football fields in size off the ground, which is approximately 450 feet, but when he submitted his CMS report, he claimed the object was 21 to 100 feet off the ground. I asked the witness if there were any other witnesses and he stated 'no.' I inquired whether there was any missing time and again he said no."

Orem is a city in Utah County, Utah, population 84,324.

OCTOBER 4

Washington witness says UFO was 'transparent'

A Washington witness at Sammamish reported watching a silent, low-flying, wedge-shaped object over Pine Lake, according to testimony in Case 95356.

The event occurred at 8 p.m. on October 4, 2018.

"Last night a UFO flew directly over my home when I was walking my dog," the witness stated. "I've recreated a Photoshop piece showing what it looked like as best I can. Even if I had had a camera, I would not have captured it, because it was just too dark. It was wedge-shaped, sort of like the black triangle types that can be found online, but not really—more arrowhead-shaped with no wings. Actually, very similar to the shape of a Star Wars Imperial Star Destroyer. It was very ghost-like, almost transparent-looking, as if it was cloaked where you could just make out the edges. Somewhat lighter than the night sky. If

it hadn't been for the faint cool-colored lights on it, I would have completely missed it, even though it was flying relatively low. When I first saw it, I had no idea what it was, I simply had no reference point for such a thing. I immediately thought it was maybe one of the black triangle UFOs that are commonly sighted, but it didn't look like the ones I've seen online. I definitely thought that it was either absolutely alien or some sort of super high-tech, secret military craft based on alien technology. At the time there were one or two other planes in the sky when this thing went by, but not close or chasing it. In the picture I've attached, the point of view was as if looking straight up at the bottom of it flying directly overhead, flying straight in the direction of the pointy end from right to left. It was probably no more than a couple of hundred yards up in the sky, but difficult to tell exactly, moving pretty quickly and totally silent. It was also pretty big. I would estimate it was probably as big as a commercial airplane but probably not bigger than a Goodyear blimp. There were several faint lights, not much brighter than the surrounding stars, but not in the configuration of the black triangle UFOs that are often depicted. This happened at 8 p.m. exactly. It was flying north to south and gliding quickly about the speed of a low-flying plane before landing; however, I had enough time to see it clearly. It probably took five seconds for it to travel from the time I saw it directly overhead until I couldn't make it out on the horizon, perhaps a mile or two off. It was awesome at first and then my rational brain kicked in and it freaked me out and made the hairs on my arms stand up straight. The strange thing is exactly an hour later, at 9 p.m., I came outside to look for it again and I saw another UFO, or perhaps several flying in formation. They appeared to be faint, glowing orbs that were also cool-colored, also gliding quickly, but again absolutely moving silently through the sky in a bow-shaped pattern. They were flying from a southeasterly to a north-westerly direction, a bit more to the west of the first one I saw earlier. There was a helicopter with a red light on it flying over at the same time I saw these orbs. It was not a private, small helicopter but a powerful one, but I couldn't make out any colors if there were any. This UFO was amazing, too, but definitely not as absolutely spectacular as the first. There was definitely something weird going on out here in the PNW skies last night. It was a nice clear night last night."

Washington MUFON State Section Director Allen Thompson closed this case as an Unknown-Other.

"The witness was very forthcoming and sincere in relating his experience," Thompson stated in his report. "He mentions that he has had three other sightings, none this close. He admits to feeling uneasy and vulnerable in the face of what he describes as a UFO. His health and physical condition did not change during or after his experience, so there was not any direct connection to the craft other than observance. He felt ill at ease to the point where he went inside and took his dog with him, thinking that his dog may have reacted to either his reaction or the appearance of the craft. The second sighting a short time later was made partly because he looked up at the sky, searching for a return of the first craft. Lack of noise, steady direction and traveling at a speed most airline planes would not achieve without much noise leads this FI to call it Other."

Sammamish is a city in King County, Washington, population 64,548.

California witness describes lights in triangular formation

A California witness at Rancho Mirage reported watching "eight to 10 lights in a triangle formation," according to testimony in Case 95343.

The witness was outside with a friend looking at the sky at 8:57 p.m. on October 4, 2018.

"I look at the sky four to five times a week before I go to bed and have good vision," the witness stated. "I can see satellites clearly at night moving. I was focused on a couple stars when I saw approximately eight to 10 lights in triangle formation high in the night sky for about two minutes. They were in a perfect triangle formation coming up from the horizon to nearly overhead, then they slowly came out of formation to almost a circular formation, then suddenly within two to three seconds went back into a perfect triangle formation. I followed as long as I could see before they were out of range. I know they were not Canadian geese or birds, as I know what they look like and their formation. They also were going too fast for geese. I am in the desert near Palm Springs, CA, and the sky is generally clear. I have been looking into the night sky all my life and know what I saw. At first, I thought they were geese when I saw them, but realized they were not when they came closer and were in a perfect triangle."

California MUFON Field Investigator Linda Fletchner closed this case as an Unknown Aerial Vehicle.

"Witness is credible and although this could have been a high-flying formation of military jets, I can find no evidence to prove it."

Rancho Mirage is a city in Riverside County, California, population 17,218.

Lights go out as silent UFO moves overhead

A Florida witness at Tampa reported parking lot lights going out right before a low-flying, triangular-shaped object moved overhead, according to testimony in Case 95606.

The event occurred at 10 p.m. on October 4, 2018.

"I am a security guard who spends a lot of time outside," the witness stated. "On that night, six parking lot lights at my post went out. I don't know if this is related to the object, but I do know that the resulting darkness probably enabled me to see the object. I was walking and looking up when I saw the object flying overhead, very low, with no lights or sound whatsoever. I could make out a vague triangular shape or semi-upright cone. It was moving very fast and in a straight line. Keep in mind that the object was dark against a dark sky. Have never seen a plane fly at night without lights, and it didn't have definitive wings. Not to mention, it was quite small compared to a plane. I was also struck by the lack of sound. I chased it for no more than 10 seconds or so until I lost sight of it over a tree line. I should add that there is an airport very nearby. I often see planes taking off and landing. However, this object was not flying in the direction that the planes take off and land. Its direction was more perpendicular to the airport flight path. My feelings were not fearful. It was more of a feeling of awe. I even chased it until I lost sight. I told the story to somebody, and he suggested it could have been some kind of military plane doing something 'top secret,' which could explain that it had no lights. Do military planes these days have such technology? Are military planes able to fly without lights and without sound? I genuinely would like to know. If it was not a UFO, it was still a very striking experience. Sorry, I didn't have enough time to get a picture or video."

Florida MUFON Field Investigators Diane Jacobs and Stuart Shelton closed this case as an Unknown Aerial Vehicle.

"The witness saw an object that was dark, silent, triangular in shape, solid but with fuzzy edges, moving fast in a straight line to the west (250 degrees on her compass). She believed her sighting to be suggestive of a military craft. Although Tampa International Airport is only two miles north of the sighting location, FlightRadar 24 ruled out commercial or private craft as nothing was seen within + or − 10 minutes of the sighting. The object displayed

no lights, ruling out any airplanes or helicopters. It is unlikely that a military craft would be flying without lights in such close proximity to a major airport runway, perpendicular to a flight path at such low altitude. We believe that a drone can be ruled out because, without special permission, it would not be flying near the airport."

Tampa is a major city in, and the county seat of, Hillsborough County, Florida, population 385,430.

OCTOBER 5

Colorado witness says black craft shot into space

A Colorado witness at Trinidad reported watching a fast-moving, black V-shaped object, according to testimony in Case 95364.

The witness was in a backyard "with lights out looking at planets and the glow of a nebula" at 8:15 p.m. on October 5, 2018.

"I was planning on bringing my telescope out to look at them when I first noticed what I thought was a satellite," the witness stated. "It travelled in a straight line southwest to northwest. All of a sudden it shot out into space and out of view at an incredible speed. I kept gazing at the sky when I saw a giant V-shaped, black craft with five white lights flying across the sky at an unbelievable speed. I could tell the shape of the craft as a V because it blacked the stars behind it."

Colorado MUFON Field Investigator Kevin Benham closed this case as an Unknown Aerial Vehicle.

"The witness submitted an image that was similar to what he saw," Benham stated in his report. "It was the typical chevron-shaped object with lights on the bottom. The witness promptly responded to emails and no indication of hoax on the part of the witness. From the description and image supplied, along with the unusual flight pattern, I don't believe that this was any known conventional aircraft."

Trinidad is a Home Rule Municipality that is the county seat of Las Animas County, Colorado, population 9,096.

OCTOBER 7

Maine witness says UFO hovered over treetops

A Maine witness at Saco reported watching a diamond-shaped object hovering over nearby trees, according to testimony in Case 95445.

The witness and his wife were driving home on a "well-traveled road" at 7:30 p.m. on October 7, 2018.

"Looked like a low-flying airplane until it stopped to hover above treetops," the witness stated. "My wife was talking on the phone when I noticed what looked like a plane's powerful headlight flying low in an uncommon direction. It wasn't in a usual flight path heading to any airport. I was driving east, and the object was flying south so we would have intersected within 30 seconds. I slowed down just before it crossed my path. It stopped about 50 to 100 feet above the treetops and about 100+ yards from the road.

"I had started to slow down a lot to see what it was, then I pulled over to get a better look. My wife asked me what I was doing, and I told her I saw an object hovering above the trees. Excited, she yelled out if it was a UFO as I got out of the car. I told her what it looked like, and it could be a UFO. I ran back about 200 feet and for a moment I saw a diamond-shaped craft with white and red lights at each corner and a powerful central light 'beam like' pointing downward.

"Within seconds the lights went off and it 'seemed' to vanish. The structure of the craft was obscured due to it being a flat black color, but you could see a basic structural diamond shape. Once the lights went off you could not see or hear anything.

"I was excited because it had been years since I had seen one that close. When I was a kid (10–12) a friend (15–16) and I saw one that had landed on the beach (low tide) in Saco, Maine, at dusk. It was witnessed by many people. That one was clearly visible in shape with great detail. I have never forgotten it. A couple of years ago I felt compelled to submit it to your organization along with a drawing."

"I called our friends whom we had visited earlier to tell them what I saw. I did not call anyone else. My wife was using my phone or I would have taken a picture of it."

Maine MUFON State Director Valerie C. Schultz closed this case as an Unknown Aerial Vehicle.

"The witness observed a diamond-shaped craft with white and red lights at each corner and a central light that was a powerful 'beam-like' light that pointed downward. It hovered 50 – 100 feet above the treetops without a sound or an emission. It then turned off all its lights and the witness could no longer see the object. The event location, Saco, is in an area of southern Maine near Portland where many sightings are reported. Being 17.4 miles southwest of the Portland International Jetport and National Guard base and 40.5 miles north of Pease Air Force Base, there could definitely be a military connection."

Saco is a city in York County, Maine, population 18,482.

OCTOBER 10

Triangular UFO encounter upset Washington witness

A Washington witness at Bellingham reported watching a fast-moving, triangular-shaped object with three lights, according to testimony in Case 95592.

The witness was on his way to work at a refinery near Casino at 4:30 a.m. on October 10, 2018.

"I saw a huge triangle UFO," the witness stated. "It had three lights on the side. They were red. Object was going south towards the islands. Moving fast but watched it as I drove to work for about 30 seconds."

Washington MUFON Assistant State Director Timothy Ward and State Director Maureen Morgan closed this case as an Unknown Aerial Vehicle.

"Spoke to witness at job site for about 15 minutes," Ward and Morgan stated in their report. "He told me that he saw this huge triangle with red lights on the side moving toward Lummi Island area. Witness says he watched it for about 30 seconds before it disappeared. Witness says that he never saw anything like it before and hopes to not see it again. Witness was very upset after seeing this triangle and didn't want to speak about it too much. But felt like someone should know. I assured witness that he wasn't the only one seeing triangles in this area and not to be too upset over it.

"I conclude that this witness saw what he was saying as we have had other reports of triangles in this area. Witness was visibly upset over this incident."

Bellingham is the county seat of Whatcom County, Washington, population approximately 88,500.

Fast-moving UFO reported over Atlanta

A Georgia witness at Atlanta reported watching a cigar-shaped object moving at high speed, according to testimony in Case 95682.

The witness was downtown following a meet-

ing and was standing at a bus stop on a hilly street at 2:27 p.m. on October 10, 2018.

"I saw object fly across open sky at high speed and went behind an obstruction but never emerged on flight path," the witness stated. "I had a clear view of a great expanse of sky and thought it strange that no planes were flying over as they usually do in this area. I kept scanning the horizon for more than 20 minutes and then a nearly solid, black, cigar-shaped object flew from right to left across an open area in the skyline, very low and very fast. When it went behind some buildings, I waited for it to come out from behind them in that direction in the next open area at that altitude or higher, but it never did. I was looking at it very intently and felt confused and later as I reflected on it, I realized that the object had no tail section and was flying below anything of that size that I had seen before. After the sighting, planes began passing over and around the area within 10 minutes as they normally do. These planes made noise close or distant, but not the black, cigar-shaped object. One other thing that caught my eye was a reddish webbing look or corona that was barely visible all over the object. I never thought it was a plane; I just felt stunned and confused while looking at it."

Georgia MUFON Chief Investigator Jerry Carlson closed this case as an Unknown Aerial Vehicle.

"The witness stated that he could not see any of the normal air traffic that is normally visible from that location in downtown Atlanta," Carlson wrote in his report. "Since the height of the cloud ceiling was 1,800 feet per FlightRadar24, all of the commercial arriving or departing air traffic was above the ceiling height, so therefore commercial air traffic can be eliminated. Another possibility is that this is an unknown type of military aircraft. And again, for any type of aircraft to be flying over the downtown area of a major American city, under 1,800 feet above the ground, is also very unlikely. Since the object was seen at only a 5-degree elevation above the horizon, there is a possibility that this could have been a news station or private drone seen by the witness at an edge-on view. However, since the relative size was an aspirin, and some of the largest commercial drones can be up to 4 feet in diameter, a 4-foot drone would be the relative size of an aspirin at approximately 250 feet from the witness. A smaller drone would have to be much closer to be the relative size of an aspirin. At 250 feet or less, it would be very clear to the witness that he was looking at a drone, so this can also be eliminated."

Atlanta is the capital of Georgia, population 486,290.

OCTOBER 11

Fast-moving shiny UFO reported over Georgia

A Georgia witness at Carrollton reported watching a fast-moving, "very shiny object," according to testimony in Case 95738.

The event occurred at 6:24 p.m. on October 11, 2018.

"Spotted a very shiny object in sky moving very rapidly," the witness stated. "We live next to a small airport and see planes flying over us daily, so this object was like none that I have seen before. I was playing in our pasture with my dog and a small Piper plane was flying over us at a low level, so I looked up and then noticed above that plane a very shiny object moving extremely fast. What caught my eye was how reflective it was and how fast it was going. I see jets fly over from the Atlanta airport daily but never any object like this. There was no sound coming from it like jets make. I grabbed my iPhone and started recording it. In the video it appears to go back and forth, and it is very far away but disappears rapidly in the skyline. The object moved behind the trees and

I lost sight of it. This is not my first time seeing strange things in my pasture, so I do believe the airport is some kind of attraction that draws them. I was proud for once I got some proof on video."

Georgia MUFON Chief Investigator Jerry Carlson closed this case as an Unknown Aerial Vehicle

"The object appeared similar to a commercial jet transport plane traveling at a high altitude, although there was no contrail or aircraft wings seen by the witness or recorded on the video," Carlson stated in his report. "In checking FlightRadar24 around the time of the witness sighting, no tracks of commercial aircraft could be found in the vicinity of the witness sighting, or in a similar heading of the object seen by the witness. It is clear that the object seen by the witness (and verified by the witness video) is an aerial craft traveling at a high altitude at a high speed. If the craft had wings, they were much too small to be seen by the witness or recorded on the video. Since it is not possible to obtain the tracking data of military aircraft, there is a possibility that this object was some type of military aircraft; however, there is no other evidence of this. Therefore, since no other explanation can explain the identity of this craft, the above classification must be made."

Carrollton is the county seat of Carroll County, Georgia, population 26,815.

OCTOBER 12

Triangular UFO 'fast moving' over California skies

A California witness at Citrus Heights reported watching a fast-moving, triangular-shaped object that hovered above her vehicle, according to testimony in Case 95590.

The witness and her husband and a friend were playing Pokémon Go in the grocery lot near her home at 1:01 a.m. on October 12, 2018.

"Very busy city near a shopping mall," the witness stated. "Craft flew up into our view in distance about 15 miles from us. Suddenly within two to four minutes, the craft was right above our car. We opened the moon roof to see and it was so close we could see the craft outline. Its lights were positioned in a triangular shape but lightly resembled the 'Enterprise.' I know, 'the Enterprise? Really?' Yes, really. The disk portion of the craft had a light on top and the 'wings' had lights atop them as well, giving it a triangular look (like three lights in a triangle pattern with the point at the top.) As close as it was it produced no sound like a helicopter or other aircraft. It was very fast. It had no specific destination it seemed. It almost acted as if it was just 'checking things out.' It randomly flashed in no specific pattern and seemed to 'dodge' a commercial aircraft as it flew near the area we were in. It could turn on a dime and move upward and downward in place. I saw the craft again on the 13th at the same time. When I notice it, it seems to follow us while we played Pokémon until we headed home. Then it seemed to part ways with us finally. My husband and close friend were present during both sightings. Shortly after both sightings, a second strange craft resembling a military drone with white and a red flashing light moved to the area and seemed to patrol the zone for about another hour. These things seem to ignore other aircraft unless they get too close. Then they seem to move out of the way. Or better put, move from view of other aircraft pilots."

California MUFON Assistant State Director Devlin Rugne closed this case as an Unknown Aerial Vehicle.

"I did a Google search for drone images and found only one quadcopter that was similar to the white lights that her 32-second video had in it," Rugne stated in her report. "Without talking with her to gather more info, I really

can't determine what it was. The video shows it quite far away and didn't appear as close as she said it was. At 1 a.m., it doesn't seem likely that someone would be out that late flying their drone around. Based on the description it doesn't seem like a normal conventional craft, and she put down they saw it for an hour."

Citrus Heights is a city in Sacramento County, California, population 83,301.

Multiple UFOs described over Orlando skies

A Florida witness at Orlando reported watching "a large craft and smaller, triangle crafts interacting," according to testimony in Case 95529.

The incident began at 1:45 a.m. on October 12, 2018.

"Very clear night, sky full of stars - normally never such high visibility," the witness stated. "I was watching regular air traffic fly in and out of MCO [Orlando International Airport] located just southeast of the city. I live on the 20th floor of a high-rise overlooking Lake Eola to the east. A light appeared from high in the sky, not a point source that resembles a star, this was almost an omni light source and it was a hazy, white blue in color. The blur of light quickly sped across the entire horizon in a matter of seven to 10 seconds. It had to be traveling thousands of miles an hour. At first, I thought it might be a shooting star, but it moved with intelligence, banking and changing direction as if it were piloted. As it disappeared from view, I returned my gaze to the area where it originated, now to see a gigantic craft high in the atmosphere. This shape appeared to be an extruded triangle in shape with seven points of light on all its sides and a dim red light at its corners. The shape maneuvered briefly in the sky, so I could tell it was a dimensional object and not a field of lights or flares. This shape slowly dissipated into the sky, and within a matter of seconds, it had completely disappeared. I ran inside to grab my iPhone to document anything further. Upon returning, I looked up directly above my building to see a black triangle zooming by overhead. This craft was close enough that I could see its whole shape as it rotated and spun with dull lights on each edge of the craft. The object then banked towards where the larger ship was earlier, and to my astonishment- it reappeared for a matter of seconds as this smaller craft flew in its direction. But again within a matter of seconds, everything seemed to slowly shift away into nothing."

Florida MUFON Field Investigator David Toon closed this case as an Unknown Aerial Vehicle.

"The witness reported an unusual series of three different sightings near and above the high-rise building where he lives in a relatively short period of time," Toon stated in his report. "The witness is educated and employed at Universal Studios. He describes the series of sightings starting with watching aircraft operations in the distance at Orlando International Airport. The report is detailed and unusual in that each of the three objects reported was separate but possibly related to each other in origin of sighting and direction of flight. Flightradar24 did not show any aircraft in this area during this time. The relationship of proximity and timing of all three objects within sight of the witness in a relatively short period of time offers no indication of man-made flight or characteristics. The details offered in subsequent witness correspondence helped form my opinion these objects could not be correlated to any known phenomenon or craft."

Orlando is a city in and county seat of Orange County, Florida, population 2,509,831.

OCTOBER 13

UFO moves close to Canadian witness

A Canadian witness at Stoney Creek reported

a very low-flying, boomerang-shaped UFO, according to testimony in Case 98344.

The witness was cooking in an 11th floor apartment at 8:58 p.m. on October 13, 2018.

"My apartment was getting smoky, so I went to open the door," the witness stated. "As I opened the balcony door, I was already starting to walk back to the kitchen until I noticed that something in the air felt very wrong and not right. It was a very dark night and there is a lot of forest in my area. As I went to the balcony and looked into the sky, I noticed an object that I thought was a cloud moving towards me. I thought it was a cloud because the object literally blended into the sky. I could hardly see the object at first, but then I noticed this object was moving in my direction and its elevation dropped incredibly fast. Then it dropped so low that it felt like it was barely above the height I was at. The craft had five lights come on out of nowhere, and it slowly moved over top of the townhouses across the road from my building. I called out, 'hey' and waved to get the craft's attention but nothing happened. The craft slowly moved towards the Devil's Punchbowl (southwest towards Hamilton Mountain) until it was out of my sight of vision. This craft was within 100 feet from me, maybe a little more. Its elevation seemed like it was barely above me. Like I said, I could have thrown a baseball at the craft, that's how close it was. It was so dark I could not tell if there were windows or not. The five lights on the bottom of the craft were all evenly spaced. The craft looked very similar to a picture of the Phoenix Lights."

Canada MUFON Chief Investigator Ryan Stacey closed this case as an Unknown Aerial Vehicle.

"I believe the witness to be extremely credible and rational," Stacey stated in his report. "The daytime photo shows no obstructions, and the witness best describes seeing something that has previously been classified as Unknown in a different part of the world. Either the witness wants to believe that this is the same object, or the witness did see something quite unusual and is using the Phoenix Lights as reference. Either way, I am unable to determine what this is."

Stoney Creek is a community in the city of Hamilton in the Canadian province of Ontario.

OCTOBER 15

California witness reports large 'invisible ship'

A California witness at Sonora reported hearing and feeling "an extremely large, invisible ship," according to testimony in Case 95599.

The event occurred at 5 p.m. on October 15, 2018.

"It was a beautiful day yesterday on our Northern California ranch," the witness stated. "Not a cloud in the sky. For some reason I was so compelled to be outside. This is unusual for me. At approximately 4 p.m. I was on the phone with my mother-in-law. I was standing on our front patio, which is off the master bedroom at the opposite end of the house where my husband and three young children were. I heard this weird rumble. I started to look around and then whoosh—right over my head—I felt this ship go right over me with such a force. It wasn't a normal jet noise. It was completely invisible. Again, there were no clouds. I ran around the corner where my family was, and they were all completely freaked out. We heard two loud gunshots after that. We have a neighbor who is a little off his rocker and a Native American. I should probably ask him what he was shooting at. Possibly the sky. We seemed to be the only ones who experienced this. It doesn't surprise me though. I have had many sightings and experiences. This scares the pants off me though. It was a rough night to sleep, to say the least. I just want to stress how massive this thing was. I could feel the weight and shape of it. I didn't

have to see it. It was like a giant, rectangular, flat ship and left us trembling. I am a born-again, spirit-filled believer and I do know that the name of Jesus is powerful. Darkness must flee at his name. I'm not claiming to know these are fallen beings and their ships. For all I know it could be government. I've never shared any of my experiences and sightings before now. But this one was so unique I had to share."

California MUFON Assistant State Director Devlin Rugne closed this case as Unknown Aerial Vehicle.

"What she and her family experienced was nothing conventional," Rugne stated in her report. "I am closing this out as an Unknown Aerial Vehicle (UAV) because some kind of invisible craft flew over their house at a low altitude that created a whoosh sound and a pressure."

Sonora is the county seat of Tuolumne County, California, population 4,903.

OCTOBER 16

Saucer-shaped UFO hovers over Wyoming campsite

A Wyoming witness at Midwest reported watching a green, glowing ball about the size of a basketball hovering near a campsite, according to testimony in Case 95874.

The witness was camped 15 miles west of Midwest and was staying in a canvas tent at 9:53 p.m. on October 16, 2018.

"I couldn't sleep and was sitting in my truck when I saw two large, saucer-shaped craft moving vertically in unison on the horizon," the witness stated. "I then noticed a green glowing object about the size of a baseball, within 50 yards of me. There was something resembling a bag of about two feet in length below the ball, but I could never get a clear look at it."

The witness watched this object, which was moving within 40 to 400 yards of the tent for nearly one hour.

"I tried repeatedly to figure out what this object was doing, with no success. It would go from hovering to vibrating to moving very fast, seemingly at random and with no discernible purpose. I remember saying aloud to myself, 'this cannot be real.' As if it heard me or read my thought, it immediately moved east approximately 400 yards, then returned to hover over me at approximately 40 yards."

The witness recalls the object's movement as a "blur."

"I remember saying aloud, 'okay, you're not fake.' It hovered there for a moment, and this was the only time during the encounter that I felt uneasy or threatened. Shortly thereafter it returned to its random movements."

The witness then returned to the tent to wake up a hunting partner, but with no luck.

"I returned to my truck and this is where my memory stops. I woke up in my sleeping bag the next morning. My hunting partner asked if I'd tried to wake him, saying something about lights. I told him it was nothing, just a meteor. At that point I was sure he wouldn't believe me. I have a feeling of losing time and memory. My eyes were irritated and red for two days afterward. My throat and mouth were extremely sore for four or five days, and my lower lip appeared burned, turning white, then peeling, with five small scabs on it. My ears also rang for several days. I have never had any previous UFO experiences and this episode has left me quite unnerved."

Wyoming MUFON State Director Richard Beckwith and Field Investigator Gregory Vasquez closed this case as an Unknown – Other.

"Based on the initial witness statement, two large saucer craft were first seen, then a green orb that moved quickly from 40 to 400 feet from the witness," Beckwith and Vasquez stated in their report. "The area was reported to be about 15 miles west of Midwest, WY, which is both remote and isolated. The time of the sighting is being roughly approximated to be 9:35 p.m. for the purpose of weather data, due to the report stating that the friend of the witness was sleeping in the tent at the time. There are a number of airports around that area, and without further information from the witness, the two saucer-like craft cannot be verified as potential conventional aircraft or unknown aerial vehicles (UAVs). The focus of this investigation is based on the green object or orb, which was close to the witness and therefore likely better identified by him. Due to the remoteness of the location and the close proximity to the witness, the object was not likely a drone, which would be heard.

"The physical effects may be coincidental to the sighting, but without further discussion with the witness, are not able to be verified. Based on the submitted description of the green object or orb, the disposition of the case is Unknown – Other."

Midwest is a town in Natrona County, Wyoming, population 404.

OCTOBER 17

Cigar-shaped UFO described over Virginia skies

A Virginia witness at Richmond reported watching a "small, white, cigar-shaped object that moved slowly across the sky," according to testimony in Case 95653.

The witness stepped outside at work for a cigarette at 6:15 p.m. on October 17, 2018.

"It was about a year ago when I first saw the strange object in the sky," the witness stated. "At first, I thought it could be a really high airplane, but I could clearly see there were no wings on it and it wasn't making any sound at all. Plus, it seemed to be moving too slowly to stay in the sky if it was a plane. It looked like an airplane fuselage moving at the speed of a blimp. I have seen them on four or five different occasions, and it has always been in the evening around 6-7 p.m. The objects are usually moving west to east, except today it was moving south to north. The object appears to be white, cigar-shaped and the size of it from my perspective is about the size of a tic-tac. It makes no sound or contrail and moves in a slow, straight line. It is visible until it goes behind a building or trees and out of view. A couple of times a second one has appeared."

Virginia MUFON Field Investigator Victor B. Rodriguez closed this case as an Unknown Aerial Vehicle.

"Witness failed to corroborate by allowing a personal interview," Rodriguez stated in his report. "However, the video and still photos substantiate his reported statement. Photo is remarkably similar to one taken in 2017 in the same area."

Richmond is the capital of Virginia, population 204,214.

OCTOBER 18

UK witness describes hovering bright sphere

A United Kingdom witness at Mercaston reported a hovering, bright, sphere-shaped object that quickly moved away, according to testimony in Case 95673.

The incident occurred at 8:25 p.m. on October 18, 2018.

"Tonight, was a perfectly clear sky," the witness stated. "My eye was caught by a bright, spherical object in the southeast in the distance. I thought it was the moon, but the moon was a half-moon clearly visible to the south-southwest. This sphere was three to four times brighter and visibly two to three times larger than the moon (had the moon been full). I went outside and watched the sphere hover for three to four minutes, taking several pictures on my iPhone. After it hovered, pulsating slowly, it sped off at huge velocity, but still silent, before disappearing from view in an instant. While it sped off it appeared to leave a pulsating trail, then stopped for an instant before it then totally vanished from view. While this was going on, I could clearly see many planes in the distance and at high altitude. The local airport is 15 miles or so away, and we see many, many planes each and every night and day. Even the planes that fly over closely would typically be visible with all three lights—white, green and red—but even the closest of these lights would appear as about two to five percent of the size of this object. About 1992, I witnessed three similar objects in the same location. They hovered for longer, weren't quite as bright and moved off at high speed to the east. They were also silent and about the same size."

United Kingdom MUFON National Director Jack Turnbull closed this case as an Unknown Aerial Vehicle.

"Spoke to the witness on October 19, 2018," Turnbull wrote in his report. "He saw something in the night sky described as follows: Large, bright, around six degrees off where the moon was in view. It remained in sight for about three minutes, after which it moved very suddenly left and then up and in an instant vanishing in due course. This was his second encounter with something unusual, the previous one being in 1992. He admitted being well-versed regarding this subject, his opinion being that on the balance of probability there is strange stuff moving about in our skies. Sounded very credible. Conclusion: witnessed an unidentified aerial object, type unknown."

Mercaston is a hamlet in Derbyshire, England.

OCTOBER 21

UFO described hovering over Wisconsin corn field

A Wisconsin witness at Belleville reported watching a "metallic object" hovering over a corn field, according to testimony in Case 95770.

The witness was driving southbound toward Belleville/New Glarus from a landscaping job in Middleton at 5:30 p.m. on October 21, 2018.

"I crossed the Sugar River bridge just before Montrose Road," the witness stated. "At that time to my right I could see an object/light over the corn field, between Walter Road and Highway 92. I thought it was very odd. This light seemed to be very low for a plane and was not moving at all. I took my first right onto Walter Road to get a better view. As I approached the turn onto Walter Road, I noticed that it was not a light. This object was so metallic/chrome it shone like a light. It was stationary at about helicopter altitude over this cornfield. I watched it for about 15 seconds after I was able to pull over. As I was trying to decipher the exact shape of the object, it appeared to become almost thinner until I could see a small dot and then nothing. This happened in just seconds, if even that. I couldn't have been the only person to see this. The highway was very busy. And there were no clouds in sight. It was a perfectly clear sky. I have no idea what this was. However, this is what I saw and exactly how it happened."

Wisconsin MUFON State Director Zelia Edgar closed this case as an Unknown-Other.

"Around 5:30 the evening of October 21, 2018, a man was driving home from a landscaping job, passing near the Belleville/New Glarus area, when he rounded a corner and saw a low, brightly illuminated object hovering completely motionlessly over a field to his right. He took the next right turn and pulled over. He described the object as the size of an aspirin to his view, hovering completely still about a half-mile away and at the same altitude of a helicopter or crop-duster plane. The witness stated that the object appeared to be metallic, chrome-like, so brightly illuminated by the sun that he could barely make out its shape, which he described as vaguely spherical. The object then proceeded to evaporate, completely vanishing where it was. The whole event, from first sighting the object to it vanishing, took about a minute. After the witness got back on the road, about 15 minutes later, a semi-truck driver, pulled over alongside the road, was pointing up at the sky. The witness is unsure whether it is connected, though I would like to make note of the coincidence if it is not.

"Because of the detailed description of the sighting afforded by the proximity of the witness to the object, and described to me in the witness interview, it is my conclusion that this man did observe an anomalous aerial object."

Belleville is a village in Dane and Green counties, Wisconsin, population 2,385.

OCTOBER 22

Two UFOs reported over small Mississippi town

A Mississippi witness at Pass Christian reported watching a "grayish, oval-shaped, elongated form" moving slowly followed by a smaller, disc-shaped object, according to testimony in Case 95806.

The incident occurred at 9:30 a.m. on October 22, 2018.

"An Apache helicopter passed by at low altitude, speeding from the west in the Gulf Coast's airspace," the witness stated. "Minutes later, a grayish, oval-shaped, elongated form passed by considerably slowly leaving ominous atmospheric anomalies in its wake. Minutes later, another smaller, disc-shaped object passed by leaving an atmospheric anomaly."

Mississippi MUFON CAG Manager John A. Gagnon closed this case as an Unknown Aerial Vehicle.

"The witness provided one video clip, which showed an object passing by the camera person's location. The object was not discernible. Witness responded and stated the anomaly was smoke in a triangle hole shape that appeared behind the object. This statement made no sense and the witness did not attempt to clarify it. The object in the video clip was too far away to identify."

Pass Christian is a city in Harrison County, Mississippi, population 4,613.

OCTOBER 23

Two disc-shaped UFOs reported over Pennsylvania

A Pennsylvania witness at California reported watching a silverish-white, glowing disc, according to testimony in Case 95826.

The witness was outside at 12:52 p.m. on October 23, 2018, walking from the California University of Pennsylvania campus to the Borough of California near the intersection of Green and Third Streets to play the lottery.

"Saw a flash in the sky that caught my attention," the witness stated. "When I looked up, I observed two silvery-white disks that were glowing and moving toward the west-northwest. When I pulled out my phone to take a video they disappeared."

Pennsylvania MUFON Field Investigator Dean LaSalvia closed this case as an Unknown Aerial Vehicle.

"I contacted the witness at his residence," LaSalvia wrote in his report. "Just past Booker Towers he saw a flash that caught his eye. He looked up and observed two, silvery-white, glowing disks traveling in a west-northwest

direction. He described the objects as metallic-looking, plate-shaped, about the size of a quarter in the sky, traveling below the clouds about the same speed as a plane. He observed the objects for about 15 seconds and when he went to record the objects with his cell phone they were gone. He stated one object was slightly ahead of the other."

"A check was made with California Borough Police to see if there had been other reports of the flying disks. At this time there have been no other reports made.

"When asked if it could have been a meteor that he saw, he explained that they had no glowing tail and that they were plate-shaped. He also stated that the objects made no sound, so he ruled out drones."

"Without any photos or other witness testimony, it is undetermined what the witness may have observed."

California is a borough in Washington County, Pennsylvania, population 6,795.

OCTOBER 25

Ohio disc-shaped UFO disappears and reappears

An Ohio witness near Dilles Bottom, Ohio, reported watching a fast-moving, gray disc-shaped UFO, according to testimony in Case 96048.

The witness was driving southbound along Route 2 in West Virginia, across the river from Dilles Bottom, at 6:30 p.m. on October 25, 2018.

"I noticed a fast-moving, large, featureless disc streaking above Dilles Bottom, Ohio," the witness stated. "It was distinctly gray against a blue sky. All clouds were white only. There were no clouds. It disappeared and reappeared five times in a span of less than 10 seconds.

It slowed each time it reappeared. It became stationary at an altitude of a few hundred feet above a hill. It then disappeared completely. The sky had broken clouds, but the disk appeared in the clear blue sky. It was about 300 feet in diameter. No lights were observed. As it descended, the bottom of the disc appeared to create some kind of thin discharge all over the visible bottom of the disk. This discharge-like smoke disappeared over the edges of the disk."

Ohio MUFON Field Investigator Tim Kelly closed this case as an Unknown Aerial Vehicle.

"The details of the report, describing the object as being in a clear blue sky, progressively appearing in different attitudes as it intermittently transitioned back and forth from visible to invisible, is very strange," Kelly wrote in his report. "FI, via Google Earth Street View, 'drove' the section of road the witness was on at the time. There are a number of trees at certain points on the road he was travelling; however, witness claims that the large majority of his travel occurred in an area that was clear of trees. Per Stellarium, at the time, the sun was about one degree below the west-southwestern horizon. Witness during interview stated that at times while the object was rotating/rolling, the sun seemed to be brightly reflecting off its surface. This would suggest that the object was not a small, low-flying, very close nearby object such as a drone, with its underside being hit by the sun's rays, since direct sun rays would have likely been blocked by the hills between the witness's vehicle and the setting sun. The adjacent hills between the witness's vehicle location and the sun are close by the road and are approximately 400 feet higher than the road surface, which is only about 30 feet above the level of the adjacent river. FI checked the web for photos/availability of drones/RC aircraft whose physical appearance was same as the report, but FI could not locate anything. Checked local newspaper/TV station stories, but no report of anything. Checked local city and county police, but call logs have no UFO reports. No MADAR match.

"Conditions and Candidates considered: A nearby model airplane or consumer drone: Unlikely. Shape inconsistent. Also, apparent size would likely have varied greatly during sighting. Also, the invisibility issue.

"Witness Credibility: Witness is 65 years old. Has an MBA. Accounting. Witness provided full background info in CMS. CMS data and interview info are coherent. Witness seems sincere and credible.

Conclusion: Based on the CMS data, interview and FI analysis, there appears to be no reasonable natural or man-made explanation."

Dilles Bottom is an unincorporated community in Belmont County, Ohio.

Hovering orb reported over small NY town

A New York witness at Montezuma reported watching a hovering orb that slowly ascended into the clouds, according to testimony in Case 95880.

The witness was driving eastbound along I-90 between exits 41 and 40 at about 7:10 p.m. on October 25, 2018.

"I saw to the southeast, in front of me as I drove, an orb of light," the witness stated. "It was, from my position sitting in the driver's seat, about the size of a quarter in the sky, and at about 50 degrees above the horizon. I had passed the eagle statue in Montezuma National Wildlife Refuge already. It hovered for a few moments, not moving. It sort of flickered, but it did not blink or flash lights of any kind. I could not see any red/green lights. The orb's light reflected off the clouds. It slowly rose straight up into the sky, continuing to throw light on the clouds around it. It eventually disappeared behind/through the clouds. I kept watching but no other show of light appeared. As for my reactions and actions, I just kept driving and watching, perhaps a bit irresponsibly. I felt stunned, in awe, and tried to scrutinize the light to see if it was a plane, helicopter, or cellphone tower in an unexpected place. I drive this route home frequently, and I was surprised to see a light where I wasn't used to seeing it. If I had not heard of a similar sighting before, I would not have considered it a potential UFO sighting."

New York MUFON Field Investigator Mary Fancher closed this case as an Unknown Aerial Vehicle.

"I believe the witness saw something unusual," Fancher wrote in her report. "Since she drives that route regularly, she's aware of the normal objects that might be in the sky. This caught her attention."

Montezuma is a town in Cayuga County, New York, population 1,277.

OCTOBER 26

Philadelphia witness had good view of UFO

A Pennsylvania witness at Philadelphia reported watching a hovering orb that eventually flew away, according to testimony in Case 95886.

The witness was in South Philadelphia at 11 p.m. on October 26, 2018.

"I was holding my three-month-old son and looking out my north-facing third floor windows," the witness stated. "There is an airport nearby and I see loads of helicopters and drones, but this was different than anything I have seen in the seven years that I have lived here."

The witness said he sees many objects from the master bedroom window on the third floor.

"I have five windows that face north, south, and west and I have no curtains since I like to see the city views. What I saw was a large, bright red, glowing orb about 11-30 feet in diameter that hovered erratically and changed colors every 30 to 60 seconds. It changed from completely red to completely green then completely blue. It was red most of the time and I don't think it was a sequential pattern; I believe it was random because I saw more red and green than blue."

The witness said the orb was flying east, and then it would hover and stay completely still.

"It then changed direction and flew west very quickly and disappeared. The total viewing was about five minutes. I've scoured the news and have seen no other accounts of this, which is perplexing because there should be multiple witnesses. South Philly is a busy area on a Friday night because of the cheesesteak places that tourists line up at. I'm hoping someone else out there saw this as well."

MUFON Pennsylvania Field Investigator William Morse closed this case as an Unknown-Other.

"The object changed color from red to green to blue," Morse stated in his report. "The color did not come from a light or lights on the object; the entire object was the color described. She watched as the object flew in the northwest and west quadrant of her viewing area for five to six minutes at 'helicopter level,' and then the object flew off to the northwest.

"The witness indicated that she has an excellent view of the Philadelphia skyline, and that she is familiar with the aircraft that are commonly in the skies in that area, but that she has never seen anything like what she reported. The evening of the sighting was rainy with several overcast cloud layers. The skies were 2,800 broken, 3,600 broken, and 4,300 overcast.

"The only aircraft activity recorded on FlightRadar24 was American Airlines flight 551, an Airbus 319 aircraft that departed from PHL at 11:02 p.m. en route to Detroit. This aircraft appeared to the south of the witness and traveled to the northwest. It was in the northwest quadrant of the witness's viewing area at 11:06 p.m. as it turned left and departed to the northwest, but it was only in that area for no more than two minutes and would not have matched the sighting description given by the witness. The aircraft was at 3,500 feet, much higher than the altitude reported by the witness, and above the 2,800-foot overcast layer. If this had been the object seen by the witness, the right wing of the aircraft would have been the only wing visible, and the navigation light on that side would have been green. The only red light visible might have been an anti-collision light that would have been either flashing white or flashing red, not steady red as reported by the witness.

"With the multiple overcast cloud layers that night and the 4,300-foot overcast layer, it would have been impossible for the witness to see any astronomical objects, and had it been visible, the only astronomical object that could have been mistaken for the object was Vega, but at 11 p.m. that night Vega was still at 25 degrees above the horizon, and remained above the northwest horizon well after midnight that evening.

"Because of the inability to identify the object, this case is closed with a disposition of "Other."

Philadelphia is the largest city in Pennsylvania, population 1,584,138.

Icelandic witness describes 'glowing circle' over church

An Icelandic witness at Reykjavík reported watching a glowing circle with "five, human-like beings" inside hovering over a church, according to testimony in Case 96858.

The witness was walking home at 11:10 p.m. on October 26, 2018.

"I walk a path that intersects another path that leads all the way up to the church," the witness stated. "There are trees on both sides of this path that leads to the church and both sides are bordered with tall trees, but there is a nice 20-30 meters between the trees on each side. I often walk that path home late at night after hanging out with my friend, and I always turn to look at the church. This time I could see a glowing circle and the outer perimeter of this circle was split into four sections, and I knew that I was seeing something not of this world. One-quarter had a silver or chromium-type color. One-quarter had a very gray color, almost like a storm cloud. The other quarter had the lightest green color I have ever seen. The final quarter was light blue like the sea in Spain and other tropical waters, but it was not transparent. The circle had to have been about 50 meters in diameter. It was hovering about 80 meters above the church tower, which is about 15 to 25 meters tall. My distance from the thing was about 130 meters. I could see inside the circle; it had four sections that were illuminated by a white light, which came from a light source on the roof of the dome. I saw five human-like beings that I estimated to be about 1.5 to 5 meters tall. They were skinny-like people who had been starved to the brink of death. They had no distinct outlines and appeared to move without moving their legs, of which they had two. I could not make out a face on those beings as I was way too far away, but they each had what looked like a human head, except it appeared to have no ears. The beings stayed in that chamber or room for about three minutes, and they would move around like there was a glass floor under them. During the time I felt stunned. My muscles were not tense, but I could not move. I tried to move my hands and walk closer, but my body just refused to. It was a very calm experience, and at no time did I feel threatened or scared. I was mostly stunned. When the beings were gone, it took about 20 seconds until the craft moved straight up about 300 meters, and then it stopped and moved up at an angle, going so fast it left a trail of rainbow-colored light like a meteor, except the trail started 450 meters above me and became smaller the farther it went up. It pretty much just disappeared into the darkness of the clear skies. When it was gone, I was just processing it and then I said to myself, 'That was quite the spectacle,' in my native language. I have told a few friends, parents, my priest and my girlfriend. My priest believes me and a few of my friends but my parents and my girlfriend laughed at it. I don't know how to feel about this encounter as it was such a calm experience and nothing significant happened during it. I have a lot of questions and I hope this can help me and others find answers."

The MUFON International Director of Investigations for Iceland, Steve Hudgeons, closed this case as Unknown-Other.

Reykjavík is the capital and largest city of Iceland, population 128,793.

OCTOBER 28

Low-flying UFO reported over California base

A California witness at Sacramento reported watching a triangular-shaped UFO with three lights in each corner, according to testimony in Case 96472.

The event occurred on October 28, 2018.

"Friends and I carpool together," the witness stated. "We went to his [sic] house to drive our cars back home. A lot of shooting stars were seen that night. As I was getting in my car I looked up and saw a triangular UFO with lights on each corner. I believe it belongs to the Air Force as there is a base nearby. These kind, if UFOs, are seen in California near Air Force bases. The object was pretty close to the ground. It moved as fast as a plane, maybe slower. My friend also saw this object. We

watched until it was out of our line of view. The lights did not blink, but the object was a flat triangle, so at times it seemed to have parts of the UFO disappear. This was all after midnight. I've seen objects like lights disappearing out of nowhere, or a light moving in random crazy locations, unlike a satellite. This was the first time I saw an object, and can say for certain it was not a plane or an aircraft that was recognizable."

California MUFON Field Investigator Valerie Benko closed this case as an Unknown Aerial Vehicle.

"I was not able to reach the witness," Benko stated in her report. "I tried emailing and calling but as stated above [in an earlier part of her report not appearing here—ed.] the witness provided MUFON with the wrong phone number and a second phone number that just rings no matter how many times you try calling. I am going to close this case out as an unknown UAV because the witness reported observing a triangular-shaped craft. We do not have any proof that this belongs to the Air Force at this time. The witness suggested in the report he filed with MUFON that this could be a UFO from an Air Force base. I will update this case should I receive any more information or if the witness should contact me."

Sacramento is the capital city of California and the seat of Sacramento County, population 501,334.

OCTOBER 30

Michigan witness says disc UFO hovered over house

A Michigan witness at Tecumseh reported watching a hovering disc just above the roof, according to testimony in Case 96776.

The witness took the dog outside at 2 a.m. on October 30, 2018.

"In my hand I had my little flashlight pointed toward the ground," the witness stated. "I heard the wind blowing very strongly but I did not feel any wind. Finally, I noticed that the tall pine tree on the east side of the backyard was frantically whipping around. Toby did his thing and we headed southward across our patio toward the back door of our one-story home. I looked up and, to my surprise, a craft hovered about two meters above our roof. My mouth dropped open as I stood there almost paralyzed. The left side of the craft appeared to be in-line with the top of the comb of our home. After staring at it for about 15 or 20 seconds, the craft shot off eastward toward Lake Erie, making a sucking sound as it went. As I stared at its tail end, with the exception of a small tail-like fin, it appeared to be about the same width as its length. In about three or four seconds it was out of sight.

"The craft had no lights but rather appeared as a dark, solid object against the clear bluish sky line.

"The next day, I looked at the roof again and, using the many roof vents as reference points, I surmised its length to be about 40 feet.

"Note: From our home to Toledo is about 30 miles. Then we have another 150 miles to Dayton - the location of Wright-Patterson Air Force Base. Of course, if one goes in a straight line, it has to be shorter. On the other hand, as fast as it traveled, this thing could go anywhere it desired in a fraction of our time.

"In addition, my neighbor on the west says he was in the Air Force and was assigned to Area 51 for a while. Sometimes he brings the subject up, starts trembling, and then says he saw and experienced things that no human should have to see. I am a retired pastor and a Vietnam veteran."

Michigan MUFON Field Investigator Judith E. Kulka and Chief Investigator Daniel Snow closed this case as an Unknown-Other.

"Using Occam's Rule that the simplest of two or more competing theories is preferable and that an explanation for unknown phenomena should first be attempted in terms of what is already known, 'entities must not be multiplied beyond necessity,' Kulka and Snow stated in their report. "The visual characteristics, flight path inclination, travel speed and object size do not violate the premise this event was stimulated by Chinese sky lanterns, since none of the actions described in this event are outside the capabilities of a flame heat source, fireproof paper, floating sky lantern balloon. The reported wind data is consistent with the object's observed travel path."

Tecumseh is a small city in Lenawee County, Michigan, population 8,521.

Ohio witness says cigar-shaped object hovered above road

An Ohio witness at Benton reported watching a "large cylinder" hovering over a roadway, according to testimony in Case 96019.

The witness was driving southbound along Route 14 just south of Benton towards Salem at 7:40 p.m. on October 30, 2018.

"Saw a large, cigar-shaped object the size of a 747 hovering over the road in front of me," the witness stated. "As I was approaching the area it was flashing red and yellow lights. When I got almost up under it, it ascended straight up and disappeared."

Ohio MUFON Field Investigator Scott Miller closed this case as an Unknown Aerial Vehicle.

"I found the witness to be credible and reported as they remembered the event," Miller stated in his report."

Benton is an unincorporated community in Texas Township, Crawford County, Ohio.

NJ witness says hovering triangle was 'huge'

A New Jersey witness at Jackson Township reported watching a large, hovering, triangular-shaped object with flashing lights at the tips of each point, according to testimony in Case 96033.

The witness was at Six Flags amusement park at 8:30 p.m. on October 30, 2018.

"I looked to the right and saw a huge, hovering object," the witness stated. "At first, we thought it was a drone, blimp or satellite and then we realized how massive the object was. It was huge. It was large and dark black, making no noise at all. It had flashing lights on the three tips of the triangle and a top part similar to a diamond shape. After watching for a minute or so trying to grasp what it was, it slowly crept forward and then it was gone, and I couldn't see it anymore."

New Jersey MUFON State Section Director Robert Spearing closed this case as an Unknown Aerial Vehicle.

"Used flightradar24.com to discern if any known objects were over Great Flags at 8:30 p.m. on October 30," Spearing wrote in his report. "Nothing within 20 miles, 30 minutes before until 30 minutes after. Flights avoid the area. All the earmarks of a traditional, low-flying, slow-flying, massive, black triangle."

Jackson Township is a township in Ocean County, New Jersey, population 54,856.

UFO approaches 50 feet from Indiana witness

An Indiana witness at Michigan City, Indiana, reported watching a triangular-shaped UFO just 50 feet away, according to testimony in Case 98437.

The witness was walking down the pier on Lake Michigan on October 30, 2018.

"It was cloudy and, when I made it to the lighthouse, I was sitting and watched the craft come out of the mist about 50 feet from me," the witness stated. "I was able to see the gray entity inside the craft. A beam of light hit me. I felt frozen and I could feel the energy in my head. I felt them taking everything I have learned. I could see myself in school learning. I could see everything I ever learned. I suddenly felt myself in freeze [sic] as the light stopped. Suddenly the craft took off towards Chicago, up in the air high. When it was by me it was only about 50 feet from me and about three feet from the water of Lake Michigan. When it took off it headed high in the sky towards Chicago. I had dreams and sketched a picture of what I saw."

Indiana MUFON Jeremy Efroymson closed this case as an Unknown Aerial Vehicle.

"Witness reiterated his statement and added detail," Efroymson stated in his report. "Said he was frozen with fear. The ET telepathically communicated with him, replaying moments of his life while telling him 'Everything is going to be okay.' There was a cloudy mist or fog over the water. The craft appeared suddenly. At first, he saw just a bright light. He could see a gray alien in the cockpit, operating a see-through control panel. The craft slowly backed up and then took off toward Chicago. The lights went out one at a time. The craft was 50 feet away and five feet over the waves. It was chevron-shaped. Forty feet in front, 60 on the sides, and 120 feet in the back.

"The witness was definitely scared by what he saw. He had a close-up look at the craft and its occupant, a 'gray alien.' He also provided a detailed sketch of the chevron-shaped craft and of the hand of the occupant."

Michigan City is a city in LaPorte County, Indiana, population 31,479.

OCTOBER 31

NC witness videotapes triangular UFO

A North Carolina witness at Selma reported watching and videotaping "a massive triangle" UFO flying at some distance over his house, according to testimony in Case 96052.

The witness was outside walking a dog at 9:45 p.m. on October 31, 2018.

"Noticed some strange red lights in the sky," the witness stated. "They were shaped like a triangle. I had my phone in my hand, so I filmed the whole event. It was a massive triangle-shaped craft. At first I thought it was a group of planes, but I quickly dismissed that. The object was huge and was blocking out the stars as it passed. There was no sound."

"I could not actually make out the object and the video doesn't show it as well as I could see it, but it was blocking out the stars inside the three lights, so I assume that the shape was a giant triangle. I can't actually determine the speed, but it was rather high, about cruising altitude for military jets that fly in the area (Selma is near Cherry Point, Bragg, and Pope). It's not uncommon to see Chinooks, F18s and F16s flying in the area, best guess is 500-700 knots. I did not see any other aircraft in the area before or after. I was born in 1980, I have a bachelor's degree, and I am a police officer (prior Air Force)."

North Carolina MUFON Field Investigator Linda Larsen closed this case as an Unknown Aerial Vehicle.

"He said he had worked with and seen many drones during his time in the military, but because of its high altitude and size he felt certain it was not a drone. Also, this is the second UFO that he had witnessed. In about 1990, he was with his mother in a parking lot and saw a triangle-shaped UFO. Other people in the parking lot saw it also. It was not report-ed to anyone at the time. He said he was very interested in becoming a Field Investigator for MUFON.

"After doing searches for all types and patterns of lights on drones, I could not find any that would have been that large and with lights in that pattern. After speaking with the witness (whom I found very knowledgeable on the subject and had military experience in that area) I felt due to its apparent distance and size that it most likely was not a drone. Also, there are two similar cases reported to the NUFORC website and also may be possibilities that the same object may have been seen by others."

Selma is a town in Johnston County, North Carolina, population 6,073.

NOVEMBER 2018

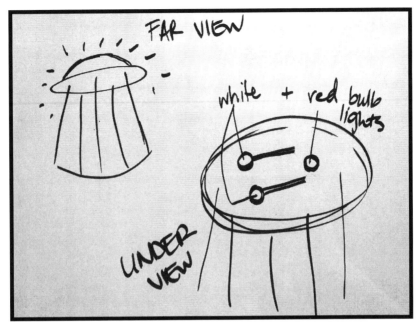

Case 96140 witness illustration. November 3, 2018.

NOVEMBER 2

Silent triangular UFO reported over Thailand

A Thai witness at Pattaya reported watching "a dull, black, triangle-shaped" object flying under 1,500 feet, according to testimony in Case 96088.

The witness and a girlfriend were standing on a 27th floor balcony facing north toward Bangkok at 9:30 p.m. on November 2, 2018.

"We both saw a dull, black, triangle-shaped craft approaching from the north at 1500 feet away from us to the west travelling at a constant speed and horizontal flight," the witness stated. "The craft had dull, dim, orange-colored, rectangular panels in each corner—three

in total. It made no sound. It had no usual aircraft ID lighting. It was totally silent—no engine or any sounds coming from it. We both clearly observed the craft for approximately 10 to 15 seconds. It was not an aircraft in the normal sense. The craft flew north to south and we lost sight as it passed across in front of our building. We regularly see aircraft flying over us from Bangkok Airport, so we are well aware of the characteristic shapes, take-off and flight ID lighting and flight paths of planes in this area. This was not a plane."

MUFON International Director of Investigations for Thailand, Steve Hudgeons Jr., closed this case as an Unknown Aerial Vehicle.

Pattaya is on the east coast of the Gulf of Thailand, population approximately 1,000,000.

NOVEMBER 3

UFO hovers over Oregon interstate highway

An Oregon witness at Walker reported a "Saturn-like" object hovered briefly over an interstate highway, according to testimony in Case 96140.

The witness was driving home from Eugene to Cottage Grove about midnight on November 3, 2018.

"Disc-shaped spacecraft ahead of me and its path came from the east as it approached," the witness stated. "It briefly hovered over the freeway and was glowing bright, white light, with the light beam underneath the same color. As I drove toward it and got closer, I could also see two white and one red, bulb-like lights on the bottom of the craft right before I drove under it and continued south before pulling over. Elevation-wise, I saw it up higher initially. It gradually decreased in elevation and was only about as high up as the top of a four- to five-story building before I passed it. By the time I pulled over and looked behind me for the spacecraft, it had disappeared."

Oregon MUFON Field Investigator Kellie Graham and State Director Thomas Bowden closed this case as an Unknown Aerial Vehicle.

"Found the witness forthcoming, pleasant and credible," Graham and Bowden stated in their report. "FI attempted to get additional witnesses through the local news agency the Register Guard, the local Eugene, OR, news source, and was unable to get the agency to post. At this time, no other reports or witnesses have been found (NUFORC, MUFON, and Internet searches). FI searched for fireballs in area and found none (www.amsmeteors.org). Contacted the local Eugene, OR, police and Oregon State Police for any sightings reported and/or police or military activity in the air in the area and was told there was none in the area on the date of reported sighting."

Walker is an unincorporated community in Lane County, Oregon.

NOVEMBER 4

Hovering disc-shaped UFO reported over Virginia

A Virginia witness at Luray reported watching a hovering "silver, shiny, disc-shaped" object, according to testimony in Case 96375.

The witness was driving from Philadelphia back to Greensboro, NC, at 3:20 p.m. on November 4, 2018.

"I'm not exactly sure how long I was driving, but the sky was clear and blue," the witness stated. "I remember being impressed by the views since I'm not used to seeing such big and vast mountain ranges. I know I was near the Shenandoah State Park because I kept seeing billboards for the exits to the caves and campgrounds. As I was driving, I looked up to the upper left of my windshield and was watching something that caught me off guard since it was silver, disk-like and not moving. I wondered if it was an airplane, but it was not moving at all. Maybe after a few seconds it shot off in a flash (flying behind me, which would be north) leaving no trail. I didn't see anything in the rearview mirror. I had music playing, so I have no idea about whether or not it made a sound. My reaction was both a surprised and happy one. It felt cool being able to see something like that since I've never seen something like that happen before."

Virginia MUFON Field Investigator Norman Gagnon closed this case as an Unknown Aerial Vehicle.

"The witness was well-educated, presented a very credible and straightforward report with nothing embellished," Gagnon stated in his report.

Luray is a town in and the county seat of Page

County, Virginia, population 4,895.

NOVEMBER 5, 2018

'Rotating' triangular UFO reported over Oregon

An Oregon witness at Newport reported watching "a flying, triangle-shaped craft that seemed to rotate as it flew by," according to testimony in Case 96204.

The witness was standing outside an apartment building at about 10:30 p.m. on November 5, 2018.

"While I was chatting with my neighbor, I just happened to look at the sky because it was so clear out tonight," the witness stated. "I noticed what at first seemed to be like a falling star. As it moved southwest along the coast, I realized that it was a scalene-shaped craft with a star-like light at each point. As it flew, it seemed to rotate. It would quickly flash each time it would rotate, and the triangle would seem to be facing a different direction, meanwhile still heading straight south down the coast. I watched it quickly fly over me. And then over a nearby building and out of my sight. I was standing there almost in a daze with my mouth open saying to my neighbor as it was flying by, 'Oh my God, what am I looking at right now?' As fast as I said that, it was gone. I felt like part of me knew that it was coming and that's why I happened to stay outside for a few more moments after walking my dog."

Oregon MUFON Field Investigator Kellie Graham and State Director Thomas Bowden closed this case as an Unknown Aerial Vehicle.

"Field Investigator found this witness pleasant and forthcoming," Graham and Bowden stated in their report. "Even though FI had trouble contacting the witness for an interview, credible also. FI contacted the Newport Police Department and inquired if there had been any reports of unknown objects on the beach around the date of this sighting and they had none. FI also asked the police department if they would be informed of any military operations in their area. They said that they would be, and that none had been reported. FI asked the police about flares being dropped on the beach and was once again told no. FI researched several web sites, including YouTube, about flying lighted kites at night and was unable to find an image close to the reported object. Lighted kites tend to have many lights for the biggest display they can get, not like the three, star-like lights on the reported object. FI found on beachconnection.net that there is no driving on the beach in Newport, OR, which if the speed of the object is to be believed, would exclude a car pulling a large, lighted kite down the beach. The object sighted was too slow and low to be a known plane and did not have the sound of the blades of a helicopter as the sighting has no sound associated with it. The object does not have the characteristics of a meteor, and according to amsmeteors.org, there were no meteor reports in the date range of November 4 to 6, 2018, in Oregon. FI found a NUFORC report of similar sighting the day before, November 4, 2018, 8:18 p.m. in Oceanside, OR. Distance between cities is 70 miles."

Newport is a city in Lincoln County, Oregon, population 10,117.

NOVEMBER 6

Triangular UFO reported hovering over Mississippi

A Mississippi witness at Hattiesburg reported watching a hovering, triangular-shaped object that quickly moved away, according to testimony in Case 96200.

The witness was driving home from work at 5:54 p.m. on November 6, 2018.

"On the outskirts of Hattiesburg, about one-half mile from home, my granddaughter and I witnessed a triangular object lit in green and white lights come from the left and stop briefly in front of us before it flew at an incredible speed forwards ahead of us into the dark sky and disappeared in a couple of seconds," the witness stated. "No sound was heard, but the radio was turned up so could not have heard if it did."

Mississippi MUFON CAG Investigator Jon Furr closed this case as an Unknown Aerial Vehicle.

"The witness saw a triangular object with lights at each corner fly over the car while driving home," Furr stated in his report. "The only evidence provided is the witness testimony, which was consistent. There is a military base in the area, so there could have been a military aircraft in the area. There is an airport in Hattiesburg that had flights going through there regularly, also. I believe this was, most likely, an airplane of some sort. As I do not have a specific flight at the time of the sighting, I am going with the witness account and closing this case."

Hattiesburg is a city primarily in Forrest County (where it is the county seat) and extending west into Lamar County, Mississippi, population 45,989.

Chevron-shaped UFO under 500 feet over Texas

A Texas witness at San Antonio reported and photographed a low-flying, chevron-shaped object, according to testimony in Case 96207.

The witness was in San Antonio for a business seminar and had stepped away to do some shopping at 8:25 p.m. on November 6, 2018.

"When I got back into my vehicle to pull out of the parking lot, I looked up and saw a large, chevron-inverted, V-shaped 'airplane' with a white, flashing light at the V point flying low

and slow, no sound," the witness stated. "I couldn't believe my eyes—it was so low and over highway 1604 going southwest along the road right next to a large shopping center area with a lot of lights and cars. I excitedly grabbed my iPhone to try and video and photograph it. Strange how my video didn't record or get the multiple photos I was taking but did get one 'live' iPhone photo, which shows the object (changed shape/color!) as a yellow-orange disc that appears to be a fluid energy source. Only way I can describe it. I tried to follow it in my car, but it disappeared, to my dismay."

Texas MUFON Chief Investigator Kenneth Jordan closed this case as an Unknown Aerial Vehicle.

"One photo to analyze," Jordan wrote in his report. "Object was solid with no discernible wings or navigation lights. Chevron shape could not be verified, nor could it be dismissed. Object is unusual and exact origin is unknown. Using witness's statement and available local information and photo analysis, this FI cannot determine the origin of the object observed, and the movement and description provided do not lend identification of normal aircraft, not to mention the low altitude and low speed."

San Antonio is the seat of Bexar County, Texas, population approximately 1.5 million.

Large boomerang-shaped UFO reported over Idaho

An Idaho witness at Boise reported watching a large, silent, boomerang-shaped object at 8,000 feet, according to testimony in Case 96312.

The witness was outside helping a friend hook on to a camp trailer at 9 p.m. on November 6, 2018.

"I looked up to see what appeared to be a crescent of dim, bluish light in the sky just slightly to the northeast of me," the witness stated. "After watching a second, I noticed it was moving. It was very large. As it got closer, I could see a dark object moving behind the light. As it got a little closer, I could see clearly that it was a boomerang-shaped craft moving silently at around 200 knots. It seemed to put off a light glow all around the craft. Brighter in the front. Almost like a static glow. It had no lights. I would have missed it if it wasn't for the glow. Once it was just about overhead, it turned west, and I lost it to the horizon. I got video but it's on my iPhone and too dark to see. May be able to pull an image out with enhancements. Three of us clearly witnessed it. It was at about 8,000 feet. It had to be close to a half-mile across. Watched it for about a minute. This all happened a mile away from the Boise Airport and Gowen Field Air National Guard Base. My family has owned and flown small planes my entire life so I'm pretty confident in the altitude and speed it was traveling. It came from the northeast flying southwest and turned directly west. I had him shut off his truck lights to try and get better video. I don't think I caught anything worthwhile, but I attached it. Don't know if it was ours or something from off-planet. It was there, it was real, it was unconventional."

Idaho MUFON State Director James Millard closed this case as an Unknown Aerial Vehicle.

"Witness description of object supports no image on video," Millard wrote in his report.

Boise is the capital and most populous city in Idaho, and is the county seat of Ada County, population 205,671.

NOVEMBER 7

'Metallic orb' group reported near Las Vegas

A Nevada witness at Las Vegas reported watching a group of "metallic orbs" changing positions as they flew, according to testimony in Case 96230.

The witness was outside around noon listening to a radio approximately seven miles east of Nellis Air Force Base at noon on November 7, 2018.

"I observed what, at first, I thought was a very large metallic plane (747 or larger) with occasional reflecting lights coming from it," the witness stated. "I couldn't really focus on it at first. It was about two miles north of me where I first observed the object/objects heading east. It seemed to be more of a blur at first, so I grabbed my binoculars and watched it through the binoculars. That's when I observed it more clearly and realized that the reason I couldn't focus clearly on it was because it was a 'group' of up to about 11 to 14, orb-like, shiny, metallic objects flying in a group, continually changing positions within the group.

"They were traveling much faster than the jetliners that fly into or out of the airports in Las Vegas. The sun was behind me. For a moment I thought it was a group of jets flying in a very tight formation, but when I was watching them through the binoculars, they appeared to be metallic, shiny orbs with something protruding out of them at different angles. That many aircraft couldn't change position that quickly and fly so close to each other without some kind of mishap. Plus, there was no sound coming from them. When I last saw them, they had almost immediately changed into two strings with three or four of them on the top string and about six or more of them on the lower string (upper and lower).

"The other two or three were leading the way in a curved pattern. Trying to describe their last position is that if you draw a backwards 'C' and add more to the lower part of the letter. Draw it with double the length in the lower string as that of the top section. By the time I finally got out the camcorder they were long gone. On a side note: I don't use illegal drugs or use alcohol. Also, I am a trained observer as

I was a member of the Civil Air Patrol."

Nevada MUFON State Director Sue Countiss and CAG Investigator Michael Barrette closed this case as an Unknown-Other.

"Made attempt to contact witness - no response," Countiss and Barrette wrote in their report. "Conclusion is based on witness statement."

Las Vegas is the county seat of Clark County, Nevada, population 648,224.

Washington UFO hovers before shooting away

A Washington witness at Lacey reported watching an object that hovered momentarily before shooting away, according to testimony in Case 96229.

The witness was driving home from work at 6:03 p.m. "in pitch black" on November 7, 2018.

"I was pulling out of the school driveway," the witness stated, "and I stopped to check for cars. And while stopped at the exit to the school, a green light shot past above my car, hovering for maybe a couple of seconds. It had a green unwavering light."

The witness at first thought it was fireworks.

"But then it was too big and stayed way too long for it to be a firework. It's also November. The object was long and almost clear, but black, and then I don't know where it went. The light vanished and after that I had this feeling one gets after passing out where your whole body feels like it was hit by a truck. And I forgot what I was doing, and my whole body felt like Jell-O for the rest of the night. And on my way from dropping my boyfriend off at home I was too scared to drive back home at night."

Washington MUFON State Section Director

Aleta DeBee closed this case as an Unknown Aerial Vehicle.

"I spoke with witness on the phone for about an hour," DeBee stated in her report. "She was exiting from the back parking lot of the elementary school where she works at a day-care after school hours. As she slowed down prior to exiting, she saw a dark, cylindrical object coming towards her from the left side of her car. It was very large and very close. It was as close to the ground as the top of a streetlight, approximately as high up as a two-story house. It was shaped like a cylinder, approximately the size of two small sedans side-by-side, and as thick as a car is tall. It was silent. When it reached the front of her vision, it stopped and hovered for between 40 and 60 seconds, then seemed to flash and then disappear. She said it was huge, shaped like a cigarette, similar to the color of Flubber in the old Disney movie. The bright green light reflected on her dashboard and on the area around the car and the house across the street. Witness stated that the green light was coming only from the back side of the object, which was the side farthest from her car. The object was 'squarish' in the front end closest to her location. She stated that it looked like there was some kind of pattern on the surface of the craft.

"Witness says she felt almost like she blacked out but was conscious the whole time. She felt her body was drained, and she was hyper-ventilating. She felt as if all of her energy was drained out of her. After it left, she found herself crying.

"The car and its radio did not stop running during this incident. After the incident, the witness called her mom to describe the sighting. Later, as she was discussing it with her mother at home, her mom suggested that she report it to MUFON. Witness also said that this was usually a busy street, with people getting off work and coming home. But she saw no one during the time of the sighting.

"Field Investigators Aleta DeBee and Kathleen Wyer visited the site on December 8, 2018, and spoke with the witness as she described the close sighting. Measurements were taken for radioactivity on the car, but none were found. No visible markings on the car were found.

"Aleta DeBee visited the homes in the cul-de-sac across from the driveway from the school, as well as the police substation just north of the school, to see if anything was seen or reported. Unfortunately (but not unexpectedly) only two of the seven homes across from the school responded to my knock. Neither of the residents from those two homes had seen anything, though one told me that some people had heard about 'activity' at Mount Rainier at various times (clear view from the neighborhood, but approximately 60 miles away). Another neighbor told me he had neither seen nor heard of any UFO at all."

"This neon glowing object was very close to the witness. It 'shot out' across the left side of her vehicle, and suddenly stopped and hovered within 50 feet of her car. It stayed there for 40 seconds to a minute, and then disappeared. She needed to stop the car and recover, because she felt drained and shocked by what she saw. She was very observant and took note of the time and description. Considering the erratic movements, silence, speed and closeness, this field investigator concludes that this is a UAV – Unknown."

Lacey is a city in Thurston County, Washington, population 42,393.

'Transparent' UFO reported moving over Florida

A Florida witness at Valrico reported watching a chevron-shaped object that appeared to be transparent or cloaked, according to testimony in Case 96766.

The witness was outside sky watching with two friends at 9:30 p.m. on November 7, 2018. Six minutes after this report, a second sighting was filed with Case 96341, 187 miles away, with matching case details.

"We were sitting in their screened-in back patio porch/lanai in our gravity chairs enjoying the clear night sky and watching the stars," the witness stated. "We do this quite often and we enjoy identifying the constellations and looking for shooting stars, etc. At around 9:30 p.m., I sat up quickly because I saw a chevron, V-shaped object flying almost directly over us, moving horizontally from north to south in a straight line at a consistent speed. I shouted and pointed it out to my friends to look at, but they could not see it, even though I could clearly see it. The object was dark but looked 'transparent' or almost cloaked, but I could easily see the outline of it moving across the night sky. There were approximately seven to eight white 'beads' (glowing orbs) that appeared to be under the craft, but they could have been windows that ran the entire length of each side. There were no flashing or bright running lights - nothing but the glow of the small white orbs.

"My friends have seen a similar 'craft' before in the past and they brought out a drawing of it to show me and it looked exactly like what I saw.

"There is also a MUFON report from the same day from a gentleman in Boca Raton, FL, at 9:36 p.m. (just minutes after I saw mine), that experienced something very similar to what I had witnessed, which is why I decided to report my sighting. I was very excited to see it and did not feel threatened at all."

Florida MUFON CAG Investigator James Horne closed this case as an Unknown Aerial Vehicle.

"The witness references another case in CMS," Horne wrote in his report. "While the witness did not respond to inquiry, the case in CMS that matches is 96341. This case was reported November 13, 2018, with a time of sighting as 9:36 p.m. Duration of two minutes. The sighting was in Boca Raton.

"This Case 96766 was reported on December 3, 2018. The time of the observation was 9:30 p.m. Duration of 15 seconds. Place of observation was Valrico, Florida.

"There are multiple witnesses and the witness is credible."

Valrico is a census-designated place in Hillsborough County, Florida, population 35,545.

Second witness reports Florida chevron-type UFO

A Florida witness at Boca Raton reported watching a chevron-shaped object, according to testimony in Case 96341.

The event occurred at 9:36 p.m. on November 7, 2018.

"I am a 64-year-old male residing in Boca Raton, Florida," the witness stated. "I am reaching out to you to share a recent experience regarding an unidentified craft. Most evenings I sit by the pool in my backyard between the hours of 9 and 10 p.m. I relax for an hour or so listening to soft music and star gazing using my phone app to identify stars, constellations, etc. My wife joins me sometimes and we spot satellites, talk about the universe and re-share our 'UFO' sightings of the past.

"This particular evening, I was focused on the Pleiades and nearby and beyond stars. You know, the longer you fixate on an area, the more stars become visible, albeit faint and looking like dots. As I remained fixated in this area, it seemed as if the Pleiades cluster suddenly grew by three, four or five dots. In fact, I thought my fixation had caused me to get cross-eyed, as the faint stars appeared to multiply. As I kept looking, I realized the dots were in a perfect horizontal row and now appeared like a short string of evenly spaced beads (faint small dots of light). What's more,

the beads were moving in unison across the night sky. It was very confusing for a few seconds as my mind did not compute what I was seeing.

"After a few seconds I could see that the night sky became obscured below and somewhat forward of the light beads as the entire row of them moved. I realized then that an entire 'shadow' was moving below and in front of the string of lights (four to five dots). They were 'drifting' horizontally from left to right (north to south). By now I could clearly make out a straight, solid 'ridge' above the entire length of the lights and somewhat beyond, but the areas below and fore were diffused, and I could not discern the entire shape.

"It was clearly a craft, completely black, no running lights whatsoever. The lights appeared to be 'windows,' not undercarriage lights. It did seem to be shaped either like a chevron or else triangular, but I can't be certain because it was so diffused and stealthy. Whatever this craft is, it is not meant to be seen. I just happened to coincidentally be focused and fixated in that area when I spotted it.

"In my opinion there is no way a person can see it under normal viewing circumstances. The craft appeared to float across the night sky (no sound, of course it may have been too far to hear). I attempted to take a picture, but the phone camera screen appeared pitch black, so I decided to speed dial and called my wife, and she and my youngest son ran out in an attempt to see it, but by then it had flown/drifted over and behind the street light, and although I could still discern it moving, there was no way they could—the street light washed out the little beads that I could barely still see until even I couldn't see them anymore.

"Generally, this was a disturbing experience, mostly because it is unexplained to me. I became excited and nervous and haven't been able to let go of this experience yet. I'll be working or doing whatever when suddenly I get that butterfly feeling and see it vividly in my mind, over and over. What makes it so profound for me, is that this craft was real. I wasn't watching a movie or an illustration in a book. I now have my own 'eyewitnessed' evidence that there exists an alternate reality regarding stealth craft. I am more convinced that we, hopefully America and its allies, have very advanced 'UFO' technology. If it were alien, my biggest question will be why? There doesn't seem to be any purpose to fly such a craft on any given evening across the Atlantic coastline, because . . . what? I would accept a military flight. Maybe still developing the technology, that these are technology-enhancing test flights? Patrolling? Do you have any knowledge or information of this craft? I look forward to hearing from you. Thank you very much."

Florida MUFON Field Investigator David Toon closed this case as an Unknown Aerial Vehicle.

"I reviewed FlightRadar24 and found no aircraft with a similar flight path and speed necessary to replicate what was described in the witness's report," Toon stated in his report. "However, the sketch had so much detail, to include estimations and measurements, it became more valuable than a photograph. The witness's credibility is high due to his career field of trained observation as a scientist. His hobby of astronomy for many years also adds to the validity of what was observed near the Pleiades star cluster, which became the start point of his object observation. With Boca Raton Airport close by, aircraft traffic is also common and discernible from the witness's point of view. The description of the object and time of flight are not beyond current known technology as cloaking is possible and radar signature evasion is common with military aircraft. Silent operations are common given enough altitude or low decibel propulsion configurations."

Boca Raton is a city in Palm Beach County, Florida, population 93,235.

Disc-shaped UFO reported hovering over Lake Superior

A Minnesota witness at Duluth reported watching a disc-shaped object hovering over Lake Superior, according to testimony in Case 97286.

The 63-year-old witness was locking the front door to his parents' home at 10:40 p.m. on November 7, 2018.

"House is located approximately four blocks from Lake Superior," the witness stated. "I observed a bright, what appeared to be a star-like object in a southeast direction over the lake. It appeared larger and brighter than other stars. As I watched it, it seemed to be getting bigger and coming toward me. The brightness of it was receding as it got closer and closer until it stopped over the lake and hovered in place maybe a mile or so and 100-200 feet over the water.

"The town is on a bowl shape to the water, so it was almost straight out from me. There were a couple small tree branches of trees across the street, but they did not obstruct my view. The object was in between round and disc-shaped. It was covered with what appeared to be hollow, round, clear columns and had a central, round, spinning center; it looked like it had white and darker-colored smoke spinning inside a central core. The dark cloud/smoke-like areas were the only thing that was not bright white.

"I was frozen watching it for (what was, later by checking clock) about seven minutes. It did not move. I did. Cell phone was upstairs. Ran up to get it and ran out front door. It was gone, but appeared to be above me about 11 'o'clock position, but was almost the same size as other stars by now. It self-illuminated itself to appear to be a star. I called my friend and headed toward his house, who turned me on to his photos and stories before this happened. He has been in that house (100 feet from lake) for many years and has some evidence of anomalies over the lake.

"I told him about my incident, and he said he might have a photo of my object. The reason I did not submit right away was because I was taking care of my dying father, almost invalid mother and three dogs I kept in my Suburban to not disturb my father. Hands were full. I know I'm past my time to submit and I was going to drop it, but then sister relieved me, for a week, and he passed. Upon returning for funeral, I observed it three more times. Never that close again, but I knew now what to look for. One overcast morning it was the only visible thing in the sky, and it appeared in the same general direction. I asked my friend why he doesn't report, and he doesn't want people thinking he was nuts or something. After the reaction from my family, especially my son, I can see why. My friend produced a photo, which showed a central, reflective core and light emanating in longer rays from it and looked like it from a distance. He got the photo from a friend who claimed she was abducted by it and said grass was not growing where she was placed [sic]. I asked him if he believed her and he said, 'I don't know.' If you want to toss my report, that's fine, but I feel better that I got it out. I am a bad typist and it took me forever to type this. I am going back armed with a zoom camera next month; later."

Minnesota MUFON Field Investigator Stephen Hero closed this case as an Unknown Aerial Vehicle.

"Closed as an Unknown due to the fact that the object was sighted over Lake Superior, and has such an unusual shape," Hero stated in his report. "Also, since the object was seen over Lake Superior, that would rule out just about all commercial and military aircraft. Pilots avoid flying over water in case they may have to make an emergency landing. And the unusual shape of the craft leads me to conclude UAV."

Duluth is a major port city in Minnesota and the county seat of Saint Louis County, population 86,293.

NOVEMBER 8

NC witness, pilot friend, report UFO at treetop level

A North Carolina witness at Apex reported watching "a very large, squashed, diamond-shaped object with non-blinking lights hovering above the tree line," according to testimony from Case 96310.

The witness was outside walking dogs at 7:30 p.m. on November 8, 2018.

"Saw a very large and very slow-moving object just above the tree line," the witness stated. "It was lower than top of the radio tower, moving left to right. It then banked very slowly behind the trees and disappeared. It was shaped like a squashed diamond. It had red and green lights, in no particular pattern, and did not blink at all. There was no sound to it, either. My friend, who was with me, is a pilot. He said it was not like anything he had ever seen before. Our neighbor said she also saw it and did not know what it was. This aircraft was huge and flying at the level of the treetops. We were surprised it was so low and had no sound. I was expecting to hear a crash when it went below the tree line."

North Carolina MUFON Field Investigator Sanford Davis closed this case as an Unknown Aerial Vehicle.

"A lot of air traffic, dim lighting," Davis stated in his report. "It's some type of aircraft but both witnesses state it was 'no blimp, nothing like we've ever seen.' Checked, no other reports from any other source."

Apex is a small city in Wake County, North Carolina, population 50,451.

NOVEMBER 9

Star-like UFO captured on home security monitor

A Minnesota witness at Chaska reported watching three lights traveling at high speed captured on an outdoor weather cam, according to testimony in Case 96286.

The witness was checking his Axis Q1615 MK II outdoor weather cam footage using a laptop computer from the living room and watched footage taken about 8:15 p.m. on November 9, 2018.

"Three white lights traveling at the same speed well over a mile from my house," the witness stated. "The three distinct lights seemed to merge into a fuzzy line. Too fast for a plane, and too slow for a meteor. The lights seem to be heading in a straight line, but when you look closely, you can see the lights drop slightly, then straighten out. I lost sight of the lights because of distance and it went out of the stationary camera view. Check out my video clip and you decide what you are seeing. My reaction was a bit of curiosity. I do live near a flight path to MSP [Minneapolis-St. Paul] Airport, so I recognize lights from passenger jets when they fly nearby."

Minnesota MUFON Chief Investigator William I. McNeff closed this case as an Unknown Aerial Vehicle.

"I can't identify what the witness recorded on Nov. 9, 2018," McNeff wrote in his report. "The three lights are likely on one object, because the spacing doesn't seem to vary. Airliner windows wouldn't appear this large, I believe. No red wingtip light, no Atkins light, and no taillight are visible in the video, so it appears this craft doesn't have required aircraft lighting. As the witness stated, this object appears to be too fast for a plane and too slow for a meteor. This case is closed with a disposition of Unknown Aerial Vehicle, pending a photo analyst study."

Chaska is a city in Carver County, Minnesota, population 23,770.

Huge 'translucent' triangle reported over Missouri

A Missouri witness at Springfield reported watching a large, triangle-shaped object moving overhead that appeared to be translucent with lights along the front, according to testimony in Case 96451.

The witness was outside walking dogs with a girlfriend in the backyard at 9 p.m. on November 9, 2018.

"We were looking up at the stars, trying to spot Orion, when we saw a huge triangle fly directly overhead," the witness stated. "There was a giant V-shaped light on the front of it. It was easy to tell the craft was much larger than the V-shaped lights. It looked like watery ripples behind the lights. It reminded me of that movie 'Predator.' The craft was definitely cloaked somehow. We stared up at it, completely shocked as it flew due south out of view. It appeared to be very large, and it was utterly silent."

Missouri MUFON State Section Director Britt Faaborg closed this case as an Unknown Aerial Vehicle.

"Witness A had a close encounter in Colorado in 2007 that was reported to MUFON," Faaborg stated in her report. "Witness seems to be credible. Very detailed in description of craft (size, shape, lights, etc.) Has knowledge of astronomy since that was reason for being outside at that time."

Springfield is the county seat of Greene County, population 159,498.

NOVEMBER 10

Large, silent triangle reported over Minnesota

A Minnesota witness at Lonsdale reported watching a silent, black, triangular-shaped object with five lights, according to testimony in Case 96271.

The witness had just arrived home at 2 a.m. on November 10, 2018.

"As I walked down my driveway to check the mailbox, I looked up at the sky to view the stars," the witness stated. "A recent cold front made for excellent visibility and there were no clouds. I noticed a large, black, triangle-shaped object with five lights. One at the point of the triangle and two more on each trailing edge. I stopped walking and started watching the object. The object was completely silent. Its flight path was from the northwest to the southeast. I attempted to obtain a photo with my phone. But the picture was unable to capture the object."

Minnesota MUFON Field Investigator Dean R. De Harpporte closed this case as an Unknown Aerial Vehicle.

"Object was sighted at 2 a.m., clear weather," De Harpporte stated in his report. "Visible for only about five seconds at about 1,000 feet above the witness. It was moving faster than a normal aircraft. The large size of the object, its flat appearance, and its total silence rule out a helicopter, drone, or balloon. The witness is a surveillance supervisor and has some college. He talked rationally. He said the sighting of the object made his hair stand on end. He had seen one UFO previously in Louisiana in 1998.

"Due to the anomalous appearance, high speed of the object, and the strong impression it made on the rational witness, I have classified the object as a UAV."

Lonsdale is a city in Rice County, Minnesota, population 3,674.

'Translucent' UFO reported fast-moving over Minnesota

A Minnesota witness at Pipestone reported a V-shaped object that "seemed translucent with no lights," according to testimony in Case 96283.

The witness was outside smoking at 5 a.m. on November 10, 2018.

"It was a semi-cloudy morning," the witness stated. "A very large object moving north to south and moving at a very high rate of speed appeared in the sky for about five seconds. Its appearance was very distinct then disappeared and then appeared again faintly farther down the horizon. It was a wide V-shaped object similar to a boomerang. It was translucent in appearance. No noise was heard from the craft. The early sunrise may have caught the object, causing a translucent projection of the craft. I do not know. I'm just reporting what I saw."

Minnesota MUFON State Section Director Preston Mattke closed this case as an Unknown Aerial Vehicle.

"He indicated that the length of the observation was about 10 seconds or less and that the unknown floating craft was able to cloak itself during that observation period," Mattke stated in his report. "It was visible for some three to four seconds and then disappeared only to return to view some four seconds later. The sky cover at that altitude was quite clear, so cloud cover was ruled out as to the lack of visual for several seconds. He indicated that the floating elevation of the craft was about the height of three water towers AGL. He used the water tower comparison as the city water tower is just a half-block from his urban residence. As the tower is about 200 to 300 feet high, that would place the craft at or near 1,000 feet AGL. As it was about 5 a.m., he indicated that visual confirmation of its outline was quite defined as the sun was in the east, just on the far side of the craft, giving it a very easy to recognize image. He estimated the size of the craft to be about the area of one city block from wing tip to wing tip and the shape was a definite V or boomerang shape. He could not make out any windows or other surface structures. As its direction was north to south, roughly floating above the middle of his city block, it conforms to many reports from the Minnesota/South Dakota border that I have entered over a 10-year period. That north-to-south line along the border is a corridor of activity that repeats itself every two to three months and always a flight plan of north to south. The city of Pipestone lies just eight miles from the South Dakota border. After questioning this witness for 20 minutes and learning of his strong professional background, I have deemed his report and character to be reputable and the report should be regarded as highly reliable."

Pipestone is the county seat of Pipestone County, Minnesota, population 4,317.

NOVEMBER 11

Missouri witness says UFO made abrupt turns

A Missouri witness at Jefferson City reported watching a black, V-shaped object with six lights that made abrupt turns, according to testimony in Case 96450.

The witness was outside standing 20 feet from home observing the Taurid meteors at 2:40 a.m. on November 11, 2018.

"Scanning the sky for meteors, noticed an airplane to north, looked back over my house, suddenly noticed this large, black, V-shaped object with six lights on bottom of object," the witness stated. "I recognized it as a V-shaped craft from many videos on YouTube. It was going east and then abruptly turned south and appeared to ascend somewhat. Noticed short 'wings' on forward section, then legs lowered

in cube-shaped outline. The craft spun 360 degrees and then took off south, noting that the 'legs' were still lowered. It took me by surprise, real sure I gasped and didn't breathe until it was gone. I watched until I couldn't see it anymore, which was quick because it was black, and the night sky was dark. I wanted to be sure to watch carefully and notice every-thing about the craft. I paused and replayed it again and again in my mind, went in my house and wrote everything down."

Missouri MUFON State Section Director Charles Frieden closed this case as an Un-known Aerial Vehicle.

"Witness was very believable," Frieden wrote in his report. "She has been doing sky watches frequently since June 2018 (about six months.) This was the first object of this type she has seen, but has seen other objects in the brief time she has been watching the skies. Be-cause she was able to identify an aircraft and meteors during this same period, I am quite sure that this object was neither of those nor any other easily identified object."

Jefferson City is the capital of Missouri and the county seat of Cole County, population 43,079.

Canadian witness describes low-flying triangle

A Canadian witness at London reported watch-ing a silent, triangular-shaped object flying at low altitude, according to testimony in Case 96314.

The witness was driving at 40 km/hour east-bound along Tweedsmuir Avenue at 7:05 p.m. on November 11, 2018.

"My son (passenger) noticed a triangular-shaped object flying parallel to our car on the right side (south) and flying at about twice our speed," the witness stated. "Sighting lasted about 12 seconds. We saw six white lights reflecting on a dark, gray, triangular structure, two on each corner and a red flashing and moving light underneath on a dome in the middle. No sound and flying still at very low altitude about one-half mile south of us, then sped up. While we kept driving slowly up to Laurentian Drive we lost sight of the object because the street has 40 to 50 feet high trees on the right side."

Canada MUFON Field Investigator Ryan Stacey closed this case as an Unknown Aerial Vehicle.

"I believe the witness to be credible, and readily available to provide information," Stacey stated in his report. "Without a picture, I would suggest that this object was a drone; however, the drawing itself is unusual. The trajectory is linear and appears to be at a low altitude. I do not have any other witnesses to confirm nor deny this object in the sky. It does not look like any conventional known aircraft that I have seen."

London is a city in southwestern Ontario, Canada, population 383,822.

Utah witness says UFO was 'camouflaged'

A Utah witness at Taylorsville reported watching a "huge, black, triangular-shaped" object that appeared to be camouflaged, according to testimony in Case 96316.

The witness was outside having a cigarette and watching the stars on November 11, 2018.

"Something weird caught my attention," the witness stated. "Almost directly above my house I saw what looked like a very dark, massive, triangular shape going in a straight line from east to west over my house.

"A few things that I found strange about the whole thing are it made no sound at all and I didn't see a single light on the thing. Something I noticed about the color is that it was darker than the night sky. It had sort of a shadow-ish look to it. There were no clouds at the time so once I noticed the shape and size, I could see it pretty clear. It was larger and moved faster than any type of aircraft I have ever seen in my life. It made me very nervous. I had pretty bad chills when I was watching it fly over."

Utah MUFON State Director Michael Barrette closed this case as an Unknown-Other.

"Made attempts to contact witness to which there were not any responses," Barrette stated in his report. "There were no other witnesses to corroborate his sighting."

Taylorsville is a city in Salt Lake County, Utah, population 58,657.

NOVEMBER 12

Arizona witness describes 'camouflaged' UFO

An Arizona witness at Phoenix reported watching a cigar-shaped object with lights acting as camouflage, according to testimony in Case 96353.

The witness was northbound along Highway 51 at 7:20 p.m. on November 12, 2018.

"Suddenly I saw four lights traveling from east to west in a landing way or 45 degrees," the witness stated. "My first thought was four planes lining up for landing. My second thought was these are not planes but helicopters, one behind the other. When I was trying to figure out what the lights are, the lights were right in front of me, still at 45 degrees like landing. Suddenly changed direction going north and in that moment is when I saw the aircraft, black burned color, like a cigar or like an asteroid. Is like the lights were a mere camouflage. Even when the lights were so close, I couldn't see an aircraft, but when the lights turned north is when I saw the craft."

Arizona MUFON Field Investigators Kristine

Wulf and Marsha Beery closed this case as an Unknown Aerial Vehicle.

"Statements from the reporting witness coincided with accuracy in his story and of the craft as well as the sighting details," Wulf and Beery stated in their report. "A sketch was requested of the craft and the witness complied. I found the witness to be credible, honest, sincere and accurate in his statements made in the interviews. No deception was detected, and, all facts and data considered, I believe he witnessed a non-conventional aircraft of some kind."

Phoenix is the state capital in Maricopa County, Arizona, population 1,626,000.

NOVEMBER 13

Witness describes UFO over Haitian resort town

A Haitian witness at Labadee reported watching an object moving around the sky with multiple lights, according to testimony in Case 96764.

The witness was standing on a cruise ship deck looking out at the city prior to departure at 6:23 p.m. on November 13, 2018.

"I noticed something moving in the sky with lights on it," the witness stated. "It moved back and forth. I called for my wife, snapped a couple of photos, called for her again and then it shot up into the night really fast. It moved around like it was trying to get a footing in the sky, like it was looking for a specific spot, and then it was gone. It was dark except for the lights, a bright one on the bottom and three or four lights around the middle part. I was a bit anxious to get my wife out to see it, but by the time I went in and called her again, it left, my wife never saw it."

MUFON International Director of Investigations for Haiti Steve A. Hudgeons, Jr. closed this

case as an Unknown Aerial Vehicle.

"My first thought was a lens flare or reflection," Hudgeons stated in his report. "My second thought was no, the distance between the lights changed as it was said to be moving away."

Labadee is a port located on the northern coast of Haiti, a private resort leased to Royal Caribbean Cruises Ltd., for the exclusive use of passengers of its three cruise lines: Royal Caribbean International, Celebrity Cruises, and Azamara Club Cruises, until 2050.

NOVEMBER 14

Multiple UFOs reported over small NY town

A New York witness at Caroga Lake reported watching multiple lights in the sky followed by aircraft that may have followed them, according to testimony in Case 96378.

The events occurred beginning at 7:24 p.m. on November 14, 2018.

"First saw four lights above tree line (two sets of two) as I was driving home from work," the witness stated. "I didn't think too much of them as I believed they were probably a home up a mountain (I live in Adirondack park). As I passed the Caroga Lake Courthouse, I was shocked to see one large, circular light alone in the sky. As soon as I saw it, I knew it was something special. It appeared clear and large and was brighter than the four lights I saw previously. It had a whitish-orange glow to it and felt 'nuclear'—extremely intense glow that illuminated surrounding clouds and pulsated slightly. It resembled a small sun. I would approximate the light to have been about a mile away from me in the sky. I pulled over in the volunteer fire department parking lot, and as soon as I stopped, a second and third light appeared in sequence right next to the first. I grabbed for my cell phone to record this amazing event, but as I grabbed it, I looked up just in time to see all three lights blink out at almost the same time (split second they were gone). I called a family member that was approximately three miles down the road to tell them to go outside and look up. I hung up and turned my car around and went back to the courthouse. I got out of the vehicle and immediately saw two dull, pulsating, red lights coming from the direction of where the three bright lights were. They came quite close to me but only appeared as lights. I couldn't see an actual craft. There was a man in the parking lot whom I called to and he too saw one of the red lights (the other one was more behind him). He just said, 'Oh yeah, UFO,' and walked away towards the courthouse entrance as if he didn't care much. There were almost instantly multiple aircraft in the area and one in particular that appeared to follow the general direction of the two red lights. I believe the other aircraft appeared before the two red lights took off. These two red lights were not planes at all, totally silent and floated along in a smooth, odd manner that felt very odd. They moved quickly, but not at an unearthly speed. When I first saw the two red lights they were in a downward 'swoop' from where the white-or-ange lights were, but they eventually straightened their path and continued on until out of sight. I will never forget this event because I have no explanation of what I saw."

New York MUFON Field Investigator John Yunitis closed this case as an Unknown Aerial Vehicle.

Caroga Lake is an unincorporated community in the town of Caroga, Fulton County, New York, population 518.

Wyoming UFO expands before moving away

A Wyoming witness at Kemmerer reported watching a large light that rose up, hovered and expanded before moving away quickly, according to testimony in Case 96382.

The witness was sitting outside in a chair looking east at 9:50 p.m. on November 14, 2018.

"I saw a large light on the mountain above town," the witness stated. "The light then ascended, hovered, and expanded at least four times its original size. It began to move as a large light, speeded increasingly faster, and sped across the night sky, faster than any light or airplane I had ever seen. It reached directly overhead and disappeared to the north. My attention was drawn by the light when it enlarged. I thought it was a star at first. I was very surprised at what I witnessed. I was ap-prehensive and puzzled at the sight. It traveled in seconds, turned north and disappeared."

Wyoming MUFON State Director Richard Beckwith and CAG Director John A. Gagnon closed this case an Unknown-Other.

"The witness description does not fit any known aerial vehicle in the U.S., Chinese or Russian inventory," Beckwith and Gagnon stated in their report. "Likewise, the maneuvers are foreign to known aerial craft."

Kemmerer is the largest city in and the county seat of Lincoln County, Wyoming, population 2,656.

NOVEMBER 15

Washington witness photographs hovering object

A Washington witness at Everett reported watching and photographing a hovering object before it moved away, according to testimony in Case 97141.

The witness had just pulled up to the intersection of 19th and Broadway at 2:46 p.m. on November 15, 2018.

"Noticed people pointing up at sky," the witness stated. "Saw an object hovering in the east and took a cell phone picture. The object proceeded from the east to a southwesterly direction."

Washington MUFON State Section Director David Gordon MD closed the case as an Unknown Aerial Vehicle.

"The witness was driving home from work through Everett in an urban environment with a nearby multistory hospital two blocks to the west when he saw six people at the intersection of 19th Street and Broadway pointing up at the sky," Gordon stated in his report. "He saw a glowing, off-white object through his front windshield hovering in the east in the clear daylight sky, took a cellphone picture, and over a three-minute period watched it hover for just under one minute, then watched it move to the southwest and out of sight behind a building. He did not notice four other small objects at the time which can be seen in the photo. He heard no sound from the object.

"The object was approximately the angular size of a dime held at arm's length but unknown distance. There was no contrail. He could not see any structure and could not tell the shape, oval versus spherical, due to the glow. There was a sense that it had symmetrical appendages, however, left and right.

"On first impression on seeing the photo, I see appendages that look like wings pointing halfway toward the vertical. He denied seeing a bird or an identifiable aircraft, however. The hovering behavior could be consistent with a hawk or eagle, but the object was glowing. A quiet helicopter or drone could not be seen by the witness through the glow. No other objects are seen to glow in the photo. I assess the target object in the photo to be blurred. This can be consistent with a field propulsion effect. It is also consistent with a motion blur, but he says the object was hovering and no other object in the photo is blurred.

"So, we have an object that was interesting enough and unidentifiable enough for six peo-

ple on a sidewalk to mill about, look upward at it, and point at it. It gives off a blurred image in the daylight while stationary when other objects in the photo are sharp. It can hover and can move in a linear fashion. It is soundless. It might have appendages."

Everett is the county seat of and the largest city in Snohomish County, Washington, population 103,019.

NOVEMBER 23

Bell-shaped UFO reported over small Irish town

An Irish witness at Ballivor, County Meath, reported watching a slow-moving, bell-shaped object, according to testimony in Case 96554.

The case was filed by the witness's mother for an event that occurred at 4:55 a.m. on November 23, 2018.

"My daughter saw a bell-shaped UFO out her bedroom window," the woman stated. "The object was at an angle of around 45 degrees and hovering due south. There was a sound which she described as a cross between a jet and a helicopter. It had two red lights, which flashed on and off alternately about every second. The dome glowed very bright yellow. It rose slowly at a slight diagonal and then blinked out of existence. About five seconds later she saw a shooting star tracing an arc in a southeasterly direction. She was in bed at the time and the light drew her attention to the object. She was not wearing her glasses. She put on her glasses and saw the object clearly and immediately thought it was a UFO. She was frightened and sent me a text. She did not lose sight of the object, it just blinked out of existence like a light being switched off. The attached sketches are of the object from below, which she saw before she put on her glasses, and from the side when she had her glasses on and therefore had a clearer view of the object."

Ireland MUFON Field Investigator Charles Aylward closed this case as an Unknown-Other.

"There was no known aircraft low enough in the area," Aylward stated in his report. "This was too big for a drone and noisy as well, according to the witness. FI requested more info on angle of craft but witness never replied back. The witness seems creditable and wants to be anonymous. Her dad explained how she is very honest and can be trusted that what she saw was real. No other cases found. Initially I thought this was mistaken for a helicopter, but I couldn't find proof that a helicopter was in the area that morning. I cannot completely rule out a possible IFO, but I couldn't prove it to be an IFO. My conclusion is that, according to the witness interview, it was an unknown object in the morning."

Ballivor is a village in County Meath, Ireland, population 1,809.

NY UFO engulfs witness vehicle in light

A New York witness at Edwards reported watching an object in the sky that "descended and followed" their vehicle, according to testimony in Case 96580.

The witness was in a vehicle headed home from Christmas shopping with her mother-in-law and two-year-old son at 6:15 p.m. on November 23, 2018.

"We were on the road that I live on and it happens to be a back road," the witness stated. "I rounded a corner and there was a deer in the road, so I slowed down to a stop. As we crested the hill and started to speed up, I noticed an object in the sky on the passenger side of the vehicle. I pointed to it and noted that it looked like a planet (big and bright) but it was far too big. It stayed stationary and we pointed it out to my son, but at a certain point my mother-in-law noted that it appeared to be getting bigger and moving closer to us.

"Seconds later it was near us and we acknowledged that it was a round object with white/yellow lights and a red light on the bottom. I slowed down to look at it and by then it was huge and close to the car. It was still round but I noticed three white/yellow lights in a circular shape with a large red light in the center. It hovered over the treetops and by then it was huge, larger than my car. I got nervous and decided to start driving again, and as I started to move it moved to the other side of the road and disappeared. My mother-in-law and I were stunned and couldn't believe what we had seen. It was the strangest thing we had ever seen. We talked about it the day after it happened and recalled that while it was large and right over top of us, we never once heard any noise, and the radio was off (we had been talking). The sheer size of the object in comparison to our car was also something that we noted, as well as the lights lighting up the inside of our car briefly while it was over us. The entire encounter lasted right around two to three minutes and the incident occurred two miles from where we live."

New York MUFON Field Investigator Mary Fancher closed this case as an Unknown Aerial Vehicle.

"After emailing and speaking with the witness, I believe she and her mother-in-law saw something that can't be explained by natural causes or conventional aircraft," Fancher stated in her report. "The object was completely silent, so it couldn't have been a helicopter, and it followed them for a mile-and-a-half, demonstrating intelligent control. Unless the object was some experimental government aircraft, which is highly unlikely, I have to classify this case as an unknown."

Edwards is a town in St. Lawrence County, New York, population 1,156.

NOVEMBER 25

Irish witness describes object 'gliding over town'

An Irish witness at Gorey reported watching a "dark, slow-moving, tumbling, manta ray-shaped craft gliding over the town, according to testimony in Case 96586.

The event occurred at 8:45 a.m. on November 25, 2018.

"Sky was partial clouds with blue sky," the witness stated. "No wind, no aircraft of any kind about. Not many people or traffic about either. Myself and my wife were walking our two dogs when I happened to look up at the sky as I often do. I saw a dark/blackish object a short distance away in the sky that had just passed over us heading south. I immediately pointed it out to my wife. My best description of the shape of the craft was a dark, 'manta ray' solid shape. We watched it as it 'tumbled slowly' while it seemed to glide silently through the sky. The object was penny size at this stage. As we watched it glide away from us it seemed to change shape, but that could have been due to the tumbling motion. We watched it for about 35 seconds until it glided off out of sight towards the countryside a short distance away. In my opinion it was not a balloon as balloons are not that large, do not 'tumble' in that manner or have a blackish color. As there was no or very little wind, a balloon would not have moved that fast, even though the object was slow-moving (slow-moving for a craft but fast for a balloon)."

Ireland MUFON Field Investigator Charles Aylward closed this case as an Unknown-Other.

"As there is no physical evidence such as video or photo, it comes down to witness testimony," Aylward stated in his report. "I also spoke to the witness's wife, and she confirmed his sighting was real and she saw a diamante-shaped object moving in the same trajectory as what her husband explained. There was little wind in the area, and there was no aircraft in the area of Gorey, Wexford, at the time of the sighting. They both told me they have excellent sight, and do not need glasses. The main witness told me he did not see anyone else in the area while they saw the object. The witness also told me the object flew from north to south until out of view. We ruled out a drone, because it flew a far distance from north to south until out of their view.

"The witness brought it to my attention what they saw was the same type of object, including color and motion, as in MUFON Case# 90185.

"The eyewitness evidence concludes that the object spotted by the two eyewitnesses was not a known, identifiable flying object. What the witnesses saw was truly an unidentified flying object from their perspective. In my view, this sighting is still unexplained. I am only ruling out the possibility that it might be a drone, because of the vast distance the object travelled from north to south and that one is not allowed to operate a drone at that distance in Ireland."

Gorey is a market town in north County Wexford, Ireland, population 9822.

Bright light descends on Irish town

An Irish witness at Galway City reported watching and videotaping a bright, white light that descended and emitted different colored lights, according to testimony in Case 96616.

The witness was with his father in his father's car driving on a country road near Barna at 8:15 p.m. on November 25, 2018.

"We both saw something below the clouds move around very fast in the distance that was between three and four miles away," the witness stated. "It was at first hovering in one place before moving downwards and across our line of sight. It was unusual due to its brilliant white light and its rapid descent from cloud cover as we approached it. We both remarked how bizarre it was behaving and how it looked. As we approached its location in the car, I observed that it moved strangely, initially thinking it was a passenger plane, but my father saying it's a satellite, before saying it's something else entirely. It then paused its flight path and moved in the opposite direction. Since we were on a coast road, this meant it was now moving quickly towards the ocean bay, rather than its initial path inland. Its altitude remained just below the clouds, with short moments of dropping lower. Once we reached a beachside car park, we pulled in to get a better look at it, at which point the flying object began moving side-to-side, flashing for a few seconds a red light and then a green light intermittently. It moved quick and I could see it was still quite far away, about half a mile, indicating to me that it was in fact quite large and around the size of a passenger plane. It was pitch dark at this point with no rain and little wind and it was nighttime, so its flashing colors were clear to see even at that height among the clouds. Unfortunately, I couldn't make out the shape of the object in the dark night sky. We watched it move back and forth to our left and right vantage until it turned at a sharp 90-degree angle and began moving towards our direction. I watched the green flashing light turn into a flashing red at this point, as it moved quickly directly over our heads, occasionally being obscured by the belly of the cloud above. It moved far faster than a passenger plane certainly and was utterly silent while moving over us. This was shocking, as I was used to air traffic in the area such as planes and helicopters being very audible. It then turned off its red lights, of which I could see there were two of, and travelled down the coast towards the direction in which we came. As we turned around, I was able to briefly film it as it suddenly switched back on its original bright, white light. This light was like a huge spotlight in the sky, it was very strong and visi-

ble. It seemed to hover for a few moments and lower in altitude, until it moved farther down the coastline direction and quickly disappeared from sight. My father made the observation that it had travelled probably 10-plus miles in that time frame and that the light must have been very powerful to have been still visible. It moved more inland rather than out to sea and probably didn't get to the city nearby, but instead was moving more towards the rest of the countryside. With regard to our reactions, the turning point was really when it began flashing lights. We were both transfixed as it turned towards us and passed overhead. I had a chill down my spine knowing I was witnessing a technology I'd never seen before being displayed. It moved not unlike a bird, in that it turned and flew in all directions very easily and with grace, all without making a single sound. This being a large aircraft made it an awe-inspiring thing to look at. When it then turned back on its full, white light in the distance, the effect was unnerving in that I'd never seen a light so bright come from one vehicle. I felt like I had a spotlight focused on me, it was so piercing and white. Afterwards we discussed it and confirmed with each other that it was nothing we'd ever seen before. Neither of us believed it was a drone, plane, balloon, helicopter or anything like that. It was something very swift and unusual, with erratic flight paths and great speed, control and flying capabilities compared to normal commercial aircraft or even military aircraft that I've observed. It is fair to say that I also experienced a great deal of adrenaline watching it pass overhead. Many of my doubts about it being a UFO went away as we approached it. It was clearly a very unusual sight to anyone watching.

Ireland MUFON Field Investigator Charles Aylward closed this case as an Unknown Aerial Vehicle.

"What the witness saw was an unidentified flying object and I believe it is technology we have not seen before," Aylward stated in his report. "I couldn't prove it to be of any identifiable flying objects. My conclusion is that, according to the witness interview, his statement and video that was uploaded, that there was an unknown object in the sky that evening. Whether it was controlled by extraterrestrial or human intelligence is not known."

Galway City is a city in the province of Connacht, population 79,934.

NOVEMBER 26

Silent object reported low over Missouri

A Missouri witness at Columbia reported watching a silent, fast-moving, V-shaped object overhead, according to testimony in Case 96643.

The incident occurred at 8:02 p.m. on November 26, 2018.

"Sky was clear enough I could see stars and even two planes higher in the sky," the witness stated. "I also saw a hawk or owl fly by moments before, so I had a good reference point of looking. I was at a school, tossing Frisbee with my dog. Then very faint at first, I see this triangle or more like a V overhead, like 200 to 300 feet in the air. It almost had no lights or faint lights on the two parts of the V. At first I was like, am I seeing something? What is that? I watched it for a good 20 more seconds pass straight over the school. It was very fast and made no noise. But my eyes could clearly see this triangle, V-shaped object zoom over my head again. I could see two planes at this time higher in the sky and saw a bird clearly visible. This object was faint, almost like a ghost, but was clearly there as I watched it pass over. I can't explain. It was an eerie feeling."

Missouri MUFON State Section Director Charles Frieden closed this case as an Unknown Aerial Vehicle.

"First of all, the effect on the witness's health was passing, and he experienced 'goosebumps and felt kind of spooked,' Frieden stated in his report. "He saw both birds and an airplane at the same time as the object. The object appeared to be traveling through a mist, and he felt it would not have been visible except for the mist. His dog did not seem to notice the object, or to be affected."

Columbia is a city and the county seat of Boone County, Missouri, population 121,717.

NOVEMBER 27

CA witness says UFO was following military jets

A California witness at Santee reported watching a "dark, triangular-shaped craft with neon green circle lights," according to testimony in Case 97510.

The incident occurred about 8 p.m. on November 27, 2018.

"I live approximately 10 to 15 miles from Marine Corps Air Station Miramar," the witness stated. "Every night helicopters or Osprey fly the same route/path directly over my house out to another base in the southern California desert to the east. I always look up to see the type of aircraft, to see if it's a helicopter or an Osprey. I happened to have my camera in my garage that night after using it earlier in the day. I was in my front driveway. At approximately 7:30 to 8 p.m., I saw two F16s fly a pattern I have not seen done in the 15 years I've been at this address. They did a loop around the area and then left. Shortly after, I heard the familiar sound of the helicopters and took a look upward to see what kind they were. The helicopters appeared like they always do on the exact path and speed I was used to seeing. Directly behind the last helicopter was what appeared to be a dark, triangular craft. In each of the corners it had neon green circles that looked like neon green rings. It was extremely silent and flew right behind the second helicopter. I was stunned for a moment then ran in to get my camera. I just started shooting in the direction of the lights, but they were already pretty far to the east. I uploaded the photos onto my computer and all I was able to make out was a neon green orb and the clear white lights of the helicopters. Again, this was a silent, slow-moving, dark, triangular craft with neon green lights in the corners. The green lights were not completely solid but almost appeared like a green ring in each corner. I am very familiar with standard aircraft and this is something I've never seen before."

California MUFON Field Investigator William Crowley closed this case as Info Only.

"Witness submitted photos that were unreliable," Crowley stated in his report. "Witness not available for interview. Although sounds like craft is TR3B."

Santee is a suburban city in San Diego County, California, population 53,413.

out that the objects were still there. Each was black with a shape I cannot identify from typical geometric figures. They were hovering and flying one above the other. The smaller object hovered to another direction and was suddenly gone. The bigger object stayed to the west direction until it suddenly disappeared while I continued filming it. The problem is my camera won't stay focused. I got frustrated. I took two videos, one from my phone and the other one is from a digicam. You will hear the voices of my daughters and myself as I filmed it."

Philippines-MUFON International Director of Investigations Steve Hudgeons Jr. closed this case as an Unknown-Other.

No city name was mentioned in the report.

NOVEMBER 28

Filipino witness videotapes 'floating objects'

A Filipino witness reported "two floating objects" above the trees, according to testimony in Case 96641.

The incident occurred at 5:20 p.m. on November 28, 2018.

"My daughter called me and told me she saw two unidentified flying objects above the trees," the witness stated. "She said she got afraid upon seeing these objects. She is familiar with stories about abduction and that's the reason why she got afraid. She hurriedly told me, at first, 'I think it's gone,' then she hurriedly asked me to go upstairs and found

DECEMBER 2018

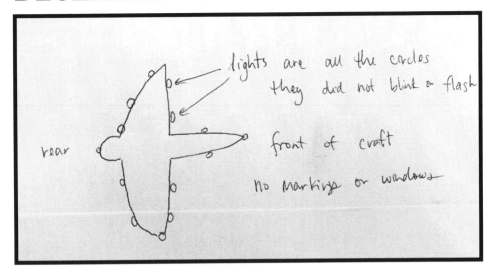

Case 97555 witness illustration. December 9, 2018.

DECEMBER 1

Texas witness says UFO landed in nearby field

A Texas witness at McKinney reported watching a UFO just 500 feet from their home that landed and left behind ground markings, according to testimony in Case 96805.

The incident occurred about midnight on December 1, 2018.

"A little background: I'm a mechanical engineer, early 30s," the witness stated. "My wife and I moved to McKinney, TX, February of 2016 and we've both witnessed/experienced weird things since we moved here. February 20, 2017, after midnight: my wife told me that she noticed green flashes in the sky in the western sky. I looked out the upstairs window that faces west and also saw the bright, green flashes in the sky. At first, I thought it could just be lightning but shortly after we heard a low rumbling/humming sound coming from above our house and it shook/vibrated the whole house. We then saw some news online

about people from Prosper, TX, witnessing the same green flashes in the sky with a loud humming sound. We were both in awe since our backyard faces west and that's where the city of Prosper is.

"On December 1, 2018 (around midnight), I was in my house in McKinney, upstairs, making music in my studio (music production is my hobby). This particular room has a window, which faces north. Next to my home I have a neighbor with a one-story home, so I have a very clear view of the open fields. Based on the aforementioned encounters, I sometimes peek outside my windows or look up the skies at night; I don't know if out of curiosity or with the expectation that I will eventually see something that can't be explained. Anyway, I got up from my chair and peeked out of the only window in this room and what I saw literally frightened me so much that I was almost paralyzed and could barely talk to myself. I started trembling and my eyes could not believe what they were seeing, but essentially what I saw was a UFO from 500 feet away, on the ground in an open field next to my neighbor's house.

It was pitch black so I could not determine its exact outline or shape, but it appeared to have an oval shape based on its lights. The thing was incredibly big and the first thought when I saw it: UFO. It had a horizontal string of extremely bright, ice-white lights with some blue in them. From my point of view, the size of each light appeared to be like a Dish Network antenna if not bigger and there were at least 20 of these lights right in the middle of this object. It also had random red lights around the horizontal lights. The red lights were smaller than the white ones. The color and brightness of these lights were so clean and powerful that I have never seen anything man-made that looks similar. As I mentioned before, these lights were ice white with some blue in them and there also appeared to be a fusing pattern inside each 'bulb.' I looked at the UFO for at least 40 seconds and my body was just processing what it was seeing. It basically looked like the UFO I had seen back in 2004 on that cruise but this time it was 500 feet from me. When you couple that with my skin markings, you can understand why I felt so scared and why it didn't even cross my mind to take a video or picture. Right after the event I was kicking myself for not doing this, but some part of me preferred to have a witness vs. a picture or video. That's why I ran downstairs and woke my wife up. It took her like a minute to go upstairs, and when we peeked out the window the UFO was still there. When I first looked at the UFO, I didn't mess with the blinds, I just peeked through its gaps. However, my wife opened the blinds to look at this thing. I then said to her, I'll go grab my binoculars (Skymaster 15x70) to get an even closer look. As soon as I walked out the room to get them, my wife yelled, 'it's moving.' I didn't get to see it move but my wife did, and she said that it moved eastbound at a very constant speed while staying low to the ground. At that point my neighbor's house blocked the view and we also didn't notice anything going up the sky either. The size of this thing is hard to tell, but if I were a guessing person and judging by

its lights, I'd say at least 30 feet wide and 16 feet tall. Five minutes later my wife convinced me to get in the car and see if we could see anything that could explain what we saw, but found nothing. I brought my 9mm with me just in case. While looking at this thing from our window, it honestly felt as if the UFO lights were pointed or aiming at our house. I still get goosebumps every time I think about this.

"The next morning, I looked out the same window to see if I could see any markings on the ground around that same area where we saw the UFO, and to my dismay, there was an evident mark of what appeared to be a burned area. I then took a picture of it with my phone through the binoculars. Also, the overall size of this mark aligned perfectly with the lights of the UFO. I then went to this open field with my wife and with a neighbor. This field is covered with two-foot-tall grass, but in the suspect landing area, the grass only had the first four inches of the stem/base sticking out, and these looked burned. The weeds/grass around the area also appeared to have experienced high winds since they were swirled and depressed. My wife and I also noticed weird circular footprints on the ground not too far away from the 'landing area.' These footprints were circular and 10 square inches in size but could be from an animal. We took pictures, nonetheless. Lastly, I researched online and the landing markings on the ground looked a lot like the Ngatea Mystery Circle picture that you can find online with two people at the scene. I don't have a drone, so I don't have above-ground pictures, but did take some ground pictures with my phone for documentation purposes, including my skin markings from a couple months ago. I also didn't take any soil/grass samples from the 'landing area' since I didn't feel comfortable bringing evidence home. It is worth noting that I also asked some of my neighbors that live next to this area to see if they had any security cameras that may have caught the UFO, but no luck. One of them did have cameras but pointed to the ground, but what's interesting is that this couple told me that they also saw a star-looking UFO in the north sky at night, about a year ago. It basically hovered for a good while and then vanished. They said that the color of the light was ice white and very bright.

"This latest close encounter experience has shaken me to my core, and I sometimes have a hard time sleeping at night, just thinking about what I've seen/experienced and re-searching UFO/skin markings, etc. I sometimes ask my wife about what we saw to see if she can provide another explanation, and she basi-cally says that she doesn't want to talk about it since this subject also scares her a lot. I hope that whoever has my case contacts me ASAP and gets to the scene to investigate before this open field is mowed as it might be owned by the city of McKinney.

Texas MUFON State Director Gary Neitzel closed this case as an Unknown Aerial Vehicle.

"This witness is an engineer working for a large defense contractor with a security clearance and when interviewed in person ap-peared to be very credible. Soil samples sent to the MUFON Lab show possible damage to plants due to unusual vibrational frequencies (see lab report #10018). It is the investigator's conclusion that a large, unknown craft either touched down or hovered in the field to the north of the witnesses' house. It may have hovered over various locations in the field. The witness saw only approximately 20 very bright, large, whitish lights with smaller, red, flickering lights surrounding them, but not the craft itself. Based on the lights the investigators estimated the craft was approximately 76 feet long."

McKinney is a city in and the county seat of Collin County, Texas, population 131,117.

DECEMBER 3

Multiple cigar-shaped UFOs described over Virginia

A Virginia witness at Toms Brook reported watching three, dull, silver, cigar-shaped objects moving in a triangular arrangement, according to testimony in Case 96755.

The witness was at work taking the trash out to a dumpster at 8:35 a.m. on December 3, 2018.

"I felt the need to look above my head," the witness stated. "I looked up and noticed three cigar-shaped objects flying silently without any jet emissions above my head at about 10,000 feet. [This scenario was revised somewhat during the subsequent witness interview; see below.—Ed.] They seemed to stop a couple of times and just hovered and then moved again, heading in a southwest direction. I heard no noise from them, but one did appear to have a filmy almost-mist around it. They seemed to change direction without any effort. I watched them for about three minutes then. I imme-diately called my wife at our home since it was in the direction of the object's travel. She called me back stating that she saw them also, but they were near three planes that were flying and as soon as she saw them it was like they knew someone was watching them. When I saw them, the planes were far behind them. The planes had jet exhaust, so they were obvious to recognize."

Virginia MUFON Field Investigator Victor Ro-driguez closed this case as an Unknown Aerial Vehicle.

"Both witnesses were interviewed by phone and appeared sincere in their responses," Ro-driguez stated in his report. "To the submitted report, the husband added the following. The two objects he saw were cigar-shaped with a flat end. They were silver-colored, and their surface was of the brightness of liquid mer-cury. The two objects appeared to be trailing an airliner but at a lower level. After watching for about three minutes, he alerted his wife by phone to look at the sky. Subsequently, he came out about 30 minutes later and this time saw one object similar to the ones seen before. This object was seen to fly into a small cloud and never came out the other side He states that he waited five minutes for an exit but that it never happened.

"The wife states that she went outside and saw three objects. One in particular was closer to her. She got the impression that the object became aware of her presence and slowed down. She describes it as having a definite structure, no windows, no wings and making no noise. She began to get the sensation of a migraine headache coming on and decided to go back inside the house.

"Neither one of the witnesses states having a similar event before."

California witness describes intelligently-controlled object

A California witness along westbound Highway 36 in Humboldt County reported a teardrop-shaped object crossing the sky and changing directions, according to testimony in Case 96773.

The incident occurred on December 3, 2018.

"I saw something in the sky and got out of the car," the witness stated. "It was a teardrop shape that shot across the sky, stopped, changed directions, and it went like northwest and went off deep into the sky like a flash of light."

California MUFON Field Investigator Jerry Gerow closed this case as an Unknown Aerial Vehicle.

"The witness was traveling by car when he spotted a strange light in the sky," Gerow stated in his report. "He pulled the car over and got out to observe. His car was facing north-

east and the light was in the west-northwest sky hovering. It then shot across in front of him to the right and then stopped, turned sort of north, and shot out of sight into the sky at incredible speed. He stated when first sighted it seemed to be shining a light into a gully. The whole sighting lasted a minute or two. Before the object flew off it was 300-350 feet off the ground and two football fields away. I asked if he had any ill effects from the sighting, and he said the object made a whirring sound or hum and the hair on his arm stood up. The witness also attached a drawing of the object to his CMS Report. The drawing shows a teardrop-shaped object with two lights towards the front, with one towards the tail, and one underneath the front section. He also said there appeared some sort of small, stubby wing-like protrusion coming from the side.

"I checked with MUFON and NUFORC and found nothing correlating. Spaceflightnow shows a SPACEX 9 launch at 10:34 that morning from Vandenberg AFB. Stellarium does not apply. The description and drawing from the witness represent a vehicle not known in domestic or military circles that I am aware of. The escape velocity is much higher than anything I am currently aware of. The changing direction shows it is intelligently controlled and not a rocket launch."

Humboldt County is a county in California, population 132,646.

DECEMBER 4

UK witness describes orange-glowing disc

A United Kingdom witness at Beaconsfield reported watching an orange-glowing disc, according to testimony in Case 96843.

The incident occurred about 6:30 a.m. on December 4, 2018.

"I work an hour's travel away from home

so I leave my house between 5 to 5:30 a.m. Monday to Friday," the witness stated. "As it was early and in December, it is dark. I arrived at work, parked my car and walked from the company car park to the office building. The walk from my car to the access point I use is around 100 feet. I got within about 30 feet of the building and what I can only describe as an orange street light glow clicked on directly above me. I looked up and saw an orange disc with a glowing red circumference was there. The emitted light glowed, clicked off and the object sped off in a northwest direction over the top of the trees on-site. The object left a brief reddish/orange trail behind it and then that also vanished. As a British army veteran, I have seen many forms of aircraft in the UK and on operational tour and I can say that whatever I saw is like no aircraft I have seen before."

United Kingdom MUFON National Director Jack Turnbull closed this case as an Unknown Aerial Vehicle.

Fast-moving teardrop UFO reported over Washington

A Washington witness at Olympia reported watching a silver, teardrop-shaped object that made a right angle and moved away quickly, according to testimony in Case 96813.

The witness was in traffic waiting for a light to turn green at 2 p.m. on December 4, 2018.

"Instead of the arrow to turn, it stayed red," the witness stated. "As I looked past the traffic light, I saw a silver craft shaped like a silver, curved teardrop flying very fast vertically, but doing a bumblebee-type ascent. The craft suddenly turned north at a right angle and shot away. My light turned green but multiple people at the light were looking at the craft."

Washington MUFON Chief Investigator Daniel Nims closed this case as an Unknown Aerial Vehicle.

"The witness's interview basically confirmed the description given, with a few more minor details," Nims wrote in his report. "The object appeared to be teardrop- or almond-shaped, with a blunt end and a narrow end, moving with the blunt end forward. The exterior of the object was silvery like an Airstream trailer. There were no external protuberances; i.e., wings, tails, cockpits, or landing gear. Aside from a glint of sunlight off the surface of the vehicle, there was no apparent lighting.

"When the witness initially saw the object, it was descending, moving toward him. It passed through a cloud. (METAR data for Olympia Airport gave a scattered layer at 1,900 feet and a broken layer at 2,900 feet.) After descending through the cloud, the object reappeared as three separate objects moving in a triangular formation. At that point the objects came to a stop and then climbed back up, moving away to the east. The object(s) moved with a weaving motion. The witness stated that they didn't move like any airplane he had ever seen.

"A check of FightRadar24 showed no aircraft activity in this area at the time of the sighting. The shape of the object was not characteristic of an aircraft or helicopter. The wind was from the north, but the object initially was moving west, then stopped and retreated to the east. This movement, along with the initial descending flight path, would not be characteristic of a Mylar balloon. The object did not show any of the frame, propellers or landing legs of a typical drone."

Olympia is the capital of Washington and the county seat of Thurston County, population 46,479.

Pennsylvania orange triangle described as fast-moving

A Pennsylvania witness at Orwigsburg reported watching an orange triangle that hovered and quickly moved away, according to testimony in Case 96829.

The witness was "outside getting coal for the coal stoker" at 8:30 p.m. on December 4, 2018.

"I then saw a big orange light," the witness stated. "I thought it was maybe a low plane on fire. Then I called my foster brothers outside to see and then it hovered from side-to-side. Then it disappeared in a quick flash. Two minutes later it reappeared in the east, hovering toward [sic] a plane. Then it flew around the plane in a 360-degree circle and then they flew apart. And the aircraft flew over the house so fast it was evident that it was unearthly, especially seeing the lights around the triangle border. Then at the end, it was in the northeast and I saw/heard two planes flying after it. And then it disappeared again in a quick flash and it never was seen again."

Pennsylvania MUFON Field Investigator Blaine Barry closed this case as an Unknown Aerial Vehicle.

Orwigsburg is a borough in Schuylkill County, Pennsylvania, population 3,061.

DECEMBER 5

Oregon witness reports seven UFOs in formation

An Oregon witness at Baker City reported watching seven, chevron-shaped objects flying in formation, according to testimony in Case 96818.

The witness was driving home at 6:10 p.m. on December 5, 2018.

"I turned onto the road my home is on and went about two blocks and looked up above the house on the hill and a noticed bright, white light and red lights above the neighbor's home," the witness stated. "At first glance I thought they were Christmas lights on top of their house. I drove a few blocks closer and realized the lights were too high in the sky

to be connected to the neighbor's house. I stopped my truck and got out. I realized then these lights were moving in sequence slightly to my left and in my direction. All the objects looked to be chevron-shaped. One white and six reddish-orange colored. The white one was in the lead and the others followed its flight pattern perfectly spaced apart. When the lead white craft got to approximately 60 degrees above the horizon, it took a rounded turn to my left and traveled west towards the mountains about five seconds and then turned directly back southeast. The six reddish-lit objects followed in perfect single file formation in perfect unison at the exact same speed behind the white-lit object. I took video on my cell phone and snapped a photo of the lead white one. They continued southeast and went out of sight over the horizon. These things made zero noise. I don't understand how these could be so big and make no sound flying over my head. They seemed as big as jet airliners but flew way too slow. I would think a jet would fall from the sky at that slow speed. Well not going to lie. I am still freaked out and don't understand what I saw. I called city police and an officer came to my home and I explained to him what I had seen. Strangest thing I have ever seen."

Oregon MUFON State Director Thomas Bowden closed this case as an Unknown Aerial Vehicle.

"This witness is very credible and was cooperative," Bowden wrote in his report. "He would have submitted a video he took; however, he has had trouble with being able to send it to me due to the file size. I decided to proceed without the video because the still photo shows something anomalous.

"There was a lot of commentary on the Facebook page of the Baker City Herald newspaper regarding lights in the sky on the night of this sighting. Many of the comments are based on little or no information on the part of the posters, but it definitely seems to indicate that the activity was unusual for this small, remote city in Eastern Oregon.

"Initially, the small, bright object in the left area of the photo looks like it could be an aircraft, but when I enlarged the image it obviously shows something that is not a normal aircraft. I searched the Internet looking at different types of lighter-than-air craft, but nothing I found was a close match to the object in the photo.

"Upon manipulating the color balance of the enlarged image, I discovered that there are more hidden details. There is a rectangular area that does not match the background sky extending downward from the object, and at the bottom edge of this rectangular zone, there are two smaller lighted objects.

"The EXIF data for this photo shows that it is an original photo that has not been modified by the submitter. After several discussions with the witness, I am fairly certain he is not involved in any attempt at deception. I am 95 percent certain that the object in this photo is an unidentified object of some kind. If someone can find a man-made object that is a close match for this object, I would really like to know about it. In the absence of a rational explanation, I am closing this case as Unknown because the object in the photo appears to be some sort of structured craft."

Baker City is a city in and the county seat of Baker County, Oregon, population 9,828.

DECEMBER 6

Giant UFO reported near Memphis Airport

A Tennessee witness at Memphis reported watching a huge, low-flying, V-shaped object followed by three Air Force jets, according to testimony in Case 96850.

The witness was driving home with a girlfriend in the car about one minute from home at approximately 5:35 p.m. on December 6, 2018.

"I saw a low-flying, very large, dark gray, V- or chevron-shaped object," the witness stated. "The object appeared to be the size of three 737 airplanes and had no visible means of propulsion nor did it make any sound as it crossed in front of us at about 800 to 1,000 feet of altitude. What made the object stand out in the failing light is the bright visible lights. I counted three on each of the corners. The sighting of the object itself was about five seconds and then I lost view of it over the tree line. The object's texture and alloy could best be described as exotic, appearing silky and seamless, unlike anything that humans are capable of building at this time. When I saw the object, I couldn't believe what was passing right in front of us so much so that I had to keep asking my girlfriend was she seeing what I was seeing and she kept confirming that she was and that it was exciting.

"About 45 seconds after we saw the object and arrived at home, we saw three Air Force fighter jets flying at about the same altitude as the object and they were very loud, to the point that I could barely hear my girlfriend talking, and they were fully armed as I could see the missiles underneath the planes as they passed directly overhead. The planes made a circle and left. My neighbor was outside when we pulled into the driveway and she said there were five planes total, but I didn't see the other two so I can only confirm the three that I saw. My neighbor did not see the object though. When we got inside the house it was all I could talk about for the rest of the night, how awesome and exciting the whole experience was."

Tennessee MUFON Field Investigator G. Kurt Veale closed this case as an Unknown-Other.

"Witnesses presented as reliable, intelligent people who seem to truly believe what they saw," Veale wrote in his report. "There were no apparent efforts to deceive and their story remained consistent. The same can be said of the main witnesses' description of prior events. Both witnesses seemed to be relieved to discuss the event with someone. Three important questions remain unanswered as this investigation concludes, if we assume the witnesses saw what they report they saw: How can any aerial object with a wingspan greater than a Boeing 747 airliner appear near the final approach path of a very busy airport, during rush hour for the airport and adjacent freeways, and not collide with other air traffic or go almost unnoticed by the flying/driving public? Based on available CMS data, why has periodic, similar activity been reported in this same area for over 30 years? Were the reported military jets acting as guides or monitors, or in pursuit of the alleged object, and does their presence during the event add credibility to the sighting reports?

"I regret that the answers to these questions cannot be answered within the scope of this investigation. Without compelling photo or video evidence, and no other means of defining the alleged object with certainty, a disposition of Unknown-Other is indicated."

Memphis is a city located along the Mississippi River in southwestern Shelby County, Tennessee, population 652,236.

Silent triangular UFO reported over California

A California witness at Red Bluff reported watching a triangular-shaped object with dim lights, according to testimony in Case 97119.

The witness had just arrived home and was walking from the garage through a back house to the main house at 7:12 p.m. on December 6, 2018.

"I looked to the northwestern sky to see stars, but immediately noticed a triangular shape, outlined by multiple, dimly lit, orange lights (three to four lights on each side of the triangle), moving from north to south in a straight line," the witness stated. "No sound was observed at this time, and I couldn't tell how far away it was or the exact size of the UFO. I only had a visual on this UFO for about 10–15 seconds as my view was blocked by trees when looking west. I had no unusual physiological or psychological symptoms. I simply was trying to recognize what I was seeing and determined I had never seen this kind of thing before. Ten minutes after seeing the UFO, I stepped outside to show my husband where I saw it, and we heard what sounded like two airplanes (but did not see any)."

California MUFON Field Investigator Jerry Gerow closed this case as an Unknown Aerial Vehicle.

"I checked NUFORC and MUFON and found nothing correlating," Gerow wrote in his report. "Spaceflightnow shows rocket launches on the fifth and sixth from China but nothing domestically. Stellarium showed nothing in the northwest sky at that time. My only evidence is the witness's word, which seems credible. The witness saw a silent, triangle-shaped object with lights down each side fly by between the trees. It possibly could be a stealth blimp that we have been hearing the military has, but nothing recognizable that I have been informed about. All things considered, I believe she saw an unknown."

Red Bluff is a city in and the county seat of Tehama County, California, population 14,076.

DECEMBER 7

Utah witness says UFO was 'very long'

A Utah witness at Wellington reported watching a long object with multiple blinking lights, according to testimony in Case 96890.

The witness was driving to Price, Utah, to buy fast food at 9:25 p.m. on December 7, 2018.

"As we were heading out of our neighborhood, I asked my boyfriend what the red dots were in the sky, as I had never seen them at our house before," the witness stated. "I just had been looking straight ahead. We had first assumed it was a radio tower's red lights. But then more lights appeared. We drove to the other side of the street and saw about 13 lights in almost perfect formation.

"The object was very long. Its lights blinked simultaneously, and it looked like one single object that was lit up and the lights were blinking. It seemed to be perfectly aligned to be more than one. We followed it from Wellington, Utah, to the Hiawatha, UT, turn out where it was very dark and watched it disappear. We all could not believe our eyes. I felt overjoyed and amazed to be privileged to witness such an event. I haven't been able to stop thinking about the lights. My boyfriend and I have been talking about it non-stop, trying to understand what we saw. There were even people pulled over on the side of the highway taking pictures. We lost sight of the object as it was going too fast to keep up with and we weren't exactly prepared to keep hunting it down with two children in the car."

Utah MUFON State Director Michael Barrette closed this case as an Unknown Aerial Vehicle.

"Spoke with witness and her boyfriend on a speaker phone," Barrette wrote in his report. "Both witnesses stated the same scenario and were excited about their sighting. The object was seen at night and the photos were taken with a cell phone. The reporting witness tried to provide an accurate description of what they saw, but the object was estimated to be one mile or more from their sighting location. I had asked the witness if she has seen any other aircraft along the same flight path as the object, but the witness stated 'no.'"

Wellington is a city in Carbon County, Utah, population 1,676.

DECEMBER 8

Virginia witness videotapes triangular UFO

A Virginia witness at Pulaski reported three lights in the form of a triangle, according to testimony in Case 97287.

The witness had just gotten into his car at 5:55 p.m. on December 8, 2018.

"My driveway runs almost exactly east-west and is slightly inclined to the west," the witness stated. "My car was pointing due west with several houses and trees between me and the western horizon. It was dark outside, and no stars were visible. Since there was a winter storm approaching that was supposed to start around midnight, I assumed there was thick cloud cover. As I started my car and turned the headlights on, I saw what appeared to be a signal flare appear from behind a house across the alley from my yard. This light reminded me of flares I'd seen in movies, where a flare was shot at night over an ocean; it was a bright pinkish-purple color. I had never seen an aircraft with this color of light. It wasn't moving very fast, and there were no changes in its speed or direction, although it was traveling behind a tree that was in between the house and the alley. All of this made me assume it was a flare. As I watched the light move from my right to left, I saw another light of the same color and intensity appear from behind the same house, appearing to follow right behind the first light. At this point I decided to shut the headlights off and turn off my car. I was still wondering why someone was firing off signal flares. This whole sequence took about 15-20 seconds. At this point I got out of the car and started walking up my driveway to the neighbor's yard. There was no sound that I could hear coming from the lights. After just one or two steps up my driveway, I realized there was an identical third light that was visible. It was hard for me to tell because of the tree that was in the way, but at the time, I thought they were all in a line and about the same distance apart. I got my phone out and started trying to get my camera in video mode. By the time I got to my neighbor's yard (about 50 feet), I realized that the lights formed what appeared to be an equilateral triangle. They were completely stationary for a few seconds, and I felt as if I was looking at the bottom of a craft, although all I could see were the three lights. The lights were bright but were not pulsing at all and they never changed color or intensity. When I finally got my phone to record, they had begun to move, but again, there was no quick acceleration or darting; the motion was very methodical. There was a guy a few houses down from where I was, and I began yelling for him to come to me because I wanted someone else to see them. By the time he got to where I was, one of the lights had disappeared to the west (possibly in cloud cover), so he only saw the last two lights. It's clear on the recording that there was no sound of aircraft. I ended the video before the last two lights completely disappeared from our view because they were no longer visible on my phone. On the video, the color of the lights doesn't appear as it looked to us in person. At the very end of the recording, you can hear the guy I called over say 'they're an odd color.' Also, my memory of it was that the bottom two lights switched sides and then the right one flew west leaving the other two to slowly fade away and finally disappear. Watching the video, that's not what happened at all; it appears the lights were all part of one object that did some kind of turn/roll and then flew east as a whole and disappeared into the cloud cover. The bright object in the foreground is a streetlight about 150–200 feet from where I was. I called the local airport and police the next day trying to see if someone had seen anything, but I was basically dismissed. I also asked the airport about the visibility/cloud cover, but again they were dismissive and told me to find it online; so unfortunately I don't have a maximum distance that the lights could've been from me, but there had to be massive cloud cover in that area because we started getting snow about 1:30 a.m. and wound up with about 16 inches by the end of the next day. I have attached the original video, a video of the same area shot during the day, several marked-up photos and photos generated by a surveying app that gives elevation, GPS, etc."

Virginia MUFON Field Investigator Norman Gagnon closed this case as an Unknown Aerial Vehicle.

Pulaski is a town in Pulaski County, Virginia, population 9,086.

DECEMBER 9

Rectangular UFO reported over Wisconsin skies

A Wisconsin witness at Wisconsin Rapids reported watching "a large, rectangular, bright object falling down," according to testimony in Case 97094.

The witness was outside moving west toward a barn at 8:20 p.m. on December 9, 2018.

"I always look up to the sky on clearer nights; stargazing is a hobby," the witness stated. "Unexpectedly, I saw a large, rectangular-shaped object, narrower ends on top and bottom stationary in the upper sky, which was extremely bright with a prism kind of look. And then it started to descend quickly straight downward, but disappeared quickly long before hitting the ground. There was no sound, and no aircraft in the area to be seen. Nothing coming up from the ground either to think something was shining upwards as any light or equipment. This was totally unexplainable. There was no burning-out of anything, no flashes or trails. It stayed bright coming down until it disappeared. It just appeared to be falling straight down and then was gone, like nothing was ever there.

"This area seems to be a hot spot. I've had a few other sightings, including a cylinder (no wings anywhere) that was low enough to see that and was huge. And a triangular shape."

Wisconsin MUFON Field Investigator Susan Birttnen closed this case as an Unknown Aerial Vehicle.

"I have worked another case with the witness; therefore, I was aware of her background and could trust her account to be accurate," Birttnen stated in her report. "In addition, I had just helped Minnesota MUFON with a case describing the same type of UAV. I emailed her a copy of the object from Minnesota and she said it looked just like what she saw."

Wisconsin Rapids is a city in and the county seat of Wood County, Wisconsin, population 18,367.

DECEMBER 10

Low-flying boomerang-type UFO photographed over West Virginia

A West Virginia witness at Scott Depot reported watching and photographing a low-flying, boomerang-shaped object, according to testimony in Case 97001.

The witness was returning home after picking up two children from Teays Valley Church of God about 8:45 p.m. on December 10.

"I was heading east on Teays Valley Road after picking up my 10- and 15-year-old boys," the witness stated. "As I approached Scott Teays Elementary heading west, I noticed bright, white lights in the sky coming straight toward us, heading east about one-half mile away. As the lights became closer, I pulled into Scott Teays Elementary facing west. I told my children in the car to look at the lights to see if they could identify the source. The lights stayed in a fixed slow motion, heading east toward us at the same elevation. Since we could

not identify the source nor hear any sound, I instructed my 15-year-old to take pictures of the object as it approached us. The object flew above us at around 500 feet or less at a slow steady pace heading east. As the object flew over and past us, we could not identify it. The object was shaped like a boomerang with white lights on the tips of the 'wings' around less than 100 feet in size. As the object was first noticed, as I was driving, the white lights were blinking. When the object flew past us the white lights became constant. There was no sound during the event. After the photos were taken, I could see on the photo a white crescent light to the left of the object."

West Virginia MUFON Assistant State Director Delmer Kelley closed this case as an Unknown Aerial Vehicle.

"Went to the location of the sighting and noted the apparent elevation, direction of travel, velocity and distance as pointed out by the witness at the location," Kelley stated in his report. "She was confident in the assessment of the shape of the craft as that of a boomerang or V-shaped object. She also was impressed by the fact that the object was completely silent and flew over at a slow, steady pace. The lights on the object were white lights.

"Four photos were taken by her son with a smart phone, but essentially no detail of significance was captured. All airplanes are required to have position lights on the tips of the wings, which are green on the right and red on the left. At no time were either red or green lights observed either during approach or departure of the craft. In view of the fact that the object did not display the characteristic lighting and motion that would likely be representative of an airplane and since no other known man-made or natural phenomena seem to fit the description as reported, this case is closed with the disposition of Unknown UAV."

Scott Depot is an unincorporated community in Putnam County, West Virginia. It is located along Crooked Creek at and downstream from the creek's intersection with Teays Valley Road. It is part of the census-designated place of Teays Valley, which is a part of the Huntington-Ashland Metropolitan Statistical Area (MSA), population about 363,000.

DECEMBER 12

Hovering triangle reported over North Carolina trees

A North Carolina witness at Reidsville reported watching a triangular-shaped object hovering over nearby trees, according to testimony in Case 97018.

The witness was driving home from a workplace in Greensboro, NC, back to Virginia on US 29 north between 11:45 p.m. and 12:30 a.m. on December 12, 2018.

"This is a trip I have taken at least twice a week since 2008," the witness stated. "It was a very clear sky that night. I appeared to see a 'falling star' or 'shooting star' and I was verbally making a wish in my car because that is always what you were told as a kid to do is wish on a star. Approximately 5-10 minutes later, I was in the Rockingham County area (a very rural area). I saw a blinking red light flashing in the distance above the tree line to the left of me, which was I think northwest. The trees blocked it some as I was approaching north, due to the aircraft being so low in the sky. As I got closer, it appeared to be very low in the sky and less than a mile away from US 29. It appeared to be just hovering there and moving very little. I knew then it wasn't a conventional airplane and my second thought was it must be a helicopter. As I got more to the side of the aircraft (still a little way away) as I was passing, I realized it wasn't making any noise like a helicopter would. I started staring at it and that's when I saw the three bright lights underneath the aircraft, one at each corner in a triangle pattern. It was very

dark, but the aircraft appeared to be a triangle due to the positioning of the lights. I was driving and trying not to wreck my car while watching something I had never seen before and saying to myself, 'What in the world is that?' I wished I could have gotten a video, but it was so late, and that highway is kind of isolated that time of night, so I didn't stop my car. In retrospect, I would have, because my husband and friends laughed when I told them. I know the aircraft was hovering because I completely passed it, and it was in my rear-view mirror to the southwest until it was completely out of my sight due to my driving away. I never saw it moving or, if it was, it was going very slow. Up to this point in my life I have never seen anything like this. I started researching online and thought I should report. I don't research or watch programs about aliens, so I had never heard of black triangle UFOs before. Another thought I had was whether or not it may be military, but I do not know why a military aircraft would be hovering in such a low-populated rural area."

North Carolina MUFON Assistant State Director Barbara Outterson closed this case as an Unknown-Other.

"My experience with the witness was very pleasant," Outterson stated in her report. "She appeared to be a very intelligent woman who had a good educational background and no exposure to paranormal or UFO-related topics. She described her life as very normal. I spent time asking her about all possible reactions she may have had during or after her sighting. She has been driving the same route for several years (back and forth to work) and has never experienced anything abnormal or remarkable. Although she did not stop to photograph or document the object she saw on the evening of December 12, 2018, she is sure that what she saw did not behave like any object she has seen before. My research did not uncover any related events or sightings on any evening during the week in question.

"With that said, I have made a potential connection between the movement of the original object(s) reported in the sighting and objects (from the NC Chinese Lantern Festival, 2018) that may have been drifting in a northwest direction for hours prior to the witness sighting over Reidsville, NC, coming from the town of Cary, NC. Under different conditions, this may have been an explanation for an 'IFO: Man-Made' disposition. Under the circumstances, I submit an 'Unknown-Other' disposition, due to an inability to disprove a solid origin for the object seen by the witness."

Reidsville is a city in Rockingham County, North Carolina, population 14,520.

Illinois witness reports 'stick creature' with four legs

An Illinois witness at St. Jacob reported watching an object crossing a highway in front of them described as a "giant walking stick with four legs," according to testimony in Case 96955.

The witness was driving home from work at approximately 3 a.m. on December 12, 2018, along Highway 4 north of Lebanon.

"I was almost to Hunter School Road when an object appeared in my headlights on the right side crossing the highway, looking like a giant walking stick with four legs. It was red wood in color and moved in approximately one second or less across the whole lighted area of my headlights. It had four legs and seemed a little elevated off the ground. It turned to me when it was almost out of view and had no face—just like a stick. Prominent color was reddish brown."

Illinois MUFON State Director Sam Maranto and Field Investigator James Heater closed this case as an Unknown-Other.

"I am reasonably certain that the submitter saw something they feel is very unusual,"

Maranto and Heater stated in their report. "The other independent report and interview were equally convincing. Though we have nothing other than their word and a statement of truth and fact and the interview was recorded. It is recommended by the standard set forth to assign the disposition assigned.

"There is a possible supporting witness account of what appears to be a similar object/creature, yet at a different location and on another day/year, yet not all that far from the submitter's location of observation."

St. Jacob is a village in Madison County, Illinois, population 1098.

Three UFOs reported low over New Jersey

A New Jersey witness at Laurel Lake reported watching three different craft that flew directly over their car and nearby trees, according to testimony in Case 97013.

The witness was heading to a meeting with a girlfriend at 6:20 p.m. on December 12, 2018.

"It flew over the road slowly," the witness stated, "directly over my car. A UFO. It flew right above the trees, rectangular in shape and four huge, white lights. Changed direction slightly. Was moving very slow. About 60 feet in length. About 20 feet wide. Then about five miles down the road saw two different craft. They both had two red lights on them. They were huge. At least a quarter-mile in length. And it looked like they were looking for the smaller craft. I was looking and stopped the car, telling my girlfriend what in the hell is that? She was acting funny, very delayed and lethargic. Almost unresponsive. I was hollering at her, 'Don't you see that?' And she said, 'Yes.' But was acting very weird. Like it wasn't sinking into her head. Very weird and the lights were a strange color of white. I would say the four lights were 8-10 feet in diameter. Lost sight of the small one over the trees as it moved farther away. The two big craft—saw them for a longer period of time. Then they disappeared. They were flying higher in the air. And, like I say, they looked like they were searching. No sound from any of them. They were no planes or helicopters. And they were not drones of any kind. Never saw anything like them before. I am a machinist and an automotive technician for over 25 years. Nothing I have ever seen before."

New Jersey MUFON Assistant State Director Ken Pfeifer closed this case as an Unknown Aerial Vehicle.

"After a long phone conversation with the witness, I will classify this case as Unknown. Witness is very credible and witness has attention to details."

Laurel Lake is an unincorporated community located within Commercial Township, in Cumberland County, New Jersey, population 2,989.

Black triangular UFO reported over St. Louis

A Missouri witness at St. Louis reported watching a "black triangle with white lights on its corners," according to testimony in Case 96983.

The witness was at work at a daycare at 6:52 p.m. on December 12, 2018.

"I took the trash out to a dumpster behind the building," the witness stated. "After I threw the trash away, I had the urge to look up into the night sky. I immediately saw a black triangular shape that had dim whitish/yellow lights on its three corners. It was lower than the cloud cover, but I am not a good enough judge of distance to say exactly how close it was. It was about the size of a guitar pick at the distance I saw it. At first, it was just rolling and rotating and moving in a southerly direction at a slow pace. Its movements were like a leaf being blown in the wind. I made a vocal exclamation, as I was rather surprised to see it, and at that

point it began moving in a northwesterly direction at a slightly faster pace. It continued to rotate and roll. It moved overhead of me, and I walked around the side of the building to keep it within sight. As I turned the corner, I noticed an airplane coming from the west (presumably the airport) and flying in an easterly direction. The triangular object moved past the airplane, made a sharp turn, and began moving in alignment with the plane. It appeared to be above and to the right of the plane, moving in a parallel line. It did this for a short period of time (about five seconds) until the plane was directly above me. It then made a 90-degree turn and began moving in a northwesterly direction. It continued to move in that direction until I was no longer able to see it, either because it was too far away or because it moved into the clouds. I recall feeling amazed, but also surprised, as I had no reason to look up into the sky, but when I had the urge to, my vision immediately locked on to the object. I'm aware of what it could have been, but it was still shocking to see. I had left my phone inside, so I do not have any evidence."

Missouri MUFON State Section Director Dana Simpson West closed this case as an Unknown Aerial Vehicle.

"Based on the interview with the witness, the shape of the craft, the unusual maneuvers of the craft, the rolling and rotating of the craft and similar cases that report the same type of rotation and rolling, I am classifying the case as an Unknown-UAV," Simpson West stated in her report.

St. Louis is a major independent city in Missouri, population 308,626.

DECEMBER 14

Multiple UFOs reported over Dominican Republic

A Dominican Republic witness at Punta Cana

reported watching "multiple shooting star-like objects followed by a very slow-flying object shaped somewhat like an airplane," according to testimony in Case 97555.

The witness and a boyfriend were standing on a rooftop terrace on the beach in Punta Cana about 9 p.m. on December 14, 2018.

"We started seeing what seemed to be like multiple shooting stars all in one area of the sky," the witness stated. "They all seemed to originate from generally the same spot but were falling in differing directions. They were also somewhat brighter and bigger (thicker, denser) than a typical falling star. Their color was a yellowish white. We probably saw somewhere between five and seven of these falling stars and then we noticed what at first seemed like a very large airplane moving very slowly through the same part of the sky. The craft was incredibly large. Bigger than any plane I've seen, including army-type cargo planes. The wings of the craft were also located further back than on a typical plane and were far longer than seemed normal. There were static lights along the edges of the wings and front of the craft. They were spaced equally along the wings, also in a way that is nothing like an airplane. The lights were white and did not flash. The body of the craft seemed to be matte, reflected no light whatsoever, had no windows like a regular plane and appeared flat. There was no dimension as there is with a regular plane. For the tremendous size of the craft, it would have had to have been extremely close to the ground - we should have been able to hear the engine at the very least. It was completely silent and moved very slowly through the sky, going in and out of very light cloud cover. At times part of the craft was behind a cloud but the tail or head of the craft was still visible. As it passed partially behind another cloud—the head of the plane and wings were still visible, with the lights showing clearly (even those behind the thin cloud)—it just disappeared. Completely gone, as if it had never been there at all. My boyfriend and I

both witnessed this. It lasted maybe a couple of minutes. Neither of us had any explanation though we tried to come up with one. It was truly incredible."

The MUFON International Director of Investigations for the Dominican Republic, Steve A. Hudgeons Jr., closed this case as an Unknown Aerial Vehicle.

DECEMBER 16

Silent triangular UFO reported over Arkansas

An Arkansas witness at Fort Smith reported watching a triangle-shaped UFO that moved overhead with no sound, according to testimony in Case 97044.

The witness was outside smoking at 7:38 p.m. on December 16, 2018.

"I noticed a triangle with dim lights at each corner," the witness stated. "It just seemed to float by silently like a balloon. It was low and moving in a straight line to the west. I got my brother-in-law to look up and he saw it too. It was kind of shocking."

Arkansas MUFON Field Investigator Arthur Lawless closed this case as an Unknown Aerial Vehicle.

"Witnesses appeared to give honest answers," Lawless stated in his report. "I rule out deception as they both wish to remain anonymous. Height and size disagreements are subjective to each individual's perception. Elevation difference one could attribute to where the object was when observed by each witness. Witness A spotted the object in the east moving west. Witness B came out after as the object was moving to the west. Object was too low and close to the witnesses to be a celestial body."

Fort Smith is the second-largest city in Arkansas and one of the two county seats of

Sebastian County, population 86,209.

DECEMBER 17

British witness describes triangle hovering over field

A British witness at Goole reported watching a triangular UFO "hovering over a field as if it was searching for something," according to testimony in Case 97065.

The witness was walking down to Goole Fields to Swinefleet to his girlfriend's house at 9:15 p.m. on December 17, 2018.

"I noticed flashing lights, which appeared to be a helicopter searching for something," the witness stated. "As I walked farther and got closer to the object, I could make out a shape. I first noticed the unusual triangular shape (isosceles) and the lights, which were apparent in each corner, flashing randomly. The object was traveling opposite to the point of the triangle, which I thought was strange as you would expect it to travel with the point streamline. The object hovered over the fields to the left of the river as I was walking to the village of Swinefleet. I was eager to capture a picture of the object on my phone; however, I had trouble opening the camera due to unusual interferences. During the sighting, I didn't feel at all nerved, which is surprising looking back on reflection. I am usually very unnerved walking in the dark and the abnormality of my lack of reaction is concerning. I lost sight of the object because it hovered into the distance [sic] and I concentrated on walking. I then turned as I came towards Swinefleet to see if it was still there and it could no longer be seen."

United Kingdom MUFON Field Investigator Robert Young closed this case as an Unknown Aerial Vehicle.

"An interesting report of the classic described flying triangle," Young wrote in his report. "If witness is telling the truth, then the object described is not your typical aircraft but an unknown object. It is interesting to note that when the young teenager wanted to take a photo of the said object, his camera wouldn't work. Maybe the object interfered with the phone on purpose so as not to be photographed?"

Goole is a town, civil parish and inland port in the East Riding of Yorkshire, England, population 19,518.

DECEMBER 23

Idaho witness describes large V-shaped object

An Idaho witness at Boise reported watching a large, V-shaped object traveling west, according to testimony in Case 97206.

The incident occurred at 11 p.m. on December 23, 2018.

"The craft was very large," the witness stated. "I estimated the length of each arm of the V to be well over the length of a commercial airliner, perhaps up to twice the length of an airliner. It made absolutely no noise, was dark, no apparent light, almost as if the entire craft was slightly glowing faintly or it could have been reflecting lights from the ground. It traveled in a straight path almost directly over my head at what I guesstimate to be well in excess of normal aircraft. I watched it until it went out of my view, which was probably 20-30 seconds.

"This is the fifth UFO I have witnessed in the past four years. The first was a glowing orb that was probably less than 100 feet above me. A few months later I witnessed a cigar-shaped craft. About six months after that I watched a V-formation of five lights. And a month or so after that I saw another V-formation of five lights. The second V-formation I saw answered one of the questions I had of the prior one, which was – Is it one craft with five lights or five separate crafts? The second sighting of the formation answered that when one of the lights veered off from the others.

"Another oddity I have witnessed on two separate occasions, as I watched what I assumed were satellites traveling across the night sky (I like to stargaze and always scan the sky for satellites, which are fairly common sightings). But on these two occasions as I watched them travel across the sky, they flared into fireballs leaving a trail of fire and then simply disappeared. If I had to make a serious guess as to what those were, I would have to say a satellite was destroyed by some type of weapon.

"It's odd to me how I could regularly look up at the stars for 45 years and see nothing and then within the past five years it has become nearly a regular thing to see UFOs."

Idaho MUFON State Director James Millard closed this case as an Unknown Aerial Vehicle.

"Based solely on the witness description, this was an Unknow UAV."

Boise is the capital and most populous city of Idaho, and is the county seat of Ada County, population 223,154.

DECEMBER 28

British witness describes UFO hovering over field

A British witness at Shrewsbury reported watching a large, slow-moving, chevron-shaped object, according to testimony in Case 97282.

The incident occurred at 1:10 a.m. on December 28, 2018.

"I'm an ex-Royal Navy petty officer and served over 20 years in the military," the witness stated. "I retired in 2015. My background was engineering and above-sea weapon systems. I have a strong knowledge of all military aircraft and have never seen anything like this before. At approximately 1:10 a.m. I had been walking my dog Jack, around fields off Gains Park Road in Shrewsbury. I wasn't able to sleep well, and the dog indicated he wanted to go out. So as the weather was fairly mild, I grabbed the dog's lead and went out. As we walked around a field that borders the A5 bypass road, I heard a strange humming noise slightly above and ahead of me. As I looked up, I could make out a very large V- or chevron-shaped object, which was literally hovering across the other side of the field I was walking around. It was black and very dull in color, with dim white lights at the tips and a red glow at the center. I estimate it to be well over 100 feet from tip to tip. Jack my dog started to get uneasy and whimpered as we walked towards it. But suddenly it started to move and as it did towards the west, a small white ball of light shot out of it towards the road. As this happened, the large chevron object shot out a clear white beam of light towards the housing estate I live in called Gains Park. The chevron then just shot off with a hum and buzzing sound towards the west, and it disappeared from sight. The whole thing lasted about 30 seconds. I would not have been able to get an image on my mobile phone, as I only have a basic one and it would not have picked up the object in the sky. I am fully aware of all military aircraft including drones, but this was like nothing I have seen before. On looking through the Internet at what I could compare it to, I would most definitely say that it was similar to the object seen over Phoenix, Arizona, in 1997."

United Kingdom MUFON National Director Jack Turnbull closed this case as Info Only.

"Unable to contact the witness," Turnbull wrote in his report.

Shrewsbury is the county town of Shropshire, England, population 71,715.

DECEMBER 31

Scottish witness reports hovering object with windows

A Scottish witness at Caithness reported watching and photographing a hovering object with windows, according to testimony in Case 97391.

The incident occurred at 3:01 a.m. on December 31, 2018.

"It was just past midnight here in North Scotland when a UFO was seen," the witness stated. "It hovered for three hours. It had windows. It was huge. Me and my wife and kids saw it. It had something looking out down to us. I have videos and photos."

United Kingdom MUFON National Director Jack Turnbull closed this case as an Unknown Aerial Vehicle.

"Witness undoubtedly saw something at close range, around 200 yards in altitude and approximately 1,000 yards away," Turnbull stated in his report. "Sent in photographs that show a strange shape with central light; however, no definition. Also saw it suspended in the air, silent. Departed at great speed. Different colors, yellow, etc., though he could see what looked like windows bigger than an aircraft. Area where seen very close to the sea."

Caithness is a historic county, registration county and lieutenancy area of Scotland.

UFO
STATISTICS

The statistics for UFO Cases of Interest were compiled to match the report selections in this edition. We pulled UFO stats for all 2018 cases reported, then showed how many of those cases actually occurred within 2018. From the 2018 cases, we listed our three chosen ways cases are closed: (a) Unknown Aerial Vehicle; (b) Unknown-Other; or (c) Info Only. From the total case reports for the entire year then, the missing data is either from cases closed as Insufficient Data or Hoax.

	Worldwide	U.S.
All reports	7,665	5,160
Unknown Aerial Vehicle	1,064	822
Unknown-Other	865	716
Info Only	998	501
2018 reports only	5,478	3,820
2018 UAVs	716	560
2018 Unknown-Other	613	519
2018 Info Only	566	284

States	All Reports	2018 Events	2018 UAV	2018 U-Other	2018 Info Only
Alabama	53	38	8	11	4
Alaska	16	2	5	1	3
Arizona	212	173	4	3	23
Arkansas	59	47	23	10	5
California	627	450	80	80	29
Colorado	175	130	15	17	10
Connecticut	40	28	3	6	6
Delaware	10	8	1	0	2
District of Columbia	12	7	2	1	2
Florida	368	285	40	26	51
Georgia	121	77	11	3	40
Hawaii	26	20	2	2	8
Idaho	51	42	10	6	6
Illinois	136	96	12	19	9
Indiana	104	72	25	25	14
Iowa	38	26	19	4	4
Kansas	29	20	7	4	2
Kentucky	67	47	18	9	0

States	All Reports	2018 Events	2018 UAV	2018 U-Other	2018 Info Only
Louisiana	60	35	7	8	12
Maine	52	39	6	12	3
Maryland	56	38	9	10	4
Massachusetts	84	63	14	16	7
Michigan	188	139	13	24	16
Minnesota	55	26	9	13	1
Mississippi	36	22	8	3	5
Missouri	118	88	62	10	3
Montana	29	24	3	7	6
Montana	23	21	4	1	1
Nebraska	18	14	2	1	2
Nevada	95	77	17	25	12
New Hampshire	28	17	8	4	0
New Jersey	122	95	39	18	33
New Mexico	81	54	1	29	15
New York	202	144	32	32	3
North Carolina	123	85	16	22	3
North Dakota	14	8	3	3	1
Ohio	169	124	23	18	13
Oklahoma	64	48	11	7	2
Oregon	139	112	29	38	7
Pennsylvania	208	163	39	33	6
Rhode Island	11	8	1	1	7
South Carolina	65	48	17	19	11
South Dakota	9	7	0	1	2
Tennessee	96	70	9	16	12
Texas	373	282	26	24	44
Utah	53	42	21	9	1
Vermont	10	6	1	0	8
Virginia	91	71	16	10	21
Washington	207	169	50	44	16
West Virginia	37	25	8	5	0
Wisconsin	91	65	18	30	6
Wyoming	15	9	2	2	1

COUNTRIES	All Reports	2018 Events	2018 UAV	2018 U-Other	2018 Info Only
Afghanistan	3	2	1	0	0
Albania	1	1	0	0	0
Algeria	4	1	0	0	2
American Samoa	0	0	0	0	0
Andorra	0	0	0	0	0
Angola	2	2	0	0	0
Anguilla	0	0	0	0	0
Antarctica	5	5	0	1	3
Antigua and Barbuda	0	0	0	0	0
Argentina	14	7	0	0	0
Armenia	1	0	0	0	0
Aruba	0	0	0	0	0
Australia	129	79	16	2	23
Austria	14	9	0	0	1
Azerbaijan	0	0	0	0	0
Bahamas	3	2	0	0	0
Bahrain	1	1	0	0	0
Bangladesh	1	1	0	0	0
Barbados	1	0	0	0	0
Belarus	1	0	0	0	0
Belgium	7	5	1	0	1
Belize	1	1	0	0	0
Benin	0	0	0	0	0
Bermuda	1	1	0	0	1
Bhutan	0	0	0	0	0
Bolivia	0	0	0	0	0
Bosnia and Herzegovina	7	2	1	0	3
Botswana	0	0	0	0	0
Bouvet Island	0	0	0	0	0
Brazil	68	43	11	0	6
British Indian Ocean Territory	0	0	0	0	0
Brunei Darussalam	0	0	0	0	0
Bulgaria	6	5	0	0	0
Burkina Faso	0	0	0	0	0

COUNTRIES	All Reports	2018 Events	2018 UAV	2018 U-Other	2018 Info Only
Burundi	0	0	0	0	0
Cambodia	1	0	0	0	0
Cameroon	0	0	0	0	0
Canada	617	384	34	40	128
Cape Verde	0	0	0	0	0
Cayman Islands	0	0	0	0	0
Central African Republic	0	0	0	0	0
Chad	0	0	0	0	0
Chile	75	63	2	7	22
China	8	3	3	0	5
Christmas Island	0	0	0	0	0
Cocos (Keeling) Islands	0	0	0	0	0
Colombia	15	11	5	1	1
Comoros	0	0	0	0	0
Congo	1	1	0	0	0
Congo, Democratic Republic	0	0	0	0	0
Cook Islands	0	0	0	0	0
Costa Rica	7	5	2	1	1
Cote D'Voire	0	0	0	0	0
Croatia	8	5	2	1	1
Cuba	3	2	0	1	1
Cyprus	3	3	0	0	1
Czech Republic	6	6	0	0	1
Denmark	6	3	0	0	1
Djibouti	0	0	0	0	0
Dominica	0	0	0	0	0
Dominican Republic	7	5	2	0	0
Ecuador	3	0	0	1	0
Egypt	2	2	1	0	0
El Salvador	3	2	1	0	0
Equatorial Guinea	0	0	0	0	0
Eritrea	0	0	0	0	0
Estonia	2	1	0	0	0
Ethiopia	0	0	0	0	0

COUNTRIES	All Reports	2018 Events	2018 UAV	2018 U-Other	2018 Info Only
Falkland Islands (Malvinas)	0	0	0	0	0
Faroe Islands	0	0	0	0	0
Fiji	1	1	0	0	0
Finland	5	4	0	0	0
France	180	97	6	12	26
French Guiana	0	0	0	0	0
French Polynesia	2	1	0	0	0
French South Territories	1	1	0	0	1
Gabon	0	0	0	0	0
Gambia	0	0	0	0	0
Georgia	1	1	0	1	0
Germany	65	48	2	0	7
Ghana	0	0	0	0	0
Gibraltar	0	0	0	0	0
Greece	9	8	3	0	0
Greenland	1	1	1	0	0
Grenada	0	0	0	0	0
Guadeloupe	1	1	0	0	0
Guam	1	0	0	0	0
Guatemala	4	3	0	1	1
Guinea	0	0	0	0	0
Guinea-Bissau	0	0	0	0	0
Guyana	1	1	0	0	0
Haiti	1	1	1	0	0
Heard Island, McDonald Islands	0	0	0	0	0
Holy See (Vatican City State)	0	0	0	0	0
Honduras	2	2	0	0	0
Hong Kong	3	3	0	0	1
Hungary	8	4	0	0	3
Iceland	4	4	0	1	0
India	52	43	6	9	3
Indonesia	1	0	1	0	0
Iran	8	5	0	0	6

COUNTRIES	All Reports	2018 Events	2018 UAV	2018 U-Other	2018 Info Only
Iraq	1	0	0	0	0
Ireland	35	26	4	2	11
Israel	5	4	0	1	4
Italy	37	18	0	0	5
Jamaica	1	1	0	0	0
Japan	10	8	0	2	3
Jordan	1	1	0	0	1
Kazakhstan	0	0	0	0	0
Kenya	3	2	0	0	0
Kiribati	1	0	0	0	0
Korea, North	1	1	0	0	0
Korea, South	11	8	0	0	0
Kuwait	0	0	0	0	0
Kyrgyzstan	1	0	0	1	0
Lao	0	0	0	0	0
Latvia	1	1	0	0	0
Lebanon	2	2	0	0	0
Lesotho	0	0	0	0	0
Liberia	1	0	0	0	0
Libyan Arab Jamahiriya	0	0	0	0	0
Liechtenstein	0	0	0	0	0
Lithuania	2	1	0	0	2
Luxembourg	1	0	0	0	0
Macao	0	0	0	0	0
Macedonia	4	0	0	1	0
Madagascar	0	0	0	0	0
Malawi	0	0	0	0	0
Malaysia	3	1	1	0	0
Maldives	1	1	0	0	1
Mali	0	0	0	0	0
Malta	3	2	1	1	0
Marshall Islands	0	0	0	0	0
Martinique	0	0	0	0	0
Mauritania	0	0	0	0	0

COUNTRIES	All Reports	2018 Events	2018 UAV	2018 U-Other	2018 Info Only
Mauritius	0	0	0	0	0
Mayotte	0	0	0	0	0
Mexico	35	24	6	6	6
Micronesia	0	0	0	0	0
Moldova	0	0	0	0	0
Monaco	0	0	0	0	0
Mongolia	1	1	0	0	1
Montserrat	0	0	0	0	0
Morocco	0	0	0	0	0
Mozambique	0	0	0	0	0
Myanmar	0	0	0	0	0
N. Mariana Islands	0	0	0	0	0
Namibia	0	0	0	0	0
Nauru	1	0	0	0	0
Nepal	2	2	0	0	0
Netherlands	24	13	0	2	4
Netherlands Antilles	0	0	0	0	0
New Caledonia	0	0	0	0	0
New Zealand	25	20	0	0	0
Nicaragua	1	0	0	0	1
Niger	0	0	0	0	0
Nigeria	1	0	1	0	0
Niue	0	0	0	0	0
Norfolk Island	0	0	0	0	0
Norway	16	11	0	0	1
Oman	4	3	1	1	0
Pakistan	3	3	1	0	1
Palau	0	0	0	0	0
Palestinian Territory Occupied	0	0	0	0	0
Panama	5	3	2	0	2
Papua New Guinea	0	0	0	0	0
Paraguay	1	0	0	0	0
Peru	10	9	0	0	3
Philippines	12	9	5	2	1

COUNTRIES	All Reports	2018 Events	2018 UAV	2018 U-Other	2018 Info Only
Pitcairn	0	0	0	0	0
Poland	20	12	0	1	0
Portugal	23	18	5	0	16
Puerto Rico	33	24	2	1	2
Qatar	0	0	0	0	0
Reunion	3	2	1	0	1
Romania	4	4	1	0	2
Russian Federation	10	5	0	0	2
Rwanda	0	0	0	0	0
Saint Helena	0	0	0	0	0
Saint Kitts and Nevis	0	0	0	0	0
Saint Lucia	0	0	0	0	0
Saint Pierre and Miquelon	0	0	0	0	0
Saint Vincent and Grenadines	0	0	0	0	0
Samoa	0	0	0	0	0
San Marino	0	0	0	0	0
Sao Tome and Principe	0	0	0	0	0
Saudi Arabia	0	0	0	0	0
Senegal	0	0	0	0	0
Serbia and Montenegro	11	10	0	0	3
Seychelles	1	1	0	0	0
Sierra Leone	0	0	0	0	0
Singapore	2	1	0	0	0
Slovakia	2	0	0	1	0
Slovenia	18	10	0	3	8
Solomon Islands	0	0	0	0	0
Somalia	0	0	0	0	0
South Africa	14	8	3	1	9
S. Georgia, S. Sandwich Islands	0	0	0	0	0
South Sudan	0	0	0	0	0
Spain	40	26	5	4	10
Sri Lanka	0	0	0	0	0
Sudan	0	0	0	0	0

COUNTRIES	All Reports	2018 Events	2018 UAV	2018 U-Other	2018 Info Only
Suriname	0	0	0	0	0
Svalbard and Jan Mayen	0	0	0	0	0
Swaziland	0	0	0	0	0
Sweden	8	7	0	3	0
Switzerland	5	4	0	0	3
Syria	0	0	0	0	0
Taiwan	1	0	0	0	0
Tajikistan	0	0	0	0	0
Tanzania	0	0	0	0	0
Thailand	7	6	4	2	0
Timor-Leste	0	0	0	0	0
Togo	0	0	0	0	0
Tokelau	0	0	0	0	0
Tonga	0	0	0	0	0
Trinidad and Tobago	0	0	0	0	0
Tunisia	2	2	1	0	0
Turkey	17	14	0	6	1
Turkmenistan	0	0	0	0	0
Turks and Caicos Islands	1	0	1	0	0
Tuvalo	0	0	0	0	0
Uganda	1	0	0	0	0
Ukraine	5	1	0	0	3
United Arab Emirates	5	5	1	0	0
United Kingdom	607	424	91	22	136
U.S. Minor Outlying Islands	1	1	0	0	0
Uruguay	4	2	1	3	0
Uzbekistan	0	0	0	0	0
Vanuatu	1	1	0	1	0
Venezuela	11	4	3	1	3
Viet Nam	2	1	0	0	1
Virgin Islands, British	0	0	0	0	0
Virgin Islands, U.S.	0	0	0	0	0
Wallis and Futuna	1	1	0	0	0
Western Sahara	0	0	0	0	0

COUNTRIES	All Reports	2018 Events	2018 UAV	2018 U-Other	2018 Info Only
Yemen	0	0	0	0	0
Zambia	0	0	0	0	0
Zimbabwe	0	1	0	0	0

UFO
RESEARCH INDEX

LOCATION INDEX: 2018

EVENT	TIME	CASE	CITY	STATE-COUNTRY	SHAPE	DISPOSITION	PAGE
Abbotsford, BC, Canada							
3.15.18	8:40 p.m.	90803	Abbotsford	BC Canada	Other	UAV	50
Ada County, Idaho							
6.17.18	11:40 p.m.	92802	Ada County	ID	Other	UAV	99
11.6.18	9 p.m.	96312	Boise	ID	Boomerang	UAV	195
12.23.18	11 p.m.	97206	Boise	ID	Triangle	UAV	229
Aiken, South Carolina							
3.31.18	9:55 p.m.	91151	Aiken	SC	Circle	Other	55
Aiken County, South Carolina							
3.31.18	9:55 p.m.	91151	Aiken	SC	Circle	Other	55
Alabama							
3.3.18	5:35 a.m.	90540	Birmingham	AL	Triangle	UAV	39
3.15.18	4 a.m.	97506	Holly Pond	AL	Triangle	UAV	49
4.5.18	9:20 p.m.	91224	Fort Payne	AL	Square/Rectangle	UAV	58
5.1.18	n/a	91829	Loxley	AL	Circle	Other	72
Alaska							
6.24.18	1:51 a.m.	92893	Anchorage County	AK	Sphere	UAV	107
Alexandria, Indiana							
7.13.18	9:30 p.m.	93410	Alexandria	IN	Sphere	Other	119
Alexandria, Maryland							
6.9.18	8:32 p.m.	92619	Alexandria	MD	Bullet/Missile	UAV	94
Allegheny County, Pennsylvania							
3.26.18	3:15 a.m.	91194	Bridgeville	PA	Boomerang	UAV	52
Anaheim, California							
7.22.18	10 p.m.	93687	Anaheim	CA	Triangle	UAV	125

EVENT	TIME	CASE	CITY	STATE-COUNTRY	SHAPE	DISPOSITION	PAGE
Ancaster, Canada							
9.12.18	n/a	95268	Ancaster	Canada	Triangle	UAV	158
Anchorage County, Alaska							
6.24.18	1:51 a.m.	92893	Anchorage County	AK	Sphere	UAV	107
Anoka County, Minnesota							
6.26.18	10:30 p.m.	92957	Fridley	MN	Sphere	Other	108
Apex, Wisconsin							
11.8.18	7:30 p.m.	96310	Apex	NC	Other	UAV	201
Arizona							
6.28.18	11:15 p.m.	93454	Buckeye	AZ	Circle	UAV	110
9.21.18	8 p.m.	98732	Sonoita	AZ	Teardrop	UAV	164
11.12.18	7:20 p.m.	96353	Phoenix	AZ	Cigar	UAV	205
Arkansas							
2.08.18	8:30 p.m.	90133	Mena	AR	Triangle	UAV	27
2.08.18	8:35 p.m.	90181	Mena	AR	Triangle	UAV	27
12.16.18	7:38 p.m.	97044	Fort Smith	AR	Triangle	UAV	228
Arkoma, Oklahoma							
5.21.18	9:59 p.m.	92164	Arkoma	OK	Triangle	UAV	79
Arncliffe, Australia							
4.15.18	1 p.m.	94668	Arncliffe	Australia	Egg	UAV	63
Ashland County, Ohio							
9.3.18	4:07 p.m.	95976	Perrysville	OH	n/a	UAV	155
Atlanta, Georgia							
10.10.18	2:27 p.m.	95682	Atlanta	GA	Cigar	UAV	176
Atlantic County, New Jersey							
6.20.18	3:15 p.m.	92849	Egg Harbor Township	NJ	Sphere	UAV	102
Attica, Indiana							
3.16.18	9:48 p.m.	90816	Attica	IN	Triangle	UAV	50
Attleboro, Massachusetts							
6.10.18	10:30 p.m.	92641	Attleboro	MA	N/A	Other	95
Australia							
4.7.18	1:30 a.m.	96086	Warracknabeal	Australia	Disc	UAV	59
4.15.18	1 p.m.	94668	Arncliffe	Australia	Egg	UAV	63

EVENT	TIME	CASE	CITY	STATE-COUNTRY	SHAPE	DISPOSITION	PAGE
Baker City, Oregon							
12.5.18	6:10 p.m.	96818	Baker City	OR	Chevron	UAV	219
Baker County, Oregon							
12.5.18	6:10 p.m.	96818	Baker City	OR	Chevron	UAV	219
Baldwin County, Alabama							
5.1.18	n/a	91829	Loxley	AL	Circle	Other	72
Baldwinsville, New York							
9.24.18	6:45 p.m.	95317	Baldwinsville	NY	Sphere	Other	165
Ballivor, Ireland							
11.23.18	4:55 a.m.	96554	Ballivor	Ireland	Triangle	Other	208
Ballymahon, Ireland							
5.18.18	4:25 a.m.	98601	Ballymahon Co. Lonford	Ireland	Saturn-like	Other	78
Bartholomew County, Indiana							
9.13.18	9 p.m.	94903	Columbus	IN	Triangle	UAV	160
Bay Shore, New York							
5.15.18	9:30 p.m.	92029	Bay Shore	NY	Sphere	Other	77
Beaconsfield, United Kingdom							
12.4.18	6:30 a.m.	96843	Beaconsfield	UK	Disc	UAV	217
Bedford County, Pennsylvania							
1.28.18	7:30 p.m.	89867	Buffalo Mills	PA	Triangle	Other	21
Belleville, Wisconsin							
10.21.18	5:30 p.m.	95770	Belleville	WI	Unknown	Other	183
Bellingham, Washington							
10.10.18	4:30 a.m.	95592	Bellingham	WA	Triangle	UAV	175
Belmont County, Ohio							
10.25.18	6:30 p.m.	96048	Dilles Bottom	OH	Egg	UAV	184
Benton, Ohio							
10.30.18	7:40 p.m.	96019	Benton	OH	Cylinder	UAV	189
Bexar County, Texas							
11.6.18	8:25 p.m.	96207	San Antonio	TX	Chevron	UAV	195
Birmingham, Alabama							
3.3.18	5:35 a.m.	90540	Birmingham	AL	Triangle	UAV	39
Black Hawk County, Iowa							
8.6.18	10:15 p.m.	93940	Waterloo	IA	Circle	UAV	132

EVENT	TIME	CASE	CITY	STATE-COUNTRY	SHAPE	DISPOSITION	PAGE
Blackstone, Massachusetts							
6.10.18	10:27 p.m.	92653	Blackstone	MA	Unknown	UAV	95
Blaine County, Idaho							
9.13.18	8:15 a.m.	94937	Hailey	ID	Square/Rectangle	UAV	159
Boca Raton, Florida							
11.7.18	9:36 p.m.	96341	Boca Raton	FL	Chevron	UAV	199
Boise, Idaho							
11.6.18	9 p.m.	96312	Boise	ID	Boomerang	UAV	195
12.23.18	11 p.m.	97206	Boise	ID	Triangle	UAV	229
Boone County, Missouri							
11.26.18	8:02 p.m.	96643	Columbia	MO	Boomerang	UAV	212
Bosnia							
4.2.18	10:27 p.m.	91182	Banja Luka	Bosnia & Herzegovina	Disc	Info Only	58
Brazil							
6.1.18	7:41 p.m.	92432	Sao Jose Dos Pinhais	Brazil	Egg	Info Only	82
Breitenbush Hot Springs							
8.1.18	9:02 p.m.	97862	Breitenbush Hot Springs	OR	Triangle	UAV	129
Bridgeville, Pennsylvania							
3.26.18	3:15 a.m.	91194	Bridgeville	PA	Boomerang	UAV	52
Bristol County, Massachusetts							
6.10.18	10:30 p.m.	92641	Attleboro	MA	N/A	Other	95
Bromsgrove, United Kingdom							
4.10.18	2:30 a.m.	96307	Bromsgrove	UK	Unknown	UAV	60
Brookline, New Hampshire							
3.28.18	3:15 a.m.	91075	Brookline	NH	Triangle	UAV	53
Brooklyn, New York							
4.22.18	5:20 p.m.	91572	Brooklyn	NY	Saturn-like	UAV	67
Brookport. Illinois							
7.17.18	10:40 p.m.	93540	Brookport	IL	Cylinder	UAV	121
Buckeye, Arizona							
6.28.18	11:15 p.m.	93454	Buckeye	AZ	Circle	UAV	110
Buffalo Mills, Pennsylvania							
1.28.18	7:30 p.m.	89867	Buffalo Mills	PA	Triangle	Other	21

EVENT	TIME	CASE	CITY	STATE-COUNTRY	SHAPE	DISPOSITION	PAGE
Bullitt County, Kentucky							
7.19.18	9:30 p.m.	97557	Mount Washington	KY	Sphere	Other	123
Burlington County, New Jersey							
10.3.18	7:30 p.m.	96637	New Lisbon	NJ	Triangle	UAV	170
Cache County, Utah							
1.6.18	10 p.m.	89385	Logan	UT	Diamond	Other	13
Caithness, United Kingdom							
12.31.18	12:10 a.m.	97391	Caithness	UK	Saturn-like	UAV	231
California							
1.3.18	6:40 p.m.	89327	Marina	CA	Sphere	Other	10
2.21.18	12:30 a.m.	90347	Sacramento	CA	Square/Rectangle	UAV	34
2.26.18	3:47 p.m.	90708	Wilmington	CA	Saturn-like	UAV	37
5.16.18	n/a	92036	Salinas	CA	Triangle	UAV	77
6.3.18	n/a	92452	Flournoy	CA	Sphere	Other	89
6.23.18	11:45 p.m.	92947	Oak Dale	CA	Fireball	UAV	105
7.2.18	2:30 p.m.	93418	Gustine	CA.	Triangle	UAV	114
7.22.18	10 p.m.	93687	Anaheim	CA	Triangle	UAV	125
8.9.18	2:40 p.m.	94827	San Diego	CA	Oval	UAV	134
8.29.18	8:15 p.m.	97227	Jamul	CA	Sphere	UAV	151
9.16.18	1:15 a.m.	94931	Kensington	CA	Unknown	Other	161
10.4.18	8:57 p.m.	95343	Rancho Mirage	CA	Boomerang	UAV	173
10.12.18	1:01 a.m.	95590	Citrus Heights	CA	Triangle	UAV	177
10.15.18	4 p.m.	95599	Sonora	CA	N/A	UAV	180
10.28.18	n/a	96472	Sacramento	CA	Triangle	UAV	188
11.27.18	8 p.m.	97510	Santee	CA	Triangle	Info Only	212
12.3.18	n/a	96773	n/a	CA	Teardrop	UAV	217
12.6.18	7:12 p.m.	97119	Red Bluff	CA	Triangle	UAV	221
California, Pennsylvania							
10.23.18	12:52 p.m.	95826	California	PA	Disc	UAV	184
Canada							
3.15.18	8:40 p.m.	90803	Abbotsford	BC Canada	Other	UAV	50
3.22.18	11:45 p.m.	91005	Coquitlam	BC Canada	Square/Rectangle	Info Only	52
4.22.18	12 a.m.	91570	Edmonton	CA	Triangle	Info Only	68

EVENT	TIME	CASE	CITY	STATE-COUNTRY	SHAPE	DISPOSITION	PAGE
5.11.18	10:20 a.m.	91939	Esquimalt	BC CA	Cigar	Info Only	74
6.2.18	10:15 p.m.	92445	London	Canada	Triangle	UAV	85
6.19.18	7:10 a.m.	92792	Joliette	Canada	Other	UAV	100
7.10.18	8:50 p.m.	93369	Newmarket	Canada	Cylinder	UAV	117
7.10.18	10 p.m.	97688	Toronto	Canada	Triangle	Other	117
7.15.18	8:06 p.m.	93445	Niagara Falls	Canada	Sphere	Other	120
9.12.18	n/a	95268	Ancaster	Canada	Triangle	UAV	158
9.25.18	10:30 p.m.	95703	Lachute	Canada	Disc	UAV	166
10.13.18	8:58 p.m.	98344	Stoney Creek	Canada	Boomerang	UAV	179
11.11.18	7:05 p.m.	96314	London	Canada	Triangle	UAV	204
Carbon County, Utah							
12.7.18	9:25 p.m.	96890	Wellington	UT	Cigar	UAV	221
Carmel, Indiana							
7.2.18	9:55 p.m.	94741	Carmel	IN	Cigar	Other	114
Caroga Lake, New York							
11.14.18	7:24 p.m.	96378	Caroga Lake	NY	Circle	UAV	206
Carolina Beach, North Carolina							
6.29.18	9:30 p.m.	93050	Carolina Beach	NC	Sphere	Other	111
Carroll County, Georgia							
10.11.18	6:24 p.m.	95738	Carrollton	GA	Blimp	UAV	177
Carroll County, Maryland							
3.10.18	11:57 p.m.	90710	Manchester	MD	Triangle	Other	45
Carrollton, Georgia							
10.11.18	6:24 p.m.	95738	Carrollton	GA	Blimp	UAV	177
Carver County, Minnesota							
11.9.18	8:18 p.m.	96286	Chaska	MN	Star-like	UAV	202
Cass County, North Dakota							
7.1.18	9:23 p.m.	93045	West Fargo	ND	Sphere	Other	113
Cassleberry, Florida							
1.4.18	6:25 a.m.	89344	Casselberry	FL	Square/Rectangle	Other	12
Caverna, Missouri							
5.3.18	10:28 p.m.	91773	Caverna	MO	Oval	UAV	72
Cayuga County, New York							
10.25.18	7:10 p.m.	95880	Montazuma	NY	Teardrop	UAV	185

EVENT	TIME	CASE	CITY	STATE-COUNTRY	SHAPE	DISPOSITION	PAGE
Cedar County, Missouri							
8.19.18	8 p.m.	94262	El Dorado Springs	MO	Disc	UAV	147
Chaska, Minnesota							
11.9.18	8:18 p.m.	96286	Chaska	MN	Star-like	UAV	202
Chatsworth, Georgia							
3.22.18	10:37 p.m.	90959	Chatsworth	GA	Triangle	UAV	51
Cherokee County, Georgia							
2.15.18	9:30 p.m.	91313	Woodstock	GA	Cylinder	UAV	33
Citrus Heights, California							
10.12.18	1:01 a.m.	95590	Citrus Heights	CA	Triangle	UAV	177
Clark County, Nevada							
1.1.18	12:05 a.m.	89317	Las Vegas	NV	Disc	UAV	8
2.23.18	7:17 p.m.	90398	Las Vegas	NV	Triangle		36
6.11.18	2:11 a.m.	92673	North Las Vegas	NV	Other	UAV	96
6.27.18	10 p.m.	92964	Mesquite	NV	Cigar	UAV	110
7.18.18	9 p.m.	93459	North Las Vegas	NV	Sphere	Other	123
8.28.18	4:15 a.m.	94461	Las Vegas	NV	Triangle	Other	151
11.7.18	12 p.m.	96230	Las Vegas	NV	Sphere	Other	196
Clark County, Washington							
9.18.18	12:25 p.m.	94996	Vancouver	WA	Unknown	UAV	162
Clark County, Wisconsin							
9.10.18	10:30 p.m.	98808	Colby	WI	Sphere	Other	157
Clay County, Missouri							
3.30.18	4:30 a.m.	91184	Excelsior Springs	MO	Triangle	UAV	54
Cobb County, Georgia							
3.6.18	9:40 p.m.	90698	Marietta	GA	Other	UAV	42
Colby, Wisconsin							
9.10.18	10:30 p.m.	98808	Colby	WI	Sphere	Other	157
Cole County, Missouri							
11.11.18	2:40 a.m.	96450	Jefferson City	MO	Chevron	UAV	204
Collin County, Texas							
12.1.18	12:00 a.m.	96805	McKinney	TX	Oval	UAV	214
Columbia, Missouri							
11.26.18	8:02 p.m.	96643	Columbia	MO	Boomerang	UAV	212

EVENT	TIME	CASE	CITY	STATE-COUNTRY	SHAPE	DISPOSITION	PAGE
Colorado							
6.7.18	10:30 p.m.	92568	Colorado Springs	CO	Other	UAV	92
8.12.18	5:06 p.m.	94086	Parker	CO	Egg	UAV	138
9.17.18	9:42 p.m.	94983	Highlands Ranch	CO	Cone	UAV	161
10.5.18	8:15 p.m.	95364	Trinidad	CO	Triangle	UAV	174
Colorado Springs, Colorado							
6.7.18	10:30 p.m.	92568	Colorado Springs	CO	Other	UAV	92
Columbia							
6.24.18	n/a	95063	Medellin	Columbia	Diamond	UAV	106
Columbus, Indiana							
9.13.18	9 p.m.	94903	Columbus	IN	Triangle	UAV	160
Contra Costa County, California							
9.16.18	1:15 a.m.	94931	Kensington	CA	Unknown	Other	161
Cook County, Illinois							
8.10.18	9:58 p.m.	94525	Tinley Park	IL	Sphere	UAV	136
Coquitlam, BC, Canada							
3.22.18	11:45 p.m.	91005	Coquitlam	BC Canada	Square/Rectangle	Info Only	52
Cospicua, Malta							
8.18.18	9:40 p.m.	96784	Cospicua	Malta	Oval	Other	146
Costa Rica							
9.14.18	8:15 a.m.	95265	Santa Elena	Costa Rica	Disc	UAV	160
Crawford County, Ohio							
10.30.18	7:40 p.m.	96019	Benton	OH	Cylinder	UAV	189
Crief, Scotland, United Kingdom							
6.2.18	3:10 p.m.	92499	Crieff, Scotland	UK	Disc	UAV	84
Cullman County, Alabama							
3.15.18	4 a.m.	97506	Holly Pond	AL	Triangle	UAV	49
Cumberland County, New Jersey							
12.12.18	6:20 p.m.	97013	Laurel Lake	NJ	N/A	UAV	226
Czech Republic							
6.1.18	11:01 p.m.	93565	Novy Jicin	Czech Republic	Triangle	Info Only	82

EVENT	TIME	CASE	CITY	STATE-COUNTRY	SHAPE	DISPOSITION	PAGE
Dallas, Oregon							
6.7.18	10:05 p.m.	92560	Dallas	OR	Square/Rectangle	UAV	91
Dane County, Wisconsin							
6.26.18	2:41 a.m.	92954	Madison	WI	Triangle	UAV	107
10.21.18	5:30 p.m.	95770	Belleville	WI	Unknown	Other	183
Darlington, United Kingdom							
1.6.18	1:50 p.m.	89370	Darlington	UK	Triangle	Info Only	12
Darrington, Washington							
7.22.18	1:42 p.m.	93732	Darrington	WA.	Disc	UAV	124
Dartford, United Kingdom							
6.3.18	7:49 p.m.	93607	Dartford	UK	Horseshoe	UAV	88
Dasmarinas, Philippines							
3.2.18	5:25 a.m.	90499	Dasmarinas	Philippines	Triangle	UAV	38
Dauphin, Pennsylvania							
2.13.18	6:40 p.m.	90221	Grantville	PA	Cigar	UAV	32
Daytona Beach, Florida							
6.9.18	9:15 p.m.	92639	Daytona Beach	FL	Sphere	UAV	94
DeKalb County, Alabama							
4.5.18	09:20 p.m.	91224	Fort Payne	AL	Square/Rectangle	UAV	58
DeKalb County, Indiana							
5.13.18	5:05 p.m.	92110	Garrett	IN	Cigar	UAV	75
Deland, Florida							
7.10.18	7:35 a.m.	93256	Deland	FL	Diamond	UAV	116
Delaware							
3.10.18	9:30 p.m.	90968	Dover	DE	Bowl	UAV	46
Derry, Pennsylvania							
2.09.18	11:18 p.m.	90175	Derry	PA	Semi-Diamond	Other	29
Dilles Bottom, Ohio							
10.25.18	6:30 p.m.	96048	Dilles Bottom	OH	Egg	UAV	184
Dominican Republic							
12.14.18	9 p.m.	97555	Punta Cana	Dominican Republic	Other	UAV	227
Dorchester County, South Carolina							
8.12.18	12:15 a.m.	97164	Ridgeville	SC	Egg	UAV	139

EVENT	TIME	CASE	CITY	STATE-COUNTRY	SHAPE	DISPOSITION	PAGE
Douglas County, Colorado							
8.12.18	5:06 p.m.	94086	Parker	CO	Egg	UAV	138
9.17.18	9:42 p.m.	94983	Highlands Ranch	CO	Cone	UAV	161
Douglas County, Nebraska							
3.3.18	11:30 p.m.	90584	Elkhorn	NE	Disc	UAV	40
Dover, Delaware							
3.10.18	9:30 p.m.	90968	Dover	DE	Bowl	UAV	46
Droitwich Spa, United Kingdom							
1.24.18	10:30 p.m.	89780	Droitwich Spa	UK	Triangle	Other	19
Dublin, Ireland							
3.29.18	5:30 p.m.	92167	Dublin	Ireland	Triangle	Info Only	53
Duluth, Minnesota							
11.7.18	10:40 p.m.	97286	Duluth	MN	Oval	UAV	200
DuPage County, Illinois							
1.3.18	9:30 p.m.	89610	St. Charles	IL	Cigar	UAV	11
Eatonville, Washington							
8.27.18	11:05 p.m.	94482	Eatonville	WA	Sphere	Other	150
Edmonton, Alberta, Canada							
4.22.18	12 a.m.	91570	Edmonton	CA	Triangle	Info Only	68
Edwards, New York							
11.23.18	6:15 p.m.	96580	Edwards	NY	Sphere	UAV	209
Egg Harbor Township, New Jersey							
6.20.18	3:15 p.m.	92849	Egg Harbor Township	NJ	Sphere	UAV	102
El Dorado Springs, Missouri							
8.19.18	8 p.m.	94262	El Dorado Springs	MO	Disc	UAV	147
Elkhorn, Nebraska							
3.3.18	11:30 p.m.	90584	Elkhorn	NE	Disc	UAV	40
Ellensburg, Washington							
1.9.18	8:45 p.m.	89498	Ellensburg	WA	Oval	UAV	15
El Paso, Texas							
8.31.18	6:35 a.m.	94699	El Paso	TX	Triangle	UAV	152
El Paso County, Colorado							
6.7.18	10:30 p.m.	92568	Colorado Springs	CO	Other	UAV	92

EVENT	TIME	CASE	CITY	STATE-COUNTRY	SHAPE	DISPOSITION	PAGE
El Paso County, Texas							
8.31.18	6:35 a.m.	94699	El Paso	TX	Triangle	UAV	152
Enterprise, Utah							
5.4.18	2:52 a.m.	91780	Enterprise	UT	Saturn-like	UAV	73
Erie County, New York							
6.3.18	1:30 a.m.	92447	Springville	NY	Saturn-like	UAV	86
6.3.18	1:30 a.m.	92447	Springville	NY	Saturn-like	UAV	86
Escambia County, Florida							
8.15.18	3:45 p.m.	94170	Pensacola	FL	Bullet/Missile	UAV	140
Esquimalt, Canada							
5.11.18	10:20 a.m.	91939	Esquimalt	BC CA	Cigar	Info Only	74
Everett, Washington							
11.15.18	2:46 p.m.	97141	Everett	WA	Other	UAV	207
Excelsior Springs, Missouri							
3.30.18	4:30 a.m.	91184	Excelsior Springs	MO	Triangle	UAV	54
Farmington, Missouri							
6.22.18	8 a.m.	93841	Farmington	MO	Triangle	UAV	104
Farmington, Wisconsin							
8.21.18	2:30 p.m.	94322	Farmington	WI	Other	UAV	148
Fayette County, Iowa							
6.9.18	1:15 a.m.	92591	Oelwein	IA	Oval	UAV	93
Flint, Texas							
8.18.18	6:35 p.m.	94292	Flint	TX	Cigar	UAV	145
Florence, Oregon							
8.5.18	3 p.m.	95040	Florence	OR	Triangle	UAV	132
Florida							
1.4.18	6:25 a.m.	89344	Casselberry	FL	Square/Rectangle	Other	12
2.04.18	7:40 a.m.	90015	Port St. Lucie	FL	Square/Rectangle	Other	24
4.1.18	6:02 p.m.	91199	New Port Richey	FL	Disc	UAV	57
4.17.18	9 p.m.	91498	Lakeland	FL	Sphere	Other	63
6.9.18	9:15 p.m.	92639	Daytona Beach	FL	Sphere	UAV	94
7.10.18	7:35 a.m.	93256	Deland	FL	Diamond	UAV	116

EVENT	TIME	CASE	CITY	STATE-COUNTRY	SHAPE	DISPOSITION	PAGE
8.15.18	3:45 p.m.	94170	Pensacola	FL	Bullet/Missile	UAV	140
8.17.18	1:30 a.m.	97678	Key West	FL	Circle	Other	143
8.17.18		97233	Key West	FL	Sphere	Other	143
10.4.18	10 p.m.	95606	Tampa	FL	Triangle	UAV	173
10.12.18	1:01 a.m.	95529	Orlando	FL	Triangle	UAV	178
11.7.18	9:30 p.m.	96766	Valrico	FL	Chevron	UAV	198
11.7.18	9:36 p.m.	96341	Boca Raton	FL	Chevron	UAV	199
Flournoy, California							
6.3.18	n/a	92452	Flournoy	CA	Sphere	Other	89
Forrest County, Mississippi							
11.6.18	5:54 p.m.	96200	Hattiesburg	MS	Triangle	UAV	194
Fort Payne, Alabama							
4.5.18	09:20 p.m.	91224	Fort Payne	AL	Square/Rectangle	UAV	58
Fort Smith, Arkansas							
12.16.18	7:38 p.m.	97044	Fort Smith	AR	Triangle	UAV	228
Fountain County, Indiana							
3.16.18	9:48 p.m.	90816	Attica	IN	Triangle	UAV	50
Franklin County, Vermont							
5.24.18	11:45 p.m.	92228	Saint Albans	VT	Triangle	Info Only	80
Franklin County, Washington							
6.20.18	8:20 p.m.	92828	Pasco	WA	Sphere	UAV	102
Fridley, Minnesota							
6.26.18	10:30 p.m.	92957	Fridley	MN	Sphere	Other	108
Fulton County, New York							
11.14.18	7:24 p.m.	96378	Caroga Lake	NY	Circle	UAV	206
Funchal, Portugal							
8.30.18	9:30 p.m.	94524	Funchal	Portugal	Triangle	UAV	152
Galway City, Ireland							
11.25.18	8:15 p.m.	96616	Galway City	Ireland	N/A	UAV	210
Garrett, Indiana							
5.13.18	5:05 p.m.	92110	Garrett	IN	Cigar	UAV	75
Georgia							
2.15.18	9:30 p.m.	91313	Woodstock	GA	Cylinder	UAV	33
3.6.18	9:40 p.m.	90698	Marietta	GA	Other	UAV	42

EVENT	TIME	CASE	CITY	STATE-COUNTRY	SHAPE	DISPOSITION	PAGE
3.22.18	10:37 p.m.	90959	Chatsworth	GA	Triangle	UAV	51
10.10.18	2:27 p.m.	95682	Atlanta	GA	Cigar	UAV	176
Germany							
5.29.18	8:50 p.m.	92387	Kronberg im Taunus	Germany	Disc	UAV	81
Gig Harbor, Washington							
8.16.18	n/a	95179	Gig Harbor	WA	Triangle	UAV	142
Glasgow, Scotland, United Kingdom							
1.24.18	8:04 p.m.	89841	Glasgow	UK	Blimp	Other	19
Godfrey, Illinois							
8.12.18	2:10 a.m.	94081	Godfrey	IL	Cigar	UAV	137
Gonzales County, Texas							
3.7.18	10:34 a.m.	90628	Gonzales County	TX	Cylinder	Other	44
Goole, United Kingdom							
12.17.18	9:15 p.m.	97065	Goole	UK	Triangle	UAV	229
Gory, Ireland							
11.25.18	8:45 a.m.	96586	Gorey	Ireland	Diamond	Other	210
Granbury, Texas							
2.10.18	11:15 a.m.	90355	Granbury	TX	Triangle/Disc	UAV	30
Grantville, Pennsylvania							
2.13.18	6:40 p.m.	90221	Grantville	PA	Cigar	UAV	32
Great Falls, Montana							
1.24.18	n/a	89785	Great Falls	MT	Circle	Info Only	20
Greece							
9.7.18	1:30 a.m.	94837	Kos Town	Greece	Chevron	UAV	155
Green County, Wisconsin							
10.21.18	5:30 p.m.	95770	Belleville	WI	Unknown	Other	183
Greene County, Missouri							
11.9.18	9 p.m.	96451	Springfield	MO	Triangle	UAV	202
Gustine, California							
7.2.18	2:30 p.m.	93418	Gustine	CA.	Triangle	UAV	114
Hailey, Idaho							
9.13.18	8:15 a.m.	94937	Hailey	ID	Square/Rectangle	UAV	159

EVENT	TIME	CASE	CITY	STATE-COUNTRY	SHAPE	DISPOSITION	PAGE
Haiti							
11.13.18	6:23 p.m.	96764	Labadee	Haiti	Diamond	UAV	206
Hamilton County, Indiana							
7.2.18	9:55 p.m.	94741	Carmel	IN	Cigar	Other	114
Hammond, Indiana							
8.10.18	7:19 p.m.	94038	Hammond	IN	Blimp	UAV	135
Hampshire County, Massachusetts							
1.2.18	5:20 p.m.	89280	Northampton	MA	Boomerang	UAV	10
Hardin County, Texas							
6.16.18	11:30 p.m.	92750	Sour Lake	TX	Triangle	UAV	97
Harris County, Texas							
4.25.18	2:30 p.m.	91628	Webster	TX	Circle	UAV	68
Harrison County, Mississippi							
10.22.18	9:30 a.m.	95806	Pass Christian	MS	Blimp	UAV	183
Harvey County, Kansas							
7.29.18	5:35 a.m.	93741	Hesston	KS	Triangle	UAV	127
Hattiesburg, Mississippi							
11.6.18	5:54 p.m.	96200	Hattiesburg	MS	Triangle	UAV	194
Heber City, Utah							
4.10.18	12 a.m.	91382	Heber City	UT	Triangle	UAV	61
Hemel Hempstead, United Kingdom							
1.17.18	3:35 a.m.	89653	Hemel Hempstead	UK	Triangle	UAV	18
Hernes, Elverum, Norway							
8.14.18	1:07 a.m.	94117	Hernes, Elverum	Norway	Other	Info Only	140
Herzegovina							
4.2.18	10:27 p.m.	91182	Banja Luka	Bosnia & Herzegovina	Disc	Info Only	58
Hesston, Kansas							
7.29.18	5:35 a.m.	93741	Hesston	KS	Triangle	UAV	127
Highlands Ranch, Colorado							
9.17.18	9:42 p.m.	94983	Highlands Ranch	CO	Cone	UAV	161
Hillsborough County, Florida							
10.4.18	10 p.m.	95606	Tampa	FL	Triangle	UAV	173
11.7.18	9:30 p.m.	96766	Valrico	FL	Chevron	UAV	198

EVENT	TIME	CASE	CITY	STATE-COUNTRY	SHAPE	DISPOSITION	PAGE
Hillsborough County, New Hampshire							
3.28.18	3:15 a.m.	91075	Brookline	NH	Triangle	UAV	53
Holly Pond, Alabama							
3.15.18	4 a.m.	97506	Holly Pond	AL	Triangle	UAV	49
Hood River, Oregon							
7.18.18	2:06 p.m.	93708	Hood River	OR	Cigar	UAV	122
Hood River County, Oregon							
7.18.18	2:06 p.m.	93708	Hood River	OR	Cigar	UAV	122
Hood County, Texas							
2.10.18	11:15 a.m.	90355	Granbury	TX	Triangle/Disc	UAV	30
Houston, Texas							
4.28.18	10:20 p.m.	91666	Houston	TX	4.28.18	UAV	20
Hudson, Illinois							
5.22.18	8:12 p.m.	92950	Hudson	IL	Other	Other	79
Hudson County, New Jersey							
8.18.18	5:15 p.m.	94231	Jersey City	NJ	Other	UAV	145
Hurricane, West Virginia							
9.12.18	1:15 a.m.	94839	Hurricane	WV	Sphere	UAV	157
Iceland							
10.26.18	11:10 p.m.	96858	Reykjavik	Iceland	Circle	Other	187
Idaho							
2.07.18	8 a.m.	90127	Shoup	ID	Teardrop	UAV	26
6.17.18	11:40 p.m.	92802	Ada County	ID	Other	UAV	99
9.13.18	8:15 a.m.	94937	Hailey	ID	Square/Rectangle	UAV	159
11.6.18	9 p.m.	96312	Boise	ID	Boomerang	UAV	195
12.23.18	11 p.m.	97206	Boise	ID	Triangle	UAV	229
Illinois							
1.3.18	9:30 p.m.	89610	St. Charles	IL	Cigar	UAV	11
5.22.18	8:12 p.m.	92950	Hudson	IL	Other	Other	79
7.17.18	10:40 p.m.	93540	Brookport	IL	Cylinder	UAV	121
8.10.18	9:58 p.m.	94525	Tinley Park	IL	Sphere	UAV	136
8.12.18	2:10 a.m.	94081	Godfrey	IL	Cigar	UAV	137
12.12.18	3 a.m.	96955	St. Jacob	IL	N/A	Other	226

EVENT	TIME	CASE	CITY	STATE-COUNTRY	SHAPE	DISPOSITION	PAGE
Indiana							
1.13.18	9:05 p.m.	89544	Indianapolis	IN	Chevron	Only	17
3.16.18	9:48 p.m.	90816	Attica	IN	Triangle	UAV	50
4.17.18	10:45 p.m.	91485	Osceola	IN	Cylinder	UAV	64
5.13.18	5:05 p.m.	92110	Garrett	IN	Cigar	UAV	75
7.2.18	9:55 p.m.	94741	Carmel	IN	Cigar	Other	114
7.13.18	9:30 p.m.	93410	Alexandria	IN	Sphere	Other	119
8.10.18	7:19 p.m.	94038	Hammond	IN	Blimp	UAV	135
8.17.18	10:30 p.m.	94217	Portage	IN	Triangle	UAV	144
9.13.18	9 p.m.	94903	Columbus	IN	Triangle	UAV	160
10.30.18	n/a	98437	Michigan City	IN	Triangle	UAV	190
Indianapolis, Indiana							
1.13.18	9:05 p.m.	89544	Indianapolis	IN	Chevron	Info Only	17
Iowa							
6.9.18	1:15 a.m.	92591	Oelwein	IA	Triangle	UAV	93
8.6.18	10:15 p.m.	93940	Waterloo	IA	Circle	UAV	132
Ireland							
3.29.18	5:30 p.m.	92167	Dublin	Ireland	Triangle	Info Only	53
5.18.18	4:25 a.m.	98601	Ballymahon Co. Lonford	Ireland	Saturn-like	Other	78
11.23.18	4:55 a.m.	96554	Ballivor	Ireland	Triangle	Other	208
11.25.18	8:45 a.m.	96586	Gorey	Ireland	Diamond	Other	210
11.25.18	8:15 p.m.	96616	Galway City	Ireland	N/A	UAV	210
Irondequoit, New York							
4.21.18	10:20 p.m.	91559	Irondequoit	NY	Chevron	UAV	66
Jackson County, North Carolina							
3.5.18	11:17 p.m.	91103	Webster	NC	Square/Rectangle	Other	40
Jackson County, Oregon							
4.5.18	11:30 p.m.	91263	Reliance	TN	Square/Rectangle	Other	59
Jackson Township, New Jersey							
10.30.18	8:30 p.m.	96033	Jackson Township	NJ	Triangle	UAV	190
Jamul, California							
8.29.18	8:15 p.m.	97227	Jamul	CA	Sphere	UAV	151

EVENT	TIME	CASE	CITY	STATE-COUNTRY	SHAPE	DISPOSITION	PAGE
Jefferson City, Missouri							
11.11.18	2:40 a.m.	96450	Jefferson City	MO	Chevron	UAV	204
Jefferson County, Alabama							
3.3.18	5:35 a.m.	90540	Birmingham	AL	Triangle	UAV	39
Jefferson County, Wisconsin							
8.21.18	2:30 p.m.	94322	Farmington	WI	Other	UAV	148
Jersey City, New Jersey							
8.18.18	5:15 p.m.	94231	Jersey City Waterfront	NJ	Other	UAV	145
Johnston County, North Carolina							
10.31.18	9:45 p.m.	96052	Selma	NC	Triangle	UAV	191
Joliette, Canada							
6.19.18	7:10 a.m.	92792	Joliette	Canada	Other	UAV	100
Kane County, Illinois							
1.3.18	9:30 p.m.	89610	St. Charles	IL	Cigar	UAV	11
Kansas							
7.29.18	5:35 a.m.	93741	Hesston	KS	Triangle	UAV	127
Kemmerer, Wyoming							
11.14.18	9:50 p.m.	96382	Kemmerer	WY	Star-like	Other	207
Kensington, California							
9.16.18	1:15 a.m.	94931	Kensington	CA	Unknown	Other	161
Kent County, Delaware							
3.10.18	9:30 p.m.	90968	Dover	DE	Bowl	UAV	46
Kentucky							
7.19.18	9:30 p.m.	97557	Mount Washington	KY	Sphere	Other	123
Key West, Florida							
8.17.18	1:30 a.m.	97678	Key West	FL	Circle	Other	143
8.17.18		97233	Key West	FL	Sphere	Other	143
King County, Washington							
7.23.18	6:30 p.m.	93587	Seattle	WA.	Circle	Other	126
10.4.18	8 p.m.	95356	Sammamish	WA	Diamond	Other	172
Kitsap County, Washington							
5.25.18	8:30 p.m.	94857	Poulsbo	WA	Square/Rectangle	UAV	80

EVENT	TIME	CASE	CITY	STATE-COUNTRY	SHAPE	DISPOSITION	PAGE
Kittitas County, Washington							
1.9.18	8:45 p.m.	89498	Ellensburg	WA	Oval	UAV	15
Knox County, Ohio							
7.31.18	1:43 a.m.	93831	Mount Vernon	OH	N/A	Other	128
Kos Town, Greece							
9.7.18	1:30 a.m.	94837	Kos Town	Greece	Chevron	UAV	155
Kronberg im Taurus, Germany							
5.29.18	8:50 p.m.	92387	Kronberg im Taunus	Germany	Disc	UAV	81
Labadee, Haiti							
11.13.18	6:23 p.m.	96764	Labadee	Haiti	Diamond	UAV	206
Lacey, Washington							
11.7.18	6:02 p.m.	96229	Lacey	WA	Cylinder	UAV	197
Lachute, Canada							
9.25.18	10:30 p.m.	95703	Lachute	Canada	Disc	UAV	166
Lake County, Indiana							
8.10.18	7:19 p.m.	94038	Hammond	IN	Blimp	UAV	135
Lakeland, Florida							
4.17.18	9 p.m.	91498	Lakeland	FL	Sphere	Other	63
Lamar County, Mississippi							
11.6.18	5:54 p.m.	96200	Hattiesburg	MS	Triangle	UAV	194
Lancaster County, Pennsylvania							
4.22.18	5:14 p.m.	91575	Manheim	PA	Other	Other	67
Lane County, Oregon							
8.5.18	3 p.m.	95040	Florence	OR	Triangle	UAV	132
11.3.18	11:59 p.m.	96140	Walker	OR	Saturn-like	UAV	193
LaPorte County, Indiana							
10.30.18	n/a	98437	Michigan City	IN	Triangle	UAV	190
Las Animas County, Colorado							
10.5.18	8:15 p.m.	95364	Trinidad	CO	Triangle	UAV	174
Las Vegas, Nevada							
1.1.18	12:05 a.m.	89317	Las Vegas	NV	Disc	UAV	8
2.23.18	7:17 p.m.	90398	Las Vegas	NV	Triangle		36
8.28.18	4:15 a.m.	94461	Las Vegas	NV	Triangle	Other	151
11.7.18	12 p.m.	96230	Las Vegas	NV	Sphere	Other	196

EVENT	TIME	CASE	CITY	STATE-COUNTRY	SHAPE	DISPOSITION	PAGE
Laurel Lake, New Jersey							
12.12.18	6:20 p.m.	97013	Laurel Lake	NJ	N/A	UAV	226
Le Flore County, Oklahoma							
5.21.18	9:59 p.m.	92164	Arkoma	OK	Triangle	UAV	79
Leesburg, Virginia							
6.4.18	n/a	97913	Leesburg	VA	Sphere	UAV	90
Lemhi County, Idaho							
2.07.18	8 a.m.	90127	Shoup	ID	Teardrop	UAV	26
Lenawee County, Michigan							
10.30.18	2 a.m.	96776	Tecumseh	MI	Disc	Other	188
Lewis County, Washington							
7.24.18	2:30 a.m.	93703	Winlock	WA.	Triangle	UAV	126
9.25.18	11:15 p.m.	95249	Silvercreek	WA	Egg	UAV	167
Lincoln County, Oregon							
8.3.18	11 p.m.	94007	Newport	OR	Other	UAV	131
11.5.18	10:30 p.m.	96204	Newport	OR	Triangle	UAV	194
Lincoln County, Wyoming							
11.14.18	9:50 p.m.	96382	Kemmerer	WY	Star-like	Other	207
Lisbon, Portugal							
5.15.18	n/a	93352	Lisbon	Portugal	Triangle	Info Only	77
Logan, Utah							
1.6.18	10 p.m.	89385	Logan	UT	Diamond	Other	13
London, Ontario, Canada							
6.2.18	10:15 p.m.	92445	London	Canada	Triangle	UAV	85
11.11.18	7:05 p.m.	96314	London	Canada	Triangle	UAV	204
London, United Kingdom							
5.1.18	11:30 p.m.	92298	London	UK	Triangle	UAV	71
9.23.18	5:40 p.m.	95215	London	UK	Triangle	UAV	165
Lonsdale, Minnesota							
11.10.18	2 a.m.	96271	Lonsdale	MN	Triangle	UAV	203
Los Lunas, New Mexico							
8.12.18	n/a	94105	Los Lunas	NM	Sphere	Other	138
Loudoun County, Virginia							
6.4.18	n/a	97913	Leesburg	VA	Sphere	UAV	90
Lowell, Massachusetts							
1.1.18	5:30 p.m.	89276	Lowell	MA	Other	UAV	9

EVENT	TIME	CASE	CITY	STATE-COUNTRY	SHAPE	DISPOSITION	PAGE
Lower Burrell, Pennsylvania							
6.19.18	7:30 p.m.	92803	Lower Burrell	PA	Cylinder	UAV	101
Loxley, Alabama							
5.1.18	n/a	91829	Loxley	AL	Circle	Other	72
Luray, Virginia							
11.4.18	3:20 p.m.	96375	Luray	VA	Disc	UAV	193
Madison, Wisconsin							
6.26.18	2:41 a.m.	92954	Madison	WI	Triangle	UAV	107
Madison County, Illinois							
8.12.18	2:10 a.m.	94081	Godfrey	IL	Cigar	UAV	137
12.12.18	3 a.m.	96955	St. Jacob	IL	N/A	Other	226
Madison County, Indiana							
7.13.18	9:30 p.m.	93410	Alexandria	IN	Sphere	Other	119
Maine							
10.7.18	7:30 p.m.	95445	Saco	ME	Diamond	UAV	175
4.21.18	9:55 p.m.	91553	Penobscot	ME	Triangle	Other	65
Malta							
8.18.18	9:40 p.m.	96784	Cospicua	Malta	Oval	Other	146
Manchester, Maryland							
3.10.18	11:57 p.m.	90710	Manchester	MD	Triangle	Other	45
Manheim, Pennsylvania							
4.22.18	5:14 p.m.	91575	Manheim	PA	Other	Other	67
Marathon County, Wisconsin							
9.10.18	10:30 p.m.	98808	Colby	WI	Sphere	Other	157
Maricopa County, Arizona							
6.28.18	11:15 p.m.	93454	Buckeye	AZ	Circle	UAV	110
11.12.18	7:20 p.m.	96353	Phoenix	AZ	Cigar	UAV	205
Marietta, Georgia							
3.6.18	9:40 p.m.	90698	Marietta	GA	Other	UAV	42
Marina, California							
1.3.18	6:40 p.m.	89327	Marina	CA	Sphere	Other	10
Marion County, Oregon							
8.1.18	9:02 p.m.	97862	Breitenbush Hot Springs	OR	Triangle	UAV	129
Maryland							
3.10.18	11:57 p.m.	90710	Manchester	MD	Triangle	Other	45

EVENT	TIME	CASE	CITY	STATE-COUNTRY	SHAPE	DISPOSITION	PAGE
6.9.18	8:32 p.m.	92619	Alexandria	MD	Bullet/Missile	UAV	94

Massac County, Illinois

7.17.18	10:40 p.m.	93540	Brookport	IL	Cylinder	UAV	121

Massachusetts

1.1.18	5:30 p.m.	89276	Lowell	MA	Other	UAV	9
1.2.18	5:20 p.m.	89280	Northampton	MA	Boomerang	UAV	10
6.6.18	1 p.m.	97168	Plymouth	MA	Blimp	Info Only	90
6.10.18	10:27 p.m.	92653	Blackstone	MA	Unknown	UAV	95
6.10.18	10:30 p.m.	92641	Attleboro	MA	N/A	Other	95

McDonald County, Missouri

5.3.18	10:28 p.m.	91773	Caverna	MO	Oval	UAV	72

McKinney, Texas

12.1.18	12:00 a.m.	96805	McKinney	TX	Oval	UAV	214

McLean County, Illinois

5.22.18	8:12 p.m.	92950	Hudson	IL	Other	Other	79

McMinnville, Oregon

6.26.18	10:04 p.m.	92936	McMinnville	OR	Oval	Other	108

Medellin, Columbia

6.24.18	n/a	95063	Medellin	Columbia	Diamond	UAV	106

Medford, Oregon

5.15.18	4:45 p.m.	92030	Medford	OR	Cylinder	UAV	76

Memphis, Tennessee

12.6.18	5:35 p.m.	96850	Memphis	TN	Chevron	Other	220

Mena, Arkansas

2.08.18	8:30 p.m.	90133	Mena	AR	Triangle	UAV	27
2.08.18	8:35 p.m.	90181	Mena	AR	Triangle	UAV	27

Mercaston, United Kingdom

10.18.18	8:25 p.m.	95673	Mercaston	UK	Sphere	UAV	182

Merced County, California

7.2.18	2:30 p.m.	93418	Gustine	CA.	Triangle	UAV	114

Mesquite, Nevada

6.27.18	10 p.m.	92964	Mesquite	NV	Cigar	UAV	110

Mexico

6.21.18	n/a	92994	San Felipe Baja Norte	Mexico	Sphere	Other	104

EVENT	TIME	CASE	CITY	STATE-COUNTRY	SHAPE	DISPOSITION	PAGE
Michigan							
3.2.18	8:30 a.m.	94597	Muskegon	MI	Square/Rectangle	UAV	38
3.14.18	5:38 p.m.	90776	Port Huron	MI	Square/Rectangle	Other	48
10.30.18	2 a.m.	96776	Tecumseh	MI	Disc	Other	188
Michigan City, Indiana							
10.30.18	n/a	98437	Michigan City	IN	Triangle	UAV	190
Middlesex County, Massachusetts							
1.1.18	5:30 p.m.	89276	Lowell	MA	Other	UAV	9
Midwest, Wyoming							
10.16.18	9:53 p.m.	95874	Midwest	WY	Sphere	UAV	180
Minnesota							
6.21.18	10:58 p.m.	92852	New Brighten	MN	Disc	UAV	103
6.26.18	10:30 p.m.	92957	Fridley	MN	Sphere	Other	108
11.7.18	10:40 p.m.	97286	Duluth	MN	Oval	UAV	200
11.9.18	8:18 p.m.	96286	Chaska	MN	Star-like	UAV	202
11.10.18	2 a.m.	96271	Lonsdale	MN	Triangle	UAV	203
11.10.18	5 a.m.	96283	Pipestone	MN	Other	UAV	203
Mississippi							
6.3.18	6:45 a.m.	92469	Panola County	MS	Cylinder	UAV	87
11.6.18	5:54 p.m.	96200	Hattiesburg	MS	Triangle	UAV	194
10.22.18	9:30 a.m.	95806	Pass Christian	MS	Blimp	UAV	183
Missouri							
2.12.18	8:05 p.m.	90205	St. Peters	MO	Square/Rectangle	UAV	31
2.12.18	n/a	90206	St. Peters	MO	Square/Rectangle	UAV	31
3.30.18	4:30 a.m.	91184	Excelsior Springs	MO	Triangle	UAV	54
5.3.18	10:28 p.m.	91773	Caverna	MO	Oval	UAV	72
6.1.18	n/a	92483	West Plains	MO	Triangle	UAV	83
6.19.18	11:15 a.m.	92800	Warrento	MO	Blimp	UAV	100
6.22.18	8 a.m.	93841	Farmington	MO	Triangle	UAV	104
8.8.18	9:45 a.m.	94049	Sunset Hills	MO	Diamond	UAV	133
8.19.18	8 p.m.	94262	El Dorado Springs	MO	Disc	UAV	147

EVENT	TIME	CASE	CITY	STATE-COUNTRY	SHAPE	DISPOSITION	PAGE
11.9.18	9 p.m.	96451	Springfield	MO	Triangle	UAV	202
11.11.18	2:40 a.m.	96450	Jefferson City	MO	Chevron	UAV	204
11.26.18	8:02 p.m.	96643	Columbia	MO	Boomerang	UAV	212
12.12.18	6:52 p.m.	96983	St. Louis	MO	Triangle	UAV	227
Monroe County, New York							
2.21.18	8:30 p.m.	90647	Rochester	NY	Triangle	UAV	35
4.21.18	10:20 p.m.	91559	Irondequoit	NY	Chevron	UAV	66
Montana							
1.24.18	n/a	89785	Great Falls	MT	Circle	Info Only	20
6.26.18	12 a.m.	95960	Noxon	MT	Disc	Other	109
Montazuma, New York							
10.25.18	7:10 p.m.	95880	Montazuma	NY	Teardrop	UAV	185
Monterey, California							
5.16.18	n/a	92036	Salinas	CA	Triangle	UAV	77
Monterey County, California							
1.3.18	6:40 p.m.	89327	Marina	CA	Sphere	Other	10
5.16.18	n/a	92036	Salinas	CA	Triangle	UAV	77
Montgomery County, Texas							
9.1.18	4:20 a.m.	94960	Porter	TX	Boomerang	UAV	154
Mount Vernon, Ohio							
7.31.18	1:43 a.m.	93831	Mount Vernon	OH	N/A	Other	128
Mount Washington, Kentucky							
7.19.18	9:30 p.m.	97557	Mount Washington	KY	Sphere	Other	123
Mt. Pleasant, Pennsylvania							
2.04.18	1:38 a.m.	90057	Mt. Pleasant	PA	Sphere	Other	23
Multnomah County, Oregon							
6.17.18	3:20 p.m.	92817	Portland	OR	Square/Rectangle	UAV	98
Munroe Falls, Ohio							
3.11.18	10 p.m.	90789	Munroe Falls	OH	Triangle	UAV	47
Murray County, Georgia							
3.22.18	10:37 p.m.	90959	Chatsworth	GA	Triangle	UAV	51
Muskegon, Michigan							
3.2.18	8:30 a.m.	94597	Muskegon	MI	Square/Rectangle	UAV	38

EVENT	TIME	CASE	CITY	STATE-COUNTRY	SHAPE	DISPOSITION	PAGE
Muskegon County, Michigan							
3.2.18	8:30 a.m.	94597	Muskegon	MI	Square/Rectangle	UAV	38
Nakhon Nayok, Thailand							
4.10.18	12 p.m.	93224	Nakhon Nayok	Thailand	Square/Rectangle	UAV	62
Natrona County, Wyoming							
10.16.18	9:53 p.m.	95874	Midwest	WY	Sphere	UAV	180
Nebraska							
3.3.18	11:30 p.m.	90584	Elkhorn	NE	Disc	UAV	40
Nevada							
1.1.18	12:05 a.m.	89317	Las Vegas	NV	Disc	UAV	8
2.23.18	7:15 p.m.	90404	Summerlin	NV	Triangle	UAV	35
2.23.18	7:17 p.m.	90398	Las Vegas	NV	Triangle	UAV	36
6.11.18	2:11 a.m.	92673	North Las Vegas	NV	Other	UAV	96
6.27.18	10 p.m.	92964	Mesquite	NV	Cigar	UAV	110
7.18.18	9 p.m.	93459	North Las Vegas	NV	Sphere	Other	123
8.27.18	4:10 a.m.	97499	Pahrump	NV	N/A	Info Only	149
8.28.18	4:15 a.m.	94461	Las Vegas	NV	Triangle	Other	151
11.7.18	12 p.m.	96230	Las Vegas	NV	Sphere	Other	196
New Brighten, Minnesota							
6.21.18	10:58 p.m.	92852	New Brighten	MN	Disc	UAV	103
New Hanover County, North Carolina							
9.8.18	n/a	96379	Wilmington	NC	Sphere	Other	156
New Hampshire							
3.28.18	3:15 a.m.	91075	Brookline	NH	Triangle	UAV	53
New Hanover County, North Carolina							
6.29.18	9:30 p.m.	93050	Carolina Beach	NC	Sphere	Other	111
New Jersey							
5.11.18	11:45 p.m.	91968	North Plainfield	NJ	Unknown	Other	75
6.2.18	5:30 p.m.	92481	Salem	NJ	Disc	Info Only	85
6.20.18	3:15 p.m.	92849	Egg Harbor Township	NJ	Sphere	UAV	102
8.18.18	5:15 p.m.	94231	Jersey City	NJ	Other	UAV	145
10.2.18	8:25 p.m.	95323	Toms River	NJ	Triangle	Other	169

EVENT	TIME	CASE	CITY	STATE-COUNTRY	SHAPE	DISPOSITION	PAGE
10.3.18	7:30 p.m.	96637	New Lisbon	NJ	Triangle	UAV	170
10.30.18	8:30 p.m.	96033	Jackson Township	NJ	Triangle	UAV	190
12.12.18	6:20 p.m.	97013	Laurel Lake	NJ	N/A	UAV	226
New Lisbon, New Jersey							
10.3.18	7:30 p.m.	96637	New Lisbon	NJ	Triangle	UAV	170
New Mexico							
8.12.18	n/a	94105	Los Lunas	NM	Sphere	Other	138
9.14.18	3:28 p.m.	94892	Santa Fe	NM	Disc	Info Only	160
New Port Richey, Florida							
4.1.18	6:02 p.m.	91199	New Port Richey	FL	Disc	UAV	57
New York							
2.21.18	8:30 p.m.	90647	Rochester	NY	Triangle	UAV	35
3.10.18	4 a.m.	95178	Woodstock	NY	Diamond	UAV	46
4.21.18	10:20 p.m.	91559	Irondequoit	NY	Chevron	UAV	66
4.22.18	5:20 p.m.	91572	Brooklyn	NY	Saturn-like	UAV	67
5.15.18	9:30 p.m.	92029	Bay Shore	NY	Sphere	Other	77
6.3.18	1:30 a.m.	92447	Springville	NY	Saturn-like	UAV	86
8.15.18	10:30 p.m.	94184	Staten Island	NY	Disc	Other	141
9.24.18	6:45 p.m.	95317	Baldwinsville	NY	Sphere	Other	165
10.25.18	7:10 p.m.	95880	Montazuma	NY	Teardrop	UAV	185
11.14.18	7:24 p.m.	96378	Caroga Lake	NY	Circle	UAV	206
11.23.18	6:15 p.m.	96580	Edwards	NY	Sphere	UAV	209
Newbury, United Kingdom							
2.13.18	9:35 p.m.	90452	Newbury	UK	Triangle	UAV	33
Newmarket, Canada							
7.10.18	8:50 p.m.	93369	Newmarket	Canada	Cylinder	UAV	117
Newport, Oregon							
8.3.18	n/a	94007	Newport	OR	Other	UAV	131
11.5.18	10:30 p.m.	96204	Newport	OR	Triangle	UAV	194
Niagara Falls, Canada							
7.15.18	8:06 p.m.	93445	Niagara Falls	Canada	Sphere	Other	120
North Carolina							
3.5.18	11:17 p.m.	91103	Webster	NC	Square/Rectangle	Other	40

EVENT	TIME	CASE	CITY	STATE-COUNTRY	SHAPE	DISPOSITION	PAGE
6.29.18	9:30 p.m.	93050	Carolina Beach	NC	Sphere	Other	111
9.8.18	n/a	96379	Wilmington	NC	Sphere	Other	156
10.31.18	9:45 p.m.	96052	Selma	NC	Triangle	UAV	191
11.8.18	7:30 p.m.	96310	Apex	NC	Other	UAV	201
12.12.18	12 a.m.	97018	Reidsville	NC	Triangle	Other	225
North Dakota							
7.1.18	9:23 p.m.	93045	West Fargo	ND	Sphere	Other	113
North Las Vegas, Nevada							
6.11.18	2:11 a.m.	92673	North Las Vegas	NV	Other	UAV	96
7.18.18	9 p.m.	93459	North Las Vegas	NV	Sphere	Other	123
North Plainfield, New Jersey							
5.11.18	11:45 p.m.	91968	North Plainfield	NJ	Unknown	Other	75
Northhampton, Massachusetts							
1.2.18	5:20 p.m.	89280	Northampton	MA	Boomerang	UAV	10
Norway							
8.14.18	1:07 a.m.	94117	Hernes, Elverum	Norway	Other	Info Only	140
Novy Jicin, Czech Republic							
6.1.18	11:01 p.m.	93565	Novy Jicin	Czech Republic	Triangle	Info Only	82
Noxon, Montana							
6.26.18	12 a.m.	95960	Noxon	MT	Disc	Other	109
Nye County, Nevada							
8.27.18	4:10 a.m.	97499	Pahrump	NV	N/A	Info Only	149
Oak Dale, California							
6.23.18	11:45 p.m.	92947	Oak Dale	CA	Fireball	UAV	105
Ocean County, New Jersey							
10.2.18	8:25 p.m.	95323	Toms River	NJ	Triangle	Other	169
10.30.18	8:30 p.m.	96033	Jackson Township	NJ	Triangle	UAV	190
Oelwein, Iowa							
6.9.18	1:15 a.m.	92591	Oelwein	IA	Oval	UAV	93
Ohio							
3.11.18	10 p.m.	90789	Munroe Falls	OH	Triangle	UAV	47
7.31.18	1:43 a.m.	93831	Mount Vernon	OH	N/A	Other	128

EVENT	TIME	CASE	CITY	STATE-COUNTRY	SHAPE	DISPOSITION	PAGE
9.3.18	4:07 p.m.	95976	Perrysville	OH	N/A	UAV	155
10.25.18	6:30 p.m.	96048	Dilles Bottom	OH	Egg	UAV	184
10.30.18	7:40 p.m.	96019	Benton	OH	Cylinder	UAV	189
Oklahoma							
5.21.18	9:59 p.m.	92164	Arkoma	OK	Triangle	UAV	79
Olympia, Washington							
12.4.18	2 p.m.	96813	Olympia	WA	Egg	UAV	218
Onondaga County, New York							
9.24.18	6:45 p.m.	95317	Baldwinsville	NY	Sphere	Other	165
Orange County, California							
7.22.18	10 p.m.	93687	Anaheim	CA	Triangle	UAV	125
Orange County, Florida							
10.12.18	1:01 a.m.	95529	Orlando	FL	Triangle	UAV	178
Oregon							
5.15.18	4:45 p.m.	92030	Medford	OR	Cylinder	UAV	76
6.7.18	10:05 p.m.	92560	Dallas	OR	Square/Rectangle	UAV	91
6.17.18	3:20 p.m.	92817	Portland	OR	Square/Rectangle	UAV	98
6.26.18	10:04 p.m.	92936	McMinnville	OR	Oval	Other	108
7.11.18	9 a.m.	93427	Pendleton	OR	Cone	UAV	118
7.11.18	10:45 a.m.	93419	Pendleton	OR	Other	UAV	118
7.18.18	2:06 p.m.	93708	Hood River	OR	Cigar	UAV	122
8.1.18	9:02 p.m.	97862	Breitenbush Hot Springs	OR	Triangle	UAV	129
8.3.18	11 p.m.	94007	Newport	OR	Other	UAV	131
8.5.18	3 p.m.	95040	Florence	OR	Triangle	UAV	132
11.3.18	11:59 p.m.	96140	Walker	OR	Saturn-like	UAV	193
11.5.18	10:30 p.m.	96204	Newport	OR	Triangle	UAV	194
12.5.18	6:10 p.m.	96818	Baker City	OR	Chevron	UAV	219
Orem, Utah							
10.3.18	9:40 p.m.	98214	Orem	UT	Cigar	UAV	171
Orfordville, Wisconsin							
1.8.18	5:20 p.m.	89435	Orfordville	WI	Triangle	UAV	14
Orlando, Florida							
10.12.18	1:01 a.m.	95529	Orlando	FL	Triangle	UAV	178

EVENT	TIME	CASE	CITY	STATE-COUNTRY	SHAPE	DISPOSITION	PAGE
Orrington, Maine							
4.21.18	9:55 p.m.	91553	Orrington	ME	Triangle	Other	65
Orwigsburg, Pennsylvania							
12.4.18	8:30 p.m.	96829	Orwigsburg	PA	Triangle	UAV	218
Osceola, Indiana							
4.17.18	10:45 p.m.	91485	Osceola	IN	Cylinder	UAV	64
Page County, Virginia							
11.4.18	3:20 p.m.	96375	Luray	VA	Disc	UAV	193
Pahrump, Nevada							
8.27.18	4:10 a.m.	97499	Pahrump	NV	N/A	Info Only	149
Palm Beach County, Florida							
11.7.18	9:36 p.m.	96341	Boca Raton	FL	Chevron	UAV	199
Panola County, Mississippi							
6.3.18	6:45 a.m.	92469	Panola County	MS	Cylinder	UAV	87
Parker, Colorado							
8.12.18	5:06 p.m.	94086	Parker	CO	Egg	UAV	138
Pasco, Washington							
6.20.18	8:20 p.m.	92828	Pasco	WA	Sphere	UAV	102
Pasco County, Florida							
4.1.18	6:02 p.m.	91199	New Port Richey	FL	Disc	UAV	57
Pass Christian, Mississippi							
10.22.18	9:30 a.m.	95806	Pass Christian	MS	Blimp	UAV	183
Pattaya, Thailand							
11.2.18	9:30 p.m.	96088	Pattaya	Thailand	Triangle	UAV	192
Pendleton, Oregon							
7.11.18	9 a.m.	93427	Pendleton	OR	Cone	UAV	118
7.11.18	10:45 a.m.	93419	Pendleton	OR	Other	UAV	118
Pennsylvania							
1.9.18	7:05 p.m.	89450	Wrightsville	PA	Triangle	UAV	14
1.28.18	7:30 p.m.	89867	Buffalo Mills	PA	Triangle	Other	21
2.04.18	1:38 a.m.	90057	Mt. Pleasant	PA	Sphere	Other	23
2.09.18	11:18 p.m.	90175	Derry	PA	Semi-Diamond	Other	29
2.13.18	6:40 p.m.	90221	Grantville	PA	Cigar	UAV	32
3.26.18	3:15 a.m.	91194	Bridgeville	PA	Boomerang	UAV	52

EVENT	TIME	CASE	CITY	STATE-COUNTRY	SHAPE	DISPOSITION	PAGE
4.22.18	5:14 p.m.	91575	Manheim	PA	Other	Other	67
6.19.18	7:30 p.m.	92803	Lower Burrell	PA	Cylinder	UAV	101
10.23.18	12:52 p.m.	95826	California	PA	Disc	UAV	184
10.26.18	11 p.m.	95886	Philadelphia	PA	Cylinder	UAV	186
12.4.18	8:30 p.m.	96829	Orwigsburg	PA	Triangle	UAV	218
Penobscot County, Maine							
4.21.18	9:55 p.m.	91553	Orrington	ME	Triangle	Other	65
Pensacola, Florida							
8.15.18	3:45 p.m.	94170	Pensacola	FL	Bullet/Missile	UAV	140
Perrysville, Ohio							
9.3.18	4:07 p.m.	95976	Perrysville	OH	N/A	UAV	155
Philadelphia, Pennsylvania							
10.26.18	11 p.m.	95886	Philadelphia	PA	Cylinder	UAV	186
Philippines							
3.2.18	5:25 a.m.	90499	Dasmarinas	Philippines	Triangle	UAV	38
9.19.18	9 p.m.	94990	Unknown	Philippines	Triangle	UAV	163
11.28.18	5:20 p.m.	96641	Unknown	Philippines	Unknown	Other	213
Phoenix, Arizona							
11.12.18	7:20 p.m.	96353	Phoenix	AZ	Cigar	UAV	205
Pierce County, Washington							
8.16.18	n/a	95179	Gig Harbor	WA	Triangle	UAV	142
8.27.18	11:05 p.m.	94482	Eatonville	WA	Sphere	Other	150
11.10.18	5 a.m.	96283	Pipestone	MN	Other	UAV	203
Pipestone County, Minnesota							
11.10.18	5 a.m.	96283	Pipestone	MN	Other	UAV	203
Plymouth, Massachusetts							
6.6.18	1 p.m.	97168	Plymouth	MA	Blimp	Info Only	90
Plymouth County, Massachusetts							
6.6.18	1 p.m.	97168	Plymouth	MA	Blimp	Info Only	90
Polk County, Arkansas							
2.08.18	8:30 p.m.	90133	Mena	AR	Triangle	UAV	27
2.08.18	8:35 p.m.	90181	Mena	AR	Triangle	UAV	27
Polk County, Florida							
4.17.18	9 p.m.	91498	Lakeland	FL	Sphere	Other	63

EVENT	TIME	CASE	CITY	STATE-COUNTRY	SHAPE	DISPOSITION	PAGE
Polk County, Oregon							
6.7.18	10:05 p.m.	92560	Dallas	OR	Square/Rectangle	UAV	91
Polk County, Tennessee							
4.5.18	11:30 p.m.	91263	Reliance	TN	Square/Rectangle	Other	59
Portage, Indiana							
8.17.18	10:30 p.m.	94217	Portage	IN	Triangle	UAV	144
Porter County, Indiana							
8.17.18	10:30 p.m.	94217	Portage	IN	Triangle	UAV	144
Port Huron, Michigan							
3.14.18	5:38 p.m.	90776	Port Huron	MI	Square/Rectangle	Other	48
Port St. Lucie							
2.04.18	7:40 a.m.	90015	Port St. Lucie	FL	Square/Rectangle	Other	24
Port Talbot, United Kingdom							
8.19.18	10 p.m.	98200	Port Talbot	UK	Triangle	Info Only	148
Porter, Texas							
9.1.18	4:20 a.m.	94960	Porter	TX	Boomerang	UAV	154
Portland, Oregon							
6.17.18	3:20 p.m.	92817	Portland	OR	Square/Rectangle	UAV	98
Portugal							
5.15.18	n/a	93352	Lisbon	Portugal	Triangle	Info Only	77
8.30.18	9:30 p.m.	94524	Funchal	Portugal	Triangle	UAV	152
Poulsbo, Washington							
5.25.18	8:30 p.m.	94857	Poulsbo	WA	Square/Rectangle	UAV	80
Pulaski, Virginia							
12.8.18	5:55 p.m.	97287	Pulaski	VA	Triangle	UAV	222
Pulaski County, Virginia							
12.8.18	5:55 p.m.	97287	Pulaski	VA	Triangle	UAV	222
Punta Cana, Dominican Republic							
12.14.18	9 p.m.	97555	Punta Cana	Dominican Republic	Other	UAV	227

EVENT	TIME	CASE	CITY	STATE-COUNTRY	SHAPE	DISPOSITION	PAGE
Putnam County, West Virginia							
9.12.18	1:15 a.m.	94839	Hurricane	WV	Sphere	UAV	157
12.10.18	8:45 p.m.	97001	Scott Depot	WV	Boomerang	UAV	224
Ramsey County, Minnesota							
6.21.18	10:58 p.m.	92852	New Brighten	MN	Disc	UAV	103
Rancho Mirage, California							
10.4.18	8:57 p.m.	95343	Rancho Mirage	CA	Boomerang	UAV	173
Ray County, Missouri							
3.30.18	4:30 a.m.	91184	Excelsior Springs	MO	Triangle	UAV	54
Red Bluff, California							
12.6.18	7:12 p.m.	97119	Red Bluff	CA	Triangle	UAV	221
Reidsville, North Carolina							
12.12.18	12 a.m.	97018	Reidsville	NC	Triangle	Other	225
Reliance, Tennessee							
4.5.18	11:30 p.m.	91263	Reliance	TN	Square/Rectangle	Other	59
Reykjavik, Iceland							
10.26.18	11:10 p.m.	96858	Reykjavik	Iceland	Circle	Other	187
Rice County, Minnesota							
11.10.18	2 a.m.	96271	Lonsdale	MN	Triangle	UAV	203
Richmond, Virginia							
10.17.18	6:15 p.m.	95653	Richmond	VA	Cylinder	UAV	181
Ridgeville, South Carolina							
8.12.18	12:15 a.m.	97164	Ridgeville	SC	Egg	UAV	139
Riverside County, California							
10.4.18	8:57 p.m.	95343	Rancho Mirage	CA	Boomerang	UAV	173
Rochester, New York							
2.21.18	8:30 p.m.	90647	Rochester	NY	Triangle		35
Rock County, Wisconsin							
1.8.18	5:20 p.m.	89435	Orfordville	WI	Triangle	UAV	14
Rockingham County, North Carolina							
12.12.18	12 a.m.	97018	Reidsville	NC	Triangle	Other	225
Saco, Maine							
10.7.18	7:30 p.m.	95445	Saco	ME	Diamond	UAV	175

EVENT	TIME	CASE	CITY	STATE-COUNTRY	SHAPE	DISPOSITION	PAGE
Sacramento, California							
2.21.18	12:30 a.m.	90347	Sacramento	CA	Square/Rectangle	UAV	34
10.28.18	n/a	96472	Sacramento	CA	Triangle	UAV	188
Sacramento County, California							
2.21.18	12:30 a.m.	90347	Sacramento	CA	Square/Rectangle	UAV	34
10.12.18	1:01 a.m.	95590	Citrus Heights	CA	Triangle	UAV	177
10.28.18	n/a	96472	Sacramento	CA	Triangle	UAV	188
Salem, New Jersey							
6.2.18	5:30 p.m.	92481	Salem	NJ	Disc	Info Only	85
Salem County, New Jersey							
6.2.18	5:30 p.m.	92481	Salem	NJ	Disc	Info Only	85
Salinas, California							
5.16.18	n/a	92036	Salinas	CA	Triangle	UAV	77
Salt Lake County, Utah							
3.6.18	10:42 a.m.	93750	West Jordan	UT	Cylinder	UAV	41
11.11.18	n/a	96316	Taylorsville	UT	Triangle	Other	205
Sammamish, Washington							
10.4.18	8 p.m.	95356	Sammamish	WA	Diamond	Other	172
San Antonio, Texas							
7.9.18	n/a	96065	San Antonio	TX	Triangle	Other	116
11.6.18	8:25 p.m.	96207	San Antonio	TX	Chevron	UAV	195
San Diego, California							
8.9.18	2:40 p.m.	94827	San Diego	CA	Oval	UAV	134
San Diego County, California							
8.9.18	2:40 p.m.	94827	San Diego	CA	Oval	UAV	134
8.29.18	8:15 p.m.	97227	Jamul	CA	Sphere	UAV	151
11.27.18	8 p.m.	97510	Santee	CA	Triangle	Info Only	212
San Felipe Baja Norte, Mexico							
6.21.18	n/a	92994	San Felipe Baja Norte	Mexico	Sphere	Other	104
Sanders County, Montana							
6.26.18	6.26.18	6.26.18	6.26.18	6.26.18	6.26.18	6.26.18	6.26.18
Santa Cruz County, Arizona							
9.21.18	8 p.m.	98732	Sonoita	AZ	Teardrop	UAV	164

EVENT	TIME	CASE	CITY	STATE-COUNTRY	SHAPE	DISPOSITION	PAGE
Santa Elena, Costa Rica							
9.14.18	8:15 a.m.	95265	Santa Elena	Costa Rica	Disc	UAV	160
Santa Fe, New Mexico							
9.14.18	3:28 p.m.	94892	Santa Fe	NM	Disc	Info Only	160
Santee, California							
11.27.18	8 p.m.	97510	Santee	CA	Triangle	Info Only	212
Sao Jose Dos Pinhais, Brazil							
6.1.18	7:41 p.m.	92432	Sao Jose Dos Pinhais	Brazil	Egg	Info Only	82
Schuylkill County, Pennsylvania							
12.4.18	8:30 p.m.	96829	Orwigsburg	PA	Triangle	UAV	218
Scott Depot, West Virginia							
12.10.18	8:45 p.m.	97001	Scott Depot	WV	Boomerang	UAV	224
Seattle, Washington							
7.23.18	6:30 p.m.	93587	Seattle	WA.	Circle	Other	126
Sebastian County, Arkansas							
12.16.18	7:38 p.m.	97044	Fort Smith	AR	Triangle	UAV	228
Selma, North Carolina							
10.31.18	9:45 p.m.	96052	Selma	NC	Triangle	UAV	191
Seminole County, Florida							
1.4.18	6:25 a.m.	89344	Casselberry	FL	Square/Rectangle	Other	12
Shelby County, Tennessee							
12.6.18	5:35 p.m.	96850	Memphis	TN	Chevron	Other	220
Shrewsbury, United Kingdom							
12.28.18	1:10 a.m.	97282	Shrewsbury	UK	Chevron	Info Only	230
Shoup, Idaho							
2.07.18	8 a.m.	90127	Shoup	ID	Teardrop	UAV	26
Silvercreek, Washington							
9.25.18	11:15 p.m.	95249	Silvercreek	WA	Egg	UAV	167
Smith County, Texas							
8.18.18	6:35 p.m.	94292	Flint	TX	Cigar	UAV	145
Snohomish County, Washington							
7.22.18	1:42 p.m.	93732	Darrington	WA	Disc	UAV	124
11.15.18	n/a	97141	Everett	WA	Other	UAV	207

EVENT	TIME	CASE	CITY	STATE-COUNTRY	SHAPE	DISPOSITION	PAGE
Somerset County, New Jersey							
5.11.18	11:45 p.m.	91968	North Plainfield	NJ	Unknown	Other	75
Sonoita, Arizona							
9.21.18	8 p.m.	98732	Sonoita	AZ	Teardrop	UAV	164
Sonora, California							
10.15.18	4 p.m.	95599	Sonora	CA	N/A	UAV	180
Sour Lake, Texas							
6.16.18	11:30 p.m.	92750	Sour Lake	TX	Triangle	UAV	97
South Carolina							
3.31.18	9:55 p.m.	91151	Aiken	SC	Circle	Other	55
8.12.18	12:15 a.m.	97164	Ridgeville	SC	Egg	UAV	139
Springfield, Missouri							
11.9.18	9 p.m.	96451	Springfield	MO	Triangle	UAV	202
Springville, New York							
6.3.18	1:30 a.m.	92447	Springville	NY	Saturn-like	UAV	86
St. Albans, Vermont							
5.24.18	11:45 p.m.	92228	Saint Albans	VT	Triangle	Info Only	80
St. Charles, Illinois							
1.3.18	9:30 p.m.	89610	St. Charles	IL	Cigar	UAV	11
St. Charles County, Missouri							
2.12.18	8:05 p.m.	90205	St. Peters	MO	Square/Rectangle	UAV	31
2.12.18	n/a	90206	St. Peters	MO	Square/Rectangle	UAV	31
St. Clair County, Michigan							
3.14.18	5:38 p.m.	90776	Port Huron	MI	Square/Rectangle	Other	48
St. Francois County, Missouri							
6.22.18	10:30 p.m.	96204	Farmington	MO	Triangle	UAV	104
St. Jacob, Illinois							
12.12.18	3 a.m.	96955	St. Jacob	IL	Triangle	Other	226
St. Joseph County, Indiana							
4.17.18	10:45 p.m.	91485	Osceola	IN	Cylinder	UAV	64
St. Lawrence County, New York							
11.23.18	6:15 p.m.	96580	Edwards	NY	Sphere	UAV	209

EVENT	TIME	CASE	CITY	STATE-COUNTRY	SHAPE	DISPOSITION	PAGE
St. Louis, Missouri							
12.12.18	6:52 p.m.	96983	St. Louis	MO	Triangle	UAV	227
St. Louis County, Minnesota							
11.7.18	10:40 p.m.	97286	Duluth	MN	Oval	UAV	200
St. Louis County, Missouri							
8.8.18	9:45 a.m.	94049	Sunset Hills	MO	Diamond	UAV	133
St. Lucie County, Florida							
2.04.18	7:40 a.m.	90015	Port St. Lucie	FL	Square/Rectangle	Other	24
St. Peters, Missouri							
2.12.18	8:05 p.m.	90205	St. Peters	MO	Square/Rectangle	UAV	31
2.12.18	n/a	90206	St. Peters	MO	Square/Rectangle	UAV	31
Stanislaus County, California							
6.23.18	11:45 p.m.	92947	Oak Dale	CA	Fireball	UAV	105
Staten Island, New York							
8.15.18	n/a	94184	Staten Island	NY	Disc	Other	141
Stevens County, Washington							
2.08.18	1:07 p.m.	94350	Valley	WA	Disc	UAV	26
Stonehouse, United Kingdom							
4.19.18	10:30 p.m.	91752	Stonehouse	UK	Triangle	Info Only	64
Stoney Creek, Hamilton, Ontario, Canada							
10.13.18	8:58 p.m.	98344	Stoney Creek	Canada	Boomerang	UAV	179
Suffolk County, New York							
5.15.18	9:30 p.m.	92029	Bay Shore	NY	Sphere	Other	77
Summerlin, Nevada							
2.23.18	7:15 p.m.	90404	Summerlin	NV	Triangle	UAV	35
Summit County, Ohio							
3.11.18	10 p.m.	90789	Munroe Falls	OH	Triangle	UAV	47
Sunset Hills, Missouri							
8.8.18	9:45 a.m.	94049	Sunset Hills	MO	Diamond	UAV	133
Tampa, Florida							
10.4.18	10 p.m.	95606	Tampa	FL	Triangle	UAV	173
Taylorsville, Utah							
11.11.18	n/a	96316	Taylorsville	UT	Triangle	Other	205

EVENT	TIME	CASE	CITY	STATE-COUNTRY	SHAPE	DISPOSITION	PAGE
Tecumseh, Michigan							
10.30.18	2 a.m.	96776	Tecumseh	MI	Disc	Other	188
Tehama County, California							
6.3.18	n/a	92452	Flournoy	CA	Sphere	Other	89
12.6.18	7:12 p.m.	97119	Red Bluff	CA	Triangle	UAV	221
Tennessee							
4.5.18	11:30 p.m.	91263	Reliance	TN	Square/Rectangle	Other	59
12.6.18	5:35 p.m.	96850	Memphis	TN	Chevron	Other	220
Texas							
2.10.18	11:15 a.m.	90355	Granbury	TX	Triangle/Disc	UAV	30
3.7.18	10:34 a.m.	90628	Gonzales County	TX	Cylinder	Other	44
4.25.18	2:30 p.m.	91628	Webster	TX	Circle	UAV	68
4.28.18	10:20 p.m.	91666	Houston	TX	Other	UAV	70
6.16.18	11:30 p.m.	92750	Sour Lake	TX	Triangle	UAV	97
7.9.18	n/a	96065	San Antonio	TX	Triangle	Other	116
8.18.18	6:35 p.m.	94292	Flint	TX	Cigar	UAV	145
8.31.18	6:35 a.m.	94699	El Paso	TX	Triangle	UAV	152
9.1.18	4:20 a.m.	94960	Porter	TX	Boomerang	UAV	154
11.6.18	8:25 p.m.	96207	San Antonio	TX	Chevron	UAV	195
12.1.18	12:00 a.m.	96805	McKinney	TX	Oval	UAV	214
Thailand							
4.10.18	12 p.m.	93224	Nakhon Nayok	Thailand	Square/Rectangle	UAV	62
11.2.18	9:30 p.m.	96088	Pattaya	Thailand	Triangle	UAV	192
Thurston County, Washington							
11.7.18	6:02 p.m.	96229	Lacey	WA	Cylinder	UAV	197
12.4.18	2 p.m.	96813	Olympia	WA	Egg	UAV	218
Tinley Park, Illinois							
8.10.18	9:58 p.m.	94525	Tinley Park	IL	Sphere	UAV	136
Toms Brook, Virginia							
12.3.18	8:35 a.m.	96755	Toms Brook	VA	Cylinder	UAV	216
Toms River, New Jersey							
10.2.18	8:25 p.m.	95323	Toms River	NJ	Triangle	Other	169

EVENT	TIME	CASE	CITY	STATE-COUNTRY	SHAPE	DISPOSITION	PAGE
Toronto, Ontario, Canada							
7.10.18	10 p.m.	97688	Toronto	Canada	Triangle	Other	117
Trinidad, Colorado							
10.5.18	8:15 p.m.	95364	Trinidad	CO	Triangle	UAV	174
Tuolumne County, California							
10.15.18	4 p.m.	95599	Sonora	CA	N/A	UAV	180
Ulster County, New York							
3.10.18	4 a.m.	95178	Woodstock	NY	Diamond	UAV	46
Umatilla County, Oregon							
7.11.18	9 a.m.	93427	Pendleton	OR	Cone	UAV	118
7.11.18	10:45 a.m.	93419	Pendleton	OR	Other	UAV	118
United Kingdom							
1.6.18	1:50 p.m.	89370	Darlington	UK	Triangle	Info Only	12
1.17.18	3:35 a.m.	89653	Hemel Hempstead	UK	Triangle	UAV	18
1.24.18	8:04 p.m.	89841	Glasgow	UK	Blimp	Other	19
1.24.18	10:30 p.m.	89780	Droitwich	UK	Triangle	Other	19
1.26.18	8:15 p.m.	91153	Unknown	UK	Sphere	UAV	20
2.04.18	6:27 p.m.	90097	Windsor	UK	Triangle	Info Only	25
2.13.18	10 p.m.	90452	Newbury	UK	Triangle	UAV	33
4.10.18	2:30 a.m.	96307	Bromsgrove	UK	Unknown	UAV	60
4.19.18	10:30 p.m.	91752	Stonehouse	UK	Triangle	Info Only	64
5.1.18	11:30 p.m.	92298	London	UK	Triangle	UAV	71
6.2.18	3:10 p.m.	92499	Crieff, Scotland	UK	Disc	UAV	84
6.3.18	7:49 p.m.	93607	Dartford	UK	Horseshoe	UAV	88
7.3.18	1:30 a.m.	93128	Wrexham	UK	Orb	UAV	115
8.19.18	10 p.m.	98200	Port Talbot	UK	Triangle	Info Only	148
9.20.18	7:45 p.m.	95065	Unknown	UK	Disc	UAV	163
9.23.18	5:40 p.m.	95215	London	UK	Triangle	UAV	165
10.18.18	8:25 p.m.	95673	Mercaston	UK	Sphere	UAV	182
12.4.18	6:30 a.m.	96843	Beaconsfield	UK	Disc	UAV	217
12.17.18	9:15 p.m.	97065	Goole	UK	Triangle	UAV	229
12.28.18	1:10 a.m.	97282	Shrewsbury	UK	Chevron	Info Only	230
12.31.18	12:10 a.m.	97391	Caithness	UK	Saturn-like	UAV	231
Utah							
1.6.18	10 p.m.	89385	Logan	UT	Diamond	Other	13

EVENT	TIME	CASE	CITY	STATE-COUNTRY	SHAPE	DISPOSITION	PAGE
3.6.18	10:42 a.m.	93750	West Jordan	UT	Cylinder	UAV	41
4.10.18	12 a.m.	91382	Heber City	UT	Triangle	UAV	61
5.4.18	2:52 a.m.	91780	Enterprise	UT	Saturn-like	UAV	73
10.3.18	9:40 p.m.	98214	Orem	UT	Cigar	UAV	171
11.11.18	n/a	96316	Taylorsville	UT	Triangle	Other	205
12.7.18	9:25 p.m.	96890	Wellington	UT	Cigar	UAV	221
Utah County, Utah							
10.3.18	9:40 p.m.	98214	Orem	UT	Cigar	UAV	171
Valencia County, New Mexico							
8.12.18	n/a	94105	Los Lunas	NM	Sphere	Other	138
Valley, Washington							
2.08.18	1:07 p.m.	94350	Valley	WA	Disc	UAV	26
Valrico, Florida							
11.7.18	9:30 p.m.	96766	Valrico	FL	Chevron	UAV	198
Vancouver, Washington							
9.18.18	12:25 p.m.	94996	Vancouver	WA	Unknown	UAV	162
Vermont							
5.24.18	11:45 p.m.	92228	Saint Albans	VT	Triangle	Info Only	80
Virginia							
6.4.18	n/a	97913	Leesburg	VA	Sphere	UAV	90
10.17.18	6:15 p.m.	95653	Richmond	VA	Cylinder	UAV	181
11.4.18	3:20 p.m.	96375	Luray	VA	Disc	UAV	193
12.3.18	8:35 a.m.	96755	Toms Brook	VA	Cylinder	UAV	216
12.8.18	5:55 p.m.	97287	Pulaski	VA	Triangle	UAV	222
Volusia County, Florida							
6.9.18	9:15 p.m.	92639	Daytona Beach	FL	Sphere	UAV	94
7.10.18	7:35 a.m.	93256	Deland	FL	Diamond	UAV	116
Wake County, North Carolina							
11.8.18	7:30 p.m.	96310	Apex	NC	Other	UAV	201
Walker, Oregon							
11.3.18	11:59 p.m.	96140	Walker	OR	Saturn-like	UAV	193
Warracknabeal, Australia							
4.7.18	1:30 a.m.	96086	Warracknabeal	Australia	Disc	UAV	59
Warren County, Missouri							
6.19.18	11:15 a.m.	92800	Warrento	MO	Blimp	UAV	100

EVENT	TIME	CASE	CITY	STATE-COUNTRY	SHAPE	DISPOSITION	PAGE
Warrento, Missouri							
6.19.18	11:15 a.m.	92800	Warrento	MO	Blimp	UAV	100
Wasatch County, Utah							
4.10.18	12 a.m.	91382	Heber City	UT	Triangle	UAV	61
Washington							
1.9.18	8:45 p.m.	89498	Ellensburg	WA	Oval	UAV	15
2.08.18	1:07 p.m.	94350	Valley	WA	Disc	UAV	26
5.25.18	8:30 p.m.	94857	Poulsbo	WA	Square/Rectangle	UAV	80
6.20.18	8:20 p.m.	92828	Pasco	WA	Sphere	UAV	102
7.22.18	1:42 p.m.	93732	Darrington	WA.	Disc	UAV	124
7.23.18	6:30 p.m.	93587	Seattle	WA.	Circle	Other	126
7.24.18	2:30 a.m.	93703	Winlock	WA.	Triangle	UAV	126
8.16.18	n/a	95179	Gig Harbor	WA	Triangle	UAV	142
8.27.18	11:05 p.m.	94482	Eatonville	WA	Sphere	Other	150
9.18.18	12:25 p.m.	94996	Vancouver	WA	Unknown	UAV	162
9.25.18	11:15 p.m.	95249	Silvercreek	WA	Egg	UAV	167
10.4.18	8 p.m.	95356	Sammamish	WA	Diamond	Other	172
10.10.18	4:30 a.m.	95592	Bellingham	WA	Triangle	UAV	175
11.7.18	6:02 p.m.	96229	Lacey	WA	Cylinder	UAV	197
11.15.18	2:46 p.m.	97141	Everett	WA	Other	UAV	207
12.4.18	2 p.m.	96813	Olympia	WA	Egg	UAV	218
Washington County, Pennsylvania							
10.23.18	12:52 p.m.	95826	California	PA	Disc	UAV	184
Waterloo, Iowa							
8.6.18	10:15 p.m.	93940	Waterloo	IA	Circle	UAV	132
Webster, North Carolina							
3.5.18	11:17 p.m.	91103	Webster	NC	Square/Rectangle	Other	40
Webster, Texas							
4.25.18	2:30 p.m.	91628	Webster	TX	Circle	UAV	68
Wellington, Utah							
12.7.18	9:25 p.m.	96890	Wellington	UT	Cigar	UAV	221
West Fargo, North Dakota							
7.1.18	9:23 p.m.	93045	West Fargo	ND	Sphere	Other	113

EVENT	TIME	CASE	CITY	STATE-COUNTRY	SHAPE	DISPOSITION	PAGE
West Jordan, Utah							
3.6.18	10:42 a.m.	93750	West Jordan	UT	Cylinder	UAV	41
West Plains, Missouri							
6.1.18	n/a	92483	West Plains	MO	Triangle	UAV	83
West Virginia							
9.12.18	1:15 a.m.	94839	Hurricane	WV	Sphere	UAV	157
12.10.18	8:45 p.m.	97001	Scott Depot	WV	Boomerang	UAV	224
Westmoreland County, Pennsylvania							
2.04.18	1:38 a.m.	90057	Mt. Pleasant	PA	Sphere	Other	23
2.09.18	11:18 p.m.	90175	Derry	PA	Semi-Diamond	Other	29
6.19.18	7:30 p.m.	92803	Lower Burrell	PA	Cylinder	UAV	101
Whatcom County, Washington							
10.10.18	4:30 a.m.	95592	Bellingham	WA	Triangle	UAV	175
Wilmington, California							
2.26.18	3:47 p.m.	90708	Wilmington	CA	Saturn-like	UAV	37
Wilmington, North Carolina							
9.8.18	n/a	96379	Wilmington	NC	Sphere	Other	156
Windsor, United Kingdom							
2.04.18	6:27 p.m.	90097	Windsor	UK	Triangle	Info Only	25
Winlock, Washington							
7.24.18	2:30 a.m.	93703	Winlock	WA.	Triangle	UAV	126
Wisconsin							
1.8.18	5:20 p.m.	89435	Orfordville	WI	Triangle	UAV	14
6.26.18	2:41 a.m.	92954	Madison	WI	Triangle	UAV	107
8.21.18	2:30 p.m.	94322	Farmington	WI	Other	UAV	148
9.10.18	10:30 p.m.	98808	Colby	WI	Sphere	Other	157
10.21.18	5:30 p.m.	95770	Belleville	WI	Unknown	Other	183
12.9.18	8:20 p.m.	97094	Wisconsin Rapids	WI	Square/Rectangle	UAV	223
Wisconsin Rapids, Wisconsin							
12.9.18	8:20 p.m.	97094	Wisconsin Rapids	WI	Square/Rectangle	UAV	223
Wood County, Wisconsin							
12.9.18	8:20 p.m.	97094	Wisconsin Rapids	WI	Square/Rectangle	UAV	223

EVENT	TIME	CASE	CITY	STATE-COUNTRY	SHAPE	DISPOSITION	PAGE
Woodstock, Georgia							
2.15.18	9:30 p.m.	91313	Woodstock	GA	Cylinder	UAV	33
Woodstock, New York							
3.10.18	4 a.m.	95178	Woodstock	NY	Diamond	UAV	46
Worcester County, Massachusetts							
6.10.18	10:27 p.m.	92653	Blackstone	MA	Unknown	UAV	95
Wrexham, United Kingdom							
7.3.18	1:30 a.m.	93128	Wrexham	UK	Orb	UAV	115
Wrightsville, Pennsylvania							
1.9.18	7:05 p.m.	89450	Wrightsville	PA	Triangle	UAV	14
Wyoming							
10.16.18	9:53 p.m.	95874	Midwest	WY	Sphere	UAV	180
11.14.18	9:50 p.m.	96382	Kemmerer	WY	Star-like	Other	207
Yamhill County, Oregon							
6.26.18	10:04 p.m.	92936	McMinnville	OR	Oval	Other	108

OBJECT INDEX: 2018

EVENT	TIME	CASE	CITY	STATE-COUNTRY	SHAPE	DISPOSITION	PAGE
Altitude, under 100 feet							
1.3.18	6:40 p.m.	89327	Marina	CA	Sphere	Other	10
1.4.18	6:25 a.m.	89344	Casselberry	FL	Square/Rectangle	Other	12
1.6.18	10 p.m.	89385	Logan	UT	Diamond	Other	13
1.24.18	10:30 p.m.	89780	Droitwich Spa	UK	Triangle	Other	19
3.6.18	10:42 a.m.	93750	West Jordan	UT	Cylinder	UAV	41
3.14.18	5:38 p.m.	90776	Port Huron	MI	Square/Rectangle	Other	48
3.15.18	4 a.m.	97506	Holly Pond	AL	Triangle	UAV	49
3.28.18	3:15 a.m.	91075	Brookline	NH	Triangle	UAV	53
4.5.18	11:30 p.m.	91263	Reliance	TN	Square/Rectangle	Other	59
4.10.18	2:30 a.m.	96307	Bromsgrove	UK	Unknown	UAV	60
4.17.18	10:45 p.m.	91485	Osceola	IN	Cylinder	UAV	64
4.28.18	10:20 p.m.	91666	Houston	TX	Other	UAV	70
5.3.18	10:28 p.m.	91773	Caverna	MO	Oval	UAV	72
5.4.18	2:52 a.m.	91780	Enterprise	UT	Saturn-like	UAV	73
5.11.18	11:45 p.m.	91968	North Plainfield	NJ	Unknown	Other	75
5.15.18	9:30 p.m.	92029	Bay Shore	NY	Sphere	Other	77
5.18.18	4:25 a.m.	98601	Ballymahon Co. Lonford	Ireland	Saturn-like	Other	78
5.21.18	9:59 p.m.	92164	Arkoma	OK	Triangle	UAV	79
6.2.18	10:15 p.m.	92445	London	Canada	Triangle	UAV	85
6.3.18	n/a	92452	Flournoy	CA	Sphere	Other	89
6.7.18	10:30 p.m.	92568	Colorado Springs	CO	Other	UAV	92
6.9.18	1:15 a.m.	92591	Oelwein	IA	Oval	UAV	93
6.9.18	8:32 p.m.	92619	Alexandria	MD	Bullet/Missile	UAV	94
6.11.18	2:11 a.m.	92673	North Las Vegas	NV	Other	UAV	96
6.19.18	11:15 a.m.	92800	Warrento	MO	Blimp	UAV	100
6.20.18	3:15 p.m.	92849	Egg Harbor Township	NJ	Sphere	UAV	102

EVENT	TIME	CASE	CITY	STATE-COUNTRY	SHAPE	DISPOSITION	PAGE
6.21.18	n/a	92994	San Felipe Baja Norte	Mexico	Sphere	Other	104
6.26.18	2:41 a.m.	92954	Madison	WI	Triangle	UAV	107
6.26.18	10:30 p.m.	92957	Fridley	MN	Sphere	Other	108
6.26.18	12 a.m.	95960	Noxon	MT	Disc	Other	109
7.3.18	1:30 a.m.	93128	Wrexham	UK	Orb	UAV	115
7.13.18	9:30 p.m.	93410	Alexandria	IN	Sphere	Other	119
7.15.18	8:06 p.m.	93445	Niagara Falls	Canada	Sphere	Other	120
7.17.18	10:40 p.m.	93540	Brookport	IL	Cylinder	UAV	121
7.19.18	9:30 p.m.	97557	Mount Washington	KY	Sphere	Other	123
8.1.18	9:02 p.m.	97862	Breitenbush Hot Springs	OR	Triangle	UAV	129
8.6.18	10:15 p.m.	93940	Waterloo	IA	Circle	UAV	132
8.12.18	n/a	94105	Los Lunas	NM	Sphere	Other	138
8.12.18	12:15 a.m.	97164	Ridgeville	SC	Egg	UAV	139
8.14.18	1:07 a.m.	94117	Hernes, Elverum	Norway	Other	Info Only	140
8.15.18	3:45 p.m.	94170	Pensacola	FL	Bullet/Missile	UAV	140
8.16.18	n/a	95179	Gig Harbor	WA	Triangle	UAV	142
8.17.18	1:30 a.m.	97678	Key West	FL	Circle	Other	143
8.17.18	10:30 p.m.	94217	Portage	IN	Triangle	UAV	144
9.10.18	10:30 p.m.	98808	Colby	WI	Sphere	Other	157
9.12.18	1:15 a.m.	94839	Hurricane	WV	Sphere	UAV	157
9.13.18	8:15 a.m.	94937	Hailey	ID	Square/Rectangle	UAV	159
9.24.18	6:45 p.m.	95317	Baldwinsville	NY	Sphere	Other	165
9.25.18	10:30 p.m.	95703	Lachute	Canada	Disc	UAV	166
10.3.18	7:30 p.m.	96637	New Lisbon	NJ	Triangle	UAV	170
10.7.18	7:30 p.m.	95445	Saco	ME	Diamond	UAV	175
10.12.18	1:01 a.m.	95590	Citrus Heights	CA	Triangle	UAV	177
10.16.18	9:53 p.m.	95874	Midwest	WY	Sphere	UAV	180
10.18.18	8:25 p.m.	95673	Mercaston	UK	Sphere	UAV	182
10.30.18	2 a.m.	96776	Tecumseh	MI	Disc	Other	188
10.30.18	8:30 p.m.	96033	Jackson Township	NJ	Triangle	UAV	190
10.30.18	n/a	98437	Michigan City	IN	Triangle	UAV	190

EVENT	TIME	CASE	CITY	STATE-COUNTRY	SHAPE	DISPOSITION	PAGE
11.7.18	6:02 p.m.	96229	Lacey	WA	Cylinder	UAV	197
11.8.18	7:30 p.m.	96310	Apex	NC	Other	UAV	201
11.23.18	6:15 p.m.	96580	Edwards	NY	Sphere	UAV	209
11.28.18	5:20 p.m.	96641	Unknown	Philippines	Unknown	Other	213
12.1.18	12:00 a.m.	96805	McKinney	TX	Oval	UAV	214
12.12.18	6:20 p.m.	97013	Laurel Lake	NJ	N/A	UAV	226
Altitude, under 500 feet							
1.2.18	5:20 p.m.	89280	Northampton	MA	Boomerang	UAV	10
1.9.18	7:05 p.m.	89450	Wrightsville	PA	Triangle	UAV	14
1.13.18	9:05 p.m.	89544	Indianapolis	IN	Chevron	Info Only	17
1.17.18	3:35 a.m.	89653	Hemel Hempstead	UK	Triangle	UAV	18
2.04.18	7:40 a.m.	90015	Port St. Lucie	FL	Square/Rectangle	Other	24
2.07.18	8 a.m.	90127	Shoup	ID	Teardrop	UAV	26
2.09.18	11:18 p.m.	90175	Derry	PA	Semi-Diamond	Other	29
2.12.18	8:05 p.m.	90205	St. Peters	MO	Square/Rectangle	UAV	31
2.15.18	9:30 p.m.	91313	Woodstock	GA	Cylinder	UAV	33
2.21.18	12:30 a.m.	90347	Sacramento	CA	Square/Rectangle	UAV	34
2.23.18	7:15 p.m.	90404	Summerlin	NV	Triangle		35
3.2.18	5:25 a.m.	90499	Dasmarinas	Philippines	Triangle	UAV	38
3.5.18	11:17 p.m.	91103	Webster	NC	Square/Rectangle	Other	40
3.6.18	9:40 p.m.	90698	Marietta	GA	Other	UAV	42
3.10.18	11:57 p.m.	90710	Manchester	MD	Triangle	Other	45
3.10.18	4 a.m.	95178	Woodstock	NY	Diamond	UAV	46
3.11.18	10 p.m.	90789	Munroe Falls	OH	Triangle	UAV	47
3.22.18	10:37 p.m.	90959	Chatsworth	GA	Triangle	UAV	51
3.26.18	3:15 a.m.	91194	Bridgeville	PA	Boomerang	UAV	52
3.30.18	4:30 a.m.	91184	Excelsior Springs	MO	Triangle	UAV	54
3.31.18	9:55 p.m.	91151	Aiken	SC	Circle	Other	55
4.22.18	5:20 p.m.	91572	Brooklyn	NY	Saturn-like	UAV	67
4.22.18	12 a.m.	91570	Edmonton	CA	Triangle	Info Only	68
5.1.18	n/a	91829	Loxley	AL	Circle	Other	72

EVENT	TIME	CASE	CITY	STATE-COUNTRY	SHAPE	DISPOSITION	PAGE
5.11.18	10:20 a.m.	91939	Esquimalt	Canada	Cigar	Info Only	74
5.13.18	5:05 p.m.	92110	Garrett	IN	Cigar	UAV	75
5.15.18	n/a	93352	Lisbon	Portugal	Triangle	Info Only	77
5.16.18	n/a	92036	Salinas	CA	Triangle	UAV	77
5.22.18	8:12 p.m.	92950	Hudson	IL	Other	Other	79
5.24.18	11:45 p.m.	92228	Saint Albans	VT	Triangle	Info Only	80
6.1.18	11:01 p.m.	93565	Novy Jicin	Czech Republic	Triangle	Info Only	82
6.3.18	6:45 a.m.	92469	Panola County	MS	Cylinder	UAV	87
6.6.18	1 p.m.	97168	Plymouth	MA	Blimp	Info Only	90
6.10.18	10:27 p.m.	92653	Blackstone	MA	Unknown	UAV	95
6.10.18	10:30 p.m.	92641	Attleboro	MA	n/a	Other	95
6.11.18	2:11 a.m.	92673	North Las Vegas	NV	Other	UAV	96
6.16.18	11:30 p.m.	92750	Sour Lake	TX	Triangle	UAV	97
6.17.18	11:40 p.m.	92802	Ada County	ID	Other	UAV	99
6.23.18	11:45 p.m.	92947	Oak Dale	CA	Fireball	UAV	105
7.1.18	9:23 p.m.	93045	West Fargo	ND	Sphere	Other	113
7.2.18	9:55 p.m.	94741	Carmel	IN	Cigar	Other	114
7.2.18	9:55 p.m.	94741	Carmel	IN	Cigar	Other	114
7.9.18	n/a	96065	San Antonio	TX	Triangle	Other	116
7.22.18	10 p.m.	93687	Anaheim	CA	Triangle	UAV	125
7.23.18	6:30 p.m.	93587	Seattle	WA.	Circle	Other	126
7.29.18	5:35 a.m.	93741	Hesston	KS	Triangle	UAV	127
8.3.18	11 p.m.	94007	Newport	OR	Other	UAV	131
8.5.18	3 p.m.	95040	Florence	OR	Triangle	UAV	132
8.10.18	7:19 p.m.	94038	Hammond	IN	Blimp	UAV	135
8.15.18	10:30 p.m.	94184	Staten Island	NY	Disc	Other	141
8.18.18	5:15 p.m.	94231	Jersey City	NJ	Other	UAV	145
8.19.18	8 p.m.	94262	El Dorado Springs	MO	Disc	UAV	147
8.19.18	10 p.m.	98200	Port Talbot	UK	Triangle	Info Only	148
8.27.18	11:05 p.m.	94482	Eatonville	WA	Sphere	Other	150
9.13.18	9 p.m.	94903	Columbus	IN	Triangle	UAV	160
9.16.18	1:15 a.m.	94931	Kensington	CA	Unknown	Other	161
9.17.18	9:42 p.m.	94983	Highlands Ranch	CO	Cone	UAV	161

EVENT	TIME	CASE	CITY	STATE-COUNTRY	SHAPE	DISPOSITION	PAGE
9.19.18	9 p.m.	94990	Unknown	Philippines	Triangle	UAV	163
9.25.18	11:15 p.m.	95249	Silvercreek	WA	Egg	UAV	167
10.3.18	9:40 p.m.	98214	Orem	UT	Cigar	UAV	171
10.13.18	8:58 p.m.	98344	Stoney Creek	Canada	Boomerang	UAV	179
10.15.18	4 p.m.	95599	Sonora	CA	n/a	UAV	180
10.21.18	5:30 p.m.	95770	Belleville	WI	Unknown	Other	183
10.23.18	12:52 p.m.	95826	California	PA	Disc	UAV	184
10.25.18	6:30 p.m.	96048	Dilles Bottom	OH	Egg	UAV	184
10.26.18	11:10 p.m.	96858	Reykjavik	Iceland	Circle	Other	187
10.30.18	7:40 p.m.	96019	Benton	OH	Cylinder	UAV	189
11.3.18	11:59 p.m.	96140	Walker	OR	Saturn-like	UAV	193
11.5.18	10:30 p.m.	96204	Newport	OR	Triangle	UAV	194
11.6.18	5:54 p.m.	96200	Hattiesburg	MS	Triangle	UAV	194
11.6.18	8:25 p.m.	96207	San Antonio	TX	Chevron	UAV	195
11.7.18	10:40 p.m.	97286	Duluth	MN	Oval	UAV	200
11.9.18	9 p.m.	96451	Springfield	MO	Triangle	UAV	202
11.12.18	7:20 p.m.	96353	Phoenix	AZ	Cigar	UAV	205
11.13.18	6:23 p.m.	96764	Labadee	Haiti	Diamond	UAV	206
11.25.18	8:45 a.m.	96586	Gorey	Ireland	Diamond	Other	210
11.26.18	8:02 p.m.	96643	Columbia	MO	Boomerang	UAV	212
11.27.18	8 p.m.	97510	Santee	CA	Triangle	Info Only	212
12.1.18	12:00 a.m.	96805	McKinney	TX	Oval	UAV	214
12.3.18	n/a	96773	n/a	CA	Teardrop	UAV	217
12.8.18	5:55 p.m.	97287	Pulaski	VA	Triangle	UAV	222
12.9.18	8:20 p.m.	97094	Wisconsin Rapids	WI	Square/Rectangle	UAV	223
12.10.18	8:45 p.m.	97001	Scott Depot	WV	Boomerang	UAV	224
12.12.18	3 a.m.	96955	St. Jacob	IL	N/A	Other	226
12.17.18	9:15 p.m.	97065	Goole	UK	Triangle	UAV	229
12.28.18	1:10 a.m.	97282	Shrewsbury	UK	Chevron	Info Only	230
12.31.18	12:10 a.m.	97391	Caithness	UK	Saturn-like	UAV	231
Altitude, under 1,000 feet							
1.1.18	12:05 a.m.	89317	Las Vegas	NV	Disc	UAV	8
1.9.18	8:45 p.m.	89498	Ellensburg	WA	Oval	UAV	15
2.08.18	8:30 p.m.	90133	Mena	AR	Triangle	UAV	27

EVENT	TIME	CASE	CITY	STATE-COUNTRY	SHAPE	DISPOSITION	PAGE
2.23.18	7:17 p.m.	90398	Las Vegas	NV	Triangle	UAV	36
3.2.18	8:30 a.m.	94597	Muskegon	MI	Square/Rectangle	UAV	38
3.3.18	5:35 a.m.	90540	Birmingham	AL	Triangle	UAV	39
4.15.18	1 p.m.	94668	Arncliffe	Australia	Egg	UAV	63
5.1.18	11:30 p.m.	92298	London	UK	Triangle	UAV	71
4.5.18	11:30 p.m.	91263	Reliance	TN	Square/Rectangle	Other	59
5.15.18	4:45 p.m.	92030	Medford	OR	Cylinder	UAV	76
5.25.18	8:30 p.m.	94857	Poulsbo	WA	Square/Rectangle	UAV	80
6.1.18	7:41 p.m.	92432	Sao Jose Dos Pinhais	Brazil	Egg	Info Only	82
6.20.18	8:20 p.m.	92828	Pasco	WA	Sphere	UAV	102
6.27.18	10 p.m.	92964	Mesquite	NV	Cigar	UAV	110
6.28.18	11:15 p.m.	93454	Buckeye	AZ	Circle	UAV	110
6.29.18	9:30 p.m.	93050	Carolina Beach	NC	Sphere	Other	111
7.22.18	1:42 p.m.	93732	Darrington	WA.	Disc	UAV	124
8.8.18	9:45 a.m.	94049	Sunset Hills	MO	Diamond	UAV	133
8.10.18	9:58 p.m.	94525	Tinley Park	IL	Sphere	UAV	136
8.12.18	2:10 a.m.	94081	Godfrey	IL	Cigar	UAV	137
8.18.18	6:35 p.m.	94292	Flint	TX	Cigar	UAV	145
8.18.18	9:40 p.m.	96784	Cospicua	Malta	Oval	Other	146
8.29.18	8:15 p.m.	97227	Jamul	CA	Sphere	UAV	151
9.7.18	1:30 a.m.	94837	Kos Town	Greece	Chevron	UAV	155
10.2.18	8:25 p.m.	95323	Toms River	NJ	Triangle	Other	169
10.4.18	8 p.m.	95356	Sammamish	WA	Diamond	Other	172
10.4.18	8:57 p.m.	95343	Rancho Mirage	CA	Boomerang	UAV	173
10.5.18	8:15 p.m.	95364	Trinidad	CO	Triangle	UAV	174
10.10.18	4:30 a.m.	95592	Bellingham	WA	Triangle	UAV	175
10.10.18	2:27 p.m.	95682	Atlanta	GA	Cigar	UAV	176
10.12.18	1:01 a.m.	95529	Orlando	FL	Triangle	UAV	178
10.17.18	6:15 p.m.	95653	Richmond	VA	Cylinder	UAV	181
10.22.18	9:30 a.m.	95806	Pass Christian	MS	Blimp	UAV	183
10.28.18	n/a	96472	Sacramento	CA	Triangle	UAV	188

EVENT	TIME	CASE	CITY	STATE-COUNTRY	SHAPE	DISPOSITION	PAGE
11.4.18	3:20 p.m.	96375	Luray	VA	Disc	UAV	193
11.7.18	9:30 p.m.	96766	Valrico	FL	Chevron	UAV	198
11.7.18	9:36 p.m.	96341	Boca Raton	FL	Chevron	UAV	199
11.10.18	2 a.m.	96271	Lonsdale	MN	Triangle	UAV	203
11.10.18	5 a.m.	96283	Pipestone	MN	Other	UAV	203
11.11.18	2:40 a.m.	96450	Jefferson City	MO	Chevron	UAV	204
11.11.18	7:05 p.m.	96314	London	Canada	Triangle	UAV	204
11.14.18	7:24 p.m.	96378	Caroga Lake	NY	Circle	UAV	206
11.14.18	9:50 p.m.	96382	Kemmerer	WY	Star-like	Other	207
11.23.18	4:55 a.m.	96554	Ballivor	Ireland	Triangle	Other	208
11.25.18	8:15 p.m.	96616	Galway City	Ireland	n/a	UAV	210
12.3.18	8:35 a.m.	96755	Toms Brook	VA	Cylinder	UAV	216
12.4.18	2 p.m.	96813	Olympia	WA	Egg	UAV	218
12.4.18	8:30 p.m.	96829	Orwigsburg	PA	Triangle	UAV	218
12.5.18	6:10 p.m.	96818	Baker City	OR	Chevron	UAV	219
12.6.18	5:35 p.m.	96850	Memphis	TN	Chevron	Other	220
12.7.18	9:25 p.m.	96890	Wellington	UT	Cigar	UAV	221
12.12.18	6:52 p.m.	96983	St. Louis	MO	Triangle	UAV	227
12.16.18	7:38 p.m.	97044	Fort Smith	AR	Triangle	UAV	228

Behavior, alien being appeared inside vehicle

| 3.3.18 | 11:30 p.m. | 90584 | Elkhorn | NE | Disc | UAV | 40 |

Behavior, arranged in semi-circle

| 1.1.18 | 5:30 p.m. | 89276 | Lowell | MA | Other | UAV | 9 |

Behavior, ball of light appeared inside vehicle

| 3.3.18 | 11:30 p.m. | 90584 | Elkhorn | NE | Disc | UAV | 40 |

Behavior, ejected smaller object

| 8.10.18 | 9:58 p.m. | 94525 | Tinley Park | IL | Sphere | UAV | 136 |

Behavior, diamond formation

| 1.9.18 | 7:05 p.m. | 89450 | Wrightsville | PA | Triangle | UAV | 14 |

Behavior, disappeared instantly

| 1.1.18 | 5:30 p.m. | 89276 | Lowell | MA | Other | UAV | 9 |
| 2.21.18 | 8:30 p.m. | 90647 | Rochester | NY | Triangle | | 35 |

Behavior, flew on side

| 9.14.18 | 8:15 a.m. | 95265 | Santa Elena | Costa Rica | Disc | UAV | 160 |

EVENT	TIME	CASE	CITY	STATE-COUNTRY	SHAPE	DISPOSITION	PAGE
Behavior, followed witness							
4.10.18	2:30 a.m.	96307	Bromsgrove	UK	Unknown	UAV	60
5.4.18	2:52 a.m.	91780	Enterprise	UT	Saturn-like	UAV	73
6.3.18	n/a	92452	Flournoy	CA	Sphere	Other	89
11.23.18	6:15 p.m.	96580	Edwards	NY	Sphere	UAV	209
Behavior, hovered							
1.1.18	5:30 p.m.	89276	Lowell	MA	Other	UAV	9
1.2.18	5:20 p.m.	89280	Northampton	MA	Boomerang	UAV	10
1.4.18	6:25 a.m.	89344	Casselberry	FL	Square/Rectangle	Other	12
1.6.18	10 p.m.	89385	Logan	UT	Diamond	Other	13
1.9.18	8:45 p.m.	89498	Ellensburg	WA	Oval	UAV	15
1.24.18	n/a	89785	Great Falls	MT	Circle	Info Only	20
2.04.18	1:38 a.m.	90057	Mt. Pleasant	PA	Sphere	Other	23
2.07.18	8 a.m.	90127	Shoup	ID	Teardrop	UAV	26
2.12.18	8:05 p.m.	90205	St. Peters	MO	Square/Rectangle	UAV	31
2.21.18	12:30 a.m.	90347	Sacramento	CA	Square/Rectangle	UAV	34
2.23.18	7:17 p.m.	90398	Las Vegas	NV	Triangle	UAV	36
2.26.18	3:47 p.m.	90708	Wilmington	CA	Saturn-like	UAV	37
3.10.18	4 a.m.	95178	Woodstock	NY	Diamond	UAV	46
3.11.18	10 p.m.	90789	Munroe Falls	OH	Triangle	UAV	47
3.14.18	5:38 p.m.	90776	Port Huron	MI	Square/Rectangle	Other	48
3.22.18	10:37 p.m.	90959	Chatsworth	GA	Triangle	UAV	51
4.1.18	6:02 p.m.	91199	New Port Richey	FL	Disc	UAV	57
4.2.18	10:27 p.m.	91182	Banja Luka	Bosnia & Herzegovina	Disc	Info Only	58
4.5.18	11:30 p.m.	91263	Reliance	TN	Square/Rectangle	Other	59
4.7.18	1:30 a.m.	96086	Warracknabeal	Australia	Disc	UAV	59
4.22.18	5:14 p.m.	91575	Manheim	PA	Other	Other	67
5.1.18	n/a	91829	Loxley	AL	Circle	Other	72
5.11.18	11:45 p.m.	91968	North Plainfield	NJ	Unknown	Other	75
5.21.18	9:59 p.m.	92164	Arkoma	OK	Triangle	UAV	79
5.22.18	8:12 p.m.	92950	Hudson	IL	Other	Other	79

EVENT	TIME	CASE	CITY	STATE-COUNTRY	SHAPE	DISPOSITION	PAGE
6.3.18	6:45 a.m.	92469	Panola County	MS	Cylinder	UAV	87
6.6.18	1 p.m.	97168	Plymouth	MA	Blimp	Info Only	90
6.7.18	10:30 p.m.	92568	Colorado Springs	CO	Other	UAV	92
6.11.18	2:11 a.m.	92673	North Las Vegas	NV	Other	UAV	96
6.19.18	7:10 a.m.	92792	Joliette	Canada	Other	UAV	100
6.20.18	8:20 p.m.	92828	Pasco	WA	Sphere	UAV	102
6.21.18	10:58 p.m.	92852	New Brighten	MN	Disc	UAV	103
6.23.18	11:45 p.m.	92947	Oak Dale	CA	Fireball	UAV	105
6.24.18	n/a	95063	Medellin	Columbia	Diamond	UAV	106
6.26.18	2:41 a.m.	92954	Madison	WI	Triangle	UAV	107
6.29.18	9:30 p.m.	93050	Carolina Beach	NC	Sphere	Other	111
7.1.18	9:23 p.m.	93045	West Fargo	ND	Sphere	Other	113
7.10.18	7:35 a.m.	93256	Deland	FL	Diamond	UAV	116
7.15.18	8:06 p.m.	93445	Niagara Falls	Canada	Sphere	Other	120
7.18.18	2:06 p.m.	93708	Hood River	OR	Cigar	UAV	122
7.19.18	9:30 p.m.	97557	Mount Washington	KY	Sphere	Other	123
8.1.18	9:02 p.m.	97862	Breitenbush Hot Springs	OR	Triangle	UAV	129
8.9.18	2:40 p.m.	94827	San Diego	CA	Oval	UAV	134
8.10.18	7:19 p.m.	94038	Hammond	IN	Blimp	UAV	135
8.10.18	9:58 p.m.	94525	Tinley Park	IL	Sphere	UAV	136
8.15.18	10:30 p.m.	94184	Staten Island	NY	Disc	Other	141
8.16.18	n/a	95179	Gig Harbor	WA	Triangle	UAV	142
8.17.18	10:30 p.m.	94217	Portage	IN	Triangle	UAV	144
8.21.18	2:30 p.m.	94322	Farmington	WI	Other	UAV	148
8.31.18	6:35 a.m.	94699	El Paso	TX	Triangle	UAV	152
9.10.18	10:30 p.m.	98808	Colby	WI	Sphere	Other	157
9.12.18	1:15 a.m.	94839	Hurricane	WV	Sphere	UAV	157
9.12.18	n/a	95268	Ancaster	Canada	Triangle	UAV	158
9.14.18	3:28 p.m.	94892	Santa Fe	NM	Disc	Info Only	160
9.20.18	7:45 p.m.	95065	Unknown	UK	Disc	UAV	163
9.25.18	10:30 p.m.	95703	Lachute	Canada	Disc	UAV	166
10.7.18	7:30 p.m.	95445	Saco	ME	Diamond	UAV	175
10.12.18	1:01 a.m.	95590	Citrus Heights	CA	Triangle	UAV	177

EVENT	TIME	CASE	CITY	STATE-COUNTRY	SHAPE	DISPOSITION	PAGE
10.18.18	8:25 p.m.	95673	Mercaston	UK	Sphere	UAV	182
10.21.18	5:30 p.m.	95770	Belleville	WI	Unknown	Other	183
10.25.18	6:30 p.m.	96048	Dilles Bottom	OH	Egg	UAV	184
10.25.18	7:10 p.m.	95880	Montazuma	NY	Teardrop	UAV	185
10.26.18	11 p.m.	95886	Philadelphia	PA	Cylinder	UAV	186
10.30.18	2 a.m.	96776	Tecumseh	MI	Disc	Other	188
10.30.18	7:40 p.m.	96019	Benton	OH	Cylinder	UAV	189
10.30.18	8:30 p.m.	96033	Jackson Township	NJ	Triangle	UAV	190
11.3.18	11:59 p.m.	96140	Walker	OR	Saturn-like	UAV	193
11.4.18	3:20 p.m.	96375	Luray	VA	Disc	UAV	193
11.6.18	5:54 p.m.	96200	Hattiesburg	MS	Triangle	UAV	194
11.7.18	6:02 p.m.	96229	Lacey	WA	Cylinder	UAV	197
11.7.18	10:40 p.m.	97286	Duluth	MN	Oval	UAV	200
11.8.18	7:30 p.m.	96310	Apex	NC	Other	UAV	201
11.14.18	9:50 p.m.	96382	Kemmerer	WY	Star-like	Other	207
11.15.18	2:46 p.m.	97141	Everett	WA	Other	UAV	207
11.23.18	6:15 p.m.	96580	Edwards	NY	Sphere	UAV	209
11.25.18	8:15 p.m.	96616	Galway City	Ireland	N/A	UAV	210
11.28.18	5:20 p.m.	96641	Unknown	Philippines	Unknown	Other	213
12.3.18	8:35 a.m.	96755	Toms Brook	VA	Cylinder	UAV	216
12.3.18	n/a	96773	n/a	CA	Teardrop	UAV	217
12.4.18	8:30 p.m.	96829	Orwigsburg	PA	Triangle	UAV	218
12.8.18	5:55 p.m.	97287	Pulaski	VA	Triangle	UAV	222
12.9.18	8:20 p.m.	97094	Wisconsin Rapids	WI	Square/Rectangle	UAV	223
12.12.18	12 a.m.	97018	Reidsville	NC	Triangle	Other	225
12.17.18	9:15 p.m.	97065	Goole	UK	Triangle	UAV	229
12.31.18	12:10 a.m.	97391	Caithness	UK	Saturn-like	UAV	231
Behavior, hovered inside cloud							
2.08.18	1:07 p.m.	94350	Valley	WA	Disc	UAV	26
3.14.18	5:38 p.m.	90776	Port Huron	MI	Square/Rectangle	Other	48
4.25.18	2:30 p.m.	91628	Webster	TX	Circle	UAV	68
Behavior, hovered over highway or roadway							
1.2.18	5:20 p.m.	89280	Northampton	MA	Boomerang	UAV	10

EVENT	TIME	CASE	CITY	STATE-COUNTRY	SHAPE	DISPOSITION	PAGE
3.11.18	10 p.m.	90789	Munroe Falls	OH	Triangle	UAV	47
3.15.18	8:40 p.m.	90803	Abbotsford	BC Canada	Other	UAV	50
4.22.18	5:14 p.m.	91575	Manheim	PA	Other	Other	67
11.3.18	11:59 p.m.	96140	Walker	OR	Saturn-like	UAV	193
11.6.18	8:25 p.m.	96207	San Antonio	TX	Chevron	UAV	195
12.12.18	3 a.m.	96955	St. Jacob	IL	n/a	Other	226
Behavior, hovered over power lines							
3.15.18	8:40 p.m.	90803	Abbotsford	BC Canada	Other	UAV	50
Behavior, hovered over power plant							
4.17.18	9 p.m.	91498	Lakeland	FL	Sphere	Other	63
Behavior, landed							
3.3.18	11:30 p.m.	90584	Elkhorn	NE	Disc	UAV	40
4.10.18	2:30 a.m.	96307	Bromsgrove	UK	Unknown	UAV	60
5.15.18	9:30 p.m.	92029	Bay Shore	NY	Sphere	Other	77
6.26.18	12 a.m.	95960	Noxon	MT	Disc	Other	109
12.1.18	12 a.m.	96805	McKinney	TX	Oval	UAV	214
Behavior, merged with another object							
7.18.18	2:06 p.m.	93708	Hood River	OR	Cigar	UAV	122
7.23.18	6:30 p.m.	93587	Seattle	WA.	Circle	Other	126
Behavior, moved in and out of water							
8.17.18	1:30 a.m.	97678	Key West	FL	Circle	Other	143
8.17.18	n/a	97233	Key West	FL	Sphere	Other	143
Behavior, moved into aura or portal							
3.31.18	9:55 p.m.	91151	Aiken	SC	Circle	Other	55
Behavior, objects flew into it							
4.17.18	10:45 p.m.	91485	Osceola	IN	Cylinder	UAV	64
Behavior, returned to witness							
2.04.18	6:27 p.m.	90097	Windsor	UK	Triangle	Info Only	25
Behavior, objects flew out of it							
3.6.18	10:42 a.m.	93750	West Jordan	UT	Cylinder	UAV	41
Behavior, split							
7.23.18	6:30 p.m.	93587	Seattle	WA.	Circle	Other	126
Behavior, square formation							
6.20.18	3:15 p.m.	92849	Egg Harbor Township	NJ	Sphere	UAV	102

EVENT	TIME	CASE	CITY	STATE-COUNTRY	SHAPE	DISPOSITION	PAGE
Behavior, string formation							
2.04.18	1:38 a.m.	90057	Mt. Pleasant	PA	Sphere	Other	23
Behavior, tilted to side							
4.5.18	11:30 p.m.	91263	Reliance	TN	Square/Rectangle	Other	59
Behavior, triangle pattern							
7.15.18	8:06 p.m.	93445	Niagara Falls	Canada	Sphere	Other	120
Behavior, turned over							
4.1.18	6:02 p.m.	91199	New Port Richey	FL	Disc	UAV	57
Behavior, vertical pattern							
6.29.18	9:30 p.m.	93050	Carolina Beach	NC	Sphere	Other	111
Color, black							
1.6.18	1:50 p.m.	89370	Darlington	UK	Triangle	Info Only	12
1.9.18	7:05 p.m.	89450	Wrightsville	PA	Triangle	UAV	14
1.24.18	10:30 p.m.	89780	Droitwich Spa	UK	Triangle	Other	19
1.24.18	n/a	89785	Great Falls	MT	Circle	Info Only	20
2.04.18	7:40 a.m.	90015	Port St. Lucie	FL	Square/Rectangle	Other	24
2.08.18	8:30 p.m.	90133	Mena	AR	Triangle	UAV	27
2.10.18	11:15 a.m.	90355	Granbury	TX	Triangle/Disc	UAV	30
2.12.18	8:05 p.m.	90205	St. Peters	MO	Square/Rectangle	UAV	31
2.13.18	10 p.m.	90452	Newbury	UK	Triangle	UAV	33
3.2.18	8:30 a.m.	94597	Muskegon	MI	Square/Rectangle	UAV	38
3.15.18	4 a.m.	97506	Holly Pond	AL	Triangle	UAV	49
3.15.18	8:40 p.m.	90803	Abbotsford	BC Canada	Other	UAV	50
3.26.18	3:15 a.m.	91194	Bridgeville	PA	Boomerang	UAV	52
3.29.18	5:30 p.m.	92167	Dublin	Ireland	Triangle	Info Only	53
4.1.18	6:02 p.m.	91199	New Port Richey	FL	Disc	UAV	57
4.5.18	9:20 p.m.	91224	Fort Payne	AL	Square/Rectangle	UAV	58
4.19.18	10:30 p.m.	91752	Stonehouse	UK	Triangle	Info Only	64
4.21.18	9:55 p.m.	91553	Orrington	ME	Triangle	Other	65

EVENT	TIME	CASE	CITY	STATE-COUNTRY	SHAPE	DISPOSITION	PAGE
4.22.18	12 a.m.	91570	Edmonton, Alberta	CA	Triangle	Info Only	68
4.28.18	10:20 p.m.	91666	Houston	TX	Other	UAV	70
5.1.18	11:30 p.m.	92298	London	UK	Triangle	UAV	71
4.5.18	11:30 p.m.	91263	Reliance	TN	Square/Rectangle	Other	59
4.5.18	11:30 p.m.	91263	Reliance	TN	Square/Rectangle	Other	59
5.15.18	n/a	93352	Lisbon	Portugal	Triangle	Info Only	77
6.1.18	7:41 p.m.	92432	Sao Jose Dos Pinhais	Brazil	Egg	Info Only	82
6.2.18	10:15 p.m.	92445	London	Canada	Triangle	UAV	85
6.3.18	1:30 a.m.	92447	Springville	NY	Saturn-like	UAV	86
6.9.18	1:15 a.m.	92591	Oelwein	IA	Oval	UAV	93
6.16.18	11:30 p.m.	92750	Sour Lake	TX	Triangle	UAV	97
6.20.18	3:15 p.m.	92849	Egg Harbor Township	NJ	Sphere	UAV	102
6.20.18	8:20 p.m.	92828	Pasco	WA	Sphere	UAV	102
6.24.18	n/a	95063	Medellin	Columbia	Diamond	UAV	106
7.24.18	2:30 a.m.	93703	Winlock	WA.	Triangle	UAV	126
8.1.18	9:02 p.m.	97862	Breitenbush Hot Springs	OR	Triangle	UAV	129
8.12.18	n/a	94105	Los Lunas	NM	Sphere	Other	138
8.15.18	10:30 p.m.	94184	Staten Island	NY	Disc	Other	141
8.18.18	5:15 p.m.	94231	Jersey City	NJ	Other	UAV	145
8.19.18	10 p.m.	98200	Port Talbot	UK	Triangle	Info Only	148
9.3.18	4:07 p.m.	95976	Perrysville	OH	n/a	UAV	155
9.13.18	8:15 a.m.	94937	Hailey	ID	Square/Rectangle	UAV	159
9.25.18	11:15 p.m.	95249	Silvercreek	WA	Egg	UAV	167
10.5.18	8:15 p.m.	95364	Trinidad	CO	Triangle	UAV	174
10.30.18	8:30 p.m.	96033	Jackson Township	NJ	Triangle	UAV	190
11.2.18	9:30 p.m.	96088	Pattaya	Thailand	Triangle	UAV	192
11.7.18	6:02 p.m.	96229	Lacey	WA	Cylinder	UAV	197
11.7.18	9:36 p.m.	96341	Boca Raton	FL	Chevron	UAV	199
11.10.18	2 a.m.	96271	Lonsdale	MN	Triangle	UAV	203

EVENT	TIME	CASE	CITY	STATE-COUNTRY	SHAPE	DISPOSITION	PAGE
11.11.18	n/a	96316	Taylorsville	UT	Triangle	Other	205
11.28.18	5:20 p.m.	96641	Unknown	Philippines	Unknown	Other	213
12.12.18	6:52 p.m.	96983	St. Louis	MO	Triangle	UAV	227
12.28.18	1:10 a.m.	97282	Shrewsbury	UK	Chevron	Info Only	230
Color, blue							
1.24.18	8:04 p.m.	89841	Glasgow	UK	Blimp	Other	19
5.4.18	2:52 a.m.	91780	Enterprise	UT	Saturn-like	UAV	73
5.11.18	10:20 a.m.	91939	Esquimalt	BC CA	Cigar	Info Only	74
7.23.18	6:30 p.m.	93587	Seattle	WA.	Circle	Other	126
9.8.18	n/a	96379	Wilmington	NC	Sphere	Other	156
9.23.18	5:40 p.m.	95215	London	UK	Triangle	UAV	165
10.26.18	11 p.m.	95886	Philadelphia	PA	Cylinder	UAV	186
Color, brown							
4.10.18	12 p.m.	93224	Nakhon Nayok	Thailand	Square/Rectangle	UAV	62
5.25.18	8:30 p.m.	94857	Poulsbo	WA	Square/Rectangle	UAV	80
Color, fluorescent							
1.6.18	1:50 p.m.	89370	Darlington	UK	Triangle	Info Only	12
Color, gold							
2.10.18	11:15 a.m.	90355	Granbury	TX	Triangle/Disc	UAV	30
4.7.18	1:30 a.m.	96086	Warracknabeal	Australia	Disc	UAV	59
4.17.18	10:45 p.m.	91485	Osceola	IN	Cylinder	UAV	64
Color, gray							
1.1.18	12:05 a.m.	89317	Las Vegas	NV	Disc	UAV	8
1.3.18	6:40 p.m.	89327	Marina	CA	Sphere	Other	10
1.24.18	8:04 p.m.	89841	Glasgow	UK	Blimp	Other	19
1.17.18	3:35 a.m.	89653	Hemel Hempstead	UK	Triangle	UAV	18
2.10.18	11:15 a.m.	90355	Granbury	TX	Triangle/Disc	UAV	30
2.12.18	8:05 p.m.	90205	St. Peters	MO	Square/Rectangle	UAV	31
3.11.18	10 p.m.	90789	Munroe Falls	OH	Triangle	UAV	47
5.11.18	10:20 a.m.	91939	Esquimalt	BC CA	Cigar	Info Only	74
6.6.18	1 p.m.	97168	Plymouth	MA	Blimp	Info Only	90

EVENT	TIME	CASE	CITY	STATE-COUNTRY	SHAPE	DISPOSITION	PAGE
6.7.18	10:05 p.m.	92560	Dallas	OR	Square/Rectangle	UAV	91
8.10.18	7:19 p.m.	94038	Hammond	IN	Blimp	UAV	135
9.1.18	4:20 a.m.	94960	Porter	TX	Boomerang	UAV	154
10.22.18	9:30 a.m.	95806	Pass Christian	MS	Blimp	UAV	183
10.25.18	6:30 p.m.	96048	Dilles Bottom	OH	Egg	UAV	184
11.11.18	7:05 p.m.	96314	London	Canada	Triangle	UAV	204
Color, green							
1.6.18	1:50 p.m.	89370	Darlington	UK	Triangle	Info Only	12
10.26.18	11 p.m.	95886	Philadelphia	PA	Cylinder	UAV	186
Color, metal							
1.3.18	9:30 p.m.	89610	St. Charles	IL	Cigar	UAV	11
Color, orange							
2.15.18	9:30 p.m.	91313	Woodstock	GA	Cylinder	UAV	33
4.17.18	9 p.m.	91498	Lakeland	FL	Sphere	Other	63
6.9.18	9:15 p.m.	92639	Daytona Beach	FL	Sphere	UAV	94
6.10.18	10:30 p.m.	92641	Attleboro	MA	n/a	Other	95
7.18.18	9 p.m.	93459	North Las Vegas	NV	Sphere	Other	123
8.3.18	11 p.m.	94007	Newport	OR	Other	UAV	131
8.27.18	11:05 p.m.	94482	Eatonville	WA	Sphere	Other	150
9.10.18	10:30 p.m.	98808	Colby	WI	Sphere	Other	157
11.14.18	7:24 p.m.	96378	Caroga Lake	NY	Circle	UAV	206
12.4.18	6:30 a.m.	96843	Beaconsfield	UK	Disc	UAV	217
12.4.18	8:30 p.m.	96829	Orwigsburg	PA	Triangle	UAV	218
Color, red							
1.26.18	8:15 p.m.	91153	Unknown	UK	Sphere	UAV	20
3.31.18	9:55 p.m.	91151	Aiken	SC	Circle	Other	55
6.9.18	9:15 p.m.	92639	Daytona Beach	FL	Sphere	UAV	94
9.10.18	10:30 p.m.	98808	Colby	WI	Sphere	Other	157
9.12.18	1:15 a.m.	94839	Hurricane	WV	Sphere	UAV	157
10.26.18	11 p.m.	95886	Philadelphia	PA	Cylinder	UAV	186
12.12.18	3 a.m.	96955	St. Jacob	IL	n/a	Other	226
Color, silver							
2.08.18	1:07 p.m.	94350	Valley	WA	Disc	UAV	26
3.10.18	9:30 p.m.	90968	Dover	DE	Bowl	UAV	46
4.22.18	5:20 p.m.	91572	Brooklyn	NY	Saturn-like	UAV	67

EVENT	TIME	CASE	CITY	STATE-COUNTRY	SHAPE	DISPOSITION	PAGE
4.25.18	2:30 p.m.	91628	Webster	TX	Circle	UAV	68
5.18.18	4:25 a.m.	98601	Ballymahon Co. Lonford	Ireland	Saturn-like	Other	78
6.4.18	n/a	97913	Leesburg	VA	Sphere	UAV	90
6.4.18	n/a	97913	Leesburg	VA	Sphere	UAV	90
8.8.18	9:45 a.m.	94049	Sunset Hills	MO	Diamond	UAV	133
8.15.18	3:45 p.m.	94170	Pensacola	FL	Bullet/Missile	UAV	140
8.21.18	2:30 p.m.	94322	Farmington	WI	Other	UAV	148
9.21.18	8 p.m.	98732	Sonoita	AZ	Teardrop	UAV	164
10.23.18	12:52 p.m.	95826	California	PA	Disc	UAV	184
10.26.18	11 p.m.	95886	Philadelphia	PA	Cylinder	UAV	186
11.4.18	3:20 p.m.	96375	Luray	VA	Disc	UAV	193
12.3.18	8:35 a.m.	96755	Toms Brook	VA	Cylinder	UAV	216
12.4.18	2 p.m.	96813	Olympia	WA	Egg	UAV	218
Color, white							
3.3.18	5:35 a.m.	90540	Birmingham	AL	Triangle	UAV	39
3.6.18	10:42 a.m.	93750	West Jordan	UT	Cylinder	UAV	41
3.30.18	4:30 a.m.	91184	Excelsior Springs	MO	Triangle	UAV	54
4.15.18	1 p.m.	94668	Arncliffe	Australia	Egg	UAV	63
6.24.18	1:51 a.m.	92893	Anchorage County	AK	Sphere	UAV	107
7.9.18	n/a	96065	San Antonio	TX	Triangle	Other	116
7.11.18	9 a.m.	93427	Pendleton	OR	Cone	UAV	118
7.11.18	10:45 a.m.	93419	Pendleton	OR	Other	UAV	118
8.17.18	1:30 a.m.	97678	Key West	FL	Circle	Other	143
9.14.18	3:28 p.m.	94892	Santa Fe	NM	Disc	Info Only	160
10.17.18	6:15 p.m.	95653	Richmond	VA	Cylinder	UAV	181
10.23.18	12:52 p.m.	95826	California	PA	Disc	UAV	184
11.15.18	2:46 p.m.	97141	Everett	WA	Other	UAV	207
Light color, amber							
6.27.18	10 p.m.	92964	Mesquite	NV	Cigar	UAV	110
Light color, blue							
1.3.18	6:40 p.m.	89327	Marina	CA	Sphere	Other	10
1.17.18	3:35 a.m.	89653	Hemel Hempstead	UK	Triangle	UAV	18

EVENT	TIME	CASE	CITY	STATE-COUNTRY	SHAPE	DISPOSITION	PAGE
2.09.18	11:18 p.m.	90175	Derry	PA	Semi-Diamond	Other	29
3.6.18	10:42 a.m.	93750	West Jordan	UT	Cylinder	UAV	41
3.11.18	10 p.m.	90789	Munroe Falls	OH	Triangle	UAV	47
3.22.18	10:37 p.m.	90959	Chatsworth	GA	Triangle	UAV	51
3.29.18	5:30 p.m.	92167	Dublin	Ireland	Triangle	Info Only	53
5.11.18	11:45 p.m.	91968	North Plainfield	NJ	Unknown	Other	75
6.21.18	10:58 p.m.	92852	New Brighten	MN	Disc	UAV	103
10.3.18	9:40 p.m.	98214	Orem	UT	Cigar	UAV	171
Light color, gold							
4.22.18	5:20 p.m.	91572	Brooklyn	NY	Saturn-like	UAV	67
Light color, green							
2.09.18	11:18 p.m.	90175	Derry	PA	Semi-Diamond	Other	29
2.26.18	3:47 p.m.	90708	Wilmington	CA	Saturn-like	UAV	37
3.29.18	5:30 p.m.	92167	Dublin	Ireland	Triangle	Info Only	53
4.21.18	10:20 p.m.	91559	Irondequoit	NY	Chevron	UAV	66
5.4.18	2:52 a.m.	91780	Enterprise	UT	Saturn-like	UAV	73
5.22.18	8:12 p.m.	92950	Hudson	IL	Other	Other	79
6.10.18	10:27 p.m.	92653	Blackstone	MA	Unknown	UAV	95
6.11.18	2:11 a.m.	92673	North Las Vegas	NV	Other	UAV	96
6.21.18	10:58 p.m.	92852	New Brighten	MN	Disc	UAV	103
10.16.18	9:53 p.m.	95874	Midwest	WY	Sphere	UAV	180
11.6.18	5:54 p.m.	96200	Hattiesburg	MS	Triangle	UAV	194
11.7.18	6:02 p.m.	96229	Lacey	WA	Cylinder	UAV	197
11.8.18	7:30 p.m.	96310	Apex	NC	Other	UAV	201
11.25.18	8:15 p.m.	96616	Galway City	Ireland	N/A	UAV	210
11.27.18	8 p.m.	97510	Santee	CA	Triangle	Info Only	212
12.1.18	12:00 a.m.	96805	McKinney	TX	Oval	UAV	214
Light color, lead							
1.3.18	6:40 p.m.	89327	Marina	CA	Sphere	Other	10
Light color, multiple							
5.3.18	10:28 p.m.	91773	Caverna	MO	Oval	UAV	72
Light color, orange							
1.6.18	10 p.m.	89385	Logan	UT	Diamond	Other	13

EVENT	TIME	CASE	CITY	STATE-COUNTRY	SHAPE	DISPOSITION	PAGE
2.09.18	11:18 p.m.	90175	Derry	PA	Semi-Diamond	Other	29
4.1.18	6:02 p.m.	91199	New Port Richey	FL	Disc	UAV	57
5.1.18	11:30 p.m.	92298	London	UK	Triangle	UAV	71
5.1.18	n/a	91829	Loxley	AL	Circle	Other	72
5.4.18	2:52 a.m.	91780	Enterprise	UT	Saturn-like	UAV	73
5.18.18	4:25 a.m.	98601	Ballymahon Co. Lonford	Ireland	Saturn-like	Other	78
7.2.18	9:55 p.m.	94741	Carmel	IN	Cigar	Other	114
7.15.18	8:06 p.m.	93445	Niagara Falls	Canada	Sphere	Other	120
9.7.18	1:30 a.m.	94837	Kos Town	Greece	Chevron	UAV	155
12.6.18	7:12 p.m.	97119	Red Bluff	CA	Triangle	UAV	221
Light color, pink							
3.6.18	10:42 a.m.	93750	West Jordan	UT	Cylinder	UAV	41
5.18.18	4:25 a.m.	98601	Ballymahon Co. Lonford	Ireland	Saturn-like	Other	78
Light color, red							
1.3.18	6:40 p.m.	89327	Marina	CA	Sphere	Other	10
1.4.18	6:25 a.m.	89344	Casselberry	FL	Square/Rectangle	Other	12
1.6.18	10 p.m.	89385	Logan	UT	Diamond	Other	13
1.9.18	8:45 p.m.	89498	Ellensburg	WA	Oval	UAV	15
1.28.18	7:30 p.m.	89867	Buffalo Mills	PA	Triangle	Other	21
1.17.18	3:35 a.m.	89653	Hemel Hempstead	UK	Triangle	UAV	18
2.09.18	11:18 p.m.	90175	Derry	PA	Semi-Diamond	Other	29
2.13.18	10 p.m.	90452	Newbury	UK	Triangle	UAV	33
2.23.18	7:15 p.m.	90404	Summerlin	NV	Triangle		35
3.2.18	8:30 a.m.	94597	Muskegon	MI	Square/Rectangle	UAV	38
3.10.18	11:57 p.m.	90710	Manchester	MD	Triangle	Other	45
3.11.18	10 p.m.	90789	Munroe Falls	OH	Triangle	UAV	47
3.15.18	4 a.m.	97506	Holly Pond	AL	Triangle	UAV	49
3.22.18	10:37 p.m.	90959	Chatsworth	GA	Triangle	UAV	51
4.5.18	09:20 p.m.	91224	Fort Payne	AL	Square/Rectangle	UAV	58

EVENT	TIME	CASE	CITY	STATE-COUNTRY	SHAPE	DISPOSITION	PAGE
4.21.18	9:55 p.m.	91553	Orrington	ME	Triangle	Other	65
5.1.18	11:30 p.m.	92298	London	UK	Triangle	UAV	71
5.4.18	2:52 a.m.	91780	Enterprise	UT	Saturn-like	UAV	73
4.5.18	11:30 p.m.	91263	Reliance	TN	Square/Rectangle	Other	59
5.15.18	9:30 p.m.	92029	Bay Shore	NY	Sphere	Other	77
5.16.18	n/a	92036	Salinas	CA	Triangle	UAV	77
5.18.18	4:25 a.m.	98601	Ballymahon Co. Lonford	Ireland	Saturn-like	Other	78
5.22.18	8:12 p.m.	92950	Hudson	IL	Other	Other	79
6.3.18	1:30 a.m.	92447	Springville	NY	Saturn-like	UAV	86
6.3.18	7:49 p.m.	93607	Dartford	UK	Horseshoe	UAV	88
6.7.18	10:30 p.m.	92568	Colorado Springs	CO	Other	UAV	92
6.9.18	1:15 a.m.	92591	Oelwein	IA	Oval	UAV	93
6.11.18	2:11 a.m.	92673	North Las Vegas	NV	Other	UAV	96
6.21.18	10:58 p.m.	92852	New Brighten	MN	Disc	UAV	103
6.26.18	10:04 p.m.	92936	McMinnville	OR	Oval	Other	108
6.26.18	10:30 p.m.	92957	Fridley	MN	Sphere	Other	108
7.15.18	8:06 p.m.	93445	Niagara Falls	Canada	Sphere	Other	120
7.24.18	2:30 a.m.	93703	Winlock	WA.	Triangle	UAV	126
7.29.18	5:35 a.m.	93741	Hesston	KS	Triangle	UAV	127
8.10.18	9:58 p.m.	94525	Tinley Park	IL	Sphere	UAV	136
8.16.18	n/a	95179	Gig Harbor	WA	Triangle	UAV	142
9.25.18	10:30 p.m.	95703	Lachute	Canada	Disc	UAV	166
10.3.18	9:40 p.m.	98214	Orem	UT	Cigar	UAV	171
10.7.18	7:30 p.m.	95445	Saco	ME	Diamond	UAV	175
10.10.18	4:30 a.m.	95592	Bellingham	WA	Triangle	UAV	175
10.30.18	7:40 p.m.	96019	Benton	OH	Cylinder	UAV	189
10.31.18	9:45 p.m.	96052	Selma	NC	Triangle	UAV	191
11.8.18	7:30 p.m.	96310	Apex	NC	Other	UAV	201
11.11.18	7:05 p.m.	96314	London	Canada	Triangle	UAV	204
11.14.18	7:24 p.m.	96378	Caroga Lake	NY	Circle	UAV	206
11.25.18	8:15 p.m.	96616	Galway City	Ireland	n/a	UAV	210
12.5.18	6:10 p.m.	96818	Baker City	OR	Chevron	UAV	219
12.12.18	6:20 p.m.	97013	Laurel Lake	NJ	n/a	UAV	226

EVENT	TIME	CASE	CITY	STATE-COUNTRY	SHAPE	DISPOSITION	PAGE
Light, turquoise							
4.1.18	6:02 p.m.	91199	New Port Richey	FL	Disc	UAV	57
Light color, white							
1.4.18	6:25 a.m.	89344	Casselberry	FL	Square/ Rectangle	Other	12
1.8.18	5:20 p.m.	89435	Orfordville	WI	Triangle	UAV	14
1.9.18	8:45 p.m.	89498	Ellensburg	WA	Oval	UAV	15
1.24.18	10:30 p.m.	89780	Droitwich Spa	UK	Triangle	Other	19
1.28.18	7:30 p.m.	89867	Buffalo Mills	PA	Triangle	Other	21
2.04.18	6:27 p.m.	90097	Windsor	UK	Triangle	Info Only	25
2.13.18	6:40 p.m.	90221	Grantville	PA	Cigar	UAV	32
2.13.18	10 p.m.	90452	Newbury	UK	Triangle	UAV	33
2.21.18	8:30 p.m.	90647	Rochester	NY	Triangle		35
2.26.18	3:47 p.m.	90708	Wilmington	CA	Saturn-like	UAV	37
3.6.18	9:40 p.m.	90698	Marietta	GA	Other	UAV	42
3.10.18	9:30 p.m.	90968	Dover	DE	Bowl	UAV	46
3.11.18	10 p.m.	90789	Munroe Falls	OH	Triangle	UAV	47
3.22.18	10:37 p.m.	90959	Chatsworth	GA	Triangle	UAV	51
3.29.18	5:30 p.m.	92167	Dublin	Ireland	Triangle	Info Only	53
3.30.18	4:30 a.m.	91184	Excelsior Springs	MO	Triangle	UAV	54
4.17.18	9 p.m.	91498	Lakeland	FL	Sphere	Other	63
4.19.18	10:30 p.m.	91752	Stonehouse	UK	Triangle	Info Only	64
4.21.18	9:55 p.m.	91553	Orrington	ME	Triangle	Other	65
5.3.18	10:28 p.m.	91773	Caverna	MO	Oval	UAV	72
5.11.18	11:45 p.m.	91968	North Plainfield	NJ	Unknown	Other	75
6.2.18	10:15 p.m.	92445	London	Canada	Triangle	UAV	85
6.3.18	1:30 a.m.	92447	Springville	NY	Saturn-like	UAV	86
6.7.18	10:05 p.m.	92560	Dallas	OR	Square/ Rectangle	UAV	91
6.7.18	10:30 p.m.	92568	Colorado Springs	CO	Other	UAV	92
6.9.18	8:32 p.m.	92619	Alexandria	MD	Bullet/ Missile	UAV	94
6.11.18	2:11 a.m.	92673	North Las Vegas	NV	Other	UAV	96

EVENT	TIME	CASE	CITY	STATE-COUNTRY	SHAPE	DISPOSITION	PAGE
6.21.18	n/a	92994	San Felipe Baja Norte	Mexico	Sphere	Other	104
6.27.18	10 p.m.	92964	Mesquite	NV	Cigar	UAV	110
7.29.18	5:35 a.m.	93741	Hesston	KS	Triangle	UAV	127
8.1.18	9:02 p.m.	97862	Breitenbush Hot Springs	OR	Triangle	UAV	129
8.8.18	9:45 a.m.	94049	Sunset Hills	MO	Diamond	UAV	133
8.12.18	12:15 a.m.	97164	Ridgeville	SC	Egg	UAV	139
8.17.18	10:30 p.m.	94217	Portage	IN	Triangle	UAV	144
8.18.18	9:40 p.m.	96784	Cospicua	Malta	Oval	Other	146
9.16.18	1:15 a.m.	94931	Kensington	CA	Unknown	Other	161
9.21.18	8 p.m.	98732	Sonoita	AZ	Teardrop	UAV	164
10.2.18	8:25 p.m.	95323	Toms River	NJ	Triangle	Other	169
10.7.18	7:30 p.m.	95445	Saco	ME	Diamond	UAV	175
10.12.18	1:01 a.m.	95529	Orlando	FL	Triangle	UAV	178
11.3.18	11:59 p.m.	96140	Walker	OR	Saturn-like	UAV	193
11.6.18	5:54 p.m.	96200	Hattiesburg	MS	Triangle	UAV	194
11.6.18	8:25 p.m.	96207	San Antonio	TX	Chevron	UAV	195
11.11.18	7:05 p.m.	96314	London	Canada	Triangle	UAV	204
11.23.18	6:15 p.m.	96580	Edwards	NY	Sphere	UAV	209
12.1.18	12:00 a.m.	96805	McKinney	TX	Oval	UAV	214
12.5.18	6:10 p.m.	96818	Baker City	OR	Chevron	UAV	219
12.10.18	8:45 p.m.	97001	Scott Depot	WV	Boomerang	UAV	224
12.12.18	6:52 p.m.	96983	St. Louis	MO	Triangle	UAV	227
12.28.18	1:10 a.m.	97282	Shrewsbury	UK	Chevron	Info Only	230
Light color, yellow							
2.08.18	8:30 p.m.	90133	Mena	AR	Triangle	UAV	27
2.13.18	10 p.m.	90452	Newbury	UK	Triangle	UAV	33
10.30.18	7:40 p.m.	96019	Benton	OH	Cylinder	UAV	189
11.23.18	6:15 p.m.	96580	Edwards	NY	Sphere	UAV	209
Light intensity, no light							
1.1.18	12:05 a.m.	89317	Las Vegas	NV	Disc	UAV	8
Light motion, blinking							
1.28.18	7:30 p.m.	89867	Buffalo Mills	PA	Triangle	Other	21
2.12.18	8:05 p.m.	90205	St. Peters	MO	Square/Rectangle	UAV	31

EVENT	TIME	CASE	CITY	STATE-COUNTRY	SHAPE	DISPOSITION	PAGE
3.10.18	11:57 p.m.	90710	Manchester	MD	Triangle	Other	45
3.10.18	4 a.m.	95178	Woodstock	NY	Diamond	UAV	46
3.15.18	4 a.m.	97506	Holly Pond	AL	Triangle	UAV	49
4.5.18	09:20 p.m.	91224	Fort Payne	AL	Square/Rectangle	UAV	58
6.21.18	10:58 p.m.	92852	New Brighten	MN	Disc	UAV	103
Light motion, flashing							
1.3.18	6:40 p.m.	89327	Marina	CA	Sphere	Other	10
1.4.18	6:25 a.m.	89344	Casselberry	FL	Square/Rectangle	Other	12
1.8.18	5:20 p.m.	89435	Orfordville	WI	Triangle	UAV	14
1.17.18	3:35 a.m.	89653	Hemel Hempstead	UK	Triangle	UAV	18
2.13.18	10 p.m.	90452	Newbury	UK	Triangle	UAV	33
3.14.18	5:38 p.m.	90776	Port Huron	MI	Square/Rectangle	Other	48
3.22.18	10:37 p.m.	90959	Chatsworth	GA	Triangle	UAV	51
3.30.18	4:30 a.m.	91184	Excelsior Springs	MO	Triangle	UAV	54
4.5.18	11:30 p.m.	91263	Reliance	TN	Square/Rectangle	Other	59
5.15.18	9:30 p.m.	92029	Bay Shore	NY	Sphere	Other	77
6.7.18	10:30 p.m.	92568	Colorado Springs	CO	Other	UAV	92
6.26.18	10:04 p.m.	92936	McMinnville	OR	Oval	Other	108
8.1.18	9:02 p.m.	97862	Breitenbush Hot Springs	OR	Triangle	UAV	129
9.18.18	12:25 p.m.	94996	Vancouver	WA	Unknown	UAV	162
10.12.18	1:01 a.m.	95590	Citrus Heights	CA	Triangle	UAV	177
10.30.18	7:40 p.m.	96019	Benton	OH	Cylinder	UAV	189
10.30.18	8:30 p.m.	96033	Jackson Township	NJ	Triangle	UAV	190
11.6.18	8:25 p.m.	96207	San Antonio	TX	Chevron	UAV	195
11.11.18	7:05 p.m.	96314	London	Canada	Triangle	UAV	204
11.25.18	8:15 p.m.	96616	Galway City	Ireland	n/a	UAV	210
12.1.18	12:00 a.m.	96805	McKinney	TX	Oval	UAV	214
Object motion, flickered							
10.25.18	7:10 p.m.	95880	Montazuma	NY	Teardrop	UAV	185

EVENT	TIME	CASE	CITY	STATE-COUNTRY	SHAPE	DISPOSITION	PAGE
Light motion, glowing							
5.18.18	4:25 a.m.	98601	Ballymahon Co. Lonford	Ireland	Saturn-like	Other	78
6.26.18	10:04 p.m.	92936	McMinnville	OR	Oval	Other	108
7.2.18	9:55 p.m.	94741	Carmel	IN	Cigar	Other	114
8.6.18	10:15 p.m.	93940	Waterloo	IA	Circle	UAV	132
8.18.18	9:40 p.m.	96784	Cospicua	Malta	Oval	Other	146
10.23.18	12:52 p.m.	95826	California	PA	Disc	UAV	184
10.26.18	11 p.m.	95886	Philadelphia	PA	Cylinder	UAV	186
10.26.18	11:10 p.m.	96858	Reykjavik	Iceland	Circle	Other	187
11.3.18	11:59 p.m.	96140	Walker	OR	Saturn-like	UAV	193
11.6.18	9 p.m.	96312	Boise	ID	Boomerang	UAV	195
Light motion, pulsating							
1.9.18	7:05 p.m.	89450	Wrightsville	PA	Triangle	UAV	14
1.9.18	8:45 p.m.	89498	Ellensburg	WA	Oval	UAV	15
3.10.18	9:30 p.m.	90968	Dover	DE	Bowl	UAV	46
3.29.18	5:30 p.m.	92167	Dublin	Ireland	Triangle	Info Only	53
4.10.18	2:30 a.m.	96307	Bromsgrove	UK	Unknown	UAV	60
6.3.18	1:30 a.m.	92447	Springville	NY	Saturn-like	UAV	86
6.27.18	10 p.m.	92964	Mesquite	NV	Cigar	UAV	110
9.18.18	12:25 p.m.	94996	Vancouver	WA	Unknown	UAV	162
10.3.18	7:30 p.m.	96637	New Lisbon	NJ	Triangle	UAV	170
10.18.18	8:25 p.m.	95673	Mercaston	UK	Sphere	UAV	182
Light motion, ripple							
6.9.18	8:32 p.m.	92619	Alexandria	MD	Bullet/Missile	UAV	94
Light motion, shimmering							
5.11.18	11:45 p.m.	91968	North Plainfield	NJ	Unknown	Other	75
5.18.18	4:25 a.m.	98601	Ballymahon Co. Lonford	Ireland	Saturn-like	Other	78
Light motion, strobing							
4.21.18	9:55 p.m.	91553	Orrington	ME	Triangle	Other	65
Movement, bumblebee							
12.4.18	2 p.m.	96813	Olympia	WA	Egg	UAV	218
Movement, disappeared in place							
2.04.18	1:38 a.m.	90057	Mt. Pleasant	PA	Sphere	Other	23

EVENT	TIME	CASE	CITY	STATE-COUNTRY	SHAPE	DISPOSITION	PAGE
6.20.18	8:20 p.m.	92828	Pasco	WA	Sphere	UAV	102
Movement, falling leaf or feather							
7.9.18	n/a	96065	San Antonio	TX	Triangle	Other	116
7.17.18	10:40 p.m.	93540	Brookport	IL	Cylinder	UAV	121
Movement, floated							
7.11.18	9 a.m.	93427	Pendleton	OR	Cone	UAV	118
Movement, glided							
3.29.18	5:30 p.m.	92167	Dublin	Ireland	Triangle	Info Only	53
Movement, rotated							
2.12.18	8:05 p.m.	90205	St. Peters	MO	Square/Rectangle	UAV	31
3.11.18	10 p.m.	90789	Munroe Falls	OH	Triangle	UAV	47
4.10.18	12 p.m.	93224	Nakhon Nayok	Thailand	Square/Rectangle	UAV	62
5.1.18	11:30 p.m.	92298	London	UK	Triangle	UAV	71
6.11.18	2:11 a.m.	92673	North Las Vegas	NV	Other	UAV	96
7.10.18	8:50 p.m.	93369	Newmarket	Canada	Cylinder	UAV	117
8.30.18	9:30 p.m.	94524	Funchal	Portugal	Triangle	UAV	152
11.5.18	10:30 p.m.	96204	Newport	OR	Triangle	UAV	194
Movement, shot away							
6.3.18	6:45 a.m.	92469	Panola County	MS	Cylinder	UAV	87
6.9.18	9:15 p.m.	92639	Daytona Beach	FL	Sphere	UAV	94
Movement, side-to-side							
11.25.18	8:15 p.m.	96616	Galway City	Ireland	n/a	UAV	210
12.4.18	8:30 p.m.	96829	Orwigsburg	PA	Triangle	UAV	218
Movement, skipped							
7.2.18	2:30 p.m.	93418	Gustine	CA.	Triangle	UAV	114
Movement, spinning							
6.17.18	11:40 p.m.	92802	Ada County	ID	Other	UAV	99
8.12.18	n/a	94105	Los Lunas	NM	Sphere	Other	138
Movement, swirling							
1.26.18	8:15 p.m.	91153	Unknown	UK	Sphere	UAV	20
Movement, tumbling							
11.25.18	8:45 a.m.	96586	Gorey	Ireland	Diamond	Other	210
Movement, twisting and turning							
6.3.18	7:49 p.m.	93607	Dartford	UK	Horseshoe	UAV	88

EVENT	TIME	CASE	CITY	STATE-COUNTRY	SHAPE	DISPOSITION	PAGE
Movement, weaving motion							
12.4.18	2 p.m.	96813	Olympia	WA	Egg	UAV	218
Movement, wobble							
4.22.18	5:20 p.m.	91572	Brooklyn	NY	Saturn-like	UAV	67
Multiple							
1.1.18	12:05 a.m.	89317	Las Vegas	NV	Disc	UAV	8
1.1.18	5:30 p.m.	89276	Lowell	MA	Other	UAV	9
1.3.18	6:40 p.m.	89327	Marina	CA	Sphere	Other	10
1.6.18	1:50 p.m.	89370	Darlington	UK	Triangle	Info Only	12
1.9.18	7:05 p.m.	89450	Wrightsville	PA	Triangle	UAV	14
1.26.18	8:15 p.m.	91153	Unknown	UK	Sphere	UAV	20
2.04.18	1:38 a.m.	90057	Mt. Pleasant	PA	Sphere	Other	23
2.04.18	6:27 p.m.	90097	Windsor	UK	Triangle	Info Only	25
2.08.18	8:30 p.m.	90133	Mena	AR	Triangle	UAV	27
2.10.18	11:15 a.m.	90355	Granbury	TX	Triangle/Disc	UAV	30
2.12.18	8:05 p.m.	90205	St. Peters	MO	Square/Rectangle	UAV	31
3.6.18	10:42 a.m.	93750	West Jordan	UT	Cylinder	UAV	41
3.7.18	10:34 a.m.	90628	Gonzales County	TX	Cylinder	Other	44
3.10.18	9:30 p.m.	90968	Dover	DE	Bowl	UAV	46
3.16.18	9:48 p.m.	90816	Attica	IN	Triangle	UAV	50
5.11.18	10:20 a.m.	91939	Esquimalt	BC CA	Cigar	Info Only	74
5.15.18	9:30 p.m.	92029	Bay Shore	NY	Sphere	Other	77
6.4.18	n/a	97913	Leesburg	VA	Sphere	UAV	90
6.7.18	10:30 p.m.	92568	Colorado Springs	CO	Other	UAV	92
6.11.18	2:11 a.m.	92673	North Las Vegas	NV	Other	UAV	96
6.19.18	7:30 p.m.	92803	Lower Burrell	PA	Cylinder	UAV	101
6.20.18	3:15 p.m.	92849	Egg Harbor Township	NJ	Sphere	UAV	102
6.24.18	n/a	95063	Medellin	Columbia	Diamond	UAV	106
6.26.18	10:30 p.m.	92957	Fridley	MN	Sphere	Other	108
7.3.18	1:30 a.m.	93128	Wrexham	UK	Orb	UAV	115
7.18.18	2:06 p.m.	93708	Hood River	OR	Cigar	UAV	122

EVENT	TIME	CASE	CITY	STATE-COUNTRY	SHAPE	DISPOSITION	PAGE
7.22.18	10 p.m.	93687	Anaheim	CA	Triangle	UAV	125
8.10.18	9:58 p.m.	94525	Tinley Park	IL	Sphere	UAV	136
8.15.18	10:30 p.m.	94184	Staten Island	NY	Disc	Other	141
8.17.18	1:30 a.m.	97678	Key West	FL	Circle	Other	143
8.18.18	6:35 p.m.	94292	Flint	TX	Cigar	UAV	145
8.27.18	11:05 p.m.	94482	Eatonville	WA	Sphere	Other	150
9.12.18	n/a	95268	Ancaster	Canada	Triangle	UAV	158
9.13.18	9 p.m.	94903	Columbus	IN	Triangle	UAV	160
9.14.18	8:15 a.m.	95265	Santa Elena	Costa Rica	Disc	UAV	160
9.14.18	3:28 p.m.	94892	Santa Fe	NM	Disc	Info Only	160
9.24.18	6:45 p.m.	95317	Baldwinsville	NY	Sphere	Other	165
10.12.18	1:01 a.m.	95529	Orlando	FL	Triangle	UAV	178
10.16.18	9:53 p.m.	95874	Midwest	WY	Sphere	UAV	180
10.22.18	9:30 a.m.	95806	Pass Christian	MS	Blimp	UAV	183
10.23.18	12:52 p.m.	95826	California	PA	Disc	UAV	184
11.7.18	12 p.m.	96230	Las Vegas	NV	Sphere	Other	196
11.14.18	7:24 p.m.	96378	Caroga Lake	NY	Circle	UAV	206
11.28.18	5:20 p.m.	96641	Unknown	Philippines	Unknown	Other	213
12.3.18	8:35 a.m.	96755	Toms Brook	VA	Cylinder	UAV	216
12.4.18	2 p.m.	96813	Olympia	WA	Egg	UAV	218
12.5.18	6:10 p.m.	96818	Baker City	OR	Chevron	UAV	219
12.12.18	6:20 p.m.	97013	Laurel Lake	NJ	N/A	UAV	226
12.14.18	9 p.m.	97555	Punta Cana	Dominican Republic	Other	UAV	227

Shape, barbell

EVENT	TIME	CASE	CITY	STATE-COUNTRY	SHAPE	DISPOSITION	PAGE
6.7.18	10:30 p.m.	92568	Colorado Springs	CO	Other	UAV	92

Shape, bell

EVENT	TIME	CASE	CITY	STATE-COUNTRY	SHAPE	DISPOSITION	PAGE
8.3.18	11 p.m.	94007	Newport	OR	Other	UAV	131
11.23.18	4:55 a.m.	96554	Ballivor	Ireland	Triangle	Other	208

Shape, black wing

EVENT	TIME	CASE	CITY	STATE-COUNTRY	SHAPE	DISPOSITION	PAGE
1.2.18	5:20 p.m.	89280	Northampton	MA	Boomerang	UAV	10

Shape, blimp

EVENT	TIME	CASE	CITY	STATE-COUNTRY	SHAPE	DISPOSITION	PAGE
6.19.18	11:15 a.m.	92800	Warrento	MO	Blimp	UAV	100
10.11.18	6:24 p.m.	95738	Carrollton	GA	Blimp	UAV	177
10.22.18	9:30 a.m.	95806	Pass Christian	MS	Blimp	UAV	183

EVENT	TIME	CASE	CITY	STATE-COUNTRY	SHAPE	DISPOSITION	PAGE
Shape, boomerang							
3.26.18	3:15 a.m.	91194	Bridgeville	PA	Boomerang	UAV	52
9.1.18	4:20 a.m.	94960	Porter	TX	Boomerang	UAV	154
10.4.18	8:57 p.m.	95343	Rancho Mirage	CA	Boomerang	UAV	173
10.13.18	8:58 p.m.	98344	Stoney Creek	Canada	Boomerang	UAV	179
11.6.18	9 p.m.	96312	Boise	ID	Boomerang	UAV	195
11.26.18	8:02 p.m.	96643	Columbia	MO	Boomerang	UAV	212
12.10.18	8:45 p.m.	97001	Scott Depot	WV	Boomerang	UAV	224
Shape, bowl							
3.10.18	9:30 p.m.	90968	Dover	DE	Bowl	UAV	46
Shape, chevron							
1.13.18	9:05 p.m.	89544	Indianapolis	IN	Chevron	Info Only	17
4.21.18	10:20 p.m.	91559	Irondequoit	NY	Chevron	UAV	66
9.7.18	1:30 a.m.	94837	Kos Town	Greece	Chevron	UAV	155
11.6.18	8:25 p.m.	96207	San Antonio	TX	Chevron	UAV	195
11.7.18	9:30 p.m.	96766	Valrico	FL	Chevron	UAV	198
11.7.18	9:36 p.m.	96341	Boca Raton	FL	Chevron	UAV	199
11.11.18	2:40 a.m.	96450	Jefferson City	MO	Chevron	UAV	204
12.5.18	6:10 p.m.	96818	Baker City	OR	Chevron	UAV	219
12.6.18	5:35 p.m.	96850	Memphis	TN	Chevron	Other	220
12.28.18	1:10 a.m.	97282	Shrewsbury	UK	Chevron	Info Only	230
Shape, cigar							
1.3.18	9:30 p.m.	89610	Saint Charles	IL	Cigar	UAV	11
2.13.18	6:40 p.m.	90221	Grantville	PA	Cigar	UAV	32
5.11.18	10:20 a.m.	91939	Esquimalt	BC CA	Cigar	Info Only	74
5.13.18	5:05 p.m.	92110	Garrett	IN	Cigar	UAV	75
6.6.18	1 p.m.	97168	Plymouth	MA	Blimp	Info Only	90
6.27.18	10 p.m.	92964	Mesquite	NV	Cigar	UAV	110
7.2.18	9:55 p.m.	94741	Carmel	IN	Cigar	Other	114
7.18.18	2:06 p.m.	93708	Hood River	OR	Cigar	UAV	122
8.12.18	2:10 a.m.	94081	Godfrey	IL	Cigar	UAV	137
10.3.18	9:40 p.m.	98214	Orem	UT	Cigar	UAV	171
10.10.18	2:27 p.m.	95682	Atlanta	GA	Cigar	UAV	176
10.17.18	6:15 p.m.	95653	Richmond	VA	Cylinder	UAV	181
11.12.18	7:20 p.m.	96353	Phoenix	AZ	Cigar	UAV	205

EVENT	TIME	CASE	CITY	STATE-COUNTRY	SHAPE	DISPOSITION	PAGE
12.7.18	9:25 p.m.	96890	Wellington	UT	Cigar	UAV	221
Shape, circle							
1.24.18	n/a	89785	Great Falls	MT	Circle	Info Only	20
3.31.18	9:55 p.m.	91151	Aiken	SC	Circle	Other	55
5.1.18	n/a	91829	Loxley	AL	Circle	Other	72
6.28.18	11:15 p.m.	93454	Buckeye	AZ	Circle	UAV	110
8.6.18	10:15 p.m.	93940	Waterloo	IA	Circle	UAV	132
8.17.18	1:30 a.m.	97678	Key West	FL	Circle	Other	143
10.26.18	11:10 p.m.	96858	Reykjavik	Iceland	Circle	Other	187
11.14.18	7:24 p.m.	96378	Caroga Lake	NY	Circle	UAV	206
Shape, cone							
7.11.18	9 a.m.	93427	Pendleton	OR	Cone	UAV	118
9.17.18	9:42 p.m.	94983	Highlands Ranch	CO	Cone	UAV	161
Shape, cross							
6.11.18	2:11 a.m.	92673	North Las Vegas	NV	Other	UAV	96
Shape, cube							
6.17.18	11:40 p.m.	92802	Ada County	ID	Other	UAV	99
Shape, cylinder							
2.15.18	9:30 p.m.	91313	Woodstock	GA	Cylinder	UAV	33
3.7.18	10:34 a.m.	90628	Gonzales County	TX	Cylinder	Other	44
4.17.18	10:45 p.m.	91485	Osceola	IN	Cylinder	UAV	64
4.5.18	11:30 p.m.	91263	Reliance	TN	Square/Rectangle	Other	59
6.3.18	6:45 a.m.	92469	Panola County	MS	Cylinder	UAV	87
7.10.18	8:50 p.m.	93369	Newmarket	Canada	Cylinder	UAV	117
8.18.18	6:35 p.m.	94292	Flint	TX	Cigar	UAV	145
10.26.18	11 p.m.	95886	Philadelphia	PA	Cylinder	UAV	186
10.30.18	7:40 p.m.	96019	Benton	OH	Cylinder	UAV	189
11.7.18	6:02 p.m.	96229	Lacey	WA	Cylinder	UAV	197
12.3.18	8:35 a.m.	96755	Toms Brook	VA	Cylinder	UAV	216
Shape, delta							
2.10.18	11:15 a.m.	90355	Granbury	TX	Triangle/Disc	UAV	30

EVENT	TIME	CASE	CITY	STATE-COUNTRY	SHAPE	DISPOSITION	PAGE
Shape, diamond							
2.09.18	11:18 p.m.	90175	Derry	PA	Semi-Diamond	Other	29
3.6.18	9:40 p.m.	90698	Marietta	GA	Other	UAV	42
3.10.18	4 a.m.	95178	Woodstock	NY	Diamond	UAV	46
6.11.18	2:11 a.m.	92673	North Las Vegas	NV	Other	UAV	96
6.24.18	n/a	95063	Medellin	Columbia	Diamond	UAV	106
7.10.18	7:35 a.m.	93256	Deland	FL	Diamond	UAV	116
8.8.18	9:45 a.m.	94049	Sunset Hills	MO	Diamond	UAV	133
10.4.18	8 p.m.	95356	Sammamish	WA	Diamond	Other	172
10.7.18	7:30 p.m.	95445	Saco	ME	Diamond	UAV	175
11.8.18	7:30 p.m.	96310	Apex	NC	Other	UAV	201
11.13.18	6:23 p.m.	96764	Labadee	Haiti	Diamond	UAV	206
11.25.18	8:45 a.m.	96586	Gorey	Ireland	Diamond	Other	210
Shape, disc							
1.1.18	12:05 a.m.	89317	Las Vegas	NV	Disc	UAV	8
2.08.18	1:07 p.m.	94350	Valley	WA	Disc	UAV	26
2.10.18	11:15 a.m.	90355	Granbury	TX	Triangle/Disc	UAV	30
2.26.18	3:47 p.m.	90708	Wilmington	CA	Saturn-like	UAV	37
3.3.18	11:30 p.m.	90584	Elkhorn	NE	Disc	UAV	40
4.1.18	6:02 p.m.	91199	New Port Richey	FL	Disc	UAV	57
4.2.18	10:27 p.m.	91182	Banja Luka	Bosnia & Herzegovina	Disc	Info Only	58
4.7.18	1:30 a.m.	96086	Warracknabeal	Australia	Disc	UAV	59
4.22.18	5:20 p.m.	91572	Brooklyn	NY	Saturn-like	UAV	67
5.29.18	8:50 p.m.	92387	Kronberg im Taunus	Germany	Disc	UAV	81
6.2.18	3:10 p.m.	92499	Crieff, Scotland	UK	Disc	UAV	84
6.21.18	10:58 p.m.	92852	New Brighten	MN	Disc	UAV	103
6.26.18	12 a.m.	95960	Noxon	MT	Disc	Other	109
7.22.18	1:42 p.m.	93732	Darrington	WA.	Disc	UAV	124
8.15.18	10:30 p.m.	94184	Staten Island	NY	Disc	Other	141
9.14.18	8:15 a.m.	95265	Santa Elena	Costa Rica	Disc	UAV	160
9.14.18	3:28 p.m.	94892	Santa Fe	NM	Disc	Info Only	160

EVENT	TIME	CASE	CITY	STATE-COUNTRY	SHAPE	DISPOSITION	PAGE
9.20.18	7:45 p.m.	95065	Unknown	UK	Disc	UAV	163
10.22.18	9:30 a.m.	95806	Pass Christian	MS	Blimp	UAV	183
10.23.18	12:52 p.m.	95826	California	PA	Disc	UAV	184
10.25.18	6:30 p.m.	96048	Dilles Bottom	OH	Egg	UAV	184
10.30.18	2 a.m.	96776	Tecumseh	MI	Disc	Other	188
11.4.18	3:20 p.m.	96375	Luray	VA	Disc	UAV	193
11.7.18	10:40 p.m.	97286	Duluth	MN	Oval	UAV	200
12.4.18	6:30 a.m.	96843	Beaconsfield	UK	Disc	UAV	217
Shape, Donut							
1.6.18	1:50 p.m.	89370	Darlington	UK	Triangle	Info Only	12
8.12.18	n/a	94105	Los Lunas	NM	Sphere	Other	138
Shape, egg							
8.12.18	12:15 a.m.	97164	Ridgeville	SC	Egg	UAV	139
9.25.18	11:15 p.m.	95249	Silvercreek	WA	Egg	UAV	167
Shape, giant moth							
8.28.18	4:15 a.m.	94461	Las Vegas	NV	Triangle	Other	151
Shape, globe							
7.19.18	9:30 p.m.	97557	Mount Washington	KY	Sphere	Other	123
Shape, half moon							
3.10.18	9:30 p.m.	90968	Dover	DE	Bowl	UAV	46
Shape, horseshoe							
6.3.18	7:49 p.m.	93607	Dartford	UK	Horseshoe	UAV	88
Shape, lunar lander							
4.22.18	5:14 p.m.	91575	Manheim	PA	Other	Other	67
Shape, missile							
6.9.18	8:32 p.m.	92619	Alexandria	MD	Bullet/Missile	UAV	94
8.15.18	3:45 p.m.	94170	Pensacola	FL	Bullet/Missile	UAV	140
Shape, morphed							
5.18.18	4:25 a.m.	98601	Ballymahon Co. Lonford	Ireland	Saturn-like	Other	78
6.3.18	7:49 p.m.	93607	Dartford	UK	Horseshoe	UAV	88
8.18.18	6:35 p.m.	94292	Flint	TX	Cigar	UAV	145
8.21.18	2:30 p.m.	94322	Farmington	WI	Other	UAV	148
10.2.18	8:25 p.m.	95323	Toms River	NJ	Triangle	Other	169

EVENT	TIME	CASE	CITY	STATE-COUNTRY	SHAPE	DISPOSITION	PAGE
Shape, orb							
1.3.18	6:40 p.m.	89327	Marina	CA	Sphere	Other	10
1.26.18	8:15 p.m.	91153	Unknown	UK	Sphere	UAV	20
2.04.18	1:38 a.m.	90057	Mt. Pleasant	PA	Sphere	Other	23
4.17.18	9 p.m.	91498	Lakeland	FL	Sphere	Other	63
5.15.18	9:30 p.m.	92029	Bay Shore	NY	Sphere	Other	77
6.3.18	n/a	92452	Flournoy	CA	Sphere	Other	89
6.4.18	n/a	97913	Leesburg	VA	Sphere	UAV	90
6.9.18	9:15 p.m.	92639	Daytona Beach	FL	Sphere	UAV	94
7.1.18	9:23 p.m.	93045	West Fargo	ND	Sphere	Other	113
7.3.18	1:30 a.m.	93128	Wrexham	UK	Orb	UAV	115
7.15.18	8:06 p.m.	93445	Niagara Falls	Canada	Sphere	Other	120
7.18.18	9 p.m.	93459	North Las Vegas	NV	Sphere	Other	123
8.10.18	9:58 p.m.	94525	Tinley Park	IL	Sphere	UAV	136
8.12.18	5:06 p.m.	94086	Parker	CO	Egg	UAV	138
8.17.18	n/a	97233	Key West	FL	Sphere	Other	143
8.27.18	11:05 p.m.	94482	Eatonville	WA	Sphere	Other	150
10.2.18	8:25 p.m.	95323	Toms River	NJ	Triangle	Other	169
10.25.18	7:10 p.m.	95880	Montazuma	NY	Teardrop	UAV	185
10.26.18	11 p.m.	95886	Philadelphia	PA	Cylinder	UAV	186
11.7.18	12 p.m.	96230	Las Vegas	NV	Sphere	Other	196
Shape, oval							
1.1.18	12:05 a.m.	89317	Las Vegas	NV	Disc	UAV	8
1.9.18	8:45 p.m.	89498	Ellensburg	WA	Oval	UAV	15
6.9.18	1:15 a.m.	92591	Oelwein	IA	Oval	UAV	93
8.9.18	2:40 p.m.	94827	San Diego	CA	Oval	UAV	134
8.18.18	9:40 p.m.	96784	Cospicua	Malta	Oval	Other	146
10.22.18	9:30 a.m.	95806	Pass Christian	MS	Blimp	UAV	183
Shape, rectangle							
2.04.18	7:40 a.m.	90015	Port St. Lucie	FL	Square/Rectangle	Other	24
2.12.18	8:05 p.m.	90205	St. Peters	MO	Square/Rectangle	UAV	31
2.21.18	12:30 a.m.	90347	Sacramento	CA	Square/Rectangle	UAV	34
3.5.18	11:17 p.m.	91103	Webster	NC	Square/Rectangle	Other	40

EVENT	TIME	CASE	CITY	STATE-COUNTRY	SHAPE	DISPOSITION	PAGE
3.14.18	5:38 p.m.	90776	Port Huron	MI	Square/Rectangle	Other	48
3.22.18	11:45 p.m.	91005	Coquitlam	BC Canada	Square/Rectangle	Info Only	52
4.5.18	09:20 p.m.	91224	Fort Payne	AL	Square/Rectangle	UAV	58
4.5.18	11:30 p.m.	91263	Reliance	TN	Square/Rectangle	Other	59
4.10.18	12 p.m.	93224	Nakhon Nayok	Thailand	Square/Rectangle	UAV	62
5.25.18	8:30 p.m.	94857	Poulsbo	WA	Square/Rectangle	UAV	80
6.7.18	10:05 p.m.	92560	Dallas	OR	Square/Rectangle	UAV	91
6.17.18	3:20 p.m.	92817	Portland	OR	Square/Rectangle	UAV	98
9.13.18	8:15 a.m.	94937	Hailey	ID	Square/Rectangle	UAV	159
10.15.18	4 p.m.	95599	Sonora	CA	Square/Rectangle	UAV	180
12.9.18	8:20 p.m.	97094	Wisconsin Rapids	WI	Square/Rectangle	UAV	223
Shape, round							
4.25.18	2:30 p.m.	91628	Webster	TX	Circle	UAV	68
5.18.18	4:25 a.m.	98601	Ballymahon Co. Lonford	Ireland	Saturn-like	Other	78
6.3.18	1:30 a.m.	92447	Springville	NY	Saturn-like	UAV	86
Shape, Saturn							
11.3.18	11:59 p.m.	96140	Walker	OR	Saturn-like	UAV	193
Shape, saucer							
8.6.18	10:15 p.m.	93940	Waterloo	IA	Circle	UAV	132
8.18.18	5:15 p.m.	94231	Jersey City	NJ	Other	UAV	145
8.19.18	8 p.m.	94262	El Dorado Springs	MO	Disc	UAV	147
10.16.18	9:53 p.m.	95874	Midwest	WY	Sphere	UAV	180
Shape, shapeshifting							
1.1.18	12:05 a.m.	89317	Las Vegas	NV	Disc	UAV	8
2.04.18	6:27 p.m.	90097	Windsor	UK	Triangle	Info Only	25
4.17.18	10:45 p.m.	91485	Osceola	IN	Cylinder	UAV	64
11.6.18	8:25 p.m.	96207	San Antonio	TX	Chevron	UAV	195

EVENT	TIME	CASE	CITY	STATE-COUNTRY	SHAPE	DISPOSITION	PAGE
Shape, sphere							
6.20.18	8:20 p.m.	92828	Pasco	WA	Sphere	UAV	102
6.21.18	n/a	92994	San Felipe Baja Norte	Mexico	Sphere	Other	104
6.24.18	1:51 a.m.	92893	Anchorage County	AK	Sphere	UAV	107
6.26.18	10:30 p.m.	92957	Fridley	MN	Sphere	Other	108
7.15.18	8:06 p.m.	93445	Niagara Falls	Canada	Sphere	Other	120
7.19.18	9:30 p.m.	97557	Mount Washington	KY	Sphere	Other	123
8.12.18	n/a	94105	Los Lunas	NM	Sphere	Other	138
8.27.18	11:05 p.m.	94482	Eatonville	WA	Sphere	Other	150
8.29.18	8:15 p.m.	97227	Jamul	CA	Sphere	UAV	151
9.8.18	n/a	96379	Wilmington	NC	Sphere	Other	156
9.10.18	10:30 p.m.	98808	Colby	WI	Sphere	Other	157
9.24.18	6:45 p.m.	95317	Baldwinsville	NY	Sphere	Other	165
10.16.18	9:53 p.m.	95874	Midwest	WY	Sphere	UAV	180
10.18.18	8:25 p.m.	95673	Mercaston	UK	Sphere	UAV	182
11.7.18	12 p.m.	96230	Las Vegas	NV	Sphere	Other	196
11.23.18	6:15 p.m.	96580	Edwards	NY	Sphere	UAV	209
Shape, square							
2.12.18	8:05 p.m.	90205	St. Peters	MO	Square/Rectangle	UAV	31
3.2.18	8:30 a.m.	94597	Muskegon	MI	Square/Rectangle	UAV	38
3.5.18	11:17 p.m.	91103	Webster	NC	Square/Rectangle	Other	40
12.9.18	8:20 p.m.	97094	Wisconsin Rapids	WI	Square/Rectangle	UAV	223
Shape, star-like							
5.18.18	4:25 a.m.	98601	Ballymahon Co. Lonford	Ireland	Saturn-like	Other	78
11.9.18	8:18 p.m.	96286	Chaska	MN	Star-like	UAV	202
11.14.18	9:50 p.m.	96382	Kemmerer	WY	Star-like	Other	207
12.14.18	9 p.m.	97555	Punta Cana	Dominican Republic	Other	UAV	227
Shape, teardrop							
2.07.18	8 a.m.	90127	Shoup	ID	Teardrop	UAV	26

EVENT	TIME	CASE	CITY	STATE-COUNTRY	SHAPE	DISPOSITION	PAGE
9.21.18	8 p.m.	98732	Sonoita	AZ	Teardrop	UAV	164
10.25.18	7:10 p.m.	95880	Montazuma	NY	Teardrop	UAV	185
12.3.18	n/a	96773	n/a	CA	Teardrop	UAV	217
12.4.18	2 p.m.	96813	Olympia	WA	Egg	UAV	218
Shape, tic-tac							
4.15.18	1 p.m.	94668	Arncliffe	Australia	Egg	UAV	63
6.24.18	n/a	95063	Medellin	Columbia	Diamond	UAV	106
Shape, tower							
4.28.18	10:20 p.m.	91666	Houston	TX	Other	UAV	70
Shape, triangle							
1.1.18	12:05 a.m.	89317	Las Vegas	NV	Disc	UAV	8
1.3.18	6:40 p.m.	89327	Marina	CA	Sphere	Other	10
1.6.18	1:50 p.m.	89370	Darlington	UK	Triangle	Info Only	12
1.9.18	7:05 p.m.	89450	Wrightsville	PA	Triangle	UAV	14
1.17.18	3:35 a.m.	89653	Hemel Hempstead	UK	Triangle	UAV	18
1.24.18	10:30 p.m.	89780	Droitwich Spa	UK	Triangle	Other	19
1.28.18	7:30 p.m.	89867	Buffalo Mills	PA	Triangle	Other	21
2.04.18	6:27 p.m.	90097	Windsor	UK	Triangle	Info Only	25
2.08.18	8:30 p.m.	90133	Mena	AR	Triangle	UAV	27
2.08.18	8:35 p.m.	90181	Mena	AR	Triangle	UAV	27
2.10.18	11:15 a.m.	90355	Granbury	TX	Triangle/Disc	UAV	30
2.13.18	10 p.m.	90452	Newbury	UK	Triangle	UAV	33
2.21.18	8:30 p.m.	90647	Rochester	NY	Triangle	Other	35
2.23.18	7:15 p.m.	90404	Summerlin	NV	Triangle	UAV	35
3.2.18	5:25 a.m.	90499	Dasmarinas	Philippines	Triangle	UAV	38
3.3.18	5:35 a.m.	90540	Birmingham	AL	Triangle	UAV	39
3.10.18	11:57 p.m.	90710	Manchester	MD	Triangle	Other	45
3.11.18	10 p.m.	90789	Munroe Falls	OH	Triangle	UAV	47
3.15.18	4 a.m.	97506	Holly Pond	AL	Triangle	UAV	49
3.22.18	10:37 p.m.	90959	Chatsworth	GA	Triangle	UAV	51
3.28.18	3:15 a.m.	91075	Brookline	NH	Triangle	UAV	53
3.29.18	5:30 p.m.	92167	Dublin	Ireland	Triangle	Info Only	53
3.30.18	4:30 a.m.	91184	Excelsior Springs	MO	Triangle	UAV	54

EVENT	TIME	CASE	CITY	STATE-COUNTRY	SHAPE	DISPOSITION	PAGE
4.10.18	12 a.m.	91382	Heber City	UT	Triangle	UAV	61
4.17.18	10:45 p.m.	91485	Osceola	IN	Cylinder	UAV	64
4.19.18	10:30 p.m.	91752	Stonehouse	UK	Triangle	Info Only	64
4.21.18	9:55 p.m.	91553	Orrington	ME	Triangle	Other	65
4.22.18	12 a.m.	91570	Edmonton, Alberta	CA	Triangle	Info Only	68
5.1.18	11:30 p.m.	92298	London	UK	Triangle	UAV	71
5.15.18	n/a	93352	Lisbon	Portugal	Triangle	Info Only	77
5.16.18	n/a	92036	Salinas	CA	Triangle	UAV	77
5.21.18	9:59 p.m.	92164	Arkoma	OK	Triangle	UAV	79
5.24.18	11:45 p.m.	92228	Saint Albans	VT	Triangle	Info Only	80
6.1.18	7:41 p.m.	92432	Sao Jose Dos Pinhais	Brazil	Egg	Info Only	82
6.1.18	11:01 p.m.	93565	Novy Jicin	Czech Republic	Triangle	Info Only	82
6.1.18	n/a	92483	West Plains	MO	Triangle	UAV	83
6.2.18	10:15 p.m.	92445	London	Canada	Triangle	UAV	85
6.16.18	11:30 p.m.	92750	Sour Lake	TX	Triangle	UAV	97
6.22.18	8 a.m.	93841	Farmington	MO	Triangle	UAV	104
6.26.18	2:41 a.m.	92954	Madison	WI	Triangle	UAV	107
7.2.18	2:30 p.m.	93418	Gustine	CA.	Triangle	UAV	114
7.9.18	n/a	96065	San Antonio	TX	Triangle	Other	116
7.10.18	10 p.m.	97688	Toronto	Canada	Triangle	Other	117
7.22.18	10 p.m.	93687	Anaheim	CA	Triangle	UAV	125
7.24.18	2:30 a.m.	93703	Winlock	WA.	Triangle	UAV	126
7.29.18	5:35 a.m.	93741	Hesston	KS	Triangle	UAV	127
8.1.18	9:02 p.m.	97862	Breitenbush Hot Springs	OR	Triangle	UAV	129
8.5.18	3 p.m.	95040	Florence	OR	Triangle	UAV	132
8.16.18	n/a	95179	Gig Harbor	WA	Triangle	UAV	142
8.17.18	10:30 p.m.	94217	Portage	IN	Triangle	UAV	144
8.19.18	10 p.m.	98200	Port Talbot	UK	Triangle	Info Only	148
8.28.18	4:15 a.m.	94461	Las Vegas	NV	Triangle	Other	151
8.30.18	9:30 p.m.	94524	Funchal	Portugal	Triangle	UAV	152
8.31.18	6:35 a.m.	94699	El Paso	TX	Triangle	UAV	152
9.12.18	n/a	95268	Ancaster	Canada	Triangle	UAV	158

EVENT	TIME	CASE	CITY	STATE-COUNTRY	SHAPE	DISPOSITION	PAGE
9.13.18	9 p.m.	94903	Columbus	IN	Triangle	UAV	160
10.2.18	8:25 p.m.	95323	Toms River	NJ	Triangle	Other	169
10.3.18	7:30 p.m.	96637	New Lisbon	NJ	Triangle	UAV	170
10.4.18	8:57 p.m.	95343	Rancho Mirage	CA	Boomerang	UAV	173
10.4.18	10 p.m.	95606	Tampa	FL	Triangle	UAV	173
10.5.18	8:15 p.m.	95364	Trinidad	CO	Triangle	UAV	174
10.10.18	4:30 a.m.	95592	Bellingham	WA	Triangle	UAV	175
10.12.18	1:01 a.m.	95590	Citrus Heights	CA	Triangle	UAV	177
10.12.18	1:01 a.m.	95529	Orlando	FL	Triangle	UAV	178
10.28.18	n/a	96472	Sacramento	CA	Triangle	UAV	188
10.30.18	8:30 p.m.	96033	Jackson Township	NJ	Triangle	UAV	190
10.30.18	n/a	98437	Michigan City	IN	Triangle	UAV	190
10.31.18	9:45 p.m.	96052	Selma	NC	Triangle	UAV	191
11.2.18	9:30 p.m.	96088	Pattaya	Thailand	Triangle	UAV	192
11.5.18	10:30 p.m.	96204	Newport	OR	Triangle	UAV	194
11.6.18	5:54 p.m.	96200	Hattiesburg	MS	Triangle	UAV	194
11.9.18	9 p.m.	96451	Springfield	MO	Triangle	UAV	202
11.10.18	2 a.m.	96271	Lonsdale	MN	Triangle	UAV	203
11.11.18	7:05 p.m.	96314	London	Canada	Triangle	UAV	204
11.11.18	n/a	96316	Taylorsville	UT	Triangle	Other	205
11.27.18	8 p.m.	97510	Santee	CA	Triangle	Info Only	212
12.4.18	8:30 p.m.	96829	Orwigsburg	PA	Triangle	UAV	218
12.6.18	7:12 p.m.	97119	Red Bluff	CA	Triangle	UAV	221
12.8.18	5:55 p.m.	97287	Pulaski	VA	Triangle	UAV	222
12.12.18	12 a.m.	97018	Reidsville	NC	Triangle	Other	225
12.12.18	6:52 p.m.	96983	St. Louis	MO	Triangle	UAV	227
12.16.18	7:38 p.m.	97044	Fort Smith	AR	Triangle	UAV	228
12.17.18	9:15 p.m.	97065	Goole	UK	Triangle	UAV	229
12.23.18	11 p.m.	97206	Boise	ID	Triangle	UAV	229
Shape, V							
3.16.18	9:48 p.m.	90816	Attica	IN	Triangle	UAV	50
11.10.18	5 a.m.	96283	Pipestone	MN	Other	UAV	203
Size, 737 aircraft							
12.6.18	5:35 p.m.	96850	Memphis	TN	Chevron	Other	220

EVENT	TIME	CASE	CITY	STATE-COUNTRY	SHAPE	DISPOSITION	PAGE
Size, 747 aircraft							
10.30.18	7:40 p.m.	96019	Benton	OH	Cylinder	UAV	189
Size, acre							
6.3.18	1:30 a.m.	92447	Springville	NY	Saturn-like	UAV	86
Size, aircraft carrier							
1.9.18	8:45 p.m.	89498	Ellensburg	WA	Oval	UAV	15
6.7.18	10:05 p.m.	92560	Dallas	OR	Square/rectangle	UAV	91
8.29.18	8:15 p.m.	97227	Jamul	CA	Sphere	UAV	151
Size, airliner							
12.23.18	11 p.m.	97206	Boise	ID	Triangle	UAV	229
Size, basketball							
1.3.18	6:40 p.m.	89327	Marina	CA	Sphere	Other	10
2.07.18	8 a.m.	90127	Shoup	ID	Teardrop	UAV	26
Size, bigger than airplane							
5.1.18	11:30 p.m.	92298	London	UK	Triangle	UAV	71
8.15.18	10:30 p.m.	94184	Staten Island	NY	Disc	Other	141
Size, bigger than car							
11.23.18	6:15 p.m.	96580	Edwards	NY	Sphere	UAV	209
Size, big as a small car							
2.12.18	8:05 p.m.	90205	St. Peters	MO	Square/Rectangle	UAV	31
Size, car							
3.6.18	9:40 p.m.	90698	Marietta	GA	Other	UAV	42
3.14.18	5:38 p.m.	90776	Port Huron	MI	Square/Rectangular	Other	48
11.7.18	6:02 p.m.	96229	Lacey	WA	Cylinder	UAV	197
Size, bus							
5.13.18	5:05 p.m.	92110	Garrett	IN	Cigar	UAV	75
Size, city block							
11.10.18	5 a.m.	96283	Pipestone	MN	Other	UAV	203
Size, cruise ship							
8.12.18	2:10 a.m.	94081	Godfrey	IL	Cigar	UAV	137
Size, football field							
2.23.18	7:15 p.m.	90404	Summerlin	NV	Triangle	UAV	35
3.6.18	10:42 a.m.	93750	West Jordan	UT	Cylinder	UAV	41

EVENT	TIME	CASE	CITY	STATE-COUNTRY	SHAPE	DISPOSITION	PAGE
3.30.18	4:30 a.m.	91184	Excelsior Springs	MO	Triangle	UAV	54
4.17.18	10:45 p.m.	91485	Osceola	IN	Cylinder	UAV	64
4.21.18	10:20 p.m.	91559	Irondequoit	NY	Chevron	UAV	66
6.3.18	n/a	92452	Flournoy	CA	Sphere	Other	89
Size, four times a helicopter							
1.8.18	5:20 p.m.	89435	Orfordville	WI	Triangle	UAV	14
Size, grew larger							
2.04.18	1:38 a.m.	90057	Mt. Pleasant	PA	Sphere	Other	23
Size, house							
1.28.18	7:30 p.m.	89867	Buffalo Mills	PA	Triangle	Other	21
6.7.18	10:30 p.m.	92568	Colorado Springs	CO	Other	UAV	92
Size, large							
1.9.18	8:45 p.m.	89498	Ellensburg	WA	Oval	UAV	15
2.08.18	1:07 p.m.	94350	Valley	WA	Disc	UAV	26
10.15.18	4 p.m.	95599	Sonora	CA	n/a	UAV	180
Size, large airplane							
1.24.18	10:30 p.m.	89780	Droitwich Spa	UK	Triangle	Other	19
Size, mile							
6.6.18	1 p.m.	97168	Plymouth	MA	Blimp	Info Only	90
Size, over a half-acre							
1.24.18	n/a	89785	Great Falls	MT	Circle	Info Only	20
Size, passenger plane							
11.25.18	8:15 p.m.	96616	Galway City	Ireland	N/A	UAV	210
Size, stadium							
3.6.18	10:42 a.m.	93750	West Jordan	UT	Cylinder	UAV	41
Size, tractor trailer							
3.3.18	11:30 p.m.	90584	Elkhorn	NE	Disc	UAV	40
3.22.18	11:45 p.m.	91005	Coquitlam	BC Canada	Square/ Rectangle	Info Only	52
Size, yoga balls							
1.3.18	6:40 p.m.	89327	Marina	CA	Sphere	Other	10
Sound, buzzing							
3.10.18	11:57 p.m.	90710	Manchester	MD	Triangle	Other	45

EVENT	TIME	CASE	CITY	STATE-COUNTRY	SHAPE	DISPOSITION	PAGE
3.22.18	11:45 p.m.	91005	Coquitlam	BC Canada	Square/Rectangle	Info Only	52
Sound, humming							
3.10.18	11:57 p.m.	90710	Manchester	MD	Triangle	Other	45
3.28.18	3:15 a.m.	91075	Brookline	NH	Triangle	UAV	53
4.5.18	11:30 p.m.	91263	Reliance	TN	Square/Rectangle	Other	59
12.28.18	1:10 a.m.	97282	Shrewsbury	UK	Chevron	Info Only	230
Sound, loud							
3.15.18	8:40 p.m.	90803	Abbotsford	BC Canada	Other	UAV	50
Sound, mechanical trumpet							
8.12.18	2:10 a.m.	94081	Godfrey	IL	Cigar	UAV	137
Sound, pulsating							
1.4.18	6:25 a.m.	89344	Casselberry	FL	Square Rectangle	Other	12
1.9.18	8:45 p.m.	89498	Ellensburg	WA	Oval	UAV	15
4.22.18	12 a.m.	91570	Edmonton, Alberta	CA	Triangle	Info Only	68
Sound, roar							
8.5.18	3 p.m.	95040	Florence	OR	Triangle	UAV	132
Sound, rumble							
10.15.18	4 p.m.	95599	Sonora	CA	N/A	UAV	180
Sound, sucking							
10.30.18	2 a.m.	96776	Tecumseh	MI	Disc	Other	188
Sound, swish							
7.17.18	10:40 p.m.	93540	Brookport	IL	Cylinder	UAV	121
Structure, central pillar of light							
1.17.18	3:35 a.m.	89653	Hemel Hempstead	UK	Triangle	UAV	18
Structure, central, round spinning center							
11.7.18	10:40 p.m.	97286	Duluth	MN	Oval	UAV	200
Structure, dome							
1.17.18	3:35 a.m.	89653	Hemel Hempstead	UK	Triangle	UAV	18
2.04.18	6:27 p.m.	90097	Windsor	UK	Triangle	Info Only	25
6.3.18	1:30 a.m.	92447	Springville	NY	Saturn-like	UAV	86

EVENT	TIME	CASE	CITY	STATE-COUNTRY	SHAPE	DISPOSITION	PAGE
8.18.18	9:40 p.m.	96784	Cospicua	Malta	Oval	Other	146
9.14.18	3:28 p.m.	94892	Santa Fe	NM	Disc	Info Only	160
9.17.18	9:42 p.m.	94983	Highlands Ranch	CO	Cone	UAV	161
Structure, hollow, round, clear columns							
11.7.18	10:40 p.m.	97286	Duluth	MN	Oval	UAV	200
Structure, legs lowered in cube-shaped outline							
11.11.18	2:40 a.m.	96450	Jefferson City	MO	Chevron	UAV	204
Structure, outer ring; inner ring							
7.3.18	1:30 a.m.	93128	Wrexham	UK	Orb	UAV	115
Structure, pipes or valves							
3.29.18	5:30 p.m.	92167	Dublin	Ireland	Triangle	Info Only	53
Structure, rectangular panels in three corner colored orange							
11.2.18	9:30 p.m.	96088	Pattaya	Thailand	Triangle	UAV	192
Structure, red glowing band							
7.24.18	2:30 a.m.	93703	Winlock	WA.	Triangle	UAV	126
Structure, rounded edges							
8.5.18	3 p.m.	95040	Florence	OR	Triangle	UAV	132
8.15.18	3:45 p.m.	94170	Pensacola	FL	Bullet/Missile	UAV	140
Structure, symmetrical appendages							
11.15.18	2:46 p.m.	97141	Everett	WA	Other	UAV	207
Structure, tail-like fin							
10.30.18	2 a.m.	96776	Tecumseh	MI	Disc	Other	188
Structure, tapering aft							
6.19.18	11:15 a.m.	92800	Warrento	MO	Blimp	UAV	100
Structure, tip was tapered							
8.18.18	9:40 p.m.	96784	Cospicua	Malta	Oval	Other	146
Structure, wings							
3.10.18	11:57 p.m.	90710	Manchester	MD	Triangle	Other	45
12.14.18	9 p.m.	97555	Punta Cana	Dominican Republic	Other	UAV	227
Structure, wings, short on the forward section							
11.11.18	2:40 a.m.	96450	Jefferson City	MO	Chevron	UAV	204
Surface, angular							
4.10.18	12 p.m.	93224	Nakhon Nayok	Thailand	Square/Rectangle	UAV	62

EVENT	TIME	CASE	CITY	STATE-COUNTRY	SHAPE	DISPOSITION	PAGE
Surface, arched ribs							
1.17.18	3:35 a.m.	89653	Hemel Hempstead	UK	Triangle	UAV	18
Surface, aura							
4.22.18	12 a.m.	91570	Edmonton, Alberta	CA	Triangle	Info Only	68
Surface, breathing							
3.29.18	5:30 p.m.	92167	Dublin	Ireland	Triangle	Info Only	53
Surface, chrome							
8.15.18	3:45 p.m.	94170	Pensacola	FL	Bullet/Missile	UAV	140
Surface, cloaking							
2.08.18	1:07 p.m.	94350	Valley	WA	Disc	UAV	26
5.1.18	11:30 p.m.	92298	London	UK	Triangle	UAV	71
7.2.18	2:30 p.m.	93418	Gustine	CA.	Triangle	UAV	114
7.10.18	7:35 a.m.	93256	Deland	FL	Diamond	UAV	116
8.8.18	9:45 a.m.	94049	Sunset Hills	MO	Diamond	UAV	133
8.12.18	2:10 a.m.	94081	Godfrey	IL	Cigar	UAV	137
8.19.18	8 p.m.	94262	El Dorado Springs	MO	Disc	UAV	147
9.1.18	4:20 a.m.	94960	Porter	TX	Boomerang	UAV	154
9.19.18	9 p.m.	94990	Unknown	Philippines	Triangle	UAV	163
10.2.18	8:25 p.m.	95323	Toms River	NJ	Triangle	Other	169
10.4.18	8 p.m.	95356	Sammamish	WA	Diamond	Other	172
10.15.18	4 p.m.	95599	Sonora	CA	n/a	UAV	180
10.28.18	n/a	96472	Sacramento	CA	Triangle	UAV	188
11.7.18	9:30 p.m.	96766	Valrico	FL	Chevron	UAV	198
11.9.18	9 p.m.	96451	Springfield	MO	Triangle	UAV	202
11.10.18	5 a.m.	96283	Pipestone	MN	Other	UAV	203
11.11.18	n/a	96316	Taylorsville	UT	Triangle	Other	205
11.12.18	7:20 p.m.	96353	Phoenix	AZ	Cigar	UAV	205
11.26.18	8:02 p.m.	96643	Columbia	MO	Boomerang	UAV	212
Surface, com trail behind							
3.6.18	10:42 a.m.	93750	West Jordan	UT	Cylinder	UAV	41
Surface, dark							
1.9.18	7:05 p.m.	89450	Wrightsville	PA	Triangle	UAV	14

EVENT	TIME	CASE	CITY	STATE-COUNTRY	SHAPE	DISPOSITION	PAGE
Surface, door							
3.6.18	10:42 a.m.	93750	West Jordan	UT	Cylinder	UAV	41
Surface, edges blurry							
2.10.18	11:15 a.m.	90355	Granbury	TX	Triangle/Disc	UAV	30
Surface, filmy mist							
12.3.18	8:35 a.m.	96755	Toms Brook	VA	Cylinder	UAV	216
Surface, flat							
1.2.18	5:20 p.m.	89280	Northampton	MA	Boomerang	UAV	10
Surface, fog around it							
3.5.18	11:17 p.m.	91103	Webster	NC	Square/Rectangle	Other	40
Surface, fuzzy							
2.10.18	11:15 a.m.	90355	Granbury	TX	Triangle/Disc	UAV	30
5.11.18	11:45 p.m.	91968	North Plainfield	NJ	Unknown	Other	75
10.4.18	10 p.m.	95606	Tampa	FL	Triangle	UAV	173
Surface, glass-like							
7.19.18	9:30 p.m.	97557	Mount Washington	KY	Sphere	Other	123
Surface, gold rays coming out							
3.31.18	9:55 p.m.	91151	Aiken	SC	Circle	Other	55
Surface, matte-like							
12.14.18	9 p.m.	97555	Punta Cana	Dominican Republic	Other	UAV	227
Surface, metal-paned glass							
3.6.18	9:40 p.m.	90698	Marietta	GA	Other	UAV	42
Surface, metallic							
1.1.18	12:05 a.m.	89317	Las Vegas	NV	Disc	UAV	8
10.21.18	5:30 p.m.	95770	Belleville	WI	Unknown	Other	183
11.7.18	12 p.m.	96230	Las Vegas	NV	Sphere	Other	196
12.4.18	2 p.m.	96813	Olympia	WA	Egg	UAV	218
Surface, misty							
5.3.18	10:28 p.m.	91773	Caverna	MO	Oval	UAV	72
Surface, pattern of black dots							
7.10.18	7:35 a.m.	93256	Deland	FL	Diamond	UAV	116

EVENT	TIME	CASE	CITY	STATE-COUNTRY	SHAPE	DISPOSITION	PAGE
Surface, perpetual kinetic motion							
6.2.18	10:15 p.m.	92445	London	Canada	Triangle	UAV	85
Surface, pink burning atmosphere							
7.9.18	n/a	96065	San Antonio	TX	Triangle	Other	116
Surface, plated							
3.29.18	5:30 p.m.	92167	Dublin	Ireland	Triangle	Info Only	53
Surface, reddish webbing							
10.10.18	2:27 p.m.	95682	Atlanta	GA	Cigar	UAV	176
Surface, reflecting light							
1.9.18	7:05 p.m.	89450	Wrightsville	PA	Triangle	UAV	14
1.17.18	3:35 a.m.	89653	Hemel Hempstead	UK	Triangle	UAV	18
6.19.18	7:10 a.m.	92792	Joliette	Canada	Other	UAV	100
7.29.18	5:35 a.m.	93741	Hesston	KS	Triangle	UAV	127
8.12.18	5:06 p.m.	94086	Parker	CO	Egg	UAV	138
8.12.18	n/a	94105	Los Lunas	NM	Sphere	Other	138
8.18.18	6:35 p.m.	94292	Flint	TX	Cigar	UAV	145
8.19.18	8 p.m.	94262	El Dorado Springs	MO	Disc	UAV	147
8.21.18	2:30 p.m.	94322	Farmington	WI	Other	UAV	148
10.11.18	6:24 p.m.	95738	Carrollton	GA	Blimp	UAV	177
Surface, seamless							
8.15.18	3:45 p.m.	94170	Pensacola	FL	Bullet/ Missile	UAV	140
Surface, shiny							
10.11.18	6:24 p.m.	95738	Carrollton	GA	Blimp	UAV	177
Surface, silvery							
8.16.18	n/a	95179	Gig Harbor	WA	Triangle	UAV	142
Surface, skin pattern							
3.29.18	5:30 p.m.	92167	Dublin	Ireland	Triangle	Info Only	53
7.2.18	2:30 p.m.	93418	Gustine	CA.	Triangle	UAV	114
Surface, smooth bottom							
3.11.18	10 p.m.	90789	Munroe Falls	OH	Triangle	UAV	47
Surface, square flaps at back							
3.15.18	4 a.m.	97506	Holly Pond	AL	Triangle	UAV	49

EVENT	TIME	CASE	CITY	STATE-COUNTRY	SHAPE	DISPOSITION	PAGE
Surface, strips of metal fluttering off it							
3.15.18	8:40 p.m.	90803	Abbotsford	BC Canada	Other	UAV	50
Surface, thin discharge dispersed							
10.25.18	6:30 p.m.	96048	Dilles Bottom	OH	Egg	UAV	184
Surface, watery ripples							
11.9.18	9 p.m.	96451	Springfield	MO	Triangle	UAV	202
Surface, windows							
2.08.18	1:07 p.m.	94350	Valley	WA	Disc	UAV	26
2.15.18	9:30 p.m.	91313	Woodstock	GA	Cylinder	UAV	33
5.4.18	2:52 a.m.	91780	Enterprise	UT	Saturn-like	UAV	73
5.13.18	5:05 p.m.	92110	Garrett	IN	Cigar	UAV	75
6.27.18	10 p.m.	92964	Mesquite	NV	Cigar	UAV	110
7.2.18	2:30 p.m.	93418	Gustine	CA.	Triangle	UAV	114
12.31.18	12:10 a.m.	97391	Caithness	UK	Saturn-like	UAV	231

SITE INDEX: 2018

EVENT	TIME	CASE	CITY	STATE-COUNTRY	SHAPE	DISPOSITION	PAGE
Additional people don't notice object							
3.22.18	10:37 p.m.	90959	Chatsworth	GA	Triangle	UAV	51
6.2.18	10:15 p.m.	92445	London	Canada	Triangle	UAV	85
Airborne, object seen during flight							
8.12.18	5:06 p.m.	94086	Parker	CO	Egg	UAV	138
Airport							
5.15.18	4:45 p.m.	92030	Medford	OR	Cylinder	UAV	76
Animal, affected							
1.9.18	8:45 p.m.	89498	Ellensburg	WA	Oval	UAV	15
8.12.18	2:10 a.m.	94081	Godfrey	IL	Cigar	UAV	137
Beam of light near witness							
6.26.18	2:41 a.m.	92954	Madison	WI	Triangle	UAV	107
Burned area on ground							
12.1.18	12:00 a.m.	96805	McKinney	TX	Oval	UAV	214
Church							
6.3.18	6:45 a.m.	92469	Panola County	MS	Cylinder	UAV	87
10.26.18	11:10 p.m.	96858	Reykjavik	Iceland	Circle	Other	187
Electronics, affected							
2.04.18	6:27 p.m.	90097	Windsor	UK	Triangle	Info Only	25
2.09.18	11:18 p.m.	90175	Derry	PA	Semi-Diamond	Other	29
4.5.18	11:30 p.m.	91263	Reliance	TN	Square/Rectangle	Other	59
4.10.18	12 a.m.	91382	Heber City	UT	Triangle	UAV	61
6.3.18	1:30 a.m.	92447	Springville	NY	Saturn-like	UAV	86
10.4.18	10 p.m.	95606	Tampa	FL	Triangle	UAV	173
12.17.18	9:15 p.m.	97065	Goole	UK	Triangle	UAV	229
Entities							
10.26.18	11:10 p.m.	96858	Reykjavik	Iceland	Circle	Other	187
10.30.18	n/a	98437	Michigan City	IN	Triangle	UAV	190
Entities, interested in bird							
6.20.18	3:15 p.m.	92849	Egg Harbor Township	NJ	Sphere	UAV	102

EVENT	TIME	CASE	CITY	STATE-COUNTRY	SHAPE	DISPOSITION	PAGE
Fireworks nearby							
1.1.18	12:05 a.m.	89317	Las Vegas	NV	Disc	UAV	8
Helicopter, followed object							
1.8.18	5:20 p.m.	89435	Orfordville	WI	Triangle	UAV	14
6.10.18	10:30 p.m.	92641	Attleboro	MA	N/A	Other	95
6.26.18	10:30 p.m.	92957	Fridley	MN	Sphere	Other	108
Helicopter, nearby							
1.9.18	7:05 p.m.	89450	Wrightsville	PA	Triangle	UAV	14
3.10.18	9:30 p.m.	90968	Dover	DE	Bowl	UAV	46
6.10.18	10:27 p.m.	92653	Blackstone	MA	Unknown	UAV	95
House, lights dimmed							
8.15.18	10:30 p.m.	94184	Staten Island	NY	Disc	Other	141
Humanoid creature, crossing road							
7.31.18	1:43 a.m.	93831	Mount Vernon	OH	N/A	Other	128
8.14.18	1:07 a.m.	94117	Hernes, Elverum	Norway	Other	Info Only	140
8.27.18	4:10 a.m.	97499	Pahrump	NV	N/A	Info Only	149
Military aircraft							
5.11.18	10:20 a.m.	91939	Esquimalt	BC CA	Cigar	Info Only	74
7.18.18	9 p.m.	93459	North Las Vegas	NV	Sphere	Other	123
11.14.18	7:24 p.m.	96378	Caroga Lake	NY	Circle	UAV	206
11.27.18	8 p.m.	97510	Santee	CA	Triangle	Info Only	212
12.4.18	8:30 p.m.	96829	Orwigsburg	PA	Triangle	UAV	218
12.6.18	5:35 p.m.	96850	Memphis	TN	Chevron	Other	220
Military base							
1.24.18	n/a	89785	Great Falls	MT	Circle	Info Only	20
5.25.18	8:30 p.m.	94857	Poulsbo	WA	Square/Rectangle	UAV	80
8.29.18	8:15 p.m.	97227	Jamul	CA	Sphere	UAV	151
9.25.18	11:15 p.m.	95249	Silvercreek	WA	Egg	UAV	167
11.6.18	5:54 p.m.	96200	Hattiesburg	MS	Triangle	UAV	194
11.7.18	12 p.m.	96230	Las Vegas	NV	Sphere	Other	196
11.27.18	8 p.m.	97510	Santee	CA	Triangle	Info Only	212
Military helicopter							
8.27.18	11:05 p.m.	94482	Eatonville	WA	Sphere	Other	150

EVENT	TIME	CASE	CITY	STATE-COUNTRY	SHAPE	DISPOSITION	PAGE
9.25.18	11:15 p.m.	95249	Silvercreek	WA	Egg	UAV	167
10.22.18	9:30 a.m.	95806	Pass Christian	MS	Blimp	UAV	183
Power lines							
7.1.18	9:23 p.m.	93045	West Fargo	ND	Sphere	Other	113
Power outage							
1.24.18	n/a	89785	Great Falls	MT	Circle	Info Only	20
Power plant							
4.17.18	9 p.m.	91498	Lakeland	FL	Sphere	Other	63
Sound, buzzing							
8.15.18	10:30 p.m.	94184	Staten Island	NY	Disc	Other	141
Sound, coyotes							
8.12.18	2:10 a.m.	94081	Godfrey	IL	Cigar	UAV	137
Sound, electrical explosion							
8.15.18	10:30 p.m.	94184	Staten Island	NY	Disc	Other	141
Sound, shook house							
12.1.18	12:00 a.m.	96805	McKinney	TX	Oval	UAV	214
Sound, wailing-screaming							
1.9.18	8:45 p.m.	89498	Ellensburg	WA	Oval	UAV	15
Trail, red-orange behind it							
12.4.18	6:30 a.m.	96843	Beaconsfield	UK	Disc	UAV	217
Vehicle, engulfed in light							
3.3.18	11:30 p.m.	90584	Elkhorn	NE	Disc	UAV	40
Vehicle, interior temperature reached 114 degrees							
3.3.18	11:30 p.m.	90584	Elkhorn	NE	Disc	UAV	40
Vehicle, overheated and stopped							
3.3.18	11:30 p.m.	90584	Elkhorn	NE	Disc	UAV	40

WITNESS INDEX: 2018

EVENT	TIME	CASE	CITY	STATE-COUNTRY	SHAPE	DISPOSITION	PAGE
Alien encounter							
3.3.18	11:30 p.m.	90584	Elkhorn	NE	Disc	UAV	40
3.6.18	9:40 p.m.	90698	Marietta	GA	Other	UAV	42
Background, aircraft enthusiast							
1.17.18	3:35 a.m.	89653	Hemel Hempstead	UK	Triangle	UAV	18
Background, air traffic controller							
1.4.18	6:25 a.m.	89344	Casselberry	FL	Square/Rectangle	Other	12
Background, engineer							
4.10.18	12 p.m.	93224	Nakhon Nayok	Thailand	Square/Rectangle	UAV	62
9.21.18	8 p.m.	98732	Sonoita	AZ	Teardrop	UAV	164
12.1.18	12:00 a.m.	96805	McKinney	TX	Oval	UAV	214
Background, flight navigator							
1.4.18	6:25 a.m.	89344	Casselberry	FL	Square/Rectangle	Other	12
Background, law enforcement							
4.22.18	5:14 p.m.	91575	Manheim	PA	Other	Other	67
Background, military							
2.10.18	11:15 a.m.	90355	Granbury	TX	Triangle/Disc	UAV	30
3.2.18	8:30 a.m.	94597	Muskegon	MI	Square/Rectangle	UAV	38
3.10.18	9:30 p.m.	90968	Dover	DE	Bowl	UAV	46
4.21.18	10:20 p.m.	91559	Irondequoit	NY	Chevron	UAV	66
6.28.18	11:15 p.m.	93454	Buckeye	AZ	Circle	UAV	110
7.9.18	n/a	96065	San Antonio	TX	Triangle	Other	116
7.18.18	2:06 p.m.	93708	Hood River	OR	Cigar	UAV	122
12.28.18	1:10 a.m.	97282	Shrewsbury	UK	Chevron	Info Only	230
Background, pilot							
1.9.18	8:45 p.m.	89498	Ellensburg	WA	Oval	UAV	15
2.10.18	11:15 a.m.	90355	Granbury	TX	Triangle/Disc	UAV	30

EVENT	TIME	CASE	CITY	STATE-COUNTRY	SHAPE	DISPOSITION	PAGE
3.2.18	8:30 a.m.	94597	Muskegon	MI	Square/Rectangle	UAV	38
3.28.18	3:15 a.m.	91075	Brookline	NH	Triangle	UAV	53
4.5.18	11:30 p.m.	91263	Reliance	TN	Square/Rectangle	Other	59
6.1.18	n/a	92483	West Plains	MO	Triangle	UAV	83
7.18.18	9 p.m.	93459	North Las Vegas	NV	Sphere	Other	123
9.25.18	10:30 p.m.	95703	Lachute	Canada	Disc	UAV	166
Background, police							
6.4.18	n/a	97913	Leesburg	VA	Sphere	UAV	90
10.31.18	9:45 p.m.	96052	Selma	NC	Triangle	UAV	191
Communicated with object							
3.31.18	9:55 p.m.	91151	Aiken	SC	Circle	Other	55
4.10.18	12 a.m.	91382	Heber City	UT	Triangle	UAV	61
6.3.18	7:49 p.m.	93607	Dartford	UK	Horseshoe	UAV	88
7.1.18	9:23 p.m.	93045	West Fargo	ND	Sphere	Other	113
8.1.18	9:02 p.m.	97862	Breitenbush Hot Springs	OR	Triangle	UAV	129
8.12.18	2:10 a.m.	94081	Godfrey	IL	Cigar	UAV	137
8.16.18	n/a	95179	Gig Harbor	WA	Triangle	UAV	142
10.2.18	8:25 p.m.	95323	Toms River	NJ	Triangle	Other	169
10.16.18	9:53 p.m.	95874	Midwest	WY	Sphere	UAV	180
10.30.18	n/a	98437	Michigan City	IN	Triangle	UAV	190
12.3.18	8:35 a.m.	96755	Toms Brook	VA	Cylinder	UAV	216
Confused							
10.10.18	2:27 p.m.	95682	Atlanta	GA	Cigar	UAV	176
Driving, or passenger in vehicle							
1.2.18	5:20 p.m.	89280	Northampton	MA	Boomerang	UAV	10
1.3.18	6:40 p.m.	89327	Marina	CA	Sphere	Other	10
1.8.18	5:20 p.m.	89435	Orfordville	WI	Triangle	UAV	14
1.13.18	9:05 p.m.	89544	Indianapolis	IN	Chevron	Info Only	17
1.24.18	10:30 p.m.	89780	Droitwich Spa	UK	Triangle	Other	19
2.04.18	6:27 p.m.	90097	Windsor	UK	Triangle	Info Only	25
2.08.18	8:30 p.m.	90133	Mena	AR	Triangle	UAV	27
2.09.18	11:18 p.m.	90175	Derry	PA	Semi-Diamond	Other	29

EVENT	TIME	CASE	CITY	STATE-COUNTRY	SHAPE	DISPOSITION	PAGE
2.12.18	8:05 p.m.	90205	St. Peters	MO	Square/Rectangle	UAV	31
2.13.18	6:40 p.m.	90221	Grantville	PA	Cigar	UAV	32
2.15.18	9:30 p.m.	91313	Woodstock	GA	Cylinder	UAV	33
2.21.18	12:30 a.m.	90347	Sacramento	CA	Square/Rectangle	UAV	34
2.23.18	7:15 p.m.	90404	Summerlin	NV	Triangle		35
3.3.18	11:30 p.m.	90584	Elkhorn	NE	Disc	UAV	40
3.5.18	11:17 p.m.	91103	Webster	NC	Square/Rectangle	Other	40
3.7.18	10:34 a.m.	90628	Gonzales County	TX	Cylinder	Other	44
3.10.18	4 a.m.	95178	Woodstock	NY	Diamond	UAV	46
3.11.18	10 p.m.	90789	Munroe Falls	OH	Triangle	UAV	47
3.15.18	8:40 p.m.	90803	Abbotsford	BC Canada	Other	UAV	50
3.22.18	10:37 p.m.	90959	Chatsworth	GA	Triangle	UAV	51
3.30.18	4:30 a.m.	91184	Excelsior Springs	MO	Triangle	UAV	54
4.2.18	10:27 p.m.	91182	Banja Luka	Bosnia & Herzegovina	Disc	Info Only	58
4.5.18	09:20 p.m.	91224	Fort Payne	AL	Square/Rectangle	UAV	58
4.10.18	2:30 a.m.	96307	Bromsgrove	UK	Unknown	UAV	60
4.15.18	1 p.m.	94668	Arncliffe	Australia	Egg	UAV	63
4.22.18	5:14 p.m.	91575	Manheim	PA	Other	Other	67
4.25.18	2:30 p.m.	91628	Webster	TX	Circle	UAV	68
5.3.18	10:28 p.m.	91773	Caverna	MO	Oval	UAV	72
5.4.18	2:52 a.m.	91780	Enterprise	UT	Saturn-like	UAV	73
5.11.18	11:45 p.m.	91968	North Plainfield	NJ	Unknown	Other	75
5.21.18	9:59 p.m.	92164	Arkoma	OK	Triangle	UAV	79
5.24.18	11:45 p.m.	92228	Saint Albans	VT	Triangle	Info Only	80
6.2.18	5:30 p.m.	92481	Salem	NJ	Disc	Info Only	85
6.3.18	1:30 a.m.	92447	Springville	NY	Saturn-like	UAV	86
6.3.18	6:45 a.m.	92469	Panola County	MS	Cylinder	UAV	87
6.9.18	8:32 p.m.	92619	Alexandria	MD	Bullet/Missile	UAV	94
6.11.18	2:11 a.m.	92673	North Las Vegas	NV	Other	UAV	96

EVENT	TIME	CASE	CITY	STATE-COUNTRY	SHAPE	DISPOSITION	PAGE
6.19.18	7:10 a.m.	92792	Joliette	Canada	Other	UAV	100
6.19.18	11:15 a.m.	92800	Warrento	MO	Blimp	UAV	100
6.20.18	3:15 p.m.	92849	Egg Harbor Township	NJ	Sphere	UAV	102
7.10.18	7:35 a.m.	93256	Deland	FL	Diamond	UAV	116
7.13.18	9:30 p.m.	93410	Alexandria	IN	Sphere	Other	119
7.18.18	2:06 p.m.	93708	Hood River	OR	Cigar	UAV	122
7.31.18	1:43 a.m.	93831	Mount Vernon	OH	n/a	Other	128
8.8.18	9:45 a.m.	94049	Sunset Hills	MO	Diamond	UAV	133
8.9.18	2:40 p.m.	94827	San Diego	CA	Oval	UAV	134
8.10.18	7:19 p.m.	94038	Hammond	IN	Blimp	UAV	135
8.12.18	12:15 a.m.	97164	Ridgeville	SC	Egg	UAV	139
8.15.18	3:45 p.m.	94170	Pensacola	FL	Bullet/ Missile	UAV	140
8.16.18	n/a	95179	Gig Harbor	WA	Triangle	UAV	142
8.17.18	10:30 p.m.	94217	Portage	IN	Triangle	UAV	144
8.19.18	8 p.m.	94262	El Dorado Springs	MO	Disc	UAV	147
8.21.18	2:30 p.m.	94322	Farmington	WI	Other	UAV	148
8.27.18	4:10 a.m.	97499	Pahrump	NV	N/A	Info Only	149
8.31.18	6:35 a.m.	94699	El Paso	TX	Triangle	UAV	152
9.13.18	8:15 a.m.	94937	Hailey	ID	Square/ Rectangle	UAV	159
9.14.18	3:28 p.m.	94892	Santa Fe	NM	Disc	Info Only	160
9.20.18	7:45 p.m.	95065	Unknown	UK	Disc	UAV	163
9.25.18	10:30 p.m.	95703	Lachute	Canada	Disc	UAV	166
10.3.18	9:40 p.m.	98214	Orem	UT	Cigar	UAV	170
10.7.18	7:30 p.m.	95445	Saco	ME	Diamond	UAV	175
10.10.18	4:30 a.m.	95592	Bellingham	WA	Triangle	UAV	175
10.12.18	1:01 a.m.	95590	Citrus Heights	CA	Triangle	UAV	177
10.21.18	5:30 p.m.	95770	Belleville	WI	Unknown	Other	183
10.25.18	6:30 p.m.	96048	Dilles Bottom	OH	Egg	UAV	184
10.25.18	7:10 p.m.	95880	Montazuma	NY	Teardrop	UAV	185
10.28.18	n/a	96472	Sacramento	CA	Triangle	UAV	188
10.30.18	7:40 p.m.	96019	Benton	OH	Cylinder	UAV	189
11.4.18	3:20 p.m.	96375	Luray	VA	Disc	UAV	193

EVENT	TIME	CASE	CITY	STATE-COUNTRY	SHAPE	DISPOSITION	PAGE
11.6.18	5:54 p.m.	96200	Hattiesburg	MS	Triangle	UAV	194
11.6.18	8:25 p.m.	96207	San Antonio	TX	Chevron	UAV	195
11.7.18	6:02 p.m.	96229	Lacey	WA	Cylinder	UAV	197
11.11.18	7:05 p.m.	96314	London	Canada	Triangle	UAV	204
11.12.18	7:20 p.m.	96353	Phoenix	AZ	Cigar	UAV	205
11.14.18	7:24 p.m.	96378	Caroga Lake	NY	Circle	UAV	206
11.15.18	2:46 p.m.	97141	Everett	WA	Other	UAV	207
11.23.18	6:15 p.m.	96580	Edwards	NY	Sphere	UAV	209
11.25.18	8:15 p.m.	96616	Galway City	Ireland	n/a	UAV	210
12.3.18	n/a	96773	n/a	CA	Teardrop	UAV	217
12.4.18	2 p.m.	96813	Olympia	WA	Egg	UAV	218
12.5.18	6:10 p.m.	96818	Baker City	OR	Chevron	UAV	219
12.6.18	5:35 p.m.	96850	Memphis	TN	Chevron	Other	220
12.7.18	9:25 p.m.	96890	Wellington	UT	Cigar	UAV	221
12.8.18	5:55 p.m.	97287	Pulaski	VA	Triangle	UAV	222
12.10.18	8:45 p.m.	97001	Scott Depot	WV	Boomerang	UAV	224
12.12.18	12 a.m.	97018	Reidsville	NC	Triangle	Other	225
Frightened							
1.24.18	8:04 p.m.	89841	Glasgow	UK	Blimp	Other	19
3.6.18	9:40 p.m.	90698	Marietta	GA	Other	UAV	42
4.2.18	10:27 p.m.	91182	Banja Luka	Bosnia & Herzegovina	Disc	Info Only	58
4.7.18	1:30 a.m.	96086	Warracknabeal	Australia	Disc	UAV	59
5.4.18	2:52 a.m.	91780	Enterprise	UT	Saturn-like	UAV	73
6.3.18	1:30 a.m.	92447	Springville	NY	Saturn-like	UAV	86
7.3.18	1:30 a.m.	93128	Wrexham	UK	Orb	UAV	115
8.12.18	12:15 a.m.	97164	Ridgeville	SC	Egg	UAV	139
9.1.18	4:20 a.m.	94960	Porter	TX	Boomerang	UAV	154
10.10.18	4:30 a.m.	95592	Bellingham	WA	Triangle	UAV	175
11.23.18	4:55 a.m.	96554	Ballivor	Ireland	Triangle	Other	208
12.1.18	12:00 a.m.	96805	McKinney	TX	Oval	UAV	214
Photos, witness captured							
1.1.18	12:05 a.m.	89317	Las Vegas	NV	Disc	UAV	8
1.9.18	8:45 p.m.	89498	Ellensburg	WA	Oval	UAV	15
2.04.18	6:27 p.m.	90097	Windsor	UK	Triangle	Info Only	25

EVENT	TIME	CASE	CITY	STATE-COUNTRY	SHAPE	DISPOSITION	PAGE
2.04.18	6:27 p.m.	90097	Windsor	UK	Triangle	Info Only	25
2.12.18	8:05 p.m.	90205	St. Peters	MO	Square/Rectangle	UAV	31
2.26.18	3:47 p.m.	90708	Wilmington	CA	Saturn-like	UAV	37
3.6.18	10:42 a.m.	93750	West Jordan	UT	Cylinder	UAV	41
5.4.18	2:52 a.m.	91780	Enterprise	UT	Saturn-like	UAV	73
5.18.18	4:25 a.m.	98601	Ballymahon Co. Lonford	Ireland	Saturn-like	Other	78
5.29.18	8:50 p.m.	92387	Kronberg im Taunus	Germany	Disc	UAV	81
6.1.18	n/a	92483	West Plains	MO	Triangle	UAV	83
6.2.18	3:10 p.m.	92499	Crieff, Scotland	UK	Disc	UAV	84
6.2.18	5:30 p.m.	92481	Salem	NJ	Disc	Only	85
6.3.18	7:49 p.m.	93607	Dartford	UK	Horseshoe	UAV	88
6.17.18	3:20 p.m.	92817	Portland	OR	Square/Rectangle	UAV	98
6.19.18	7:30 p.m.	92803	Lower Burrell	PA	Cylinder	UAV	101
6.20.18	3:15 p.m.	92849	Egg Harbor Township	NJ	Sphere	UAV	102
6.21.18	10:58 p.m.	92852	New Brighten	MN	Disc	UAV	103
6.26.18	12 a.m.	95960	Noxon	MT	Disc	Other	109
7.1.18	9:23 p.m.	93045	West Fargo	ND	Sphere	Other	113
7.2.18	9:55 p.m.	94741	Carmel	IN	Cigar	Other	114
8.10.18	7:19 p.m.	94038	Hammond	IN	Blimp	UAV	135
8.31.18	6:35 a.m.	94699	El Paso	TX	Triangle	UAV	152
9.3.18	4:07 p.m.	95976	Perrysville	OH	N/A	UAV	155
9.8.18	n/a	96379	Wilmington	NC	Sphere	Other	156
9.24.18	6:45 p.m.	95317	Baldwinsville	NY	Sphere	Other	165
11.6.18	8:25 p.m.	96207	San Antonio	TX	Chevron	UAV	195
11.15.18	2:46 p.m.	97141	Everett	WA	Other	UAV	207
12.5.18	6:10 p.m.	96818	Baker City	OR	Chevron	UAV	219
12.7.18	9:25 p.m.	96890	Wellington	UT	Cigar	UAV	221
12.10.18	8:45 p.m.	97001	Scott Depot	WV	Boomerang	UAV	224
12.31.18	12:10 a.m.	97391	Caithness	UK	Saturn-like	UAV	231

Physical, calm and restraint

| 8.12.18 | 2:10 a.m. | 94081 | Godfrey | IL | Cigar | UAV | 137 |

EVENT	TIME	CASE	CITY	STATE-COUNTRY	SHAPE	DISPOSITION	PAGE
Physical, disoriented							
2.09.18	11:18 p.m.	90175	Derry	PA	Semi-Diamond	Other	29
11.7.18	6:02 p.m.	96229	Lacey	WA	Cylinder	UAV	197
Physical, dizzy							
8.12.18	2:10 a.m.	94081	Godfrey	IL	Cigar	UAV	137
Physical, don't take a picture							
8.16.18	n/a	95179	Gig Harbor	WA	Triangle	UAV	142
Physical, ears rang							
10.16.18	9:53 p.m.	95874	Midwest	WY	Sphere	UAV	180
Physical, eyes hurt or irritated							
10.16.18	9:53 p.m.	95874	Midwest	WY	Sphere	UAV	180
Physical, felt entity was not evil							
1.24.18	8:04 p.m.	89841	Glasgow	UK	Blimp	Other	19
Physical, felt frozen							
10.30.18	n/a	98437	Michigan City	IN	Triangle	UAV	190
Physical, felt overwhelmed							
2.07.18	8 a.m.	90127	Shoup	ID	Teardrop	UAV	26
Physical, felt seen by entity							
1.24.18	8:04 p.m.	89841	Glasgow	UK	Blimp	Other	19
Physical, lower lip burned							
10.16.18	9:53 p.m.	95874	Midwest	WY	Sphere	UAV	180
Physical, mesmerized							
2.21.18	8:30 p.m.	90647	Rochester	NY	Triangle		35
Physical, migraine headache							
12.3.18	8:35 a.m.	96755	Toms Brook	VA	Cylinder	UAV	216
Physical, nausea							
4.5.18	09:20 p.m.	91224	Fort Payne	AL	Square/Rectangle	UAV	58
6.3.18	6:45 a.m.	92469	Panola County	MS	Cylinder	UAV	87
Physical, panic							
8.12.18	2:10 a.m.	94081	Godfrey	IL	Cigar	UAV	137
Physical, rage							
8.12.18	2:10 a.m.	94081	Godfrey	IL	Cigar	UAV	137
Physical, ringing in ears							
6.3.18	6:45 a.m.	92469	Panola County	MS	Cylinder	UAV	87

EVENT	TIME	CASE	CITY	STATE-COUNTRY	SHAPE	DISPOSITION	PAGE
Physical, throat and mouth sore							
10.16.18	9:53 p.m.	95874	Midwest	WY	Sphere	UAV	180
Physical, time loss							
2.09.18	11:18 p.m.	90175	Derry	PA	Semi-Diamond	Other	29
3.3.18	11:30 p.m.	90584	Elkhorn	NE	Disc	UAV	40
8.12.18	2:10 a.m.	94081	Godfrey	IL	Cigar	UAV	137
Physical, trance							
6.26.18	2:41 a.m.	92954	Madison	WI	Triangle	UAV	107
Video, witness captured							
1.1.18	12:05 a.m.	89317	Las Vegas	NV	Disc	UAV	8
1.6.18	1:50 p.m.	89370	Darlington	UK	Triangle	Info Only	12
2.07.18	8 a.m.	90127	Shoup	ID	Teardrop	UAV	26
2.09.18	11:18 p.m.	90175	Derry	PA	Semi-Diamond	Other	29
2.12.18	8:05 p.m.	90205	St. Peters	MO	Square/Rectangle	UAV	31
2.23.18	7:17 p.m.	90398	Las Vegas	NV	Triangle	UAV	36
2.26.18	3:47 p.m.	90708	Wilmington	CA	Saturn-like	UAV	37
3.10.18	11:57 p.m.	90710	Manchester	MD	Triangle	Other	45
4.28.18	10:20 p.m.	91666	Houston	TX	Other	UAV	70
4.5.18	11:30 p.m.	91263	Reliance	TN	Square/Rectangle	Other	59
6.2.18	3:10 p.m.	92499	Crieff, Scotland	UK	Disc	UAV	84
6.3.18	7:49 p.m.	93607	Dartford	UK	Horseshoe	UAV	88
6.3.18	n/a	92452	Flournoy	CA	Sphere	Other	89
6.17.18	11:40 p.m.	92802	Ada County	ID	Other	UAV	99
6.23.18	11:45 p.m.	92947	Oak Dale	CA	Fireball	UAV	105
6.24.18	n/a	95063	Medellin	Columbia	Diamond	UAV	106
6.24.18	1:51 a.m.	92893	Anchorage County	AK	Sphere	UAV	107
6.26.18	12 a.m.	95960	Noxon	MT	Disc	Other	109
7.2.18	2:30 p.m.	93418	Gustine	CA.	Triangle	UAV	114
7.10.18	8:50 p.m.	93369	Newmarket	Canada	Cylinder	UAV	117
7.11.18	9 a.m.	93427	Pendleton	OR	Cone	UAV	118
8.12.18	5:06 p.m.	94086	Parker	CO	Egg	UAV	138
9.18.18	12:25 p.m.	94996	Vancouver	WA	Unknown	UAV	162

EVENT	TIME	CASE	CITY	STATE-COUNTRY	SHAPE	DISPOSITION	PAGE
9.23.18	5:40 p.m.	95215	London	UK	Triangle	UAV	165
10.3.18	7:30 p.m.	96637	New Lisbon	NJ	Triangle	UAV	170
10.10.18	2:27 p.m.	95682	Atlanta	GA	Cigar	UAV	176
10.12.18	1:01 a.m.	95590	Citrus Heights	CA	Triangle	UAV	177
10.22.18	9:30 a.m.	95806	Pass Christian	MS	Blimp	UAV	183
10.31.18	9:45 p.m.	96052	Selma	NC	Triangle	UAV	191
11.6.18	9 p.m.	96312	Boise	ID	Boomerang	UAV	195
11.9.18	8:18 p.m.	96286	Chaska	MN	Star-like	UAV	202
11.25.18	8:15 p.m.	96616	Galway City	Ireland	N/A	UAV	210
11.28.18	5:20 p.m.	96641	Unknown	Philippines	Unknown	Other	213
12.5.18	6:10 p.m.	96818	Baker City	OR	Chevron	UAV	219

46874210R00190

Printed in Poland
by Amazon Fulfillment
Poland Sp. z o.o., Wrocław